THE DOWNSTRETCHED HAND

INDIVIDUAL DEVELOPMENT IN GEORGE MAC-DONALD'S MAJOR FANTASIES FOR CHILDREN

HELP CANNOT COME TO ONE MADE IN THE IMAGE OF GOD, SAVE IN THE OBEDIENT EFFORT OF WHAT LIFE AND POWER ARE IN HIM, FOR GOD IS ACTION. IN SUCH EFFORT ALONE IS IT POSSIBLE FOR NEED TO ENCOUNTER HELP. IT IS THE UPSTRETCHED THAT MEETS THE DOWNSTRETCHED HAND.

"A SKETCH OF INDIVIDUAL DEVELOPMENT,"
GEORGE MACDONALD, 1880

LESLEY WILLIS SMITH

The Downstretched Hand:
Individual Development in
George MacDonald's Major Fantasies for Children

Copyright © 2018 Lesley Willis Smith

Winged Lion Press
Hamden, CT

All rights reserved. Except in the case of quotations embodied in critical articles or reviews, no part of this book may be reproduced or transmitted in any form or by any means, electronic or mechanical, including photocopying, recording, or by any information storage or retrieval system, without written permission of the publisher. Contact Winged Lion Press www.WingedLionPress.com

Winged Lion Press titles may be purchased for business or promotional use or special sales.

10-9-8-7-6-5-4-3-2-1

WINGED LION PRESS

ISBN 13   978-1-935688-19-8

For Christopher with love

ACKNOWLEDGEMENTS

My thanks are due to Colin Manlove, formerly Reader in English Literature at the University of Edinburgh, for his kind support and encouragement at an early stage of this project; to Dr Juliet McMaster, English Professor Emeritus at the University of Alberta, for her unfailing moral support; and to Graham Henderson, a former student at the University of Guelph, for igniting my interest in Carl Jung. I am also grateful to Robert Trexler, of Winged Lion Press, for his help with illustrations. Most of all I thank my husband Christopher for his patience, his warm support, and his help with formatting the manuscript.

An Appreciation of *The Downstretched Hand*

This outstanding book is the first to look at George MacDonald's major fantasies for children in the light of the Bible, tracing submerged references that transform our understanding of these stories. Written in a straightforward and engaging style, the book holds the reader from first to last. Its theme is the maturation of the various protagonists of the tales, seen against a larger backcloth of death, resurrection and final judgement. Lesley Smith shows how incidents from MacDonald's personal life, often harrowing, are changed into parts of a larger holy pattern in these works. In particular she shows how the resonance of these fairy tales derives both from alchemical thought in their past, and from archetypal imagery to be described by C.G. Jung in the future. Every page of this book gives us something new or recreates the known. Above all, its humane tone gives us a MacDonald who is always immediately present, whether as wise and suffering man, or as an artist forging the new genre of fairy tale.

Colin Manlove, Author of
Scotland's Forgotten Treasure: The Visionary Novels of George MacDonald

TABLE OF CONTENTS

	Introduction	1
Part One: *At the Back of the North Wind*		
Ch 1	MacDonald's Crystal Palace Diamonds and Rubies	17
Ch 2	MacDonald's Crystal Palace Common Crystals	35
Ch 3	"Full of Quiet Wisdom" Diamond as Prophet	49
Ch 4	Diamond and North Wind A Mystical Relationship	69
Part Two: *The Princess and the Goblin*		
Ch 5	"The Princess and—We Shall See Who" The Heart of the Mystery	89
Ch 6	"All Thy Children Shall Be Taught of the LORD" The Princess Goes to School	101
Ch 7	"And Great Shall Be the Peace of Thy Children" Mission Accomplished	117
Part Three: *The Princess and Curdie*		
Ch 8	Home and Away The Mountain and the Miner	141
Ch 9	The Shadow	159
Ch 10	Gwyntystorm	171
	Conclusion	199
	Endnotes	219
	Works Cited	319
	Index	337

Then he crept out into the yard, through the door in the wall, and away to the primrose. Behind it stood North Wind, leaning over it, and looking at the flower as if she had been its mother.

"Come along," she said, jumping up and holding out her hand.

Diamond took her hand. It was cold, but so pleasant and full of life, it was better than warm. She led him across the garden. With one bound she was on the top of the wall. Diamond was left at the foot.

"Stop, stop!" he cried. "Please, I can't jump like that."

"You don't try" said North Wind, who from the top looked down a foot taller than before.

"Give me your hand again, and I will try," said Diamond.

Chapter 3, "Old Diamond"
illustration by Arthur Hughes

INTRODUCTION

"We *are* not yet; we are only *becoming*."
("Sorrow the Pledge of Joy," in *The Hope of the Gospel*, 97)

"Who in the world am I? Ah, *that's* the great puzzle!" exclaims Lewis Carroll's Alice in the second chapter of *Alice's Adventures in Wonderland*, unintentionally conflating, or almost conflating the two great questions of human life: "Who am I?" and "What does it all mean?" The first is pursued throughout the book in a way that would be frightening if it weren't funny, largely because the second is not explored at all. Personal development is reduced to a series of arbitrary size-shifts in an arbitrarily changing world, and all that is achieved is a coping mechanism for dealing with bullies such as the caterpillar who, when Alice is at her most vulnerable, puts her on the spot: "'You!' said the Caterpillar contemptuously. 'Who are *you?*'" (Ch.5). By the end of the book Alice outbullies the bullies: "'Who cares for *you?*' said Alice (she had grown to her full size by this time). 'You're nothing but a pack of cards!'" (Ch. 12). This is great entertainment, as George MacDonald's children could avouch since, at Carroll's request, the original version of the book, *Alice's Adventures Underground*, had been tried out on them;[1] but while it is reassuring to the immature self, as it provides a coping mechanism which the child reader can grasp, it does not promote maturity. To George MacDonald, on the other hand, the questions "Who am I?" and "What does it all mean?" are profoundly serious, and growth to maturity, or individuation, which is of crucial importance in his eyes, is only possible within a context of universal meaning which leads to transcendence—the possibility of oneness with God. No wonder he says, in a letter to William Cowper-Temple: "I will try to show what we might be, may be, must be, shall be—and something of the struggle to gain it," so that his books will be "true to the real and not the spoilt humanity."[2]

"I do not write for children, but for the childlike, whether of five, or fifty, or seventy-five," says MacDonald in "The Fantastic Imagination."[3] But "childlike" does not mean "childish," and the issues with which he is concerned can be treated in as great a depth in what, for the sake of convenience, I shall refer to as children's fantasies, as in works more obviously geared to adults.[4] My purpose is to examine George MacDonald's vision of the mystery of human life as it is explored in his three full-length fantasies for children, *At the Back of the North Wind* (1871), *The Princess and the Goblin* (1872) and *The*

The Downstretched Hand: Individual Development in

Princess and Curdie (1882), but within the context of his other fictional works, especially those published close to these three in time. At the heart of the mystery is the relationship between the self and God—the child and the Father, or the "upstretched" and the "downstretched hand," as MacDonald envisions it in an essay entitled "A Sketch of Individual Development."[5] And in order to explore this mystery, the human psyche, itself a mystery, must be explored as well.

Some time ago a cleric with whom I was discussing G.P. Taylor's *The Shadowmancer* observed that the many biblical and indeed specifically Christian allusions in the book would surely stamp it politically incorrect and limit its appeal. I replied that child readers would be unlikely to recognise them. "But their parents would," she objected. Their grandparents might, but many adults do not recognise such allusions in an age the secular character of which has long been established—and in the event *The Shadowmancer*, far from being disadvantaged by them, soon outsold everything except *Harry Potter*.[6] In Victorian times both biblical and specifically Christian allusions would have been widely recognised and generally, though not universally accepted, but George MacDonald sometimes went beyond allusion and was used to encountering detractors on this score: "People . . . find this great fault with me—that I turn my stories into sermons," he said. "They forget that I have a Master to serve first before I can wait upon the public."[7] Such an unambiguous statement of priorities—faith over art—is unlikely to conciliate hostile critics whether Victorian or modern. But it could hardly be otherwise for a man who could write as follows to a correspondent: "I do say that all my hope, all my joy, all my strength are in the Lord Christ and his Father; that all my theories of life and growth are rooted in him; that his truth is gradually clearing up the mysteries of this world. . . . To Him I belong heart and soul and body, and he may do with me as he will—nay, nay—I pray him to do with me as he wills: for that is my only well-being and freedom" (*GMHW* 374).

Deliberate preaching is much more evident in MacDonald's 'realistic' fiction than in his fantasy, a genre which makes preaching difficult (though it happens sometimes).[8] But the three fantasies under discussion are, like all MacDonald's works, full of religious meaning and permeated by biblical imagery, although *At the Back of the North Wind* is the only one of the three in which God is specifically mentioned. This book, a fantasy rooted in what Tolkien calls the everyday or "Primary World" (Diamond, the hero, travels by train as well as by the agency of North Wind), but embracing the "Secondary

George MacDonald's Major Fantasies for Children

World"[9] as well—desirability as well as possibility, as Tolkien puts it[10]—contains several overtly religious references. Diamond's name is associated with the Bible in the very first chapter; he speaks to a clergyman, spends a night in a cathedral, and reads the Bible, which his father Joseph discusses with the family on Sundays; while his mother, like Diamond, thinks about what she has heard in church and Joseph caps their list of friends by saying "And God for us all," after which he and Diamond "were both silent, for that was very solemn."[11]

The fact that Diamond was born in a stable indicates that he has some claim to be a Christ-figure, at least in embryo.[12] Yet it would be hard to class the book, in which children talk about dysfunctional families, physical abuse and the possibility of suicide,[13] as a work of conventional Victorian piety, though the narrator cannot resist preaching from time to time; even in *The Princess and the Goblin*, which is set in the Secondary World, Curdie's father, Peter Peterson (a name which suggests apostolic descent), makes a visit to the vicar at one point.[14] No-one, however, could accuse *The Princess and the Goblin* of being doctrinaire, though G.K. Chesterton testifies to its spiritual quality; he calls it "a book that has made a difference to my whole existence, which helped me to see things in a certain way from the start; a vision of things which even so real a revelation as a change of religious allegiance [to Roman Catholicism] has substantially only crowned and confirmed."[15] The much later and much bleaker *The Princess and Curdie*—more of a hero myth than a fairy tale, which perhaps makes it less surprising that the "note of consolatory hope that is the essence of fairy tale"[16] should be muted in it—is for the most part too enigmatic to be doctrinaire.[17]

It is a truism of MacDonald scholarship that much of his fictional writing has a strong personal or even autobiographical element, and, in his fantasies, this is particularly clear in *At the Back of the North Wind* and *The Princess and the Goblin*. Aspects of MacDonald himself appear in *At the Back of the North Wind* in many guises. The New Testament father figure, Joseph the coachman, resembles MacDonald in his poverty, his long bout of illness and, of course, his love of horses. If he is not a writer, he does teach Diamond to read.[18] In the Bloomsbury section of the book Diamond's friend, Mr. Raymond, another father figure who later becomes the employer and protector of Diamond's whole family, is actually designated the author of "The Little Lady and the Goblin Prince" (*ABNW* 341)—and he too suffers from a long illness. At The Mound this persona is eclipsed by that of the tutor (once MacDonald's own occupation) who is also the narrator.

The Downstretched Hand: Individual Development in

In *The Princess and the Goblin*, the illustrator, Arthur Hughes,[19] shows considerable astuteness in portraying MacDonald himself as Irene's king-papa—not unnaturally, as the princess is named, on one level, after MacDonald's daughter Irene (whose nickname was "Goblin").[20] By the time *The Princess and Curdie* appears, however, the directly personal element has faded with the reduced and changed roles of both Irene and her father—and so, partly in consequence of this, has a good deal of the protectiveness and consolation which characterise its predecessors and which are particularly geared to child readers.

The three fantasies were undoubtedly influenced by MacDonald's having lost, by the time of writing, not only his parents but three of his brothers and a young half-sister, so the idea of death is very strong—particularly in *At the Back of the North Wind*, but also in the *Princess* books, though in a more purely symbolic way. Some particular experiences also affected the writing of these and other books. A tour of part of Europe in the summer of 1865 had a profound effect on MacDonald which found expression in all three fantasies and most especially in *The Princess and the Goblin*. "If I hadn't climbed that tower and had a breath of divine air, I should have been ill to-day," he writes of Antwerp Cathedral in a letter to his wife Louisa: "I went up ill and came down well" (*George MacDonald and His Wife*, 348). He writes in similar terms about the cathedral at Strasbourg: "I went up the tower and up the spire. . . . I am sure the only cure for you and me and all of us is getting up, up—into the divine air. . . . How will it be when I get amongst God's steeples?" (349). In the same letter he says: "Oh how I should delight to build a cathedral—towers if nothing else" (348), and although Diamond, in *At the Back of the North Wind*, only gets as far as the clerestory, the tower is built in *The Princess and the Goblin*. Mountains, very much associated with cathedrals in MacDonald's mind, were also a major source of inspiration during this tour: "Oh, for the mountains—God's church towers!" he says (*GMHW* 348). Of the Jungfrau in particular George MacDonald writes to Louisa at length, saying, most notably, "I had seen something which raised me above my former self and made me long to rise higher yet" (352).[21] The whole setting of *The Princess and the Goblin* is a mountain and, although it has a more restricted role in *The Princess and Curdie*, the first chapter, actually entitled "The Mountain" and using the word "Alps" as part of a figure of speech (*PC* 10), describes the essential nature of a mountain in a way calculated to engage the reader's imagination.

A very different personal experience finds expression in *At the Back of the North Wind*. Diamond's voyage to the North Pole echoes

George MacDonald's Major Fantasies for Children

MacDonald's own sailing trip to Norway in the summer of 1869. He was forced to remain below decks because of an agonising abscessed knee—a condition which nearly killed him. As Louisa wrote soon afterwards with great penetration, "he had suffered greatly, and who shall say those sufferings were not for other people—in what he may hereafter write" (*GMHW* 396). The closest MacDonald actually came to Norway was being transferred to the steamer of that name[22] and taken home, when, says his son Greville, "I thought he was dead" (*GMHW* 394). This impression was obviously relayed to his father afterwards, for, in *At the Back of the North Wind*, Martha has the same impression about Diamond (*ABNW* 126).

If personal experiences play a significant part in MacDonald's work, ideas and topics of particular importance to him—sometimes arising from notable public events, for individual development, to him, must be located in the collective—have an even greater role to play. This is why the same incidents, symbols, themes and motifs recur frequently, from *Phantastes* (1858) to *Lilith* (1895), from *David Elginbrod* (1863) to *Salted with Fire* (1897), and of course in his poetry as well. Just as, when writing about the imagination, MacDonald speaks of the capacity of poetry to give a "new arrangement of thought and figure whereby the meaning contained is presented as it never was before,"[23] so his symbols and ideas—even his characters—are revisited in a way that not only reveals his fascination with them but often yields fresh insights.[24] Two books written during the period when *At the Back of the North Wind* and *The Princess and the Goblin* appeared afford an especially interesting background to them; not surprisingly, since, in an interview given in 1893, he said "I have always two novels on the stocks at once—I used to manage three."[25] One is the adult novel *Wilfrid Cumbermede*, published in 1872. The other, *Ranald Bannerman's Boyhood* (1871), the fictionalised autobiography of the author's childhood—"I do not intend to carry my story one month beyond the hour when I saw that my boyhood was gone and my youth arrived," he begins (*RB* 9)—is not of great literary value but is illuminating in many respects; and serialised as it was in *Good Words for the Young* between *At the Back of the North Wind* and *The Princess and the Goblin*, it would be surprising if it were otherwise.[26] This is where the cradle appears (to be discussed later in connection with *At the Back of the North Wind*); this is where the heavenly ceiling found in *The Princess and the Goblin* first appears: "The ceiling was a ceiling indeed; for the sun, moon, and stars lived there" (*RB* 13).[27] This, too, is one place where George MacDonald begins to articulate a great

The Downstretched Hand: Individual Development in

theme running through all his work—the integration of the total psyche through the bringing of the unconscious into consciousness; the darkness, in other words, into the light.

How much the children's fantasies meant to MacDonald is indicated by his estimate of the worth of *The Princess and the Goblin* in particular. Shortly before the serial publication of the book was finished, he wrote to his wife: "I know it is as good work as I can do, and I think will be the most complete thing of the kind I have done."[28] In my view he never wrote anything finer than *The Princess and the Goblin*, and its nominal sequel, *The Princess and Curdie*, and particularly the earlier *At the Back of the North Wind*,[29] are also outstanding (though it might be argued that *The Princess and Curdie* has less of "the one central spot of red" which, MacDonald tells Louisa, "is the life and depth . . . the thing that shows the unshowable" than the other two [*GMHW* 326]). The three fantasies are not, of course, a trilogy, and even the titles of the *Princess* books refer to different princesses—*The Princess and the Goblin* to Princess Irene and *The Princess and Curdie* to Queen Irene in her temporary reincarnation as "the old princess." But the three books are organically related; Diamond reads "the story of the Little Lady and the Goblin Prince" not long before the end of *At the Back of the North Wind* (*ABNW* 341), and the narrator of *The Princess and the Goblin* ends the book by telling the reader that "the rest of the history of *The Princess and Curdie* must be kept for another volume" (*PG* 308).

MacDonald's personal input of various kinds adds to the authenticity of the children's fantasies, but his meaning and purpose go far beyond himself. This is conveyed by the simple use of third person narration (unlike the first person narration of the unambiguously adult fantasies *Phantastes* and *Lilith*, which demands a sophisticated identification or at least a personal application on the reader's part) and by a deliberate paring of contextual memories. The library, for example, important, though obscurely so, in MacDonald's own life and a feature of most of his adult writing,[30] is almost totally absent from the major children's fantasies. It is 'phased out' gently in *At the Back of the North Wind*, in which North Wind provides a book of poetry from which Diamond learns to read; Mr. Raymond's study is a miniature library, and Diamond "gazed with some wonder at the multitude of books on the walls, and thought what a learned man Mr. Raymond must be" (*ABNW* 286)—but he is a writer and has some excuse. In *The Princess and the Goblin* libraries matter not a jot, and the only one in *The Princess and Curdie* (and then only the remains of it)

George MacDonald's Major Fantasies for Children

has been consigned to the city dump, its age having destroyed its value in the eyes of the corrupt and ignorant religious authorities (*PC* 276). Apart from this, the only mention of a book in *The Princess and Curdie* occurs when Curdie's mother is getting his breakfast "while his father sat reading to her out of an old book" (112). This is important because it locates the Petersons in a wider context than that of their family and immediate environment or even than that of their own time—just as, in the rest of the book, the individual must become rooted in a universal context. But even this shared reading is in line with the much older oral tradition specifically instanced in *The Princess and the Goblin* and appealing to both children and adults: "The king's harper, who always formed a part of his escort, was chanting a ballad which he made as he went on playing on his instrument—about the princess and the goblins, and the prowess of Curdie . . ." (*PG* 298). And in both books Irene and Curdie at intervals relate (or once, in Curdie's case, dream) their adventures and so not only inform their hearers but gain perspective on what they have lived through.[31]

Reflection on lived experience, actual or imagined, is vital to the development of understanding which is essential to the process of maturity. "Our whole life, to be life at all, must be a growth in understanding," says MacDonald in his essay "Salvation From Sin,"[32] and hence the imagery of light out of darkness which is pervasive in his writing. He is well aware that much of the self is unconscious: "Our consciousness is to the extent of our being but as the flame of the volcano to the world-gulf whence it issues," he writes in "Man's Difficulty Concerning Prayer."[33] But the gulf must be sounded. "The great fantasies, myths, and tales are . . . like dreams," says Ursula le Guin: "They speak *from* the unconscious *to* the unconscious, in the *language* of the unconscious—symbol and archetype."[34] But she also says that "[t]rue myth arises only in the process of connecting the conscious and unconscious realms,"[35] and Carl Jung thinks along similar lines: "Myths and fairy tales give expression to unconscious processes, and their retelling causes these processes to come alive again and be recollected, thus re-establishing the connection between conscious and unconscious."[36]

Much of MacDonald's work deals with this process of connection—which is, of course, the process of individuation. The theories of Carl Jung about the same process, achieved in the same way, provide valuable insight,[37] and "Light Out of Darkness," a chapter heading in *Ranald Bannerman's Boyhood*, could be the philosophy of both.[38] Some of MacDonald's own writings about the unconscious

The Downstretched Hand: Individual Development in

could almost have been written by Jung: "The being of which we are conscious, is not our full self; the extent of our consciousness of ourself is no measure of ourself; our consciousness is infinitely less than we," for example[39]—but, while Jung stops at the goal of integrating the unconscious into consciousness,[40] or individuation, George MacDonald says that individuation is a means to "the final end [of] oneness [with God]—an impossibility without it."[41]

The paradoxical result of the process of connection in MacDonald's work is that "intensification of the mystery of the real" which Ursula le Guin calls "the direction of the great myths and legends."[42] Ultimately this will promote the harmonious development of the total self in all its complexity: "Every one . . . has a beast-self—and a bird-self, and a stupid fish-self, ay, and a creeping serpent-self too—which it takes a deal of crushing to kill! In truth he has also a tree-self and a crystal-self, and I don't know how many selves more—all to get into harmony," says Mr. Raven in *Lilith,* MacDonald's final fantasy (43).

But there certainly can be no getting into harmony if the conscious self is limited by lack of awareness of the unconscious. The person in this situation will commit the cardinal sin of being commonplace, like the unfortunate Mrs. Dempster in the short story "The Butcher's Bills," who was "a very ordinary woman in that region of her which knew what she meant when she said 'I.'" Since her husband is more intelligent, he is more to blame for the complacency which thwarts development: "It is harder for me to understand," says MacDonald, "how Mr. Dempster could be so comfortable in his own mind that he never wanted to get out of it, even at the risk of being beside himself."[43]

The trouble is that getting out of one's mind is a very dangerous operation, and should never be attempted without seeking divine assistance. For one thing it would be futile, since "God must reveal, or nothing is known;"[44] for another, the conscious self might be overwhelmed by the unconscious, which would result in the destruction of individuality. Unless brought into consciousness through understanding, the necessarily non-individuated unconscious is an enemy to the development of the self—something MacDonald envisages when he pleads with God, in *Diary of an Old Soul:*

> Leave not thy son half-made in beastly guise—
> Less than a man, with more than human cries—
> An unshaped thing in which thyself cries out![45]

Yet although "our consciousness is infinitely less than we," there is no need to be afraid of its being swamped by the unconscious so long as we hold on to the "downstretched hand" of the God who is more ourselves than we are.⁴⁶ MacDonald emphasises that, even in the most obscure and terrifying areas, the one infinitely harmonious and integrated self exercises a primary function of consciousness—that of illuminating the darkness. No wonder that in *Diary of an Old Soul* he says "Thou art the only person, and I cry / Unto the father *I* of this my *I*" (August, 258). God is always calling those he has made to individuality, as is clear from his mode of relating to them: "Before him stands each, as much an individual child as if there were no one but him."⁴⁷

But individuality must ultimately develop in the context of the collective: "All communities are for the divine sake of individual life. . . . A community is the true development of individual relations," says MacDonald (*The Miracles of Our Lord*, 304). He believes that conscious and unconscious need to be integrated in both areas—a harder task in the case of the collective unconscious, as we see in *The Princess and Curdie*, and here again the work of Carl Jung, drawing as it does on myths and archetypes from many ages and cultures, is illuminating.⁴⁸ Jung's fascination with alchemy is of particular interest, especially as MacDonald sometimes appears, principally in *At the Back of the North Wind*, to be writing almost to an alchemical prescription.⁴⁹ Jung is not, of course, concerned with the defunct 'royal art' *per se*, but with what he describes in *Psychology and Alchemy* as "the signal connection between our modern psychology of the unconscious and alchemical symbolism."⁵⁰ As regards the collective unconscious, Jung's belief that Christianity has an unconscious level is especially interesting in view of MacDonald's firm conviction that conscious and unconscious, on the personal or collective levels, can only be integrated through the agency of God. In Jung's view the symbolic structures developed by the proponents of alchemy are "rather like an undercurrent to the Christianity that ruled on the surface. It is to this surface as the dream is to consciousness, and just as the dream compensates the conflicts of the conscious mind, so alchemy endeavours to fill in the gaps left open by the Christian tension of opposites"—that is, good and evil (*PA* par. 26).

"All George MacDonald's writings were consistent, communicating the same essential truth—that in everything God was to be seen," says Michael Phillips.⁵¹ This is much more overtly the case in the adult novels than in the children's fantasies; but then, as John Pridmore says, "[t]o educate the spirit of the child we may well talk about God, but we do not have to."⁵² *Robert Falconer*, a novel written

The Downstretched Hand: Individual Development in

very shortly before *At the Back of the North Wind*, treats in detail of the protagonist's developing belief and trust in God. In *At the Back of the North Wind*, however, Diamond's belief in God is completely taken for granted. He grows in trust—but this can be done without any type of theological reasoning. The approach is totally different from that of the adult works, as it is in *The Princess and the Goblin* and *The Princess and Curdie;* but the children's fantasies are nevertheless excellent vehicles for the exploration of that relationship between God and the self which, to MacDonald, is the means of integration of the mature psyche.

Not only can children's books accommodate the tastes of adult readers—some of whom, "in virtue of their hearts being young and old both at once, discern more in the children's books than the children themselves," says MacDonald in *Ranald Bannerman's Boyhood* (182)—but they are ideally suited to the depiction of dawning consciousness: "I cannot tell any better than most of my readers how and when I began to come awake, or what it was that wakened me," says Ranald Bannerman (12).[53] And *At the Back of the North Wind*, *The Princess and the Goblin* and *The Princess and Curdie*, explore the work of individuation—the task which faces the protagonists, as it does every person—in large part through incorporating the development of major biblical themes which are integrated into the structure of MacDonald's own myth. *At the Back of the North Wind* owes much to prophecy, particularly, though by no means exclusively, to the Book of Daniel (the first book in the Old Testament to teach, specifically and in detail, the doctrine of the resurrection); *The Princess and the Goblin*, though drawing a great deal on the prophet Isaiah,[54] is influenced most especially by the Gospel and first epistle of St. John; and *The Princess and Curdie* draws mainly on Revelation, which in turn draws on the books of Daniel and Ezekiel.[55] The imagery of Ezekiel, with an undercurrent (suitably toned down) of his prophecies, may be said to link all three fantasies —and the twenty-second chapter of the Second Book of Samuel (a prophet who was, when a child, called in the night by a celestial voice) abounds in images which, found in close proximity, also link all three books: "The LORD is my rock, and my fortress, and my deliverer," sings King David after victory in a series of battles, and he goes on to describe him as "the God of my rock. . . my high tower, and my refuge, my saviour; thou savest me from violence" (vv 2, 3). He describes the Lord's answer to his original cry of distress:

> There went up a smoke out of his nostrils, and fire out of his mouth devoured; coals were kindled by it.
>
> He bowed the heavens also, and came down; and darkness was under his feet.
>
> And he rode upon a cherub, and did fly; and he was seen upon the wings of the wind.
>
> And he made darkness pavilions round about him, dark waters, and thick clouds of the skies,
>
> Through the brightness before him were coals of fire kindled.
>
> The LORD thundered from heaven, and the most High uttered his voice.
>
> And he sent out arrows, and scattered them; lightning, and discomfited them.
>
> (2 Sam. 22:9-15)

Psalm 104 also says that God "walketh upon the wings of the wind" (v.3) and, as 2 Samuel 22 is "essentially a duplicate of Psalm 18," [56] it is not surprising that many of the images in Samuel are found in this psalm of King David: "There went up a smoke out of [the Lord's] nostrils, and fire out of his mouth devoured: coals were kindled by it. . . . And he rode upon a cherub, and did fly: yea, he did fly upon the wings of the wind. . . . At the brightness that was before him his thick clouds passed, hail stones and coals of fire./The LORD also thundered in the heavens, and the Highest gave his voice; hail stones and coals of fire./ Yea, he sent out his arrows, and scattered them; and he shot out lightnings, and discomfited them" (Ps 18: vv. 8, 10, 12, 13, 14). But some of the images in 2 Samuel 22 are even closer to MacDonald's fantasies, for "thou wilt light my candle" in Psalm 18 (v.28) becomes, in 2 Samuel 22, "thou art my lamp, O LORD" (v.29), and the chapter ends by proclaiming: "He is the tower of salvation for his king" (v.51).

To oversimplify, the first of the three books under discussion deals with death, the second with resurrection and the third with the Last Judgement—a switch from the individual to the public domain—and psychologically there is a progression from the childhood innocence of the first two books to the guilt, expiation and reformation of the third. But most important is the fact that, at a very profound level, the three fantasies are about the relationship of the human soul with God in the persons of the Trinity, and the divine association—not identification—is with the Father in *At the Back of the North Wind*, in which an intermediary is necessary;[57] with the Son in *The Princess and*

The Downstretched Hand: Individual Development in

the Goblin, in which the Word is made flesh; and with the Holy Spirit in *The Princess and Curdie*, the book in which supernatural help is most veiled (as is indicated by Queen Irene's apparent demotion, until the last chapter, to "the old princess," a process connected with the loss of her name; St Thomas Aquinas, writing of the Holy Spirit, says "non habet nomen proprium").[58] This may not have been MacDonald's intention when he began to write,[59] but such a development is not at all surprising in view of his passionate belief in the Trinity, the most distinctive and fundamental of all Christian doctrines.[60]

"The best thing you can do for your fellow, next to rousing his conscience, is—not to give him things to think about, but to wake up things that are in him; or say, to make him think things for himself," says MacDonald in "The Fantastic Imagination" (*A Dish of Orts*, 319); and—from *Phantastes* onwards—he is waking up things that are in himself as well as in his reader. This is why MacDonald puts the hypothetical reader of his fairy tales, who asks how he can be sure of ascertaining the author's meaning and not simply finding his own, on a level with himself: "It may be better that you should read your meaning into it.... your meaning may be superior to mine" (*Orts* 316-317) As for children: "They find what they are capable of finding, and more would be too much" (317)—though there is nothing to say that they won't be capable of more as they mature.

But whatever the age of his readers, MacDonald's purpose is always to promote the wholeness of the self. This is one reason why even in his fairy tales ("my so-called Fairy Tales," as he once described them[61]), George MacDonald is generally concerned with miracle, which involves an essential change, rather than with magic, which involves the manipulation of reality and of the person: "Magic exercises a *compulsion* that prevails over the conscious mind and will of the victim: an alien will rises up in the bewitched and proves stronger than his ego," says Jung.[62] But miracle is very different: "*Lux in tenebris* is the essence of the miracle in the world," says Max Luthi,[63] and MacDonald's aim, in the children's fantasies as in all his works, is always to bring light out of darkness, whether the light grows in the protagonist himself, as in *At the Back of the North Wind*, or in Queen Irene's lamp, as in *The Princess and the Goblin*—or whether, as in *The Princess and Curdie*, it remains on the metaphysical level described in *The Miracles of Our Lord*: "The future lies dark before us, with an infinite hope in the darkness."[64] But "the dark is only the box [God] keeps his bright things in," says the dying child Mark Raymount in *Weighed and Wanting* (600). And the light in every case comes from

George MacDonald's Major Fantasies for Children

"the Father of lights, yea even of 'The Light of the World.'"[65]

Endnotes to Introduction on page 219

PART I

"Come up, Diamond," it said. "It's all ready. I'm waiting for you."

He looked out of the bed, and saw a gigantic, powerful, but most lovely arm -- with a hand whose fingers were nothing the less ladylike that they could have strangled a boa-constrictor, or choked a tigress off its prey -- stretched down through a big hole in the roof. Without a moment's hesitation he reached out his tiny one, and laid it in the grand palm before him.

Chapter 5, "The Summer-House"
illustration by George S. Graves

CHAPTER 1

MacDonald's Crystal Palace: Diamonds and Rubies

"What is your name, little boy?" [the voice] asked.
"Diamond," answered Diamond, under the bed-clothes.
"What a funny name!" *(ABNW* 9)

And it is, in any ordinary sense. But Diamond's name is as multi-faceted as the jewel, for he is both a boy with a distinctive and developing character and a mandala, or universal symbol of integration and wholeness[1]—at least in process, for, as MacDonald says in *The Hope of the Gospel*, "we *are* not yet, we are only *becoming.*"[2] The diamond is the *lapis*, or stone, "whose prism contains all the hues of the rainbow"[3] and is therefore the ultimate symbol of completeness; in *Unspoken Sermons* MacDonald even says that "every human being is like a facet cut in the great diamond" which is God himself.[4]

The depiction of Diamond involves three layers of authorial input. One is drawn from real life, for his character owes a great deal to MacDonald's son Maurice;[5] one is influenced by MacDonald's reading, and especially by Paul Dombey in Charles Dickens's *Dombey and Son*;[6] and one—the most crucial—is the product of MacDonald's imagination on both the symbolic and realistic levels.

An important dimension of the symbolic meaning of Diamond's name derives from what may be described as the collective consciousness, part and parcel of Tolkien's "Primary World, Reality" which, like the "Secondary World" of fantasy,[7] figures largely in the book. Less than twenty years before the publication of *At the Back of the North Wind*, the most famous diamond on earth—the Koh-i-Noor, or "Mountain of Light"—was brought to Britain from India, was given to Queen Victoria and was a major exhibit in the Great Exhibition of 1851 in the newly-constructed Crystal Palace, a showplace for the development of commerce, industry and technology, not only in Britain and her Empire but in countries around the world.[8] The Exhibition was enormously popular. Among the approximately six million visitors[9] were members of the MacDonald family, including George MacDonald himself[10]—and he would have found nothing to deprecate in this display.[11] Indeed, he wrote to his father using the Great Exhibition as an inducement to visit Arundel: "Please do come.

You could come while the Exhibition was open."¹²

In view of MacDonald's love of jewels—"My father's delight in gems was wonderful. They were to him symbolic," says Greville MacDonald¹³—it is not strange that the Koh-i-Noor Diamond should have been to him, as it was to many others, the most fascinating exhibit of all. As a contemporary correspondent of *The Times* reported:

> The Koh-i-Noor is at present decidedly the lion of the Exhibition. A mysterious interest seems to be attached to it, and now that so many precautions have been resorted to, and so much difficulty attends its inspection, the crowd is enormously enhanced, and the policemen at either end of the covered entrance have much trouble in restraining the struggling and impatient multitude. ["Koh-i-Noor," in *Wikipedia*]

Public interest in the jewel was if anything reinforced from about 1855, when newspapers were coming into their own—John Sutherland calls it "the explosive growth of a national press"¹⁴—and this interest was reflected and perpetuated in novels. In Wilkie Collins's *The Moonstone*, published (in *All the Year Round*) a little before *At the Back of the North Wind*, the moonstone is based partly on the Koh-i-Noor, as attested by Collins in his preface to the first complete edition in 1868. He describes it as reputedly "one of the sacred gems of India" and as "the subject of a prediction, which prophesied certain misfortune to the persons who should divert it from its ancient uses."¹⁵ This by no means lessened the fascination of the jewel. MacDonald himself mentions it in his much later novel *Mary Marston* (1881); describing the dishonest character of Lady Malice (what a name!) he says that "had she been certain of escaping discovery, she would have slipped the koh-i-noor into her belt-pouch" (*MM* 87). What happens in *At the Back of the North Wind* is that MacDonald transforms the allegedly stolen Koh-i-Noor, enormously valuable yet reputedly accursed and therefore taboo, into a blessing precious beyond price—the living child who is at the heart of the book.

"What a funny name!" says North Wind (*ABNW* 9)—surely the understatement of the book, but it does open the subject on the level of a child's understanding. And what a funny conversation, taking place as it does between North Wind and a little boy in "the Primary World, Reality," a world in which London street names are accurately given and the protagonist for some time drives a cab and carefully reckons up his fares. Yet Diamond's surname is never given—something much more common in fairy tales. The narrator himself says "I have seen this world . . . look as strange as ever I saw Fairyland" (17), and strange things happen in it.[16] MacDonald accentuates the strangeness of the first conversation between wind and boy by explaining that Diamond's father, a coachman, named him after a favourite horse (2): "He is Old Diamond, and I am Young Diamond," Diamond says (9).[17] Boy and horse relate primarily to Joseph the coachman rather than to each other—"he's Big Diamond, and I'm Little Diamond; and I don't know which of us my father likes best"(10)—though their personal relationship develops as Diamond matures. And both horse and boy must, with Mr. Raymond, eventually become part of a symbolic trinity of diamonds—body, spirit and mind, with their concomitant functions of sensation, meditation and imagination—in which it is imperative that the horse should take the lowest place.[18]

The diamond is rich in connotation in *At the Back of the North Wind* and we are soon made aware that that when it comes to Young Diamond, at least, the name has a meaning more complex than anything his father intended. When North Wind first visits Diamond she tells him almost immediately that she already knows his name and has even defended its suitability to (one presumes) a visiting cleric:

> "Don't you remember that day when the man was finding fault with your name—how I blew the window in?"
>
> "Yes, yes," answered Diamond, eagerly. "Our window opens like a door, right over the coach-house door. And the wind—you, ma'am—came in, and blew the Bible out of the man's hands, and the leaves went all flutter flutter on the floor, and my mother picked it up and gave it back to him open, and there—"
>
> "Was your name in the Bible,—the sixth stone in the high priest's breast-plate."

If Diamond is disappointed with this explanation—"'Oh!—a stone, was it?' said Diamond. 'I thought it had been a horse—I did'" (13)—it is rewarding for the reader. The reference is to the breastplate of Aaron, the first high priest, as described in the Book of Exodus:

> And thou shalt set in it settings of stones, even four rows of stones: the first row shall be a sardius, a topaz, and a carbuncle: this shall be the first row.
>
> And the second row shall be an emerald, a sapphire, and a diamond. (Exodus 28: 17-18, and see 39: 10-11).

But if Diamond is to achieve the symbolic fullness of his name he must begin by coming to terms with the animal who lives in the stable beneath him and who, in MacDonald's eyes, is also more precious than

The Downstretched Hand: Individual Development in

a diamond. In an essay in *Unspoken Sermons: Series Three*, MacDonald says that while "the precious things of the earth . . . may be said to have come from [God's] hands . . . the live things come from his heart" ("The Inheritance," 613). And North Wind puts it more succinctly: "A horse is better than a stone any day" (*ABNW* 13).

At the beginning of the book Young Diamond has still to come to terms with the animal who sleeps in the stable beneath him:

> [W]hen young Diamond woke in the middle of the night, and felt the bed shaking in the blasts of the north wind, he could not help wondering whether, if the wind should blow the house down, and he were to fall through into the manger, old Diamond mightn't eat him up before he knew him in his nightgown (3).

But Diamond begins to grow close to the horse after his first encounter with North Wind. He hesitates to follow her down the dark, unfamiliar staircase to the yard and runs instead to the stable ladder with its comforting gleam of light at the bottom. And

> there was horse Diamond's great head poked out of his box on to the ladder, for he knew boy Diamond although he was in his nightgown, and wanted him to pull his ears for him. This Diamond did very gently for a minute or so . . .(15)

Ear-pulling notwithstanding, Diamond is not so wise in the ways of friendship as he later becomes, for he decides next morning to give the sleeping horse a surprise. But when he climbs onto Old Diamond's back the horse gets up with a tremendous commotion and the situation is only saved when the child gives a cry of terror:

> But then the horse stood as still as a stone, except that he lifted his head gently up, to let the boy slip down to his back. For when he heard young Diamond's cry he knew that there was nothing to kick about; for young Diamond was a good boy, and old Diamond was a good horse, and the one was all right on the back of the other. (26)

When Diamond's mother finds him he is sitting "like a knight on his steed in enchanted stall" (26)—an appropriate image for the battle in which he and Old Diamond will together be engaged, and not unduly romantic in view of the fact that when he first rides horse Diamond he rescues a distressed damsel in the shape of Nanny, a crossing-sweeper who is defending her broom from some teasing urchins (171). But the first change of any significance is that next day he forsakes his earlier game of sitting in a blanket cave before his mother's fire[19] and takes to driving two broken chairs harnessed to a cradle (29). The mother-image of the cave is not abandoned, for the cradle is a mother-image too.[20] But Diamond has also begun to enact his father's role which, when described to North Wind, was merely a future prospect: "I'm going to be a coachman" (32).

In the course of his nocturnal expeditions with North Wind Diamond never has any adventures involving horses, perhaps because he has a more exotic mode of transport, but more probably because horse and wind represent two different spheres of the unconscious—the instinctual and the spiritual[21]—and Diamond cannot, or at any rate does not make contact with both levels simultaneously. So his excursions with North Wind take place either when he is separated from Old Diamond or when the horse has faded into the background. But Old Diamond is significant in the context of young Diamond's day-to-day struggles, especially in the real battleground of Bloomsbury and the central London area. The close proximity of horse and boy in the stables of both Chiswick and Bloomsbury is important too, for without making too much of young Diamond as a Christ-figure,[22] a stable, or at least the coach house, was presumably the place of his birth.[23] Certainly it is the setting for an important stage in his growth to maturity on the night when North Wind, to encourage him to overcome his fears, says "Diamond, dear ... be a man" (67). And more important than proximity is co-operation between boy and horse, for their relationship symbolises Young Diamond's assimilation of the instinctual level of his psyche. During his first ride,

> Diamond soon found that, as he was obedient to his father, so the horse was obedient to him. . . . And another discovery he made was that, in order to guide the horse, he had in a measure to obey the horse first. If he did not yield his body to the motions of the horse's body, he could not guide him; he must fall off. (54)

This is the era of struggle for Diamond. He is in the thick of all the change and upheaval to which his family is subject when they are obliged to leave their home on the Colemans' estate in the country—a tremendous adjustment to new and less appealing surroundings (152), precarious finances and even short commons (310-11), and the delightful but certainly traumatic events of the birth of a second son just before moving to London and of a daughter while they are there. Against this background his own identity develops. Long before, in a cathedral, North Wind taught him literally to stand on his own feet (81-82), but now he must also change the lives of those around him for the better. When his family moves into the mews, Diamond does his best to "keep out the misery that was trying to get in at doors and windows" (155), begins to heal the wretchedness of the drunken cabman and his family next door (177ff), and extends his care for Nanny the crossing-sweeper, a solicitude which turns out to be even more important on the symbolic level of the book than it is to the plot—if indeed the two can be separated.

Horse Diamond cannot help Boy Diamond in these endeavours, but, when Joseph falls ill, the two diamonds share the venture of driving the cab. Young Diamond has first to saddle up the horse—"If the old horse had had the least objection to the proceeding, of course he could not have done it" (218)—and then to drive him in order to feed the family. And he proves his discretion as well as his driving ability when he takes Mr. Evans (Miss Coleman's former sweetheart, now presumed dead) to the Colemans' new house in Hoxton.[24]

During the Bloomsbury era North Wind, Diamond's great support and mentor, fades into the background: "Indeed, there was such a high wall, and there were so many houses about the mews, that North Wind seldom got into the place at all" (152). Although she continues to help in practical ways, such as blowing down a stack of chimneys to alter the direction of the cab (174-75), Diamond "could not quite satisfy himself whether the whole affair [of his first journey with her] was not a dream which he had dreamed when he was a very little boy" (174). And he finds a new mentor—Mr. Raymond, the similarity of whose name to Diamond's own is significant. For, as Freud says in *Totem and Taboo*:

> [Children] are never ready to accept a similarity between two words as having no meaning; they consistently assume that if two things are called by similar-sounding names this must imply the existence of some deep-lying point of agreement between them.[25]

This presumably applies to the childlike as well[26]—and in any case children do have a special claim on a book which first appeared in a journal designed for them.[27] Mr. Raymond is another diamond; and MacDonald is playing not only on the similarity in sound of the words "raymond" and "diamond" but on what—to adults even more than to children—is an apparent similarity of meaning, for the words suggest "light of the world" and "day of the world" respectively.[28]

By this point Diamond, as his father has discovered in the course of his illness, has become "not only useful to his family but useful to other people" (*ABNW* 251)—that is, his psyche is now centred, as it should be, in a universal context. He turns to Mr. Raymond for help when Nanny is ill, and it is thanks to him that she is conveyed from her filthy cellar to a children's hospital. Then a chain of events begins in which Mr. Raymond, his future wife, Nanny and Diamond are inextricably involved. Nanny's dream of the moon—triggered, as she says herself, by Mr. Raymond's story about Princess Daylight in which the waxing and waning of the moon are of central importance (295)—actually begins with her contemplation of the ruby ring lent her (to wear all night) by the future Mrs. Raymond:

> "[A]s she talked I kept seeing deeper and deeper into the stone. . . . I do think it was the ring that set me dreaming; for, after I had taken my tea, I leaned back, half lying and half sitting, and looked at the ring on my finger. By degrees I began to dream. The ring grew larger and larger, until at last I found that I was not looking at a red stone, but at a red sunset. . . . Why couldn't I live in the sunset instead of in that dirt?" (293)

This complements Diamond's earlier waking fantasy of living in a sunset (29); but Nanny's dream goes further. Eventually she finds herself in the garden, watching the moon which she has always loved—"She's the only thing worth looking at in our street at night" (296)—when a dog chases her into a small summer-house, reminiscent (though not to her) of the one that used to stand in the garden of The Wilderness.[29] As Diamond was fascinated by the pane of stained glass in the real summer-house, so Nanny in the dream summer-house sees "the moon beginning to shine again—but only through one of the panes—and that one was just the colour of the ruby." And just as she earlier kept looking at the ring, so now "the moon was so beautiful that [she] couldn't keep from looking at it through the red pane" (298).

Nanny's unconscious is beginning to claim her attention in this dream, in which the moon, symbolically associated with the unconscious,[30] plays so great a part: "Somehow the moon suited me exactly" (295). It can also, however, symbolise at least an aspect of the totality of the self—especially in the course of Diamond's development, throughout the book, into the *lapis invisibilitatis*.[31] Diamond's interest in the moon, already awakened by the story of Princess Daylight, is deepened by Nanny's dream—at the end of which he can even say "Perhaps if she hadn't [let out the bees], the moon might have carried her to the back of the north wind" (308). Certainly he shows an increasing interest in the moon from this point, and it is very evident in the Mound section of the book. But in the London section pride of place as mandalas must go to the diamond and the ruby, included

The Downstretched Hand: Individual Development in

by Carl Jung in his *Psychology and Religion* in a list of symbols pre-eminent in expressing "the non-human [i.e. universal] character of the totality or self" (par. 276).

Diamond begins to feel the attraction of the ruby even before he hears the story of the ring. The foundation is laid by the emphasis on roses and rose-colour in his dream of the stars *(ABNW* 233-234)— and shortly before he visits Nanny in hospital a ruby of another sort enters Diamond's life in the shape of Mr. Raymond's horse, which Joseph is to work and care for with his own horse while his master is abroad: "Oddly enough, the name of the new horse was Ruby, for he was a very red chestnut. . . . Young Diamond said they *were* rich now, with such a big diamond and such a big ruby" (290).[32] And he interrupts Nanny during the narration of her dream to point out the coincidence of Horse Ruby's having arrived at just about the same time as she borrowed the ruby ring (293).

Just as Old Diamond was part of Diamond's family before he himself was born, so Ruby precedes Nanny into the establishment. And his presence is intimately connected with her own, for Mr. Raymond stipulates that Joseph shall provide for her as for one of his own children—"so long, that is, as he had the horse" (287). But though Ruby and Nanny have a symbolic connection, they, unlike the Diamonds, have no relationship. Ruby's thoughts are entirely (and sometimes misguidedly) on his distant master, while Nanny turns out to be less exalted as a human being than Ruby, "an angel of a horse" (323), is as an animal.

There is symbolic consistency in the very lack of a parallel between the connection of Horse Diamond with Boy Diamond on the one hand and the connection of Ruby with Nanny on the other. The two Diamonds harmonise and finally enter the trinity of diamonds headed by Mr. Raymond. But the trinity is an incomplete symbol of the self, the wholeness of which must be represented by a quaternity.[33] Ruby and Nanny symbolise the fourth element (in this case the ruby) which is ambiguous and problematic, since "[t]his 'inferior' personality is made up of everything that will not fit in with, and adapt to, the laws and regulations of conscious life. It is compounded of 'disobedience'"[34]—the one thing Ruby and Nanny have in common. The sense of taboo which clings to the Koh-i-Noor and its literary descendant, the Moonstone, is projected, not onto the diamonds but onto the rubies in *At the Back of the North Wind,* though in a comparatively mild form.[35] Ruby is unconscious of or indifferent to his exploitation of those who have charge of him—but then, as

George MacDonald's Major Fantasies for Children

Job tells us, "the price of wisdom is above rubies" (Job 28:18). Yet the ruby (or sardius}, like the diamond, is a stone in the High Priest's breastplate, and though Ruby shirks working for Joseph because, as he explains to Horse Diamond, "Your master's not mine. . . . I must attend to my own master's interests" (*ABNW* 317),[36] his intentions are good. Nanny, however, is more blameable. She tells Diamond that in her dream the man in the moon "made me sit down *under a lamp that hung from the roof* [my italics][37] and gave me some bread and honey" (305). This is the beginning of a connection with the moon lady's bees[38] which promises enlightenment, since they "gather their honey from the sun and the stars" (304). But the man in the moon refuses to open their box and show them to Nanny, since "they are so bright that if one were to fly into your eye, it would blind you altogether" (305). In other words, the enlightenment of Nanny's unconscious self must begin with the humble task of cleaning the windows of the moon. Yet Nanny cannot resist opening the box "the tiniest crack" when she is alone (306), and three bees escape and have to be burned, precipitating a storm—in other words, disobedience leads to chaos.

The fourth and maverick element of the psyche is a source of energy that is, however, by no means wholly negative. It is "absent and yet present, [it] always appears in the fiery agony of the furnace and symbolizes the divine presence—succour and the completion of the work," says Jung.[39] Here Nanny and Ruby complement each other, for if Ruby, as the angel-horse which he declares himself to be (*ABNW* 320), is the "divine presence," Nanny, in "the fire of the fever" (*ABNW* 254), suffers the "fiery agony of the furnace"—even though, in *At the Back of the North Wind*, it is tempered by "the dew of tenderness" (*ABNW* 254). And when she recovers, Joseph's whole family (of which she is now part) has still much to suffer—a suffering of which Ruby is an indirect cause, although he does eventually bring "succour and the completion of the work." A heavy burden for Joseph during Mr. Raymond's absence ("No wonder, father: he's so fat," says Diamond [*ABNW* 323]), he becomes an invaluable assistant after his master's return: "Considering his fat, he exerted himself amazingly, and got over the ground with incredible speed. So willing, even anxious, was he to go now, that Joseph had to hold him quite tight" (332).

Nanny, as good and as strong as she is in spite of the disadvantage of her wretched background, suffers from a divided self. Her unconscious self knows she needs Diamond—"she had dreamed of him often" (255)—but her conscious self is only capable of shallow judgement: "Now that she could manage the baby as well as he

The Downstretched Hand: Individual Development in

[we learn when she is established in the family], she judged herself altogether his superior" (333). She never achieves her full potential and cannot pair with Diamond, whose love is of too unselfish and spiritual a nature for her fully to appreciate it. Instead she pairs with Cripple Jim, who, unlike Diamond, puts his own feelings before hers--he allows his shyness to keep him from visiting her in hospital—and who, like Nanny, allows fear and ignorance to get the upper hand, as when they are afraid of the dragonfly in the well (343) or of the thunder and lightning (350-351). Nanny does grow through her dream, but not enough; she tells Diamond that she would never open the lady's box of bees again if she had the chance—but she does not believe she ever will have another chance, and anyway, "It was only a dream" (308). Cripple Jim, for his part, is "very fond of looking at the man in the moon" (302)—but he never gets any further; not surprisingly, since the man in the moon is inferior to the moon itself: "I daren't [show you the lightning bees] . . . I have no business with them. I don't understand them," he says to Nanny (305). Failure adequately to transcend the instinctual level of the unconscious means that Nanny and Jim must be restricted on the conscious level too, and so they never realise that they owe almost everything to Diamond; they rationalise his wisdom as folly and gradually exclude him from their company.

On the animal level, however, Horse Ruby and Horse Diamond are paired, though there is much conflict and difficulty to be worked through first—particularly as Ruby deliberately, and ill-advisedly, lames himself to save his energies for his own master's service. Though Diamond does not see North Wind during the London era, he does once hear her voice; the end of the sojourn in Bloomsbury is signalled by her calling him down to the stable to listen to a conversation between the two horses,[40] who are, at this point, ill-matched both in feeling and appearance. When Diamond comes in, they are in the middle of a quarrel—or rather old Diamond is finding fault with Ruby, who, "with [his] fat and [his] shine," makes old Diamond "ashamed of being a horse" (317) and sounds for all the world like one of the prophet Jeremiah's wicked men—"They are waxen fat, they shine" (Jer. 5:28). Old Diamond has already been established as a good horse who does his duty and probably exercises a wholesome moral influence on Joseph (*ABNW* 285); the question has even been raised whether he will go to heaven (284). But he is too much of "an ignorant, rude old human horse" to understand an angel—or rather a mount for angels, for, as Ruby remarks, "there are horses in heaven for angels to ride upon, as well as other animals, lions and eagles and bulls, in more important situations" (320).[41] Ruby and Diamond are not so very far apart, however, for Ruby has been mistaken in the self-economy which has made him "as fat as a pig" (327)—an undignified condition for an angel. The very next day Mr. Raymond says "I think they make a very nice pair. If the one's too fat, the other's too lean—so that's all right" (329);[42] and "[b]efore the end of the month, Ruby had got respectably thin, and Diamond respectably stout. They really began to look fit for double harness" (333).

Until the end of the Bloomsbury section the rubies, both ring and horse, cause much uneasiness. Both jewel and animal are lent[43] and therefore of special concern to their recipients, whose cases, however, are very dissimilar; Joseph is reluctant to accept the horse, but Nanny yearns for the ring and thereby reveals her own association with the ruby element. In Nanny's dream the lady in the moon tells the little man to "take that ring off her finger. *I am sadly afraid she has stolen it*" (307)—which betrays contamination by Nanny's 'lower' unconscious, since North Wind, who sent the dream, must be well aware that the ring has not been stolen—while Joseph confesses to feeling so anxious about Mr. Raymond's horse that "when [Ruby's] between the shafts, I sit on the box *as miserable as if I'd stolen him*" (328; italics mine). There is something taboo or threatening about the rubies because the fourth dimension of the psyche which Ruby and Nanny represent is feeling; not love, but those intense emotions which, when fully experienced, tend to become unmanageable. They must be integrated into the psyche in order to give love (concern for others) the dimension of emotional warmth, but they must never predominate—which is why Ruby, though an angel, has a subordinate position in the angelic hierarchy. To begin with the red horse arouses considerable hostility, not only in old Diamond but in Joseph the coachman, who declares that he "wouldn't drive a horse that [he] didn't like" (328); yet eventually he is "reconciled to Ruby" (329), of whom his dislike has soon "so utterly vanished that he felt as if Ruby . . . had been his friend all the time" (332).[44]

If the scene in the Bloomsbury stable underlines the conflict between diamond and ruby, it is also the prelude to its resolution—and to the integration of all the symbolic elements of the book into a harmonious community. In the Mound section of *At the Back of the North Wind* there are overlapping quaternities of rubies and diamonds. Horse Diamond and Horse Ruby pull a carriage for Mr. Raymond and his wife, the owner of the ruby ring; an important link between the animal and human pairs is the fact that both the

The Downstretched Hand: Individual Development in

rubies come from Mr. Raymond. The matching of Horse Ruby and Horse Diamond, however, stops short of union, since there can be no "coniunctio"[45] where both elements are male. And this promotes the harmonious development of the psyche, for although animals, as "the instinctive forces of the unconscious," are "brought into unity within the mandala,"[46] it is imperative that the union of opposites should occur on the human or conscious level. Jung points out that "it must be reckoned a psychic catastrophe when the *ego* [consciousness] *is assimilated by the self* [total psyche]. The image of wholeness then remains in the unconscious"---i.e. the self will be dominated by the instincts.[47]

The "coniunctio" is achieved by Mr. and Mrs Raymond, the two 'diamonds' who are, respectively, the giver and the receiver of the ruby ring. Diamond, the symbolic offspring of the "chymical wedding"[48] of the red and white, the king and queen, makes up a trinity which is turned into a quaternity by the ruby element—in the same way that the overlapping trinity of diamonds (master, boy and horse) is transformed into a quaternity by Horse Ruby. Although the influence of the fourth element—the ruby—defies precise quantification, it is significant that when Joseph compares the emaciated Horse Diamond with the bloated Ruby he says "The horse is worth three of the other now" (*ABNW* 329). Nanny, too, is a witness that the diamond far outweighs the ruby, for although when she dreams of the moon (another form of the white stone) she begins by looking at it through a ruby-coloured pane of glass, she finds that "as [she] looked it got larger and larger till it filled the whole pane and outgrew it" (298). And the Mound section of *At the Back of the North Wind* focuses more and more on Diamond, the white stone.

Although he has been the principal means of drawing the little community together, Diamond paradoxically becomes a more and more solitary figure, for his increasing unworldliness distances him from everybody; in this sense, and only in this sense, he partakes of the taboo. Nanny and Jim dismiss Diamond by describing him as having "a tile loose" (an interesting echo of North Wind's having torn some tiles off the roof in order to take Diamond out to visit the cathedral [65]) or as being "God's baby" (345, 346 and elsewhere);[49] the tutor—the only character in this section, apart from Diamond, who is not one of a pair—says, when he has been talking to Diamond in his perch in the beech-tree, "A gush of reverence came over me, and with a single *good night*, I turned and left him in his nest" (345).[50] And there is a context of couples or pairs who emphasise his solitude, although three of them—his parents, his employers and the horses—recede into the background, with the partial exception of Joseph and Mrs. Raymond. Of those in the middle ground, Nanny and Jim are increasingly engrossed in each other, and Diamond's brother and sister, close to each other in age, are a sibling pair.

Diamond in a sense engineers his own dispensability—and not only because he is the proximate cause of Nanny's coming into the family. Though his isolation is greatest in the Mound section, it begins in Bloomsbury; the boy who sings to his brother that "Diamond's his nurse" (165) teaches Nanny to usurp his function, and "she had not many such lessons before she was able to perform those duties quite as well as Diamond himself" (309). And "[w]hen the second baby came, Diamond gave up his room that Nanny might be at hand to help his mother" (313). The innocent-looking comment in the Mound section that "[t]owards his father and mother, she was all they could wish" (333) is especially significant in view of Martha's earlier reliance on Diamond's help at home—"you're as good to your mother as if you were a girl" (156).[51]

The baby boy who was born when Diamond was away from home, and who is so oddly without a name, plays a special part in the distancing of his elder brother from the family, for Diamond appears actually to be grooming him as a successor. After his first assay at driving Diamond picks up the baby and sings a lullaby which begins:

>   baby baby babbing
>   your father's gone a-cabbing
>   to catch a shilling for its pence
>   to make the baby babbing dance
>   for old Diamond's a duck
>   they say he can swim
>   but the duck of diamonds
>   is baby that's him (164)

The symbolic connection between the two brothers—and the horse—is reinforced soon afterwards when the drunken cabman's wife next door identifies their nocturnal visitor as Diamond, and "a duck o' diamonds he is!" she adds (183). But Diamond identifies his brother as *the* "duck of diamonds," and therefore as the new Diamond who will grow into his full identity when his elder brother leaves.[52] The original family threesome of Joseph, Martha and Diamond has always been what Jung, in *Aion*, calls "a defective quaternity" (par. 351); and now the boy who did not want to remain in the country at the back of

The Downstretched Hand: Individual Development in

the north wind because he could not leave his mother (118-119) sees his family become a complete quaternity of father, mother, son and daughter almost (except for a spot of baby-minding) without him.

Although Diamond in a sense becomes isolated, he is anything but incomplete. As befits the "most brilliant and valuable of precious stones,"[53] he is the central mandala, or symbol of wholeness, in *At the Back of the North Wind*, and is one of the "living philosophical stones" which the alchemist Dorn urges all who seek the ultimate truth to be.[54] He transcends the paired opposites of male and female in the Mound section, even the "chymical wedding" or royal marriage of the Raymonds, who have made possible the harmonious development of the little community. Jung writes: "We shall hardly be mistaken if we assume that our mandala aspires to [be] the most complete union of opposites that is possible, including that of the masculine trinity and the feminine quaternity on the analogy of the alchemical hermaphrodite" (*Psychology and Alchemy*, par. 311). The triangular family unit of Joseph, Martha and Diamond in the Wilderness section of *At the Back of the North Wind* is intersected by the trinity of Horse Diamond, Boy Diamond (a "duck o' diamonds" [*ABNW* 183]) and baby, "the duck of diamonds" (164); and, "if the Trinity is understood as a *process* . . ." says Jung in *Psychology and Religion*, "then, by the addition of the Fourth, this process would culminate in a condition of absolute totality" (par. 290). The "process" in MacDonald's book involves a general reshuffle, for just as Ruby replaces the unnamed horse who was formerly old Diamond's stablemate (*ABNW* 148), so Nanny, closely associated with Ruby—she is to be provided for "as for one of [Joseph's] own children . . . so long . . . as he had the horse" (287)—replaces Diamond on a practical level:

> It was great fun to see Diamond teaching her how to hold the baby, and wash and dress him, and often they laughed together over her awkwardness. But she had not many such lessons before she was able to perform those duties quite as well as Diamond himself. (309)

When baby Dulcimer is born the family quaternity of Joseph, Martha, their unnamed son and their little daughter is settled in a cottage in the grounds; but Diamond, so vital to the original family unit, has moved from a "nest" under the thatch (340) to the more exalted "nest" of a tower room in the main house (341). Ever since the scene in the stable in Bloomsbury Diamond has been preparing for the role which becomes peculiarly his in the Mound section—that of the witness who, for all his love and concern, must be "[content] to see from afar"

(350). And now, from the tower, or sometimes a tree—both points of vantage from which perspective on life may be gained—Diamond symbolically affirms the wholeness of the family, for, as Jung observes in *Aion*, the complement of quaternity is unity; five, in fact, corresponds to the indistinguishability of unity and quaternity (par. 351n).

Diamond, the fifth, is a symbol of unity and totality of a very particular kind; he becomes the *lapis aethereus*, or ethereal stone (*Psychology and Alchemy*, par. 343). When North Wind first takes Diamond out with her they visit a fashionable house where a party is being held; North Wind takes the shape of a wolf and bounds upstairs to frighten a drunken nurse, and Diamond rushes after her, fully visible to the guests who regard him with well-bred surprise (*ABNW* 35). But during his first journey to North Wind's back Diamond's body undergoes a symbolic refinement, though it makes no difference to his daily occupations. One stage in the search for the philosopher's stone, the "ever-hoped-for and never-to-be-discovered 'One'," as Jung calls it, is described by the alchemist Khunrath as follows: "The spirit . . . must first be separated from its body and, after the purification of the latter, infused back into it" (*Psychology and Alchemy*, par. 165). This is what happens during the Sandwich episode, when Diamond's spirit goes to the country at the back of the north wind while his body lies in a coma at his aunt's house.

Does Diamond really leave his body behind? Apparently. But his sojourn behind North Wind's back has not been in the next world; as she tells him later, he has seen "[o]nly a picture of it" (*ABNW* 364), and the reality will be much more beautiful. Yet the vision affects him profoundly and radically alters his attitude to life and death:

> The fact was he had lived so long without any food at all at the back of the north wind, that he knew quite well that food was not essential to existence; that in fact, under certain circumstances, people could live without it well enough (136).

What this means is that Diamond believes there is a different kind of life after death—and he has already shown that, child though he is, he can now discuss death with equanimity. As for starving people, "They—they—what you call—die—don't they?" he says to his mother (134); and as for the birds who fall dead on the ground in winter, "They must die some time. They wouldn't like to be birds always" (135).

During his last journey with North Wind it becomes apparent that the symbolic purification of Diamond's body, begun when he visited North Wind's image of the country behind her back, has made him not only the *lapis aethereus* but the *lapis invisibilitatis* (*Psychology and Alchemy*, par. 343). He is quite imperceptible to the suffering woman to whom he sings about resurrection and eternity:

> "Didn't the lady hear me?" asked Diamond, when they were once more floating down with the river.
> "Oh, yes, she heard you," answered North Wind.
> "Was she frightened then?"
> "Oh, no."
> "Why didn't she look to see who it was?"
> "She didn't know you were there."
> "How could she hear me then?"
> "She didn't hear you with her ears."
> "What did she hear me with?"
> "With her heart." (*ABNW* 371-372)

The Koh-i-Noor Diamond, once on display in the Crystal Palace, was eventually set in a royal crown and is now kept in the Tower of London; MacDonald's Diamond has a different destiny.[55] When he is still in London, and has just driven the cab for the first time, Diamond dreams of the stars; they repeatedly call him by name (234-35), and to a child's consciousness they themselves resemble diamonds:

> Twinkle, twinkle, little star,
> How I wonder what you are;
> Up above the world so high,
> Like a diamond in the sky.

So goes the nursery rhyme[56]—and if proof be needed that MacDonald was familiar with it, one has only to turn to his friend Lewis Carroll's parody of the rhyme in *Alice's Adventures in Wonderland* (1865), where he compares the star to a tea-tray. Diamond's dream has to do with birth; in the Mound section of *At the Back of the North Wind*, his love of climbing trees and looking at real stars indicates that he is increasingly drawn towards eternity and willing to leave nature behind: "The earth is all behind my back," he tells the tutor (345).[57]

Diamond's "crystal-self" has always been in front (*Lilith* 43), and, like Margaret in *David Elginbrod*, he has "a soul slowly refining itself to a crystalline clearness" (*DE* 130); he becomes increasingly spiritualised until he reaches a stage which is not susceptible to further development in this world. Jung tells us that in Chinese alchemy "this state is called the 'Diamond Body' . . . which is identical with the *corpus glorificationis* of Christian tradition, the incorruptible body of resurrection."[58] And although the mystery of resurrection is only foreshadowed, not explored, in *At the Back of the North Wind*, it is evident from the tutor's remarks which close the book that Diamond has finally attained the ultimate transcendence of eternity:[59]

> I walked up the winding stair, and entered his room. A lovely figure, as white and almost as clear as alabaster, was lying on the bed. I saw at once how it was. They thought he was dead. I knew that he had gone to the back of the north wind (*ABNW* 378).

Endnotes to Chapter 1 on page 234

The hand felt its way up his arm, and, grasping it gently and strongly above the elbow, lifted Diamond from the bed. The moment he was through the hole in the roof, all the winds of heaven seemed to lay hold upon him, and buffet him hither and thither. His hair blew one way, his night-gown another, his legs threatened to float from under him, and his head to grow dizzy with the swiftness of the invisible assailant. Cowering, he clung with the other hand to the huge hand which held his arm, and fear invaded his heart.

Chapter 6, "Out in the Storm"
illustration by Arthur Hughes

CHAPTER 2

MacDonald's Crystal Palace
Common Crystals

Diamonds and rubies, with their connotations of beauty, brilliance and value, do much to bring out the meaning of the central mandala, or symbol of wholeness, in *At the Back of the North Wind*. In particular they do a very good job of telescoping together the animate and the inanimate, the personal and the non-personal, and thus (so to speak) kill four birds with two stones. But the mandala has a yet deeper meaning than the symbolism of precious stones can suggest unaided, and the full significance of Boy Diamond in *At the Back of the North Wind* cannot be understood without a detailed examination of his context. Roderick McGillis notes MacDonald's "intense gaze at a transcendent rather than an actual world,"[1] but the "actual world" is extremely important too. Diamond as mandala must, to be fully effective, develop in tandem with his growth to maturity as a living child with a unique character—and this growth is situated in a wider context, both realistic and symbolic.[2]

Many critics have observed a two-world consciousness (Primary and Secondary) in *At the Back of the North Wind*[3] and it is something that gives the book a unique value; MacDonald is showing, not a division, but the fundamental unity of life on all levels. Yet the two-world consciousness is in fact three. The entire book is permeated by the spiritual—"a something of which all human, all divine words, figures, pictures, motion-forms, are but the outer laminar spheres through which the central reality shines more or less plainly," says MacDonald (*Unspoken Sermons Series Three*, 425); and when his son Ronald points out that "[h]ere, for child and man alike, George MacDonald gives us . . . two worlds co-existent; not *here* and *there*, but both here and now," he is speaking not of Primary and Secondary but of spiritual and temporal.[4] MacDonald sees no essential conflict between material and spiritual and no threat to faith in scientific discoveries, whether in the fields of geology or of evolution. Nor is there any contradiction between fundamental unity and change. Everything is part of God's universe, like the Nature in the "changeful profusions" of which "God . . . is ever uttering himself" (*USS* 1, 15). And within the Primary World, too (to keep Tolkien's capitalisation), there is development which makes it not simply the 'ordinary' everyday world in which

The Downstretched Hand: Individual Development in

everyone knows what to expect but a world in transition—a world in which MacDonald is passionately interested and of which Diamond must be fully part.[5]

The Primary World in *At the Back of the North Wind* is particularly strong in the Bloomsbury section, in which Diamond never actually sees North Wind. This part of the book is a complement to MacDonald's novel *Guild Court, a London Story*, which appeared in volume form shortly before serial publication of *At the Back of the North Wind* began—and to some extent it complements *Robert Falconer*, which also appeared in 1868. *At the Back of the North Wind* is, in part, MacDonald's London story for children, without the guilt and disgrace which accrue to Tom Worboise in *Guild Court*, and without Tom's original shallowness and his eventual transformation. When MacDonald says that he writes, not for children, but for the childlike (*Orts* 317), this means that childlike adults can respond to his children's fiction—but not that all his adult novels are suitable for children. *Guild Court* certainly is not, as much of what transpires in it would be beyond their ken or might play to childhood insecurity; an unloving father, for example, can be coped with symbolically in fantasy or fairy tale, but would be too threatening in a story that deals with everyday life. In the Bloomsbury section of *At the Back of the North Wind* MacDonald shows that innocence can be strong enough to meet the demands and challenges of the contemporary world, even, if necessary, in its less salubrious aspects (dealt with in detail in *Robert Falconer*). A setting so uncompromisingly of the Primary World as London is best suited to demonstrate this.

For the reader of the twenty-first century it is easy to overlook the excitement caused by the expansion, even the explosion of the railway system in early to mid-Victorian England—something that made a huge difference to life for people of all classes, for the movement of travellers, rich and poor, was far greater than the promoters had anticipated.[6] In 1844 Parliament passed a law requiring railways (originally used largely to transport freight) to run at least one train a day carrying passengers at a rate of a penny a mile, and by 1868, the year in which serial publication of *At the Back of the North Wind* began, nearly all the long main line sections had been built. "I cannot convince myself that the roof of Bletchley station is more 'real' than the clouds," says Tolkien, disagreeing with a "clerk of Oxenford" who apparently thinks so—"'real life' in this context seems to fall short of academic standards," Tolkien sniffs ("On Fairy-Stories," 62). But MacDonald believes that the conditions and amenities of everyday life are as important as those of the Secondary World—and considering that until well into the last century the typical ambition of a small boy was to be an engine driver, it must have been very exciting, in mid-Victorian England, to read that Diamond had actually travelled by train (on his own, too). This might have seemed as exciting to some children as travelling on North Wind's back, but MacDonald, who is firmly in control, takes care that the trip cannot outshine his hero's more exotic adventures: "I will not describe the preparations Diamond made," says the narrator. "You would have thought he had been going on a three months' voyage. Nor will I describe the journey, for our business is now at the place." He doesn't even mention the words "train" or "railway," though Diamond's aunt, an unlikely apostle of modernity, meets her nephew at the station (*ABNW* 95).

"Our business is now at the place"—and Sandwich provides an important contextual background, for it is not only part of the Primary World but a part which reveals the overlapping of past and present in that world; not only "here and now," as Ronald MacDonald puts it, but 'then and now,' or 'then becoming now.' On the one hand the town "used to be one of the chief seaports in England" (*ABNW* 96) but is now "nearly dead of old age" (95) because left high and dry by the sea; on the other, small though it is, it is served by a railway station and is the residence of Diamond's aunt—she who sent his mother a letter inviting him to visit. Cheap postage, says Sir Llewellyn Woodward, was hardly less important than cheap travel in improving the ordinary conditions of life; before the introduction of the penny post in 1840 few poor people ever sent letters by post, and there were towns of 12,000 or so (larger than Sandwich) without post office or postman.[7] Members of Parliament franked their own and their family's letters (like Sir Thomas Bertram, in Jane Austen's *Mansfield Park* [1814]), and the cost to anyone else of sending a letter to Ireland, for example, and getting a reply, would have amounted to about a fifth of a labourer's weekly wage (Woodward, 595). Sending an invitation would have been a major undertaking only thirty years before the publication of *At the Back of the North Wind*—and so would getting a child from one place to another on his own. By the time the book appeared the general public must have been getting accustomed to these developments, but railway travel was still modern enough to be exciting.[8] So Sandwich is not only, like The Wilderness and Bloomsbury, a locus of change, but also, symbolically, a point of departure for the resurrection which is the goal towards which Diamond's whole life tends. This makes it a fit starting point for major development in the hero, and Sandwich

The Downstretched Hand: Individual Development in

also plays an important part in MacDonald's powerful evocation of his very own Crystal Palace, a symbolic context of crystals—not only precious stones, but common crystals associated with the basic needs of everyday life.

The non-precious crystals on which he focuses are coal and salt, basic components of shelter and food respectively. At the beginning of the book Joseph, Martha and Diamond are living on The Wilderness, the estate owned by Mr. Coleman, a merchant who lives next door, in more ways than one, to Mr. Dyves—an allusion to the rich man in the parable in St. Luke's Gospel who ignores the plight of Lazarus, the poor man, and is cast into hell (Luke 16:19-23). The Colemans are symbolically connected with coal, and coal and diamonds are both carbon crystals, so that at this point in *At the Back of the North Wind* we are shown the complementary aspects—black and white—of the same material.[9] This is why Diamond, on his first encounter with North Wind, goes out in the middle of the night to look at and then to enter the Colemans' house, although owing to the moral inadequacy of the Colemans there is little follow-up to this incident and its full symbolic potential is never realised.

Long before Mr. Coleman is "what himself and his wife and the world called ruined" (129), dubious speculation has compromised his honesty, "the tail of which had slipped through his fingers to the very last joint, if not beyond it" (130).[10] And, though the Colemans are described as "kind people," it is clear that the word "kind" does not necessarily denote either moral worth or emotional strength in MacDonald's vocabulary. The Colemans "did not care much about children" (21), and it has never bothered them that Diamond's family lives in poverty and what would be squalor but for Martha, who is as careful a housewife as her New Testament prototype. Their attitude results, not merely from indifference, but from a kind of disciplined meanness. Boy Diamond, riding Horse Diamond for the first time, sees Nanny sweeping a crossing before Mrs. Coleman:

> He drew Diamond's bridle in eager anxiety to see whether her outstretched hand would gather a penny from Mrs. Coleman. But she had given one at the last crossing, and the hand returned only to grasp its broom. (54)

And this is before the family loses its money! Diamond's generosity in compensating his friend with his own penny (ironically, Mrs. Coleman's gift of the day before) saves the situation, but underlines the parsimony of his mistress.[11]

George MacDonald's Major Fantasies for Children

Coal is a crystal of potential—a sort of *"prima materia"* in the alchemy of the book[12]—but in the case of the Colemans this potential is never developed. Though they could have been "more ruddy in body than rubies" (Lamentations 4:7), i.e. giving off warmth and light like the "stones of fire" in Ezekiel (28:14), they are forced to leave The Wilderness, "[t]heir visage . . . blacker than a coal," for a neighbourhood where "they are not known in the streets" (Lamentations.4:8).[13] The comparison with Jeremiah's Nazirites, or consecrated ones, is by no means fortuitous, for Mrs. Coleman has a brother who is a clergyman—the person who first put the idea of going to the land at the back of the north wind into Diamond's head (*ABNW* 91). Even Miss Coleman, the daughter of the family, who makes a friend of little Diamond and is therefore the most promising of the 'black crystals,' is actuated mainly by a combination of vanity and self-indulgence. Diamond's original mistaking of her for North Wind makes him give her a demonstration of apparently spontaneous affection, and "[s]he was so pleased that she . . . almost knelt on the floor to receive him in her arms" (22). This is natural enough, and her liking for his frank conversation is pleasing (55). But her feelings are at the mercy of circumstances, for after the storm which ruins her family and (apparently) kills her suitor, she, like her parents, appears never to give Diamond and his family another thought—though, just as "[t]he elm-tree which North Wind blew down that very night . . . crushed Miss Coleman's pretty summer-house: just so the fall of Mr. Coleman crushed the little family that lived over his coach-house and stable" (130).[14] After the disaster there is no contact between the two families until Joseph, unexpectedly seeing Mrs. and Miss Coleman, takes them up as passengers (something which results directly from Diamond's defence of Nanny on their first meeting [172]). Miss Coleman's previous fondness for Diamond now proves to have been no more than the indulgence of a weak and wounded affectivity, for she makes no move to resume her friendship with him except to tell his father that "he must come and see us, now you've found us out" (173).

Diamond correctly interprets this as a nothing-meaning remark, but this does not prevent his doing Miss Coleman a good turn when he gets the chance. One day when he is driving the cab he brings her chastened and repentant sweetheart to her door, to the astonishment of both parties—so Miss Coleman finds her heaven in Mr. Evans. At this point, however, Diamond shows that he can be hard as well as bright. Whereas his father gallantly refused to accept the fare from his former mistress, Diamond parks outside the front door (with North

The Downstretched Hand: Individual Development in

Wind's unseen assistance [248]) and gives Horse Diamond a well-deserved nosebag—a manoeuvre which brings Miss Coleman out, when her first transports are over, with a munificent five shillings.[15]

A symmetrical plot would demand the reformation and restoration of the Colemans, and if Dickens had written *At the Back of the North Wind* we should certainly have heard a great deal more about them. But they are not the focus of MacDonald's attention—"Diamond . . . is my only care" (336)—and from now on we lose sight of them altogether; they presumably remain in genteel poverty in Hoxton but are not, as Diamond observes with that shrewdness which is increasingly characteristic of him, entitled to much sympathy on this score:

> "Poor things!" said the mother [actually talking to Joseph]; "it's worse for them than it is for us. You see they've been used to such grand things, and for them to come down to a little poky house like that—it breaks my heart to think of it."
>
> "I don't know," said Diamond thoughtfully, "whether Mrs. Coleman had bells on her toes."
>
> "What do you mean, child?" said his mother.
>
> "She had rings on her fingers anyhow," returned Diamond.
>
> "Of course she had, as any lady would. What has that to do with it?"
>
> "When we were down at Sandwich," said Diamond, "you said you would have to part with your mother's ring, now we were poor."[16]

In the overall context of MacDonald's work this would be a loss of enormous symbolic significance.[17] In the present case Martha is flustered by Diamond's remark, and begins to see that her loyalty to her former employers is to some extent misplaced—or at least based on the erroneous assumption that the rich have an inherent right to stay rich: "Mrs. Coleman is none so poor as all that yet. No, thank Heaven! she's not come to that," she says. "'Is it a *great* disgrace to be poor?' asked Diamond" (175).

At the Back of the North Wind is steeped in biblical allusion—and in the Wilderness section the allusion of greatest significance, because of its bearing on coal, is to Ezekiel's king of Tyrus, a man who, though far more affluent, more influential and more exotic than Mr. Coleman, resembles him in some interesting particulars. To begin with, he is a merchant; a large part of Ezekiel 27 is devoted to a description of the number and magnificence of his ships and the merchandise they carry.

George MacDonald's Major Fantasies for Children

His pride, too, comes before a great fall. No-one could say of Mr. Coleman, as the Lord does of the king, that "[t]hou wast perfect in thy ways from the day that thou wast created, till iniquity was found in thee" (Ezekiel 28:15)—and as certainly no-one would consider Mr. Coleman an "anointed cherub" (28:14). But the symbolic significance of the Lord's lament in relation to MacDonald's book is so great that it is worth detailed attention.

The "stones of fire" in the midst of which the king walked are presumably burning coals (28:14). The associations of coal in The Wilderness are with darkness and torpor, but the allusion is nonetheless there—and it becomes plainer as the passage continues:

> By the multitude of thy merchandise they have filled the midst of thee with violence, and thou hast sinned: therefore I will cast thee as profane out of the mountain of God: and I will destroy thee, O covering cherub, from the midst of the stones of fire. (28:16)

The prophecy becomes more menacing as it goes on:

> Thou hast defiled thy sanctuaries by the multitude of thine iniquities, by the iniquity of thy traffick; therefore will I bring forth a fire from the midst of thee, it shall devour thee, and I will bring thee to ashes upon the earth in the sight of all them that behold thee. (28:18)

To find ashes in The Wilderness we need only look next door, for Mr. Dyves, or Dives, who represents exhausted potential, has burned out his *prima materia*. When Diamond suggests that Mr. Dyves' bed would afford North Wind a better view than his own, she replies: "Nobody makes a window into an ash-pit" *(ABNW* 8).[18]

But the main importance of the Lord's lament over the king, as far as *At the Back of the North Wind* is concerned, is in its bearing on Diamond himself. For the king of Tyrus, like Aaron the high priest, wears a "covering" of precious stones, and although one row of the Exodus jewels is missing the diamond is not:

> Thou hast been in Eden the garden of God; every precious stone was thy covering, the sardius [ruby], topaz, and the diamond, the beryl, the onyx and the jasper, the sapphire, the emerald, and the carbuncle, and gold. (Ezek. 28:13).

There are only three comprehensive lists of precious stones in the Bible, and they are to be found in the descriptions of the high priest's breastplate (occurring twice in the Book of Exodus), the adornment of the king in Ezekiel and the garnishing of the foundations of the New

The Downstretched Hand: Individual Development in

Jerusalem in Revelation 21:19-20. It is no accident that two of these three lists should be mentioned or alluded to in *At the Back of the North Wind*, and that the name of the protagonist—not to mention that of his father's horse—should figure in both of them. But Diamond is a "living stone" (see 1 Peter 2: 4),[19] and when the garment of the fallen trader becomes incompatible with that of the high priest it is not fitting that he adorn both. The appropriate symbolic setting for Diamond is the breastplate of the high priest, as North Wind has already intimated; there was "your name in the Bible,--the sixth stone in the high-priest's breast-plate" (*ABNW* 13).

The breastplate expresses the idea of completeness, not only because the twelve stones represent the twelve tribes of Israel, i.e. the totality of the people of God, but because the four rows represent the four seasons and therefore the totality of nature: "[B]y constant association with this symbolism, the high priest makes his own life worthy of the universal nature; his robe signifies that the whole cosmos worships with him."[20] During his prolonged association with North Wind, Diamond's own love of nature grows ever deeper and more spiritual. The lack of a natural environment in Bloomsbury causes him much suffering, although his sense of the relationship between man and animal develops considerably while he is there—and by the Mound section the tutor (the narrator as participant) believes that "little Diamond possessed the secret of life, and was himself what he was so ready to think the lowest living thing—an angel of God with something special to say or do" (*ABNW* 345).

North Wind avouches almost from the beginning that Diamond is good:

> "Good people see good things; bad people, bad things."
>
> "Then are you a bad thing?"
>
> "No. For *you* see me, Diamond, dear," said the girl. (37)

One night she takes him to a cathedral (a more spiritualised Crystal Palace for an increasingly spiritualised Diamond) where she leaves him alone while she goes to sink a ship—an experience of solitude which culminates in his falling asleep in front of the high altar, for all the world like a living sacrifice (86-87). And Diamond's goodness does not remain passive, but grows into active holiness. He becomes not only a reader of the Bible (323) but a visitor of the sick and a lover of even his drunken neighbour—who says, as Diamond takes his leave after comforting the crying baby, "I do somehow believe that wur an angel just gone . . . . He warn't wery big, and he hadn't got none o' them wingses, you know. It wur one o' them baby-angels you sees on the gravestones" (183). Small wonder that in the Mound section he inspires a "gush of reverence" (345) in the tutor, nor that the kindly but patronising nickname of "God's baby," given to Diamond first by the cabmen and then by Nanny and Jim, should be regarded by Diamond himself as a title of dignity (375). And, child as he is, he is able shortly before his death to agree with the tutor that "there is a still better love than that of the wonderful being you call North Wind" (376).

With holiness goes wisdom, and the high priest's breastplate is not only a ceremonial garment of sanctity but the "breastplate of judgment" (Exodus 28:15). Yet if by the end of *At the Back of the North Wind* Diamond can be described as "full of quiet wisdom" (345), this has to be learned. To start with North Wind teaches him in a rather didactic way: "You must not be ready to go with everything beautiful all at once, Diamond. . . . sometimes beautiful things grow bad by doing bad, and it takes some time for their badness to spoil their beauty" she says, and much more (13-14). But she is always ready to discuss and guide, and Diamond, for his part, always wants to learn and understand—and he sometimes challenges North Wind's own understanding, which, like her experience, only goes so far; as she tells him shortly before the end of the book: "There are a great many things I don't understand more than you do" (361).

Before his family leaves The Wilderness, the region of the dark crystals, Diamond, who has not been well, visits his aunt at Sandwich. Here he symbolically becomes more limpid; as St. Thomas Aquinas says, "the thing is the whiter, the less it is mixed with black,"[21] and Sandwich, a former port which has been "abandoned by its nurse, the sea" (*ABNW* 96) is, metaphorically speaking, "a salt land and not inhabited" (Jeremiah 17:6). And while he is staying here Diamond comes into contact with the positive side of salt, that most paradoxical white crystal—one which symbolises the contraries of fire and water, bitterness and wisdom[22]—not in Sandwich itself but in the course of an (apparent) journey to the country at the back of the north wind.[23] This is what Frobenius describes as the "night sea journey"[24] which is crucial if the hero is to make contact with his own unconscious, of which the sea is itself a powerful symbol.[25]

Diamond is transformed by this dream voyage, in which the Koh-i-Noor finds another Crystal Palace—the ice ridge and its hinterland. He shows such an increase of maturity and thoughtfulness that his parents are sometimes uneasy about him—he has descended so deeply into his own unconscious, indeed, that in terms of earthly time he has been 'dead to the world' for over a week,[26] and has woken to find his mother crying over him (more salt). "'Oh, Diamond, my darling! you have been so ill!' she sobbed;" but instead of continuing, as one might expect, "I was afraid you would die," she says "I thought you were dead" (*ABNW* 126).[27]

It is not altogether surprising to find, at the end of the book, that the land Diamond visits is only a picture of the real country at North Wind's back—the best she is able to project (364). For the real country is the New Jerusalem, and, as St. John says in the Book of Revelation, "I saw a new heaven and a new earth: for the first heaven and the first earth were passed away; and there was no more sea" (21:1). What is described in Revelation, as Gilbert Cope points out, is the bringing of the total self into consciousness.[28] No sea, or unconscious, is necessary any longer, and Diamond need make no voyage to arrive at the New Jerusalem; he must only "consent to be nobody" (*ABNW* 102). After his sojourn in the supposed country at North Wind's back Diamond still has much to do in order to attain the state of ultimate development, completeness and integrity of the *lapis*. But it is noteworthy that he never again mentions the sea and becomes almost obsessively interested in rivers—particularly the river at the back of the north wind whose songs he frequently sings as best his memory will allow (his interest in music and poetry begins to mature from this point).[29] He has not seen the river of the New Jerusalem—only the impression of it which North Wind has tried to give him—but he is yearning for the "pure river of water of life, clear as crystal, proceeding out of the throne of God and of the Lamb" (Rev. 22:1), which stands for the total consciousness of full self-realisation.

When he and his family move to Bloomsbury, Diamond renews his acquaintance with a different source of salt—Nanny, for whose sake he once dismounted from North Wind's hair to help the little girl get home in a storm. Nanny's salt is not found in the sea but under the earth, for she lives in Old Sal's cellar—a salt-cellar. It is intriguing that, while Diamond never actually sees or hears Old Sal, her presence is so powerful that Arthur Hughes makes her the central figure in one of his illustrations (*ABNW* 47). For salt, as Jung points out in *Mysterium Coniunctionis*, pervades everything, like the world-soul (par. 322) and in Nanny, who considers herself Sal's granddaughter and is locally known as "Sal's Nanny" (*ABNW* 206 et al.), it appears in its character as the representative of "the feminine principle of Eros, which brings everything into relationship, in an almost perfect way" (*MC* par. 322). But Nanny's femininity cannot fully develop while she lives with Old Sal, for the feminine can only differentiate itself in relation to the masculine. In the milieu of Paradise Row,[30] where Old Sal's cellar is located, a child with a father is considered a "natural curiosity" (*ABNW* 45),[31] and although she has had long-term 'maternal' contact with Cripple Jim, to whom she gives food and even money, they cannot have a peer relationship until Nanny has finally been separated from her 'grandmother.'[32]

In Old Sal herself the deadly quality of salt is paramount. Her cellar is a "dreary place" (204); it is "very dark, for the window was below the level of the street, and covered with mud, while over the grating which kept people from falling into the area, stood a chest of drawers, placed there by a dealer in second-hand furniture, which shut out almost all the light" (205). It looks almost as if Old Sal's neighbours want to shut her in—and she does seem a terrifyingly chthonic figure. Certain it is that in the dark, salt might as well be black as white (and coal is kept in cellars too). Old Sal's immediate predecessors are Widow Walker, the 'guardian' of Nancy Kennedy in *Robert Falconer* (1868), who drinks herself to death in six months on the proceeds of selling the girl (*RF* 440), and Mrs. Flanaghan, the sometime accommodator of Poppie in *Guild Court* (also published in 1868), who precipitates the loss of her 'charge' by hitting her on the head with her gin-bottle (*GC* 207). Old Sal is not, however, a minor character, as they are, but a powerful symbolic presence indissolubly linked to the earth—virtually the opposite of North Wind. She is ruled by the instincts of her unconscious, as her habitual drunkenness shows; the duality of fire and water in her is represented only by gin—no doubt from the nearby Adam and Eve pub, which aptly corresponds to her fallen nature. She has never sought the illumination of consciousness and has therefore failed to become individuated.[33]

Nanny's whole environment, Old Sal included, has made her "rough, blunt in her speech, and dirty in her person," and her face is coarse, "partly from the weather, partly from her living amongst low people, and partly from having to defend herself" (*ABNW* 254). Paradoxically, she has escaped fundamental contamination by Old Sal because mere survival has been the mainspring of their relationship— and Old Sal's shutting her out of the cellar from time to time makes it plain that even her hold on survival is precarious in that situation.[34] There has been little emotional investment by Nanny to prevent her from 'moving on,' and no-one knows better than she that her grandmother's capacity for feeling has almost been extinguished. Old Sal can no longer even work up a good spate of swearing unless someone first

The Downstretched Hand: Individual Development in

puts her into a passion of rage (her last remaining emotion): "It's no good till you do that," says Nanny, "she's so old now" (186).

Even before she meets Diamond, Nanny has begun to reject Old Sal's influence. She dislikes the mud (earth as filth) in which she works, and it is significant not only that her job as crossing-sweeper involves a rudimentary form of cleaning but that the task she dreams of is cleaning the windows of the moon (305-306). What keeps her interested in life is hope. When Diamond says that, given her circumstances, he would kill himself (an extraordinary remark in a Victorian, or indeed in any children's book), Nanny replies: "Oh no, you wouldn't! *When I think of it,* I always want to see what's coming next, and so I always wait till next is over" (51; italics mine). And Nanny draws away from Old Sal not only because of her love of life but because of her capacity for affection, or fire. Diamond discovers that Nanny is saving food and, when she can, pennies, to give to cripple Jim—"He's a good boy, is Jim, and I love Jim dearly" (189). Her name, too, suggests the nurse's role which she later adopts.

But Old Sal's cellar is unhealthy, and fire in Nanny turns to fever.[35] Salt symbolises bitterness as well as wisdom, and for Nanny, who has never had the chance to become more than street-wise, the bitterness of salt can mean death. Diamond's task is to get her away, and his gift of a lump of barley sugar (another crystal) symbolises her need of sweetness to redress the balance. And, as MacDonald says in the later *Sir Gibbie,* "no human consciousness can be *clean* unless it lies wide open to the eternal sun and the all-potent wind; until, from a dim-lighted cellar it becomes a mountain top" (*SG* 293). So Diamond, a white crystal compounded of fire and water, rescues another such crystal, homely but essential to life, and restores it to the light which makes its whiteness apparent. When Mr. Raymond tells the story of Princess Daylight, who, cursed by a wicked old fairy, can only experience waking life by the light of the moon—that is, she has been overwhelmed by her unconscious and the moon is her only hope of ever bringing it into consciousness—he is in effect recounting what has happened to Nanny. "I can't wake," murmurs Daylight when the prince asks why she cannot see the sun (*ABNW* 276), and, like her, Nanny needs a "prince" to bring her into consciousness by showing her love when she has reached her weakest point.

Jean Webb describes Diamond as an "agent for change,"[36] which he certainly becomes during the course of the book. But if Nanny needs Diamond in order to grow, Diamond also needs her, for the fire in the salt calls forth the fire in the precious stone. What in Nanny has been excessive pugnacity—"I'll box your ears," she threatens him at one point (51)—in Diamond becomes physical courage. He helps her to fight off the louts who are trying to grab her broom, [37] getting a bloodied nose for his pains, and although his efforts are not very effectual—it is Joseph who finally routs the foe—what counts is that Diamond can say "I couldn't let them behave so to a poor girl—could I, father?" (171).

Strange as it may seem, Nanny also has something to teach Diamond about love—namely forgiveness. It has never occurred to him that anyone might need his forgiveness and so he has never forgiven. This has allowed him, through an over-zealous partisanship of Nanny (he too is capable of being led astray by misplaced loyalty) to dismiss Old Sal with a general criticism on the grounds that her behaviour is stereotyped and predictable. Nanny sets this right, for as her characteristic hopefulness revives she shows that she has not only forgiven Old Sal but expects her eventually to be redeemed:

> "[H]ow. . . can anything be too good to be true?" [says Diamond]. "That's like old Sal—to say that."
>
> "Don't abuse Grannie, Diamond. She's a horrid old thing, she and her gin bottle; but she'll repent some day, and then you'll be glad not to have said anything against her."
>
> "Why?" said Diamond.
>
> "Because you'll be sorry for her."
>
> "I am sorry for her now."
>
> "Very well. That's right. She'll be sorry too. And there'll be an end of it." (296-297).

Nanny never returns to the cellar to see Old Sal or makes any inquiries about her, but her letting go of negative feeling is important. Furthermore, it is a very good thing that she has taught Diamond to forgive, for he forgives both Nanny and Jim for patronising and neglecting him.

"Perhaps the precious things of the earth, the coal and the diamonds, the iron and clay and gold, may be said to come from [God's] hands," says MacDonald (*USS* 3, 613)[38]—and it is interesting that he brackets coal and diamonds together. Coal and salt, rubies and diamonds, all come from the earth, but while the symbolic associations of precious stones can be brought clearly into focus, those of salt and coal make themselves felt, for the most part, through a general, unfocused pervasiveness; even when the reader is familiar

The Downstretched Hand

with the Bible, specific allusions such as the implied association between Mr. Coleman and the Prince of Tyrus are likely to register on the subconscious level. Nevertheless these associations are important, and by bringing them out MacDonald shows the significance of the primary world in the realm of spirit and imagination. More vital still, he is creating a context in which Primary and Secondary worlds, and therefore all levels of human experience, are not only harmonious but integrated.

Endnotes to Chapter 2 on page 247

CHAPTER 3
"Full of Quiet Wisdom"
Diamond as Prophet

If the Primary World in *At the Back of the North Wind* plays a significant part in the domains both of spirit and imagination, it follows that the converse is true. And the spiritual, in particular, plays a large part both in Diamond's everyday life and in his relationship with North Wind, for in MacDonald's view the spiritual is the most important level of human experience and must irradiate both the workaday world and the world of the imagination; it cannot be stressed too much that *At the Back of the North Wind* has to do not with two worlds, but with three. Diamond becomes more and more aware of the immanence of this third world, and through him others sense it too. There is a range of responses within the novel, depending on the psychic development of the characters—and a range of responses within the readership, for, as Raeper says, MacDonald's symbols "begin a process which acts on the unconscious mind of the reader" (*George MacDonald*, 202).

Greville MacDonald describes *At the Back of the North Wind* as "possibly the simplest of [MacDonald's] prophetic utterances" (*GMHW* 362), which may well be true; yet if the message of love and trust is simple, there is nonetheless a dense context of allusions to Old Testament prophecy in which Diamond lives and grows. Amos, Jeremiah and most of all Daniel loom especially large in *At the Back of the North Wind*, and the influence of the Book of Ezekiel is by no means confined to the resemblance between the prince or king of Tyrus, whose doom Ezekiel foretells, and Mr. Coleman; Ezekiel's "whirlwind... out of the north" (1:4) inevitably suggests North Wind, and, like other prophets, he speaks of punishment for wrongdoing and the hope of subsequent reconciliation. The Colemans' expulsion from Eden (paradoxically called The Wilderness) is just such a punishment. The proximity of Dives and Lazarus, in the shape of Mr. Dyves and the poor coachman, makes it fitting that such a disaster should have been imminent, while the fall of the elm tree in the garden telescopes the ideas of the fatal tree of Eden and the frequent biblical references to a fallen tree or branch as a metaphor of death or disaster.[1]

The meaning of the fallen tree is progressively amplified. On the morning after the great storm in which North Wind sinks Mr.

The Downstretched Hand: Individual Development in

Coleman's last ship, "there lay the little summer-house crushed to the ground, and over it the great elm-tree, which the wind had broken across, being much decayed in the middle" (*ABNW* 90). Later MacDonald elaborates on the symbolic significance of the ruin:

> The elm-tree which North Wind blew down that very night, as if small and great trials were to be gathered in one heap, crushed Miss Coleman's pretty summer-house: just so the fall of Mr. Coleman crushed the little family that lived over his coach-house and stable. (130)

And the summer house (the setting for Diamond's encounter with North Wind as "the tiniest creature" [57] in a chapter entitled "The Summer-House") has its own allusive meaning. The only building to be so denominated in the Bible[2] is found in the writings of the prophet Amos, through whom God says "I will smite the winter house with the summer house . . . and the great houses shall have an end" (Amos 3:15). This is elaborated upon later: "[The Lord] will smite the great house with breaches, and the little house with clefts" (6:11). By means of North Wind, who "had in a sense been blowing through the Colemans' house the whole of the night"(*ABNW* 128)—not to destroy Mr. Coleman, but "to look after [him], and try to make an honest man of him" (129)—others of Amos's prophecies have also been fulfilled: "I have sent among you the pestilence after the manner of Egypt: your young men have I slain with the sword, and have taken away your horses" (Amos 4:10). Miss Coleman's lungs are not strong, and on the night of the storm "North Wind had wound a few of her hairs round the lady's throat. She was considerably worse the next morning" (*ABNW* 129). After his ship is wrecked her father is obliged to sell everything, horses included, and move to a humble house in Hoxton—and, far worse, Miss Coleman's sweetheart is thought to have drowned with the other passengers. So it happens that the frequently reiterated Old Testament prophecies of death by sword, famine and pestilence[3] are to some degree fulfilled in the Colemans—and not only because of the failings of dishonesty, weakness and irresponsibility which MacDonald has described; as Amos says of those who "lie upon beds of ivory, and stretch themselves upon their couches . . . . they are not grieved for the affliction of Joseph" (6:4, 6).

As far as Joseph the coachman and his family are concerned, the Raymonds' house in Kent may well be viewed as a kind of Beulah: "I will save the house of Joseph, and I will bring them again to place them; for I have mercy upon them: and they shall be as though I had not cast them off," says the Lord through Zechariah (Zech.10:6)—and they are a lot better off at The Mound than they were in The Wilderness before the smiting of the "little house." It is actually a very long time before the reader learns that the name of Diamond's father is Joseph, perhaps because MacDonald wants to avoid making Diamond into a Christ-figure (he is more and more Christ-*like*, but that is not the same thing). "Why, Joseph! can it be you?" Mrs. and Miss Coleman exclaim when he drives them home in his cab *(ABNW* 173), and this is the first we hear of it. Even now they do not ask after Joseph's wife, and not until Ch. XXX111 do we know that she is called Martha (322)—a name that suits her admirably as a worrier about mundane matters but which disqualifies her from a role analogous to that of the Madonna. She does, however, sound like a mother, the resemblance between word and name being—if the pun may be forgiven—pronounced.

Joseph the coachman is much more like the Old Testament Joseph than the New. And the Joseph of the Old Testament, however high he rises in the Pharoah's retinue, is pre-eminently a figure of servitude. In the Wilderness section of *At the Back of the North Wind* Joseph is the faithful servant—"one of the most discreet of servants" (31)—of an unworthy master; for while Horse Diamond is shod as soon as necessary, Boy Diamond has to stay indoors for a week because "his mother had not quite saved up enough money to get him the new pair [of shoes] she so much wanted for him" (29); the Colemans have, in effect, "sold . . . the poor for a pair of shoes" (Amos 2:6). No lasting good could have come of remaining with the Colemans in the valley of The Wilderness, with its symbolically unprepossessing outside: "It was a waste kind of spot . . .bounded by an irregular wall, with a few doors in it. Outside lay broken things in general, from garden rollers to flower-pots and wine-bottles" *(ABNW* 50). And Mr. Coleman has come perilously close to the "dishonesty [that] goes very far indeed to make a man of no value—a thing to be thrown out in the dust-hole of the creation, like a bit of broken basin, or a dirty rag" (129).

The modern solution for Joseph and his family would be independence, but no particular value is attached to this in *At the Back of the North Wind* and the period spent in Bloomsbury driving his own cab, though it furthers the development of his character, is the most difficult of Joseph's life. His peace and security depend on a good master in a settled environment, and this he finds in the service of Mr. Raymond. What Joseph and Martha and their dependants need is to move to The Mound, which, if clearly to be Diamond's grave, is also one of the "little hills [which] rejoice on every side" (Psalm 65:12). For Diamond himself it is a place of perspective important

The Downstretched Hand: Individual Development in

in hero myth, elements of which are present in the book—"a place . . . from the top of which you could see the country for miles on all sides" (*ABNW* 339). And Mr. Raymond, as his name indicates, is not only 'the light of the world' but 'the king of the mound' (which had in all probability, MacDonald tells us, been built for another monarch [339]). In the setting of one of "[t]he mountains [that] shall bring peace to the people, and the little hills, by righteousness" (Psalm 72:3), Mr. Raymond, like the psalmist's king, "judge[s] the poor of the people" and "save[s] the children of the needy" (Psalm 72:4).

By far the most important biblical allusions in the book are, of course, those which bear on Diamond himself. He is chiefly remembered as the boy who travelled in North Wind's hair, yet, while nothing else captivates the imagination quite so much as this, his most important role is to be a prophet—that is, not necessarily to foretell the future but to see the truth and make others aware of it. This function is brought out in great measure by his connection with the prophet Daniel. The process by which Diamond fixes on a name for his baby sister is revealing: "The baby had not been christened yet, but Diamond, in reading his Bible, had come upon the word *dulcimer*, and thought it so pretty that ever after he called his sister Dulcimer" (*ABNW* 323).[4] This word occurs only three times in the Bible, and all three are in the third chapter of the Book of Daniel.

When Diamond goes on his second journey with North Wind the allusions to the Book of Daniel become more marked. On the night of the great storm North Wind must sink Mr. Coleman's ship, but she must also deliver Diamond from incapacitating fear—just as the prophet, in the tenth chapter of Daniel, is freed from fear by his heavenly visitant so that he may proclaim what he has seen. The setting in the two books could hardly be more different, though in each case "[the] call has the character of a supernatural experience."[5] Daniel has a daylight vision which no-one else can see. Diamond, in *At the Back of the North Wind*, wakes alone in the dark and is frightened by the noise of the storm: "For a while he could not come quite awake, for the noise kept beating him down, so that his heart was troubled and fluttered painfully. A second peal of thunder burst over his head, and almost choked him with fear" (*ABNW* 65). Relief at North Wind's arrival is short-lived, for when she lifts him out onto the roof he is overwhelmed by the violence of the storm: "Cowering he clung . . . to the huge hand which held his arm, and fear invaded his heart" (66).[6] At last "his knees failed him, and he sunk down at North Wind's feet" (68)— very like Daniel, who, in his terror at the vision, sinks to the ground unconscious: "When I heard the voice of his words, then was I in a deep sleep on my face, and my face toward the ground" (Dan. 10:9).

Daniel's visitant bears some resemblance to the storm in *At the Back of the North Wind*, since "his face [is] as the appearance of lightning," and he is also rather like North Wind, the author of the storm, for, if "the voice of his words [is] like the voice of a multitude" (Dan. 10:6), George MacDonald, in what is not one of his best pieces of writing, analyses what might well be the constituents of a multitude in North Wind's voice—ending, however, with the reflection that "it was more like [Diamond's] mother's voice than anything else in the world" (*ABNW* 67).

Diamond, like Daniel, is encouraged by the being who visits him. In the prophet's case "an hand touched me, which set me upon my knees and upon the palms of my hands" (Dan.10:10), and then the "man clothed in linen" (10:5) told him to "understand the words that I speak unto thee, and stand upright" (10:11).[7] North Wind encourages Diamond just as firmly in *At the Back of the North Wind*: "'Diamond, dear,' she said, 'be a man'" (*ABNW* 67). When he "clasped her round the column of her ankle" (68)—her arms and feet sound as impressive as those of the man in Daniel's vision, even if not "like in colour to polished brass" (Dan. 10:6)—"She instantly stooped and lifted him from the roof—up—up—into her bosom, and held him there, saying, as if to an inconsolable child—'Diamond, dear, this will never do'" (*ABNW* 68*)*.

Daniel becomes speechless from very weakness, but "one like the similitude of the sons of men touched my lips . . . . Then there came again and touched me one like the appearance of a man, and he strengthened me" (Dan. 10:16, 18). Diamond, in the cathedral, gains courage by feeling North Wind's arm about him and "putting his little mouth to the beautiful cold hand that had a hold of his" (*ABNW* 80). But Diamond is only a child, so even when he is left to conquer his fear by himself he has the encouragement of little puffs of wind to remind him that North Wind is really there, though unseen.

The night of the storm is crucial to Diamond's spiritual development, for the lonely vigil in the cathedral prepares him for his visit to the country at the back of the north wind by helping him to confront his fear of the ultimate solitude, death. Prophetic vision later emerges in his understanding of the tragedy of the fallen tree:

> Diamond almost cried to see the wilderness of green leaves, which used to be so far up in the blue air, tossing about in the breeze, and liking it best when the wind blew it most, now

The Downstretched Hand: Individual Development in

lying so near the ground, and without any hope of ever getting up into the deep air again. (90)[8]

But when the clergyman (Mrs. Coleman's brother) says that if the tree had been at the back of the north wind it would not have been blown down, Diamond points out that, though they would not have had to be sorry for it, they would not have had to be glad for it either (91-92); that is, life makes death worthwhile. His present understanding contrasts strongly with the naivete of his view of the poet's function expressed only the previous evening: "A poet is a man who is glad of something, and tries to make other people glad of it too," explains North Wind. "Ah! now I know," replies Diamond. "Like the man in the sweety-shop" (61). The post-storm Diamond would never make such a remark.

Even before the great storm Diamond discusses the meaning of suffering and death with North Wind, pressing her (like a true child) to the point where she eventually becomes distinctly uncomfortable. "I would rather not see the ship go down," he says. "And I'm afraid the poor people will cry, and I should hear them." North Wind admits that she would rather he did not hear the cry. "But how can you bear it then, North Wind?" he retorts. "For I am sure you are kind. I shall never doubt that again." Her answer, though sincere, sounds suspiciously like a platitude:

> "I will tell you how I am able to bear it, Diamond: I am always hearing, through every noise, through all the noise I am making myself even, the sound of a far-off song. I do not exactly know where it is, or what it means; and I don't hear much of it . . . but what I do hear, is quite enough to make me able to bear the cry from the drowning ship. So it would you if you could hear it."
>
> "No, it wouldn't," returned Diamond, stoutly. "For *they* wouldn't hear the music of the far-away song; and if they did, it wouldn't do them any good. You see you and I are not going to be drowned, and so *we* might enjoy it."
>
> "But you have never heard the psalm,[9] and you don't know what it is like. Somehow . . . it tells me that all is right; that it is coming to swallow up all cries."
>
> "But that won't do them any good—the people, I mean," persisted Diamond.
>
> "It must. It must," said North Wind, hurriedly. (76-77)

But after his journey to the land at her back (an expedition for which the night of the storm prepares him) Diamond can contemplate death with equanimity. "There *are* people in the world who have nothing to eat, Diamond," says his mother on the beach at Sandwich. "Then I suppose they don't stop in it any longer. They—they—what you call—die—don't they?" Diamond replies (134). The visionary experience which is all that North Wind has been able to provide for him (364) is not one of paradise, for North Wind has never seen the real country at her back; though Diamond describes it as "a very good place;" the people there "looked as if they were waiting to be gladder some day" (117),[10] and Diamond himself "began to long very much to get home again . . . for he saw his mother crying" (118). But his sojourn in the land at North Wind's back (for so we must consider it until almost the end of the book) causes him to deepen and mature to such an extent that his attitude is totally changed—a change on which MacDonald comments simply through reference to the experience: "I venture to remind [the reader] once more that Diamond had been to the back of the north wind," he says on several occasions (e.g. 202).

What Diamond has gained is understanding; not the cleverness to which Mr. Raymond is inclined to attach too much importance, and which is rebuked by Diamond's failure to understand the tree riddle—"Genius finds out truths, not tricks," says MacDonald (213)—and not the street wisdom of Nanny and Cripple Jim, but the wisdom which can be derived only from reflection on intensely-lived experience. This accession of wisdom is a vital link between Diamond and the prophet Daniel, for Daniel is above all a man of understanding, a man to whom it is given to understand others better than they do themselves and to awaken them to the word which God is speaking to them as well as to him—"that thou mightest know the thoughts of thy heart," he says to Nebuchadnezzar (Dan.2:30). This is precisely why the Book of Daniel is so important in *At the Back of the North Wind*, for understanding is of fundamental importance to George MacDonald. In *The Hope of the Gospel* he says: "Our whole life, to be life at all, must be growth in understanding" (*HG* 19).[11]

From the very first chapter North Wind, through her nocturnal visits, begins to initiate Diamond into the mysteries of life and eternity—just as, in the Bible, "the secret [was] revealed unto Daniel in a night vision" (Dan. 2:19). At first, however, it appears that the role of Daniel is that of a good psychiatrist, helping Nebuchadnezzar to bring his most deeply-buried ideas into consciousness—and it is doubtful whether this can be said of Diamond, in *At the Back of the North Wind*, with reference to anyone but himself. The king's

The Downstretched Hand: Individual Development in

immediate problem is a restless night productive of much uneasiness: "Nebuchadnezzar dreamed dreams, wherewith his spirit was troubled, and his sleep brake from him" (Dan. 2:1). He seeks an interpretation, but he has forgotten the original dream—"the thing is gone from me," he exclaims petulantly (2:8). When his wise men cannot tell him what the dream was, Nebuchadnezzar throws a tantrum and orders them all to be slaughtered. Daniel, however, steps in and saves the situation, revealing both the dream and its interpretation by praying for enlightenment (Dan. 2:17-19).[12]

Presumably Diamond reads about Nebuchadnezzar's dream before he gets to the chapter in which he finds his sister's name. The association with Daniel as visionary is inevitably there, and it is developed later on. To find the word "dulcimer" Diamond must have been reading about the casting of Shadrach, Meshach and Abednego into the burning fiery furnace (Dan. Ch.3), and this probably makes him think of his own traumatic passage through North Wind to the country at her back:

> When he reached her knees, he put out his hand to lay it on her, but nothing was there save an intense cold. He walked on. Then all grew white about him; and the cold stung him like fire. He walked on still, groping through the whiteness. It thickened about him. At last, it got into his heart, and he lost all sense. . . . It was when he reached North Wind's heart that he fainted and fell. But as he fell, he rolled over the threshold, and it was thus that Diamond got to the back of the north wind. (*ABNW* 112)[13]

This experience is a foreshadowing of his future passage to the real country at North Wind's back.

Diamond's association is basically with Daniel the prophet as the interpreter of dreams who later becomes a visionary himself [14]—especially in view of the probability that if Diamond has reached chapter three, he has also read chapters one and two. In his own case, however, things happen the other way round. He begins as a visionary, through his encounters with North Wind and especially through his journey to the country at her back—and much later he becomes, not quite an interpreter of Nanny's dream, but a commentator who tries to convince her of its fundamental truth:

> "I jumped up" [said Nanny} "and ran for a little summer-house in the corner of the garden. The dog came after me, but I shut the door in his face. It was well it had a door—wasn't it?"
>
> "You dreamed of the door because you wanted it," said

Diamond.

"No, I didn't; it came of itself. It was there, in the true dream."

"There—I've caught you!" said Diamond. "I knew you believed in the dream as much as I do." (297-298)

Going one better than Nebuchadnezzar, Nanny remembers her dream; but in spite of Diamond's encouragement and her original sense of shame at having disobeyed the moon lady, she dismisses the possibility of amendment and represses her incipient sense of the dream's importance (307-308). Like other prophets, Diamond is not always successful; in the Mound section of *At the Back of the North Wind* Nanny reverses her original remark about "the true dream" (297) and says "I never dreamed but that one, and it was nonsense enough, I'm sure. . . . Dreams ain't true" (355).

Just as Diamond's flights with North Wind had been psychologically prepared for by "those precious dreams he had so often had, in which he floated about on the air at will" (358), so the subconscious foundation for Nanny's dream was her interest in the moon, in London, as "the only thing worth looking at in our street at night" (296). But her rejection of the authenticity of her dream results in the much-diminished significance of the moon—and with it of the rest of the natural world—in her eyes: "There ain't nothing in [the country] but the sun and moon," which "ain't no count" (344). Nebuchadnezzar at least seeks an interpretation of his dream; when Nanny rejects her own dream as "nonsense" (355), it is reduced from experience to narrative and therefore produces no inner change.[15]

But Nanny's dream is not wasted. Diamond reflects on it and, by making it part of his own imaginative experience, validates hers: "It wasn't nonsense," he tells Nanny. "It was a beautiful dream—and a funny one, too, both in one." He draws from it the truth that Nanny needs to learn: "Didn't you come to grief for doing what you were told not to do? And isn't that true?" (355). And his appreciation of Nanny's dream grows, beginning with the reflection that if she hadn't been disobedient "the moon might have carried her to the back of the north wind" (308) and culminating in North Wind's revelation that she not only gave Nanny the dream but was herself the lady who sat at the window of the moon (364).[16]

Paradoxically it is in the Bloomsbury section of *At the Back of the North Wind* that the celestial bodies are most prominent in an imagined or visionary character, and, as Diamond suspects, North Wind, though never seen in this part of the book, has a lot to do

The Downstretched Hand: Individual Development in

with it. She later admits not only to sending Nanny's dream but to inspiring Mr. Raymond's story about Princess Daylight, in which the moon plays a major part, and sending Diamond's own dream of the stars (364-365). But the establishment of the little community at The Mound sees Diamond's interest in the moon reach, so to speak, its full. One evening Nanny asks him why he is climbing into his treehouse in the great beech. "I'm going up to look at the moon to-night," he responds, and the ensuing discussion reveals how entirely interest in the moon has been transferred from Nanny to Diamond:

> "You'll see the moon just as well down here", she returned.
>
> "I don't think so."
>
> "You'll be no nearer to her up there."
>
> "Oh, yes! I shall. I must be nearer her, you know. I wish I could dream as pretty dreams about her as you can, Nanny."
>
> "You silly! you never have done about that dream. . . . Do you really believe, Diamond, that there's a house in the moon, with a beautiful lady, and a crooked old man and dusters in it?"

And because his imagination is becoming more and more visionary, Diamond can simply reply:

> "If there isn't, there's something better," and vanish into the leaves (355).

This exchange takes place soon after the thunderstorm in which a branch of the beech tree is broken off by lightning (any resemblance to the fallen elm tree in The Wilderness is purely deliberate). And Nanny's not entirely good-natured warning that "You'll break your neck some day" (355) is a prophecy of death which is reinforced later the same night. Upstairs in his tower room, "he woke in the dim blue night. The moon had vanished."(357). He hears knocking at a door which he has never before been able to open—and as the passage continues the connotations of death become clear:

> The door now opened quite easily, but to his surprise, instead of a closet he found a long narrow room. The moon, which was sinking in the west, shone in at an open window at the further end. The room was low with a coved ceiling, and occupied the whole top of the house, immediately under the roof. It was quite empty. The yellow light of the half-moon streamed over the dark floor. He was so delighted at the discovery of the strange desolate moonlit place close to his own snug little room, that he began to dance and skip about the floor. (357)

The room is shaped like a coffin, and Diamond eventually dies in it (378). But now he is all but prepared to die—hence the easy opening of the door—and the "strange desolate place" has none of the terrors of a similar scene long before in Mr. Coleman's yard ("It was so dreadful to be out in the night after *everybody* was gone to bed!" [21]).

Only when North Wind takes Diamond back to The Wilderness does the moon preside over a desolation that makes Diamond afraid, and this is because North Wind, in her final act of preparation for his death, has to detach him from the past:

> Diamond ran about the lawn for a little while in the moonlight. He found part of it cut up into flower-beds, and the little summer-house with the coloured glass and the great elm-tree gone. He did not like this, and ran into the stable. There were no horses there at all. He ran upstairs. The rooms were empty. . . . He ran down the stair again, and out upon the lawn. . . . The moon was under a cloud, and all was looking dull and dismal. (373)

Diamond dies a few days later, when the moon is presumably at or near the full—so that, in a sense, the moon has been growing from a "poor thin crescent" (17) to a full moon throughout his life.

But the moon is less important to him than its context, the sky, which, when no-one and nothing else can pay him much attention, "does mind me, and thinks about me" (344). And the most important things in the sky, to Diamond, are the stars, a relationship with which, as Jung affirms, has connotations of eternity.[17] In the Book of Daniel the celestial bodies play no part until the last chapter. But shortly before the end there is a striking reference to the stars: "And they that be wise shall shine as the brightness of the firmament; and they that turn many to righteousness as the stars for ever and ever" (Dan. 12:3). Diamond, who is described as "full of quiet wisdom" *(ABNW* 345), turns many to righteousness within his small circle: "[B]efore long the bad words found themselves ashamed to come out of the men's mouths when Diamond was near," the narrator says of the cab drivers attached to the Bloomsbury stable (166), and he later comments: "I have little doubt that much of [Nanny's and Jim's] good behaviour was owing to the unconscious influence of the boy they called God's baby" (346). As regards shining like the stars, Diamond says to his new friend the tutor, "I should like to get up into the sky. Don't you think I shall, some day?" (344) "Yes, I do," the tutor replies (345)—and we remember that he is a persona of MacDonald, himself a tutor when he first moved to London.

The Downstretched Hand: Individual Development in

Any association with the prophet Daniel has connotations of the Book of Revelation.[18] MacDonald displaces the apocalyptic aspect of Daniel onto Revelation in the Bloomsbury section of *At the Back of the North Wind*, where London, the place of exile for Diamond, is linked with Babylon, Daniel's lifelong place of exile and also the "great city" of Dan. 17:18 which has still more unpleasant associations. These, or some of them, are brought out through the horses.

When Diamond and his family lived in The Wilderness, Horse Diamond had an inferior partner who was never named—"I liked [Diamond] far the best of the pair, though the other was good," says Joseph (*ABNW* 148). But Old Diamond's original partner is not the only nameless horse in *At the Back of the North Wind*, and it sometimes happens that the lack of a name, or the failure to tell it, is as interesting as any name could be. We see this clearly in a conversation between North Wind and Diamond: "Sometimes [people] call me Bad Fortune, sometimes Evil Chance, sometimes Ruin; and they have another name for me which they think the most dreadful of all," she says—and refuses to tell Diamond what that name is (363-364). It is not hard, however, to guess that the name is Death.

This conversation is anticipated in the Bloomsbury section. Diamond's first assay at driving the cab is made with Mr. Stonecrop, the owner of the yard, and his mysterious horse:

> "What's the horse's name?" whispered Diamond, as he took the reins from the man.
>
> "It's not a nice name," said Mr. Stonecrop. "You needn't call him by it. I didn't give it him. He'll go well enough without it. Give the boy a whip, Jack. I never carries one when I drives old----"
>
> He didn't finish the sentence. (162)

The suggestion that this name is Death,[19] or some associated term, is reinforced when they leave the yard, for Diamond narrowly escapes colliding with his father in Bloomsbury Square:

> "Why, Diamond, it's a bad beginning to run into your own father," cried [Joseph].
>
> "But, father, wouldn't it have been a bad ending to run into your own son?" said Diamond in return; and the two men laughed heartily. (163)

Father and son have narrowly escaped fulfilling one of the death prophecies of Jeremiah: "And I will dash them one against another, even the fathers and the sons together,' saith the LORD" (Jer. 13:14).[20]

The "nameless horse" (*ABNW* 163) is probably associated with the "pale horse" of Revelation whose rider is called Death (Rev. 6:8). In relation to Horse Diamond and Ruby, who strongly resemble two of the horses ridden by angels of the Apocalypse, the influence of Revelation is clearly discernible—and Ruby says himself that he is a horse for angels to ride on (*ABNW* 320). Revelation 6:4 says:

> And there went out another horse that was red: and power was given to him that sat thereon to take peace from the earth, and that they should kill one another: and there was given unto him a great sword.[21]

The rider of the red horse is generally thought to represent destruction, and this, by association, is the meaning of the horse itself. And we find that "things ... did not go well with Joseph from the very arrival of Ruby. It almost seemed as if the red beast had brought ill luck with him" (*ABNW* 309-310).[22] The mission of God's messengers in *At the Back of the North Wind* is not retribution, as in *Revelation*, but testing: "It was necessary I should grow fat, and necessary that good Joseph, your master, should grow lean," Ruby tells old Diamond (320),[23] sounding remarkably like the prophet Isaiah: "And in that day it shall come to pass, that the glory of Jacob [Joseph's father] shall be made thin, and the fatness of his flesh shall wax lean" (Is. 17:4).

Horse Diamond has religious significance too. Revelation 6 continues:

> And I beheld, and lo a black horse; and he that sat on him had a pair of balances in his hand.
>
> And I heard a voice in the midst of the four beasts say, A measure of wheat for a penny, and three measures of barley for a penny; and see thou hurt not the oil and the wine. (vv. 5, 6)

The rider of the black horse[24] is thought to represent famine, which, again, is associated with the horse; and if Old Diamond does not cause famine he certainly suffers from it in the London section of the book. Boy Diamond is astounded when he meets him again in Bloomsbury:

> Diamond didn't hang his head like that; yet the head that was hanging was very like the one that Diamond used to hold so high. Diamond's bones didn't show through his skin like that; but the skin they pushed out of shape so was very like Diamond's skin .... (*ABNW* 159)[25]

And although Horse Diamond's fortunes improve after his reunion with Joseph, he fares worse than ever during Ruby's stay:

The Downstretched Hand: Individual Development in

> Beside the great red round barrel Ruby, all body and no legs, Diamond looked like a clothes-horse with a skin thrown over it. There was hardly a spot of him where you could not descry some sign of a bone underneath. Gaunt and grim and weary he stood, kissing his master, and heeding no-one else. (328)[26]

With the associations of Revelation MacDonald combines allusions to the before-and-after states of the Nazarites in the Lamentations of Jeremiah: "[T]hey were more ruddy in body than rubies" (4:7) as opposed to "[t]heir visage is blacker than a coal . . . their skin cleaveth to their bones; it is withered, it is become like a stick" (4:8).

The Old Testament plagues of pestilence, famine and the sword are certainly not wanting in the Bloomsbury section of *At the Back of the North Wind*. Diamond's apparently tubercular condition is an important factor throughout the book, and culminates in his death; but Miss Coleman in the Wilderness section seems a prey to the same sort of condition and, in the Bloomsbury episode, Nanny succumbs to a fever, Joseph almost immediately does the same, and Mr. Raymond, not much later, is taken ill in Switzerland. Yet all this suffering has a positive outcome, as MacDonald suggests by his reference to 2 Corinthians: "Diamond could not help thinking of words which he had heard in the church the day before: 'Surely it is good to be afflicted;' or something like that" (*ABNW* 254; see 2 Cor. 1:6). Nanny is refined by suffering, Joseph's illness gives Diamond the chance to "[take] his place as a man who judged what was wise, and did work worth doing" (251), and the prolonging of Mr. Raymond's absence only makes him the more impressed, on his return, by Joseph's trustworthiness (330-331). The other curses, too, are turned into blessings; Ruby starts to pull his weight and famine changes into sufficiency in London and abundance at The Mound.

After Diamond's visionary sojourn at the back of the north wind, a time during which he was so ill (back at Sandwich) that his mother thought he had actually died (126), he begins to fulfil his prophetic role—the role prepared for by North Wind's teaching, by his care of Nanny on the night of the windstorm in London, by his experience of solitude in the cathedral on the night of the great storm and, most of all, by his having always been greatly loved. In this, again, he is like Daniel, whose heavenly visitant, Gabriel, says: "I am come to shew thee; *for* thou art greatly beloved: *therefore* understand the matter, and consider the vision" (Dan. 9:23; italics mine).[27] And there is nothing passive in this: "We love [God], because he first loved us," says St. John (1 John 4:19), and Diamond is loving, and therefore able to fulfil his potential, precisely because he is loved.

His role as prophet develops through poetry and song—starting with the apparently never-ending poem the wind finds for him in the book that is half-buried on the beach at Sandwich, a poem that both affirms Diamond's mystical experience and inspires him when the family is reunited in Bloomsbury: "It's all in the wind / That blows from behind" (*ABNW* 143). And "in the troubles which followed, Diamond was often heard singing; and when asked what he was singing, would answer 'One of the tunes the river at the back of the north wind sung' (116).

Many of Diamond's songs are taken from "North Wind's book" (215)—his text book when he learns to read—or from the book given to him by Mr. Raymond. Many more are nursery rhymes or songs he makes up himself, inspired largely by his baby brother and, later, his sister. As he tells Mr. Raymond, "I couldn't make a line without baby on my knee. We make them together, you know. They're just as much baby's as mine. It's he that pulls them out of me" (212). And the right poem always seems to be found when it is needed. North Wind's version of "Little Boy Blue" gives Diamond a good deal of food for thought, for, as emerges in a discussion with his mother, he recognises the truth it contains:

> "That killing of the snake looks true. It's what *I've* got to do so often."
>
> His mother looked uneasy. Diamond smiled full in her face, and added—
>
> "When baby cries and won't be happy, and when father and you talk about your troubles, I mean." (201)

Another of North Wind's poems has a special message for Diamond's mother: "Don't you remember how I bothered you about some of the words?" says Diamond (215), and repeats the poem, which deals with a mother bird's anxiety about the source of the next day's worms. But, although Diamond has previously jogged her memory about similar sentiments heard in church—"something like this, that she hadn't to eat for to-morrow as well as for to-day" (136)[28]—Martha, like the mother bird in the poem, fails to appreciate the child's wisdom: "The folly of childhood,' sighed his mother, / 'Has always been my especial bother" (216). It is left to Diamond to realise that, during his father's illness, he must be the early bird, and not until he comes back with the "worm," in the shape of fare money, does his mother begin to understand:

The Downstretched Hand: Individual Development in

> "How's father?" asked Diamond, almost afraid to ask.
>
> "Better, my child," she answered, "but uneasy about you, my dear."
>
> "Didn't you tell him I was the early bird gone out to catch the worm?"
>
> "*That* was what put it into your head, was it, you monkey?" said his mother. . . .
>
> "That or something else," answered Diamond, so very quietly that his mother held his head back and stared in his face.
>
> "Well! of all the children!" she said, and said no more. (226)

The word "uneasy," used of both Joseph and Martha in relation to things Diamond says and does, indicates the challenging nature of change—both in their perception of him and their insight into wider issues. As the modern idiom would express it, they are being moved out of their comfort zone, something they wouldn't expect to happen at the hands of a child who would normally look to them for guidance.

At The Mound Diamond's singing comes into its own, and his songs have implications for all who can understand. The tutor comments that "[a]t times they would be but bubbles blown out of a nursery rhyme" (346). But such bubbles are neither ephemeral nor trivial, for even "Little Bo Peep," in which the sheep run off into the sunset and are replaced by three times as many lambs (347-348)—one of the death prophecies that grow increasingly frequent as the book continues—merits an illuminating discussion with North Wind (360-361).[29]

The most mysterious paradox in *At the Back of the North Wind* is that the deeper the insight Diamond gains into the meaning of love—the commitment involved to the individual person, faults and all—the more his songs reveal that he is preparing to let go of all he loves in the ultimate separation of death. In the Bloomsbury section we find him singing, in "The True History of the Cat and the Fiddle," that "The dog laughed at the sport/ Till his cough cut him short" (228)—an allusion that comes very near to Diamond's own presumably tubercular condition. But the clearest rendering of his philosophy of abandonment is given in the song he sings to his little brother and sister just before the thunderstorm—the second thunderstorm of the book, and quite as important as the first:

> What would you see if I took you up
> To my little nest in the air?

> You would see the sky like a clear blue cup
>   Turned upside downwards there.
>
> What would you do if I took you there
>   To my little nest in the tree?
> My child with cries would trouble the air
>   To get what she could but see.
>
> What would you get in the top of the tree
>   For all your crying and grief?
> Not a star would you clutch of all you see—
>   You could only gather a leaf.
>
> But when you had lost your greedy grief,
>   Content to see from afar,
> You would find in your hand a withering leaf,
>   In your heart a shining star. (349-350)

There are many references in Old Testament prophecy to those who build their nests in tall trees or mountains, usually in an arrogant attempt to achieve self-sufficiency or power: "Woe to him that coveteth an evil covetousness to his house, that he may set his nest on high, that he may be delivered from the power of evil!" says Habbakuk (2:9). And such references are usually followed by the stern pronouncement that the nest-builders will be forced to descend: "Though thou shouldest make thy nest as high as the eagle, I will bring thee down from thence, saith the LORD" (Jeremiah 49:16), and Obadiah is even more emphatic: "Though thou exalt thyself as the eagle, and though thou set thy nest among the stars, thence will I bring thee down" (Ob.1:4). But Diamond's nest-building does not spring from arrogance, unless it be arrogant to say: "Aha! little squirrel . . . my nest is built higher than yours" *(ABNW* 341). His two nests—one in the beech tree and one in the tower—are to him, like the "woven nest" (39) of North Wind's hair in which he once flew, simply vantage points. And they pose no threat; he has long passed the point where "he did not dare to look over the top of the nest" (40), for after his journey to the country at the back of the north wind he can say, in the course of a discussion with his mother, that birds enduring the hardships of winter "must die some time. They wouldn't like to be birds always" (135)—i.e. death has no sting. And the security of love obtains outside the nest as well as in it: "I begin to think there are better things than being comfortable," Diamond tells North Wind when he elects to brave the storm from the crook of her arm (69). His feelings about nests are

The Downstretched Hand: Individual Development in

closer to the sentiments of Job than to the proud complacency of those whom the prophets attack, for, although Diamond does not share the nostalgia of the man from the land of Uz, the fate Job hoped for in his earlier days is very similar to that which befalls the hero of *At the Back of the North Wind*; if Diamond does not expect to "multiply [his] days as the sand," he fulfils Job's youthful anticipation that "I shall die in my nest" (Job 29:18).

"We saw a huge bough of the beech-tree in which was Diamond's nest, hanging to the ground like the broken wing of a bird," says the tutor in the course of the thunderstorm (*ABNW* 351). Diamond has only just come down from the tree, and Jim's warning that lightning might kill him does not seem illogical, reinforced as it is by the tutor's remark that a little later "I turned my steps . . . to look at the stricken beech. I saw the bough torn from the stem" (352). The fate of the beech tree is prophetic, as is consistent with the fact that, in the Old Testament, man is frequently imaged as a tree; one need look no further than Nebuchadnezzar's dream of a tree to see this (Daniel 4: 10-16). And Job, thinking of his happier past, draws an analogy between the tree and himself: "My root was spread out by the waters, and the dew lay all night upon my branch" (Job 29:19).[30] So important is the tree as an image of man in the Old Testament that the Branch is used as a Messianic title: "And there shall come forth a rod out of the stem of Jesse, and a Branch shall grow out of his roots" (Isaiah 11:1).[31]

The fall of the rotten elm tree in the storm in The Wilderness signifies the destruction of the status quo; the fall of a branch of the beech tree presages the death of Diamond—as he recognises when he immediately sings:

> The clock struck one,
> And the mouse came down.
> Dickery, dickery, dock! (351)

In both Old and New Testaments the severing of a branch from the tree usually betokens a curse: Isaiah, for example, prophesies that "the Lord, the LORD of hosts, shall lop the bough with terror" (Is. 10:33), and Jesus says that any branch that does not bear fruit will be cut away from the vine and burnt (see John 15:6).

But in *At the Back of the North Wind* the curse is turned into a blessing. For death, which seems the greatest curse, is already Diamond's friend, and in the penultimate chapter he looks forward to nothing more than her visit through the window of his tower room. When he finally goes to the real land at her back, one of Jeremiah's most frightening prophecies has been fulfilled without its sting: "For death is come up into our windows, and is entered into our palaces, to cut off the children from without" (Jer. 9:21).

Diamond's last song is about the resurrection, and he sings it to a (presumably) dying woman[32] during his last outing with North Wind:

> The sun is gone down,
> And the moon's in the sky;
> But the sun will come up,
> And the moon be laid by.
>
> The flower is asleep
> But it is not dead,
> When the morning shines,
> It will lift its head.
>
> When winter comes,
> It will die—no, no;
> It will only hide
> From the frost and the snow.
>
> Sure is the summer,
> Sure is the sun;
> The night and the winter
> Are shadows that run.
>
> (*ABNW* 371)

So although Diamond goes to what the old princess, in *The Princess and Curdie*, sings of as "the something that nobody knows" (*PC* 91), we are not afraid for him.[33] The whole gist of the book has been to promise him (and potentially the reader) that, as the final and culminating sentence of the Book of Daniel expresses it, "thou shalt rest, and stand in thy lot at the end of the days" (Dan. 12:13).

Endnotes for Chapter 3 on page 258

"What do you want me to do next, dear North Wind?" said Diamond, wishing to show his love by being obedient.

"What do you want to do yourself?"

"I want to go into the country at your back."

"Then you must go through me."

"I don't know what you mean."

"I mean just what I say. You must walk on as if I were an open door, and go right through me."

"But that will hurt you."

"Not in the least. It will hurt you though."

"I don't mind that, if you tell me to do it."

"Do it," said North Wind.

Chapter 9, "How Diamond Got To The Back Of The North Wind" illustration by Jessie Wilcox Smith

CHAPTER 4

Diamond and North Wind
A Mystical Relationship

Underlying *At the Back of the North Wind* is a powerfully sustained allusion to a passage from the Book of Job, described by MacDonald as "the most daring of all poems:"[1]

> Thou liftest me up to the wind; thou causest me to ride upon it, and dissolvest my substance.
>
> For I know that thou wilt bring me to death, and to the house appointed for all living. (Job 30:22, 23)

In MacDonald's book the focus and mood are different; Job's relationship with God is mediated, in *At the Back of the North Wind*, through the wind who is God's agent, and Job's anguish is replaced by Diamond's peace—a peace largely sourced by the resurrection to which the whole book tends.[2] And, although it is partly set in the Secondary World and Diamond is able to realise some of the wishes and desires named by Tolkien as fulfilled in fairy tales—the longing to fly like a bird, or to enjoy (even if only once) the magical understanding of the speech of other living creatures—*At the Back of the North Wind* is not a fairy tale. There is no conflict between good and evil—only the great but more mundane challenges of poverty, insecurity and illness to be faced; there is no promise to be kept and no prohibition to be violated. Nor, most emphatically, does the book feature what Tolkien describes as the "Great Escape: the Escape from Death" ("On Fairy-Stories," 67), for it is the story of a boy who makes friends with death, in the shape of North Wind, and then dies.[3] But if it is not a fairy tale *At the Back of the North Wind* is not wholly 'realistic' either; although it is largely set in the Primary World, it certainly embodies one of what Tolkien describes as the three faces of fairy stories—"the Mystical towards the Supernatural."[4] It is a mixture, though not a muddle of forms, and Diamond's approach seems the best: "Any story always tells me itself what I'm to think about it," he tells the tutor (342).

Set as it is in both Primary and Secondary Worlds—"almost without warning, we pass from one world to the other, and at times the two worlds are fused," says Robert Lee Wolff (*The Golden Key*, 148)—I must emphasise again that it is actually about three, and that the third, the spiritual world, is always immanent, although just out

The Downstretched Hand: Individual Development in

of reach. Looking at a sunset early in the book, Diamond sees that "above the fire in the sky lay a large lake of green light, above that a golden cloud, and over that the blue of the wintry heavens. And Diamond thought that, next to his own home, he had never seen any place he would like so much to live in as that sky" (*ABNW* 29). This is a hint, though no more, of the theme of resurrection—and of Diamond's as yet unknown longing for it—which underlies the whole book: "I should like to get up into the sky. Don't you think I shall, some day?" he says to the tutor when he is in fact very close to doing so (344).

The theme of resurrection makes North Wind's role even more mysterious than it would otherwise be.[5] She is that threshold to eternity from which there can be no Great Escape, but she can only encourage Diamond's progress towards something in which she herself has never participated. Yet North Wind is certainly the medium of connection between Primary and Secondary Worlds (to keep Tolkien's capitals) in *At the Back of the North Wind*.[6] This is revealed by the part she plays in sending dreams—especially, of course, to Diamond, though she also sends one to Nanny, who "never had but that one" (355) or doesn't remember the others. Diamond's dreams, though sent by North Wind, are often triggered by something that happens in the temporal world. Before his journey with North Wind on the night of the great storm, for example, Diamond sits in the Colemans' summer house, which has a little window in the side made of coloured glass (56)—a connection with the more august stained glass window in the cathedral which triggers his dream of the sham apostles (86), itself rounded off, when his eyes open, by the "little panes in the roof of his loft glimmering blue in the light of the morning" (90).[7] In Diamond, North Wind is working on a person naturally given to dreams; when he visits Nanny in hospital he says "I think I like dreams even better than fairy tales" (294), and "those precious dreams he had so often had, in which he floated about upon the air at will" (358) have prepared him for his subsequent nocturnal excursions.

Under North Wind's tutelage, however, Diamond learns to distinguish between dreams, vehicles of truth though they can be, and the reality of his encounters with her. He is in no doubt that his meeting with the stars is a dream; but since North Wind sends him this one it has much to say, not only about Diamond, but about North Wind herself, his relationship with her, and her function in the book. Strangely enough, in view of the fact that Diamond has just taken his place in a man's world by driving his father's cab, it begins with a

George MacDonald's Major Fantasies for Children

regression to an earlier phase of childhood: "He dreamed that he was running about in the twilight in the old garden" (232). Diamond does not see North Wind in Bloomsbury, and his dream shows that he is longing for her at an unconscious level: "He thought he was waiting for North Wind, but she did not come. So he would run down to the back gate, and see if she were there" (232-233). She is not there, and neither is the gate, for the garden, in dream-fashion, has changed—though, interestingly enough, the "beautiful country, not like any country he had ever been in before," is still referred to, without block capitals this time, as "the wilderness" (233).

As the dream continues it not only encourages Diamond to explore his unconscious self but touches imaginatively on eternity. The terrain is a heath covered with flowers among which roses preponderate, and it becomes clear that the roses constitute a feminine image—also, specifically, an image of the mother, who, says Jung, symbolises the unconscious.[8] Still dreaming, Diamond falls asleep under a rosebush (the mother of roses) and has another dream: "He woke, not out of his dream, but into it, thinking he heard a child's voice, calling 'Diamond, Diamond!'" The rosebushes around him, in true dream fashion, begin to behave in a way quite unlike the reality of the conscious world: "[They] were pouring out their odours in clouds. He could see the scent like mists of the same colour as the rose, issuing like a slow fountain and spreading in the air till it joined the thin rosy vapour which hung over all the wilderness" (233).

The voice that wakes Diamond comes from the stars. When Jung says that the soul comes "from the stars"[9] he might almost be describing this part of *At the Back of the North Wind*, for Diamond is now experiencing a pre-birth dream. He can only reach the stars by going down into the earth (a return to the womb), going round a rosebush which, he is advised, has got its foot in the sky (234)—that is, children are sent by heaven. He descends a stair until he reaches the opening through which the little stream that flows up the steps (another paradox) comes pouring in. Going through it, he meets a group of boy-angels who turn out to be unborn children, though he is too much of a child to realise this intellectually.

Happy though Diamond is here, he not only recognises the impermanence of the situation (each angel leaves when he finds his own personal star, his "door" to the world) but senses its incompleteness: "'I don't see any little girls,' he said at last" (239). The boy-angels (who are all left-handed)[10] have never seen any little girls, but their captain believes that they come to clean the stars while the boys are

The Downstretched Hand: Individual Development in

asleep. Their coming is, in fact, the signal for the boys to fall asleep, so that male and female—left hand and right hand—are never found conscious together; they cannot fully harmonise until they are in the 'real' world. Diamond does not associate himself with the others and thinks he will not have to fall asleep, but the proof that he was once an angel himself and has only lost his wings—as the angel captain intimates (239)—is his inability to stay awake when the girl-angels are coming: "He struggled hard .... But it was of no use. He thought he saw a glimmer of pale rosy light far up the green hill, and ceased to know" (241). The "ceased to know" is significant, for this is the third level of sleep in one session and the only one that is dreamless, though it is preceded by Diamond's glimpse of the "rosy light" which represents the unconscious. Poor Diamond—first he tries to stay awake and then to stay asleep, his hold on both consciousness and the unconscious being tenuous as yet. But he has begun the all-important task of bringing his unconscious into consciousness, though the femininity of the image suggests a complementation of the masculine which, though Diamond finds it to some extent in Nanny, he is never fully to experience—or rather which he internalises as he becomes, especially in the Bloomsbury section of the book, increasingly androgynous: "You're as good to your mother as if you were a girl," says Martha (156).

The dream is inspired by Wordsworth's "Ode: Intimations of Immortality," which MacDonald describes in *A Dish of Orts* as "that grandest ode that has ever been written."[11] The two writers do not start from the same place; MacDonald certainly could not say, with Wordsworth, that "nothing was more difficult for me in childhood than to admit the notion of death as a state applicable to my own being."[12] What is more germane to the issue is Wordsworth's interest in a prior state of existence. "[W]hen I was impelled to write this Poem on the 'Immortality of the Soul,' I took hold of the notion of pre-existence as having sufficient foundation in humanity for authorizing me to make for my purpose the best use of it I could as a Poet," he continues (280), and so he writes in the poem itself:

> Our birth is but a sleep and a forgetting:
> The Soul that rises with us, our life's Star,
> Hath had elsewhere its setting,
> And cometh from afar:
> Not in entire forgetfulness,
> And not in utter nakedness,

George MacDonald's Major Fantasies for Children

> But trailing clouds of glory do we come
> From God, who is our home . . .

George MacDonald too believes in the divine provenance of the child—"God thought about me, and so I grew"—says the baby in one of Diamond's songs (*ABNW* 324)—though he sees it in terms of preparation for existence rather than pre-existence. Diamond trails "clouds of glory" in the shape of imperfect memories of the songs the boy-angels sang; and as for Wordsworth, he bursts out:

> O joy! that in our embers
> Is something that doth live,
> That nature yet remembers
> What was so fugitive!

The "vision splendid" is not, however, doomed in Diamond's case to "die away, / And fade into the light of common day," not because Diamond dies in childhood but because in his case the vision grows more and more splendid as he grows in wisdom and understanding.

By sending the dream of "the little boys that dug for the stars" (*ABNW* 364)—superficially quite a childish and sentimental dream—North Wind shows that the basis of her relationship with Diamond has changed. She continues to feel maternal towards him, yet he must no longer seek the mother but progress towards a strength and independence which will enable him to engage in peer relationships with others. And North Wind promotes this process not only by sending the dream but by withholding her physical presence (something prefigured during the dream of the sham apostles, and for the same reason). Her apparent absence during the Bloomsbury section—she does of course intervene to make Joseph meet Mrs. and Miss Coleman (174-175) and to ensure that Miss Coleman does not go out before Mr. Evans reaches her house (248)—coincides not only with Diamond's increasingly responsible behaviour at home but with his gradual adoption of his father's role, first as pupil and then as replacement coachman when his father is ill. "Won't you come and see the cab, Diamond?" says Joseph at the beginning of this process (156). And though Martha, now and later, is reluctant to let Diamond go, his father is greatly pleased when he finds during his illness that Diamond is "quite taking his place as a man who judged what was wise, and did work worth doing" (251) Diamond's dream of the stars, Nanny's dream of the moon, Diamond's visit to the supposed country at the back of the North Wind and even Mr. Raymond's story of Princess Daylight—"I believe I had something to do with it," she says

The Downstretched Hand: Individual Development in

to Diamond (365)—all reveal the power of North Wind's imagination, which is active on many levels. But it is on the spiritual level that her imagination is of the greatest importance.[13] While the whole thrust of *At the Back of the North Wind* is towards eternity, MacDonald actually says nothing on the subject at all. There are only suggestions about the possible nature of eternity, all of them North Wind's imaginings, as, since "North Wind . . . never played anybody a trick" (89), she freely admits:

> "Would you be afraid of me if you had to go through me again?" [she asks Diamond].
>
> "No. Why should I? Indeed I should be glad enough, if it was only to get another peep of the country at your back."
>
> "You've never seen it yet."
>
> "Haven't I, North Wind? Oh! I'm so sorry! I thought I had. What did I see then?"
>
> "Only a picture of it. The real country at my real back is ever so much more beautiful than that." (364)

She herself has never seen the reality, just as she has never heard the boy-angels' song in the dream of the stars:

> "I want to ask you whether you remember the song the boy-angels sang in that dream of yours."
>
> "No. I couldn't keep it, do what I would, and I did try."
>
> "That was my fault."
>
> "How could that be, North Wind?"
>
> "Because I didn't know it properly myself, and so I couldn't teach it to you. I could only make a rough guess at something like what it would be, and so I wasn't able to make you dream it hard enough to remember it. Nor would I have done so if I could, for it was not correct. I made you dream pictures of it, though. But you will hear the very song itself when you do get to the back of—"
>
> "My own dear North Wind," said Diamond. (365)

North Wind is in the tradition of the Wise Woman, deep-rooted in Victorian fantasy and especially so in the works of George MacDonald.[14] Like all Wise Women, she has something in common with the Great Mother[15]—not only the Earth Mother, though that aspect is of considerable importance in some variations of the archetype, but a being of preternatural tenderness and authority.

George MacDonald's Major Fantasies for Children

Before Diamond sees North Wind (he is hiding under the bedclothes when she first comes through her "window"[6]), her voice strikes him as familiar: "It was a still more gentle voice now, although six times as large and loud as it had been [when she was outside], and he thought it sounded a little like his mother's" (9). And even on the night of the great storm, when North Wind's voice is tremendous, it seems to Diamond that "after all, it was more like his mother's voice than anything else in the world" (67). Perhaps this makes it all the more fitting that Diamond's meeting with North Wind constitutes a rebirth into another phase of experience and awareness: "The renewal," says Jung, "must 'happen' to him from outside, and to bring this about he is pulled through a hole in the wall at the head of his sick-bed, and now he is reborn."[16] The resemblance to what happens in Diamond's case, where a hole in the boards behind the head of his bed plays an important part, is uncanny.[17] He could alternatively, Jung goes on to say, undergo "an ablution or baptismal bath" (shades of *The Princess and the Goblin*, "The Golden Key" etc.) but the result is the same; he "miraculously changes into a semi-divine being with a new character and an altered metaphysical destiny" ("Concerning Rebirth," par. 231).

Just as Queen Irene, in *The Princess and the Goblin*, reassures the princess by establishing a flesh-and-blood connection with her from the first—"I'm your father's mother's father's mother" (*PG* 25)—North Wind establishes, during her first conversation with Diamond, a community of love between them: "'I know your mother very well,' said the lady. . . . 'I love your mother, Diamond.'" And her words suggest a knowledge that embraces Diamond too: "I was with her when you were born" (*ABNW* 13). As the book goes on North Wind is both mentor and mother, for the maturing Diamond never loses his need for unconditional love: "The yacht shall be my cradle, and you shall be my baby,"[18] she tells him as she prepares to have him transported to the North Pole (105); and when Diamond sees her at The Mound, after an interval of more than a year, she carries him to the top of the great beech tree, where "she placed him on her lap and began to hush him as if he were her own baby" (358).

The mother-child aspect of the relationship between Diamond and North Wind is—like their relationship as a whole—highly paradoxical. The question of maternal authority surfaces early in the book, for it is clear from the first that North Wind is determined to get Diamond out of bed in the middle of the night, while Martha (with the name that even sounds like 'mother')[19] is anxious to see that he stays there. North Wind is forceful, even violent in pursuing her

The Downstretched Hand: Individual Development in

purpose, as we see from the first:

> "Will you take your head out of the bed-clothes?" said the voice, just a little angrily.
>
> "No!" answered Diamond, half peevish, half frightened.
>
> The instant he said the word, a tremendous blast of wind crashed in a board of the wall, and swept the clothes off Diamond. He started up in terror. (10-11)

Later in the book, on the night North Wind goes to sink Mr. Coleman's ship, a "great blast . . ., having torn some tiles off the roof, sent a spout of wind down into [Diamond's] bed and over his face . . ."[20]—but by this time he has changed; whereas the preceding thunder "almost choked him with fear," the wind "gave him back his courage" (65).

North Wind would not have been able to win Diamond's confidence had her voice not sounded "a little like his mother's" (9). Yet Martha's strategy, in comparison with North Wind's manifestation of power, is tame; all she can do is keep checking on Diamond. For a week after his supposed sleep-walking in the Colemans' garden, "his mother watched him very carefully—going into the loft several times a night,--as often, in fact, as she woke" (28). But she does not check on him on the nights when he actually goes out, except when Diamond follows North Wind's summons and listens to Old Diamond and Ruby in the Bloomsbury stable: "He's been at his old trick of walking in his sleep. I saw him run up the stair in the middle of the night," Martha tells Joseph; but again she has "found him fast asleep in his bed" (322).

Martha's authority over Diamond, though scrupulously respected by North Wind when it has been directly asserted—"my mother has forbidden me" brings an immediate "Then don't" (60)—nonetheless begins to diminish from the first time he encounters North Wind in his loft bedroom. When she asks him to follow her, Diamond objects that "mother never would let me go [out] without shoes" (12)—and her reply that she knows his mother very well prompts Diamond, with the common sense that distinguishes him throughout the book, to challenge her: "How was it you did not know my name, then, ma'am?" He is, however, convinced by the ensuing discussion and by the time she concludes "Well, you see, I know all about you and your mother," he is quite ready to say "Yes. I will go with you" (13).

Paradoxically, Martha's very anxiety to keep Diamond in bed at night assists North Wind, for "I can't take you until you're in bed. That's the law about the children," North Wind tells him (60). On the night of the great storm,

> "You don't seem very well to-night, Diamond," said his mother.
>
> "I am quite well, mother," returned Diamond....
>
> "I think you had better go to bed," she added. (63-64)

North Wind and Martha both want the best for Diamond, but Martha has far less understanding than North Wind of what that best really is. His increasing maturity gladdens but also worries his family, and Martha tries to keep Diamond in that state of immaturity in which she thinks he will be safe. Just as his father is about to give him the treat of driving Old Diamond for the first time, she calls him back:

> Diamond got down, a little disappointed of course, and went in with his mother, who was too pleased to speak. She only took hold of his hand as tight as if she had been afraid of his running away instead of glad that he would not leave her. (161)

His ready obedience causes the owner of the stables, Mr. Stonecrop, to invite him to drive the nameless horse which seems to be associated with death—so Martha's limited vision indirectly promotes North Wind's ultimate purpose.

There is at least one mistake in *At the Back of the North Wind*—Cripple Jim is referred to as Joe at one point (255), perhaps a Freudian slip because he seems destined to be Nanny's husband, as Joe is Martha's—but it is unlikely to be a slip that Diamond's clothes should be locked in his mother's room at the time of North Wind's first visit (12) yet not when she pays her second visit a week later; "springing out of bed, [he] dressed himself as fast as ever he could" (33). This is one of those MacDonaldian inconsistencies which shift the narrative in the direction of change. It begins a process by which Diamond is freed from his mother's dominion (loving though it is)—a process essential to the development of psychological maturity. His mother, for her part, is eventually released from her need first for his dependence on her and later for his active support, so that, though deeply grieved, she will not be crushed by his death. When Diamond does die, Mrs. Raymond is his most prominent mourner; neither Martha nor Joseph is mentioned (and Martha is hardly mentioned at all, and never by name, during the whole of the Mound section).

Since North Wind's love is untrammelled by fear, she can help Diamond's capacity for love to grow deeper and more spiritual. From their first encounter she builds Diamond up with loving affirmation and soon calls forth his love in return: "I love you, and you must love me, else how did I come to love you?" he says (*ABNW* 72-73).[21] The only emotional pain the relationship causes Diamond arises from his fear, at the end of the book, that North Wind may not have empirical reality—for, since love can only exist in the context of a relationship with another, the idea of North Wind as merely an imaginary projection of his own inmost longings would devastate the boy. "Nought loves another as itself, / Nor venerates another so, / Nor is it possible to Thought / A greater than itself to know," says William Blake in "A Little Boy Lost"—but Diamond doesn't believe that and neither does MacDonald. In the event love becomes its own justification:

> "I think," said she, . . . "that if I were only a dream, you would not have been able to love me so. You love me when you are not with me, don't you?"
>
> "Indeed I do," answered Diamond . . . . "I see! I see! How could I be able to love you as I do if you weren't there at all, you know? Besides, I couldn't be able to dream anything half so beautiful all out of my own head; or if I did, I couldn't love a fancy of my own like that, could I?" (*ABNW* 363)

Perceiving love as a proof of the loved one's existence shows how tremendously Diamond's understanding of the nature of love has grown in the course of his relationship with North Wind—beyond even the great concept he enunciates in Bloomsbury: "Love makes the only myness" (325).

North Wind is, however, a living paradox. It takes time and effort for Diamond to come to terms with her occasional apparent callousness: "Why shouldn't you be as kind to her as you are to me?" he says (42) when he sees Nanny bowling along the street, the wind "worrying her like a wild beast" (41). But eventually he realises, not only that severity and love can co-exist, but that severity can actually be a manifestation of love. Diamond's efforts to reconcile his different impressions of North Wind culminate, on the night of the great storm, in a long discussion about trust, which concludes with his crying out: "How could you know how to put on such a beautiful face if you did not love me and the rest? No. You may sink as many ships as you like, and I won't say another word" (73).

The irony of the situation lies in Diamond's failure to realise that North Wind is severe to him as well as to others. "You know the one *me*, you say, and that is good," says North Wind. "Yes," Diamond replies. "Do you know the other *me* as well?" she asks, and Diamond's immediate response is "No. I can't. I shouldn't like to" (71). But in fact he is in contact with the "other me" throughout the book. From their first meeting it is clear that North Wind is killing Diamond by aggravating his (presumably) tubercular condition—and she may even have caused it as, before he met her, "the wind got in at a chink in the wall, and blew about him all night. For the back of his bed was only of boards an inch thick, and on the other side of them was the north wind" (4).

When Diamond first hears North Wind's voice through a papered-over hole in the stable wall he has a presentiment that her nearer neighbourhood will be hazardous: "[Y]ou'll give me the toothache," he expostulates. Her reply only makes sense on the spiritual level. "You shall not be the worse for it—I promise you that," she says. "You will be much the better for it."[22] Well, she doesn't give him toothache. But as soon as he tears the brown paper covering from the hole in the wall, "[i]n came a long whistling spear of cold, and struck his little naked chest" (8). The aggression of the metaphor of being struck by a spear is quite deliberate, and is reinforced when Diamond goes outside; "sharp as a knife came the wind against his little chest and his bare legs" (18). As soon as he turns round and stops trying to walk against it the apparent hostility of the wind disappears, but cold is inevitably associated with North Wind throughout. Although Diamond thinks her cold hand is "so pleasant and full of life, it was better than warm" (33), his pre-death experience of the country at North Wind's back is caused by walking through her body, for "the cold stung him like fire" (112). On his return he embraces her and, until she comes fully awake, "the cold of her bosom . . . pierced Diamond's bones" (122). When, much later, Diamond sees his friend for the last time, he becomes imbued with some of her own coldness: "I think I have been rather cold ever since," he tells the tutor (377)—and four days later he is dead.

MacDonald sees death as a profoundly positive mystery. In his short story "The Light Princess," he goes so far as to equate it with love: "Death alone from death can save. / Love is death, and so is brave / Love can fill the deepest grave."[23] Orba, in the much later novel *The Flight of the Shadow* (1891), is not given her own pony, Zoe, or life, until she has learned to ride her uncle's horse, Thanatos, or Death—an animal who is frequently called by his English name and who is even referred to as "dear old Death" occasionally (see *FS* 71, 211). MacDonald's writings consistently express this attitude; and, perhaps most poignantly, in a private poem written to his wife in 1878, a few months after their daughter Mary died, he describes death as "one wide landing to the rooms above" (*GMHW* 485).

The Downstretched Hand: Individual Development in

As it relates to Diamond, North Wind's work has all one tendency; to prepare him—physically, psychologically and spiritually—for death. The task, however, fairly bristles with paradoxes. On the one hand North Wind takes Diamond's life; on the other she is "spirit," or breath,[24] and symbolically compensates for his lung troubles by giving him the air he lacks. Certainly Diamond associates wind with life; just before entering the supposed country at North Wind's back he thinks that "[t]he air . . . seemed somehow dead, for there was not the slightest breath of wind" (110).

What North Wind essentially does is to free Diamond from fear. "I'm never frightened at things," he tells the tutor towards the end of the book (343)—but it takes a long time for him to reach this point. On the night of his first encounter with North Wind, Diamond goes outside and sees a cloud with a steep side like a precipice, and the moon, "a poor thin crescent," seems to have rolled down it: "She did not seem comfortable, for she was looking down into the deep pit waiting for her"—a universal image of death [25] which Diamond senses unconsciously. This time the narrator himself reassures Diamond (and the child reader): "[T]hat was what Diamond thought . . . . But he was quite wrong, for the moon was not afraid, and there was no pit she was going down into" (17). After this it is usually up to North Wind, not to dispel fear, but to help Diamond conquer it—while always respecting his vulnerability and giving him (where necessary) a sense of protection which progressively deepens his trust in her. She knows he could not cope with seeing her sink the ship (76) and takes him to the cathedral where they walk on a narrow gallery high up the walls: "I am afraid of falling down there," says Diamond (80), and he is not completely reassured by her promise that she would catch him if he fell—so she vanishes from sight and he has to continue alone but for puffs of wind, eventually "marching along the narrow ledge as fearless for the time as North Wind herself" (81). When he reaches the bottom of a downward stair North Wind reappears, and he admits that he wasn't brave of himself: "It was the wind that blew in my face that made me brave," he says. "You had to be taught what courage was," North Wind explains, but she adds "don't you feel as if you would try to be brave yourself next time?" (83). And so he does. After his journey to the land at the back of the North Wind Diamond's fear of death is all but conquered, and this imbues him with the calm which makes the cabmen, Nanny, and later Jim think him "silly" (ironically, however, it has a bearing on his skill as a cab driver, since, if you aren't afraid of death, you aren't afraid of anything: "[H]e never got frightened, and consequently was never in too great a hurry" [169]). Just once in the Bloomsbury section the fear of death recurs. After Diamond's first day of solo driving during his father's illness, he gets home and is greeted by his mother: "'How's father?' asked Diamond, almost afraid to ask" (226). "Almost," however, is the key word.

At The Mound, Diamond delights in the sudden thunderstorm that frightens Nanny, Jim and his baby brother ("Dulcimer crowed with pleasure" [350], but she's a very small baby). "He ain't got sense to be frightened," says Nanny. "It might kill you," says Jim. "Oh no, it mightn't!" answers Diamond, and is not in the least phased by the fact that after the next flash there was a "tearing crack" and "a huge bough of the beech tree in which was [his] nest" was left "hanging to the ground like the broken wing of a bird" (351)—in fact, he returns to the nest a little later that evening (353)..

Positive though it is in MacDonald's view, death is still a great mystery, and through North Wind he tackles its paradoxical nature; physically it is a terrifying termination, spiritually the door to eternity. In either sense MacDonald seeks not so much to elucidate the mystery of death as to make friends with it. He deliberately draws on images and archetypes with evil associations in order to deal with the almost universal tendency to equate "dreadful" with "evil"—and dreadful North Wind certainly is in human eyes. Her dreadfulness, however, seems fitting when it is linked with the dignity of God, who several times in the Old Testament is described as riding on the wind: "And he rode upon a cherub, and did fly: and he was seen upon the wings of the wind," sings David (*2 Samuel* 22:11), while the composer of Psalm 104 describes Yahweh as one who "maketh the clouds his chariot: who walketh upon the wings of the wind" (v.3). Diamond, of course, is being carried rather than riding—but then, he is a little boy.

North Wind is sometimes described (paradoxically again) in terms of witches and their animal familiars. Wolves get a particularly bad press in both Old and New Testaments, yet this is the first transformation Diamond sees her undergo (*ABNW* 35) and she does not let him forget it: "You remember I was a wolf once—don't you?" she says when they are discussing whether or not she is real (363). Sir J.G. Frazer, in *The Golden Bough: A Study in Magic and Religion*, notes that witches were thought to be able to transform themselves into animals and points out that witches and wolves were the two great foes dreaded by herdsmen in Europe. Other attributes of witches are still more interesting in connection with North Wind. They were thought, says Frazer, to be able to cause hail and thunderstorms, to raise the wind and to sink ships (yes, that too!). But most striking of all is the fact that witches and wizards were thought to keep their strength in their hair.[26] Diamond, in the storm that sinks the Colemans' ship,

> saw the threads of the lady's hair streaking [the stormy scene]. In parts indeed he could not tell which was hair and which was black storm and vapour. It seemed sometimes that all the great billows of mist-muddy wind were woven out of the crossing lines of North Wind's infinite hair, sweeping in endless intertwistings. (*ABNW* 74-75)

She herself seems to associate her hair with her conscious life: "Ever since I knew I had hair, that is, ever since it began to go out and away, that song [which tells her that all is right] has been coming nearer and nearer," she says (77).

Although North Wind's associations with witches are problematic MacDonald does not seek to dodge the difficulty. Just as he is content to let Diamond gain insight into the mystery of suffering through experience rather than through a discussion that can lead nowhere (76-77),[27] so he allows Diamond to develop confidence in North Wind's goodness simply through knowing her: "I don't think I am just what you fancy me to be," she tells him. "I have to shape myself various ways to various people. But the heart of me is true" (363). The problem, if it is one, of animal familiars is dispelled on the unconscious level by the fact that North Wind in her supernatural manifestation is never in the company of Horse Diamond. The very first time North Wind encounters Diamond she leads him out of the stable—and because he at first runs the other way and pets the horse (the less frightening of the two), he loses sight of the lady. Although it is important that Boy Diamond should conquer his initial fear of the horse, learn to work with him and finally come to understand his language, it is even more important that he should ultimately transcend Horse Diamond, as he does at The Mound. Even here, however, there is a parallel between the horse and North Wind, for last of all Diamond must transcend her and go to the "something that nobody knows" (*PC* 91). Carl Jung points out in divers places that animals can be symbols of the unconscious,[28] but he also emphasises that "it is of the greatest importance that the ego should be anchored in the world of consciousness" ("The Self," *Aion* par.46). And in *The Diary of an Old Soul*, MacDonald writes: "I am a beast until I love as God doth love"[29]—which is the transcendent state.

What most deeply underlies *At the Back of the North Wind* is the Christian mystery that love is stronger than death—and this opens up another paradox, the most baffling one of all, in the relationship between Diamond and North Wind. Shortly before Diamond dies he decides that, whatever form North Wind may take, "You would love me, and I should love you all the same" (*ABNW* 363). Yet after the Sandwich episode his greatest desire is to return to, or rather to reach, the country at North Wind's back—the one place she cannot reach. As she says:

> "The people they say I drown, I only carry away to—to—to—well, the back of the North Wind—that is what they used to call it long ago, only *I* never saw the place."
>
> "How can you carry them there if you never saw it?"
>
> "I know the way."
>
> "But how is it you never saw it?"
>
> "Because it is behind me."
>
> "But you can look round."
>
> "Not far enough to see my own back. No; I always look before me. In fact, I grow quite blind and deaf when I try to see my back. I only mind my work." (59)

North Wind, in her character of Death, cannot enter eternity: "There shall be no more death" (Revelation 21:4). But if this makes good theological sense, it does not explain why Diamond is willing to leave his beloved friend behind—and the answer, yet again, is paradoxical. In nurturing Diamond's spiritual growth, North Wind has been teaching him about the nature of love—or perhaps it would be truer to say that through their loving relationship she has nurtured his spirit. She has shown Diamond that love exists only in terms of relationships with specific individuals, and he has learned the lesson well:

> "I've been thinking about it a great deal [he tells her], and it seems to me that although any one sixpence is as good as any other sixpence, not twenty lambs would do instead of one sheep whose face you knew. Somehow, when once you've looked into anybody's eyes, right deep down into them, I mean, nobody will do for that one any more." (360)

But delight in individuals is only one side of the paradox of love. The other side is that it is not exclusive and makes for a universally loving attitude, as is underlined in the chapter entitled "Diamond's Friends" in which he discusses friends and friendship with his father (189-191). And once one has reached this point one finds yet another paradox—that it is possible not only to love an individual but also to let that individual go. Just so Diamond, during the Mound section of

The Downstretched Hand: Individual Development in

At the Back of the North Wind, eventually lets go of his parents, Horse Diamond and even (in prospect) North Wind, without at all ceasing to love them.

Because North Wind's love is not selfish she can let Diamond pass through her, not only to the country at her back but to the love from which she herself comes. This is why MacDonald presents us with the paradox (only apparent this time) that the boy who can say "I can't help being frightened to think that perhaps I am only dreaming, and you are nowhere at all. Do tell me that you are my own real beautiful North Wind" (361), can agree with the tutor, only a week or so afterwards, that "at least there is one thing you may be sure of, that there is a still better love than that of the wonderful being you call North Wind. Even if she be a dream, the dream of such a beautiful creature could not come to you by chance." Diamond appears "more thoughtful than satisfied" at this point (376)—but he knows, or rather senses, that his relationship with North Wind cannot be an end in itself; as she says when he makes his original journey to the supposed land at her back, "You must walk on as if I were an open door, and go right through me" (111). Death, which seems the ultimate curse, is Diamond's beloved, and in the Mound section of the book he looks forward to nothing more than her visits through the window of his tower room. But he is now able to let go. When he finally goes to the land at North Wind's back, some of the prophet Jeremiah's words are fulfilled without their sting: "Death is come up into our windows, and is entered into our palaces, to cut off the children from without" (Jer. 9: 21).[30]

"Most fantasies seek to conserve those things in which they take delight: indeed it is one of their weaknesses that they are tempted not to admit loss," says Colin Manlove.[31] MacDonald admits loss—but to him, loss is subsumed in what Manlove describes as "a sense of approaching promise."[32] *At the Back of the North Wind* leaves us with a sense of the unknown beyond this world, as, ultimately, does all MacDonald's fantasy. But the unknown is always envisaged as good, from the "great good" that is coming to Anodos in *Phantastes* (319) to the hardly to be dreamed of awakening of the world in MacDonald's last fantasy, *Lilith*. What he does in *At the Back of the North Wind* is to imbue Diamond, through North Wind's love, with such trust that he can abandon himself to the unknown.

There is poignancy in the idea that North Wind will not be able to experience the eternity for which she so lovingly prepares Diamond. But, in more ways than one, she "consent[s] to be nobody" (*ABNW*

102), and the fundamental message of *At the Back of the North Wind* is the same as that of the Book of Job: "Though he slay me, yet will I trust in him" (13:15).

Endnotes for Chapter 4 on page 262

PART II

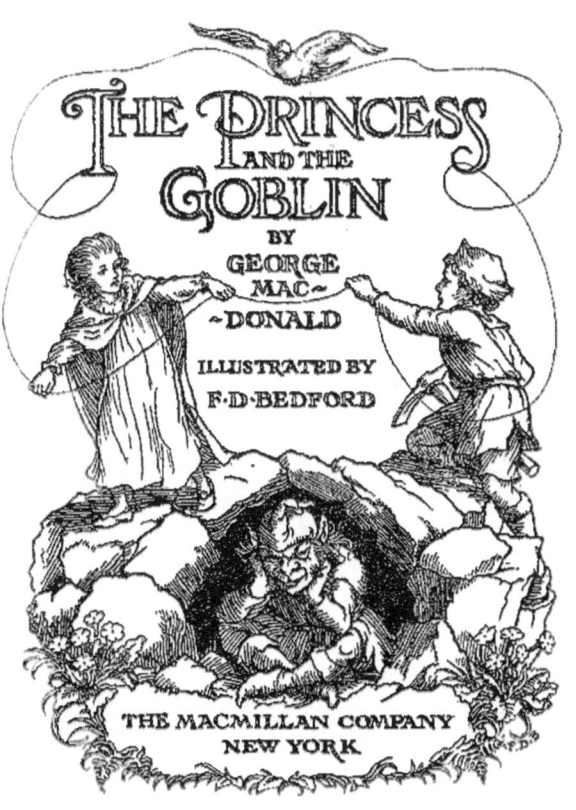

THE PRINCESS AND THE GOBLIN
BY GEORGE MAC~DONALD
ILLUSTRATED BY F·D·BEDFORD

THE MACMILLAN COMPANY
NEW YORK

When they reached a certain point, after which she could see them no more from the garden, she ran to the gate, and there stood till up they came clanging and stamping, with one more bright bugle-blast which said: 'Irene, I am come.'

By this time the people of the house were all gathered at the gate, but Irene stood alone in front of them. When the horsemen pulled up, she ran to the side of the white horse, and held up her arms. The king stooped, and took her hands. In an instant she was on the saddle, and clasped in his great strong arms.

Chapter 10, "The Princess's King-Papa"
illustration by F.D. Bedford

CHAPTER 5

"The Princess and—We shall see who"
The Heart of the Mystery

At the Back of the North Wind was swiftly followed by *The Princess and the Goblin*;[1] and Diamond's remark, shortly before his death, that he is reading the story of "the Little Lady and the Goblin Prince" (*ABNW* 341) shows that this closeness is much more than chronological. For if, as Tolkien says, "death is the theme that most inspired George MacDonald,"[2] this is always in the faith that death will be followed by resurrection. What MacDonald describes in *The Marquis of Lossie* as "the second birth—of sonship and liberty"[3] can come only after death, whether it be resurrection from physical death or from the symbolic deaths which occur in the course of daily life and on which, in *The Princess and the Goblin*, MacDonald focuses mainly through Princess Irene.[4]

Of the three fantasies in this study, *The Princess and the Goblin* is the one in which the motifs of light and darkness are of the greatest importance—from the inhabited and menacing darkness at the beginning of the book to the light shining upon the path of Curdie's family at the end, a light which even the uncomprehending Lootie can see (*PG* 307): "The people that walked in darkness have seen a great light," says Isaiah, and continues "they that dwell in the land of the shadow of death, upon them hath the light shined" (Is. 9:2).[5] The darkness, symbol of the unconscious, also symbolises death, whether of body or spirit; the light, which is incomparably more powerful, symbolises not only enlightenment but resurrection, which is, as in *At the Back of the North Wind*, the main theme of the book, though it follows a very different trajectory.

Although *The Princess and the Goblin* is not a sequel to *At the Back of the North Wind*, there is an organic relationship between them and a definite progression takes place. It is achieved by a change of perspective and a narrowing (or perhaps a broadening!) of focus, since *The Princess and the Goblin* is set entirely in the Secondary World. Within this, however, there is a night-time world and a daytime world, representing the supernatural and the natural respectively—and these worlds, distinct at the beginning of the book, must be progressively integrated. But there is no equivalent of the grinding daily round of

The Downstretched Hand: Individual Development in

the Bloomsbury section in *At the Back of the North Wind* and there are goblins and their creatures, unimaginable in The Wilderness or Bloomsbury or at The Mound. And there are even more fundamental differences between the two books. Princess Irene does not have to suffer the pressures of illness or financial necessity and Diamond's integrity is not threatened, even symbolically, by others; furthermore, Diamond lives in a setting of secure family affection and Irene does not.

"Many fairy-tale plots begin with children being cast out," says Bruno Bettelheim,[6] and this is in effect what has happened to Princess Irene, who, though born in the king's palace, is described in the first paragraph of *The Princess and the Goblin* as having been "sent soon after her birth, because her mother was not very strong, to be brought up by country people" in another part of the kingdom (9). And although the casting-out does not take one of the two forms specified by Bettelheim—either being sent out into the world or deserted— the fact remains that Irene, in spite of her entourage, is essentially vulnerable, as the taboo against her going out after dark attests. Those who are entrusted with her care are "much too afraid to let her out of the house then, even in company with ever so many attendants" (14). Her king-papa loves her dearly, but his wide-ranging national duties keep him for the most part at a distance. "It was a long time since he had been to see her," we find before the first visit (101), and in view of increasing concerns about the goblins—"[i]t was clear he was not quite comfortable about the princess" (108)—the best he can manage is to leave first six and later twelve sentries to guard the house, in other words to protect her on a conscious and pragmatic level. He pays only flying visits and never stays in the castle at night, the time of greatest danger and the time when the unconscious is symbolically dominant— and the narrator feels obliged to affirm that he is nonetheless a loving father; but for his realisation of Queen Irene's presence in the tower, "I presume [he] would have taken Irene with him that very day," we are told after his second visit (166).

The fairy-tale form allows MacDonald to respect the immaturity of his child readers and is also a suitable medium for the revelation of religious truth; as Tolkien points out in "On Fairy-Stories," "God is the Lord, of angels, and of men—and of elves" (72). According to Tolkien, however, "the essential face of Faerie" is that of "the Magical towards Nature." But in MacDonald's fairy tales, and especially in *The Princess and the Goblin*, it is that of "the Mystical towards the Supernatural" which predominates, and Tolkien himself says that

MacDonald tries to make the fairy tale "a vehicle of Mystery" (26). Indeed he does, and this mystery is profoundly religious, as is clear from the fact that the transformations and incomprehensible events in *The Princess and the Goblin*, like those in *At the Back of the North Wind* and *The Princess and Curdie*, are not the distortions of reality which magic produces.[7] Not for nothing does George MacDonald say that "the fairy tale is, in so far as it is art, revelation,"[8] and he might well have said of it, as he does of genius, that it is concerned with "truths, not tricks" (*ABNW* 213).

What seem to be magical objects almost invariably turn out to be mandalas, or symbols of wholeness, which have no magical properties at all.[9] When Irene, in *The Princess and the Goblin*, asks the Queen: "Is it because you have your crown on that you look so young?" she supposes that magic must have been at work to transform her great-great-grandmother into a young woman. But Queen Irene's response is unequivocal: "No, child . . . it is because I felt so young this evening, that I put my crown on" (*PG* 157). The crown is not a magic object; and the ring, crucial though it is to both the action and the central mystery of the book,[10] is only important because it is a gift from Queen Irene to her granddaughter and the Queen's thread is tied to it. The power is in the person, not the object, as Irene recognises when she is under the mountain: "She became more and more sure that the thread *could not have gone there of itself,* and that her grandmother must have sent it" (199-200; italics mine). Even the moon lamp draws people not to itself but to the Queen, and it is under her control: "*When I please,* I can make the lamp shine through the walls—shine so strong that it melts them away from before the sight," she says (150; italics mine). The power is in the person—the person of Queen Irene, who is at the heart of the mystery of the book.

Only when we reach the Secondary World of *The Princess and the Goblin* does evil become a factor,[11] and this is what brings in the "element of threat" which, says Bruno Bettelheim, "is crucial to the fairy tale" (*Uses of Enchantment,* 144). In *At the Back of the North Wind* there is no struggle between good and evil; Diamond is affected by the moral deficiencies of others, but he has to cope with rather than conquer them (much more the stuff of daily life). The degradation and ferocity of Old Sal, the only purely subterranean dweller to be found in *At the Back of the North Wind,* convey no sense of the purposeful malignity of the goblins who inhabit the mountain caves in *The Princess and the Goblin* and who would be the stuff of nightmare were it not that their grotesque appearance verges on the farcical. During a discussion with

The Downstretched Hand: Individual Development in

"Mr. Editor" in the last chapter of the serialised version, the child readers say: "We don't care about [like] the goblins and their nasty creatures. They frighten us—rather." [12] But the malevolent nature of the goblins cannot be overlooked, and this is why "Mr. Editor" tells his readers from the outset that "this is not a fairy story, but a goblin story."[13] And the goblins are called "demons," not only by the soldiers, who understand little of the matter (258), but by so wise a person as Curdie's mother (234).

Although it is symbolised from the first by the idea of fearsome darkness, only the goblins actually speak of death—and, as they are unaware of their own degeneration, they are only interested in the physical kind. When Curdie overhears a goblin family talking among themselves under the mountain, references to the subject come thick and fast. Speaking of the queen "from upstairs" (the goblin king's first wife), Glump, the "father-goblin" (83), says "when she died" (74), and the family discussion continues as follows: "Did she die *very* soon? They didn't tease her to death, did they?". . . "'What made her die, then?'. . . 'She died when the young prince was born'" (74-75). Death later becomes an immediate prospect when the king of the goblins and his family discuss whether it would be better to starve Curdie or to kill him at once (186-189).

Irene, however, never hears any of this. The story is set within a framework of fear, but she herself is sheltered from the terrors of death, both physical and spiritual; at their first meeting Queen Irene tells her: "I came here to take care of you" (26). Not until the story is almost finished does she realise that the goblins had planned to kidnap her as a wife for Prince Harelip, which would have been the spiritual death really to be feared. The taboo on being out after dark, which symbolises, on one level, the threatening nature of the unconscious,[14] protects her from the goblins in the short term, and the guards, placed around the house in increasing numbers once the taboo has been violated, indicate the king's sense of a need for continuing protection for his daughter—although in the event they are powerless to protect her and, but for Curdie, could not protect anybody. The "sun-people" who surround Princess Irene (186, 188) never mention either death or goblins;[15] no-one has ever told her that her mother has died, and even the reader is fobbed off with the euphemism that Irene was sent away from the royal palace soon after her birth "because her mother was not very strong" (9). This euphemistic strain is later continued by her king-papa, who says, when they are discussing her ring, that her mother has "gone where all those rings are made" (165)—that is, it comes from eternity—something Irene cannot yet understand, but which the reader, even the child reader, has presumably worked out by this time (and it must be remembered that in MacDonald's day the reality of death was far more present to children than it is now). The king, the guards and the servants are all aware of danger, but 'above ground' there is no significant reference to death (if we except Curdie's slaying of a goblin creature [246]) until, in the penultimate chapter, he realises that a flood is coming and tells the king that everyone must leave the hall at once, without explanation—"for that might make it too late for some of us" (299).

Queen Irene doesn't mention death either, except in the fairly innocuous context of chicken broth—"I never kill any of my chickens," she tells the princess (27). But one of the most extraordinary things about *The Princess and the Goblin* is that the Queen doesn't mention the goblins, those outward and visible signs of the threat of death and degeneration, from start to finish—and the goblins do not mention her. Almost as extraordinary is the fact that most readers, whether children or childlike, do not spot this, and silence on the subject, like other mysteries in this book, works on their subconscious minds; in MacDonald what is not said can be as important as what is actually said. The challenge for Irene (and later for Curdie) is to learn to believe in and trust the Queen—and a warning about the goblins would mean not only that there is something to fear, but something from which her grandmother may not be able to protect her.

The day-to-day concerns of Diamond's mother in much of *At the Back of the North Wind* are displaced, in *The Princess and the Goblin*, onto Lootie the nurse, whose love is weaker, whose fears are stronger and whose capacity for faith and understanding are less than Martha's—and who does not stand to Irene in the symbolically potent relation of mother.[16] Queen Irene is the nearest thing to a mother that the princess has, but whereas North Wind seeks Diamond out, it is Irene, in *The Princess and the Goblin*, who has to do the seeking—and in a context which, in spite of the affection of Lootie and the other servants, leaves her very much thrown back on her own devices.

The protection of the Queen, who has been in the castle as long as the princess herself, has always been behind Irene, though she has not known it. But on the conscious level—that is, downstairs—Irene is comparatively isolated, and this is emphasised by the fact that the physical sphere of action in *The Princess and the Goblin* is narrowly circumscribed. Whereas Diamond, in *At the Back of the North Wind*, moves from The Wilderness to Bloomsbury to The Mound—holidays

The Downstretched Hand: Individual Development in

in Sandwich, travels extensively in London and (as he thinks) voyages as far as the North Pole—Irene never leaves the mountain until the action of the plot is complete; her travels are limited to upstairs, downstairs and underground, with short walks on the outside of the mountain. This limitation of spatial scope is reinforced by the Queen, who seldom leaves the tower (in stark contrast to North Wind, in *At the Back of the North Wind*, whose very life is in motion). When Curdie the miner boy enters the picture Irene's context is broadened, for he represents (among other things) the outside world, and is, indeed, the first person from outside (not counting her father and the guards) whom she has ever met. This still leaves an intense focus on the relationship between Irene and her great-great-grandmother, which is the pivot on which the whole book turns.

The main sphere of action in *The Princess and the Goblin* is the interior development, both psychological and spiritual, of Princess Irene. In a 'typical' fairy tale, Curdie would be the principal character, and not merely have proved his mettle by seeing off the goblins (all in a day's work to him) when Irene and Lootie are lost on the mountain. Far from eventually needing to be rescued from the goblins by the princess, he would not only have effected his own escape but thwarted their plan to kidnap her; but at the end he is obliged to admit: "I wasn't good enough to be allowed to help you: I didn't believe you. Your grandmother took care of you without me." "She sent you to help my people, anyway," Irene adds kindly (284)—and it is obvious who is the source of power. Yet for all the fascination of the Queen, Princess Irene, as the character with whom the reader can most nearly identify, and, perhaps more important, with the greatest discoveries to make, remains the central figure in the book. But her great-great-grandmother is crucial to her metamorphosis, or rebirth—and Queen Irene is distinct from all the other manifestations of the Wise Woman that pervade MacDonald's fantasy (even the Queen Irene of *The Princess and Curdie*, who, though the same person, has a different function) and from the grandmothers who frequently appear in his adult fiction.[17]

It is tempting to argue that the Queen represents Irene at different points in her life; she has been in the castle ever since the princess arrived, she manifests herself at different ages and they both have the same name, "Irene," an anagram of the French *reine* or queen, so that Irene is a princess queen and her grandmother a queen queen, or what her granddaughter is eventually to become. While Irene is about eight years old, the Queen's rejuvenation levels off at twenty-three; since fifteen is often the age of puberty for fairy-tale heroines (Bettelheim 232), Irene + maturity = the Queen.[18] But other evidence proves that Queen Irene cannot simply be a projection of the princess. Curdie's mother saw the Queen's light through the tower walls long before the princess was born (239)—something which, the Queen says, does not happen more than five times in a hundred years (121). And Irene's father not only asked the Queen if he could name his baby daughter after her (25) but goes to see her on his second visit to the castle (166). She has, furthermore, other children: "I confess I have sometimes been afraid about my children," she tells Irene (158), though she never refers to them again.

Queen Irene is not Irene's mature self—except in the sense that Irene, though a unique individual, also stands for all maturing selves—but is associated with Jesus, the perfect self in whom all possibility of fulfilment is to be found.[19] *The Princess and the Goblin* is influenced by Isaiah (the prophet who, as Kirstin Jeffrey Johnson tells us, emphasises "the primacy of Light over darkness"[20]) and by other biblical writers, but the influence of MacDonald's beloved St. John is especially pervasive. It is worth noting that the apostle, who describes Jesus as "the Word . . . made flesh" (John 1:14), virtually identifies Jesus, the masculine Word, with the feminine Wisdom of God to be found in the Old Testament.[21]

It must be emphasised that the Queen is *associated* with Jesus but not *identified* with him. She is almost omniscient but not quite, knowing everything that happens to Curdie but being unaware that Irene has hurt her thumb on an old spindle (118) and, more importantly, unaware of what happens to the princess before she gets back to the tower after rescuing Curdie—when, that is, she is worried about her granddaughter,[22] for fear can blunt perception even in the Queen (which does not make her any less reassuring: "I've been waiting for you, . . . and beginning to think whether I had not better go and fetch you myself," she tells Irene on her return [222-223]). And while Queen Irene implies that she is nearly two thousand years old (158)—a period which dates from the lifetime of Jesus—Jesus himself says simply: "Before Abraham was, I am" (John 8:58). But the association between the Queen and Jesus is very close. The Queen does what Jesus does—not only symbolic actions such as washing Irene's feet (*PG* 120) but the spiritual ministry of comforting, healing, forgiving and saving.

The third chapter, in which Irene first meets the Queen, is entitled "The Princess and—we shall see who" (20), and subsequent pages are headed simply "The Princess and—". "Do you know my name, child?" asks the Queen (24), and when it has been established that they are both named Irene she continues: "Wouldn't you like to know who I am, child?" This goes much further than "I'm your father's mother's father's mother" (25), which is all Irene can cope with (though without understanding it) at the moment.[23] The concept of the name as something of intrinsic value has much to do, not only with the relationship between Queen Irene and her granddaughter, but with the association of Queen Irene with Jesus. Cruden, in his *Complete Concordance to the Bible*, says: "*Name* is frequently used to designate the entire person, his individuality and his power. This is usually the case when the reference is to God."[24] Perhaps the Queen is opening a deeper dimension of her name when she says "Wouldn't you like to know who I AM, child?" (*PG* 25; capitals mine), for when, on Mount Sinai, Moses asks God's name, God replies: "I AM THAT I AM; and he said, 'Thus shalt thou say unto the children of Israel, I AM hath sent me unto you'" (Exodus 3:14). In St. John's Gospel, the major Biblical influence on *The Princess and the Goblin*, there are seven special "I Ams."[25] The first chapter of this Gospel assigns a special numinosity to the name of the Messiah: "As many as received him, to them gave he power to become the sons of God, even to them that believe on his name" (John 1:12). And Queen Irene's name, "peace," is one of the Messiah's titles; Isaiah the prophet calls him "The Prince of Peace" (Is. 9:6).[26]

In the promise of peace inherent in Princess Irene's name, one of Isaiah's prophecies is fulfilled: "All thy children shall be taught of the LORD: and great shall be the peace of thy children" (54:13). Irene gains peace, as MacDonald puts it in a sermonising interpolation in *Donal Grant*, through "love and faith and obedience [which] are sides of the same prism" (*DG* 89). This is exemplified most clearly when, after Queen Irene's light has guided her home from the pitch-dark mountain, she is sitting in her grandmother's chair:

> The child sat gazing, now at the rose-fire, now at the starry walls, now at the silvery light; and a great quietness grew in her heart. If all the long-legged cats in the world had come rushing at her then, she would not have been afraid of them for a moment. How this was she could not tell;--she only knew there was no fear in her, and everything was so right and safe that it could not get in. (*PG* 151)

Although Irene is occasionally frightened after this, fear never again has the same power over her—not even when, for a few moments, she feels abandoned under the mountain.

In the course of her relationship with the Queen, Irene goes through a process analogous to that outlined by St. Paul in the relationship with Christ to which he aspires:

> That I may know him, and the power of his resurrection, and the fellowship of his sufferings, being made conformable unto his death;
>
> If by any means I might attain unto the resurrection of the dead. (Philippians 3:10-11)

Queen Irene herself need undergo no symbolic equivalent of the crucifixion because she has already died, as would have to be the case in view of the fact that she is Irene's great-great-grandmother and well over a hundred years old: "Are you a hundred?" asks Irene on their first encounter. "Yes—more than that. I am too old for you to guess," the queen replies (27), and later she tells her that "it does not happen above five times in a hundred years that anyone does see [my moon lamp]" (*PG* 121). Jesus said: "I am the resurrection and the life" (John 11:25), and the resurrection in *The Princess and the Goblin* is just as real as it is in *At the Back of the North Wind*, or even more so.[27] But it is no longer limited to something eventually to be attained by the protagonist; here it is always present in Queen Irene, pervading the whole book and working on the reader's unconscious—perhaps the less obviously because the Queen is still growing (and I reiterate that she is associated, but not identified with Jesus). It is Irene who has to go through a symbolic crucifixion, and Irene who is symbolically born again.

The goblins, on the other hand, stand for the "second death" of Revelation 20: 14 which admits of no resurrection, for not only do they suggest physical death through their underground setting and their association with darkness but they symbolise the psychological and spiritual death which is inherent in evil. Through the taboo to which fear of them gives rise, evil and death are linked. Freud, who quotes Wundt's view that "the essence of taboo is fear of demons" (*Totem and Taboo*, 58), later says:

> It is quite possible that the whole concept of demons was derived from the important relation of the living to the dead. The ambivalence inherent in that relation was expressed ... by the fact that, by the same root, it gave rise to two completely opposed psychical structures: on the one hand fear of demons and ghosts and on the other hand veneration of ancestors. (*Totem and Taboo*, 65)

The Downstretched Hand

Freud adds that demons were always regarded by primitive peoples as the spirits of those who had died recently, and who were, in their jealousy of those still alive, particularly hostile to their nearest and dearest.[28] If this idea persists in the collective unconscious—as it may well do, since it is merely another expression of the inordinate guilt which often follows the loss of a person who was at once beloved and the object of repressed hostility—it is interesting to note that Irene's mother died (apparently) in childbirth; in other words, Irene has in a manner of speaking killed her own mother to come into the world. Hence the menace of being paired with the goblin Prince Harelip, whose mother ("from upstairs") died in the same way (*PG* 74, 75), and of being permanently imprisoned underground in the region of death.

But George MacDonald's fantasy for children always comes with a layer of protective insulation. Just as the reader of *At the Back of the North Wind* knows, though Diamond does not, that a kindly policeman (a father figure with three children) follows him to Old Sal's cellar—no wonder Catherine Persyn calls it "the comfort book"[29]—so Irene, in *The Princess and the Goblin*, does not violate the taboo and come across the goblins until after she has met the Queen. Although a long time passes before she sees Queen Irene again—long enough (especially after a failed attempt to find her) to think that their first encounter must have been a dream—there still remains an unconscious residue of reassurance from that first meeting.

Irene's great task in *The Princess and the Goblin* is to grow, not only in faith in the reality of the Queen but in trust in her goodness and power; and the challenges she must face in the process, supported always by a love incomparably stronger than the malice of the goblins, are the greatest ones of all—those of death and rebirth.

Endnotes to Chapter 5 on page 267

"I should like you to take me to see my great old grandmother."

The king looked grave, and said – "What does my little daughter mean?"

"I mean the Queen Irene that lives up in the tower – the very old lady, you know, with the long hair of silver."

The king only gazed at his little princess with a look which she could not understand.

"She's got her crown in her bedroom," she went on; "but I've not been in there yet. You know she's here, don't you?"

"No," said the king, very quietly.

"Then it must be all a dream," said Irene.

    Chapter 10, "The Princess's King-Papa"
    illustration by Arthur Hughes

"But how do you get at their eggs? Where are their nests?"

The lady took hold of a little loop of string in the wall at the side of the door, and lifting a shutter showed a great many pigeon holes with nests, some with young ones and some with eggs in them. The birds came in at the other side, and she took out the eggs on this side. She closed it again quickly, lest the young ones should be frightened.

"Oh, what a nice way!" cried the princess."Will you give me an egg to eat? I'm rather hungry."

"I will some day, but now you must go back, or nursie will be miserable about you. I daresay she's looking for you everywhere."

Chapter 3, "The Princess And - We Shall See Who"
illustration by F.D. Bedford

CHAPTER 6

"All Thy Children Shall Be Taught of the LORD" (Isaiah 54:13)

Princess Irene Goes to School

"God... goes on teaching the whole [world], and bringing every man who will but turn his ear a little toward the voice that calls him, nearer and nearer to the second birth—of sonship and liberty." *The Marquis of Lossie* (77-78).

For all the importance of death in *The Princess and the Goblin*—especially the ongoing death to self which is fundamental to Christianity—MacDonald's primary purpose is to show that being born again is also a process continuous throughout life.[1] Like death to self, rebirth calls for courage, and Irene at the beginning of the book is "as brave as could be expected of a princess of her age" (*PG* 18). She knows nothing about the goblins, and her fears at this stage are the universal ones of disorientation and solitude. After climbing a "curious old stair... which looked as if never anyone had set foot upon it" (17), she "began to get frightened" in the empty passages above (18), and the references to fear multiply thick and fast; she "began to be afraid," "she was too eager and perhaps too frightened to cry for some time," "frightened as she was" (18, 19). But even before Irene finds the Queen, MacDonald reassures the reader by letting the comforting voice of the dramatized narrator frequently be heard. The second chapter is entitled "The Princess Loses Herself," and as soon as this catastrophe occurs the author remarks that "[i]t doesn't follow that she *was* lost, because she had lost herself, though" (18). The suggestion of "[h]e that findeth his life shall lose it; and he that loseth his life for my sake shall find it" (Matthew 10:39) is still more strongly brought out in Irene's subsequent remark that "I went upstairs, and I lost myself, and if I hadn't found the beautiful lady, I should never have found myself" (*PG* 33-34).[2] As Jung says in *Symbols of Transformation*, "[t]he parallel to the motif of dying and rising again is that of being lost and found again" ("The Dual Mother," par. 531)—and at this point the theme of spiritual rebirth is already emerging.

When the adventure begins, the outside world has temporarily lost its charms for the princess (since it has been raining too hard for her to go out and play) and her boredom with her toys and her "safe

The Downstretched Hand: Individual Development in

nursery" (*PG* 10) indicates not only that the fairy tale is on the level of serious fantasy but that the heroine is ready for what MacDonald calls, in *David Elginbrod*, "a . . . growth of individual being" (*DE* 419). And just as Diamond, in *At the Back of the North Wind*, has been psychologically prepared for his aerial adventures by "those precious dreams he had so often had, in which he floated about on the air at will" (*ABNW* 358)—that is, unconsciously he had been longing for his later experiences—so Irene has been prepared, with masterly unobtrusiveness, for the life-changing experience of meeting her grandmother and all that follows on from it: "She had once before been up six steps" of the "curious old stair of worm-eaten oak" which leads her to the tower (*PG* 17)—and which, though the door to it is in the nursery, Lootie has never even mentioned.

The importance of Irene's leaving the nursery to go up the old staircase is underlined by MacDonald's switching to the present tense, the immediacy of which constitutes an invitation to the reader to engage in the adventure. As in all hero myth (and there is a strong element of this in *The Princess and the Goblin*, as there is in *At the Back of the North Wind* and especially in *The Princess and Curdie*), the tower is the place of perspective which the hero must climb at some point.[3] What Irene finds at the top of the tower (though of course she does not know it) is a combination of the trinity, or the fullness of God, and the mandala, or human representation of wholeness. The doors round three sides of the landing all lead into Queen Irene's apartments, which represent the trinity of levels on which the fully developed human self, made in the image of God, must live; and this trinity of rooms forms part of a mandala, the fourth side of which is the staircase that the immature self must climb to meet the Queen.[4]

The third door on the landing (the first that Irene opens) leads to the Queen's workroom, which represents everyday reality—even though the Queen is spinning her mysterious thread in it. To see the Queen in this room requires no special gift of faith: "If I had been there, Curdie would have seen me well enough," she says after Irene rescues him from the goblins (228). Even Lootie, the nurse, would be able to see the Queen in her workroom, though if that happened "[s]he would rub her eyes, and go away and say she felt queer, and forget half of it and more, and then say it had been all a dream" (115).[5] The principal, and very important function of the workroom is to prove that Queen Irene belongs as much in the world of everyday reality as in that of transcendent mystery—though she herself is the greatest mystery of all.

George MacDonald's Major Fantasies for Children

The second door looks out onto the world of nature; through it one sees the pigeons and the night sky.[6] In *The Princess and the Goblin* it straddles Primary and Secondary Worlds, for to live in and see the natural world is not necessarily to understand it (Curdie, in *The Princess and Curdie*, is told "when you shot that arrow you did not know what a pigeon is" [*PC* 38]). This door too is opened on Irene's first visit to the Queen, for the princess has a spontaneous appreciation of the beauties of the natural world. When she sees the pigeons she asks for an egg, but she gets, not a scorpion,[7] but a postponement; the ball of thread which Queen Irene is spinning for her granddaughter, and which will be the means of her symbolic death and rebirth through rescuing Curdie, is eventually placed under one of the brooding pigeons and is "about the size of a pigeon's egg" (*PG* 151).

The first conversation between Irene and her great-great-grandmother is marked by the reassuring attitude of the Queen, who not only plays the part of a kindly adult by washing away the traces of Irene's tears but makes maturity attractive by opening up new possibilities of understanding. The discussion of the name they have in common is fascinating to Irene, who has always taken it for granted as part of herself.[8] But what undoubtedly makes the greatest impact on the princess—for she immediately begins to discuss the question—is the discovery that she is, and always has been, the principal object of the Queen's love: "I came here to take care of you" (26). To the self-centred consciousness of a child this is more surprising as a discovery than as a fact, but the reassurance gives her the confidence to begin loving in her turn.

Almost as important is the preceding sentence: "I will explain it all to you when you are older" (26). Taking the Queen as a role model in the ordinary sense of the term would not be insuperably difficult given Irene's necessarily limited view of her. Even Alice, in Lewis Carroll's *Alice's Adventures in Wonderland*, thinks along the lines of "When *I'm* a Duchess" (Ch.9), i.e. "when I'm older and more important." But the Queen makes the understanding and strength, not the power and self-sufficiency that come with maturity, seem appealing, for she again and again makes remarks such as "you are hardly old enough to understand," "it is too hot for you yet," "that you would not understand if I were to try ever so much to make you—not yet—not yet" (*PG* 114, 148, 150); words reminiscent of John 16:12, where Jesus says "I have yet many things to say unto you, but ye cannot bear them now."

The Downstretched Hand: Individual Development in

This encouragement to think of future growth might in itself be threatening were it not that, in the present, the Queen accepts Irene just as she is; and at their first meeting she is very childish, though normally and endearingly so. She fires personal questions at the Queen—"Is [living on eggs] what makes your hair so white?".... "Are you fifty?"..."Are you a hundred?" (*PG* 27) and she comments with that devastating frankness which is characteristic of early childhood:

> "Do you live in this room always?"
>
> "I don't sleep in it. I sleep on the opposite side of the landing. I sit here most of the day."
>
> "I shouldn't like it. My nursery is much prettier." (26)

The Queen lets this pass without comment. But a visit to the tower—the place of perspective—is always followed by psychological growth, and however harmless Irene's tactlessness may seem when directed at her grandmother, she learns that inadequate, anxious people can be threatened by it. In the next chapter she describes the Queen to the nurse as "much taller than you, and much prettier," and fails to realise that Lootie's "Oh, I dare say!" expresses real hurt (32). But by bedtime she realises the necessity for a soothing qualification: "[I]f you had been twice as nice-looking as you are, some king or other would have married you, and then what would have become of me?"(37) And in spite of the hurtfulness of not being believed, Irene shows increasing maturity by making allowances for Lootie's incapacity for faith:

> "Nursie," said the princess, "why won't you believe me?"
>
> "Because I can't believe you," said the nurse, getting angry again.
>
> "Ah! then, you can't help it," said Irene, "and I will not be vexed with you any more." (35)

It is after this that we hear for the first time of Irene's "pet name" for her nurse (39),[9] for she has begun to realise that Lootie cannot simply be defined by her protective role towards herself but is a person with feelings to be considered and views—however limited or unsatisfactory—to be acknowledged. As she grows in understanding Irene is already growing from princess into queen—a process later accelerated by what St. Paul might have described as entering into "the fellowship of [Queen Irene's] sufferings" (Phil. 3:10). "You must be content not to be believed for a while," says her grandmother when Curdie, after being rescued from the goblins, proves unable to see her and leaves the tower in dudgeon: "It is very hard to bear; but I have had to bear it, and shall have to bear it many a time yet" (*PG* 226).

Not until Irene has been reassured by discovering the Queen's presence in the tower—for her failure to find her again the next day, though it makes her "very thoughtful" (42), does not shake her belief in the reality of the Queen for long—is the taboo on being out after dark violated, and when this happens the precautions of fear are shown to be utterly inadequate in the face of real danger. When Lootie and Irene go for a walk up the mountain to celebrate the re-emergence of the sun on the third day of bad weather, Lootie lets Irene prolong their outing until it is too late to return to the house before dark and then, realising their predicament, she panics, they start to run and are soon lost. Irene finds it "very discomposing to see her nurse in such a fright," but before she has time to grow really frightened herself she hears the sound of whistling—whistling which changes, as Curdie approaches, into songs mocking the goblins (49-51). "If you're not afraid of them, they're afraid of you," he explains to Lootie (52),[10] but she is unable to assimilate this and her egoism surfaces when Curdie warns that to run from the goblins is to invite pursuit:

> "I don't want to run," said Irene.
>
> "You don't think of *me*," said the nurse.
>
> "Yes, I do, Lootie. The boy says they won't touch us if we don't run."
>
> "Yes, but if they know at the house that I've kept you out so late, I shall be turned away, and that would break my heart." (54-55)

Not too much should be expected from Lootie, for her role is basically that of the Greek pedagogue, a slave whose function was to keep the child in order, escort him and teach him morals, but who did not embody the ideal to be imitated by the child. This was to be found in the father (in this case, the grandmother), and when the child had matured sufficiently to assume the full status of sonship the services of the pedagogue were dispensed with[11] (as happens in Lootie's case, for she is left behind when Irene leaves with the king at the end of the book). St Paul uses the image of the pedagogue to get a point across to the Corinthians: "Though ye have ten thousand instructors in Christ, yet have ye not many fathers," he says, "for in Christ Jesus I have begotten you through the gospel. Wherefore I beseech you, be ye followers of me" (1 Cor. 4:15-16). His elaboration of the same image in the Epistle to the Galatians has a close application to *The Princess and the Goblin*:

The Downstretched Hand: Individual Development in

> Before faith came, we were kept under the law, shut up unto the faith which should afterwards be revealed.
>
> Wherefore the law was our schoolmaster to bring us unto Christ, that we might be justified by faith.
>
> But after that faith is come, we are no longer under a schoolmaster.
>
> For ye are all the children of God by faith in Christ Jesus. (Gal. 3:23-26)

This sums up both Irene's original situation and the subsequent change in her relationship with Lootie which corresponds to the development of her faith in the Queen. Before she meets her grandmother, Irene is "kept under the law" that forbids her to go out after dark and "shut up" in a "safe" nursery (*PG* 18) with an artificial sky painted on the ceiling.[12] And Lootie is the "schoolmaster" who represents the power of the law, though, unlike the pedagogue to whom the word "schoolmaster" in Galatians refers, she does not do any teaching—on this point, indeed, MacDonald exploits the flexibility of the fairy tale, for if Irene is not "taught of the LORD" she is not taught by anybody. But the role of nurse is more appropriate for Lootie anyway, since it suggests motherly care and yet, because a children's nurse was in those days a servant, carries with it an authority which can eventually be thrown off—as in fact happens when Lootie commits the cardinal sin of accusing Irene of lying, and as is endorsed by MacDonald when he entitles that chapter "Irene Behaves like a Princess" (248). That Lootie is the guardian of the law which Irene's father symbolises is clear from the housekeeper's fear of her (250)—though to a lesser degree all the servants share Lootie's function of enforcing or at least supporting the law, and, as a corollary, her perturbation when the princess, in her occasional evasions of 'custody,' shows signs of escaping its discipline.

If Irene is ignorant of the reason for the taboo against staying outside after sunset, she is well aware of the law itself—and it is striking that, after her first meeting with her great-great-grandmother, she takes the first opportunity to break it. As Freud says, "The prohibition owes its strength ... precisely to its unconscious opponent, the concealed and undiminished desire—that is to say, to an internal necessity inaccessible to conscious inspection" (*Totem and Taboo*, 30). There is no need to forbid something that no-one wants to do! When Irene and Lootie have been walking up the mountain for some time, Lootie keeps telling Irene that the sun is getting low and they should go home. But "every time, the princess begged her to go on just a little farther and a little farther" (*PG* 44), and in this way the two—influenced more and more, the longer they stay out, by the magnetic pull of the unconscious—collude in violating the taboo and thus opening the door to the 'lower' or instinctual level of the unconscious, with all its dangerous possibilities.

The impetus driving this comes originally from Irene's encounter with Queen Irene, whom she longs to see again. But it is not possible satisfactorily to make contact with only one aspect of the unconscious— the 'higher' level of the unconscious on the occasion of her meeting with the Queen—and an important reason why Irene does not find her great-great-grandmother on the second attempt is that at this point she has not yet been out in the dark, something as essential as it is dangerous if Irene is to become a fully developed individual. Even Tolkien, who supports the observance of taboos by saying "Thou shalt not—or else thou shalt depart beggared into endless regret" ("On Fairy-Stories," 33), recognises in practice the value of what he reprobates in theory, for if Bilbo and his companions in *The Hobbit* had obeyed the stern and repeated injunction not to leave the path in Mirkwood they would have ended up in a swamp. The fascination of the taboo in fairy tales derives from the necessity to take a tremendous risk in order to realise one's potential—or else to be mired in the swamp of safety and non-development. Through disobeying the law, Irene not only encounters the goblins for the first time but also meets Curdie, who, as a miner, represents on one level the positive aspects of the 'lower' unconscious.

The taboo cannot, however, be violated with impunity. Though Irene herself will be "justified by faith" (Romans 5:1), Lootie will not; for, as St. Paul puts it, "as many as are of the works of the law are under the curse: for it is written, Cursed is every one that continueth not in all things which are written in the book of the law to do them" (Galatians 3:10). "That's against the law," Curdie tells her sternly: "It must be your fault" (*PG* 53). And, as Lootie has good cause to fear, she is held accountable by Irene's king-papa, the source of law in the kingdom (not for nothing does he travel the country to keep "a constant lookout for the ablest and best men to put into office" and dismiss anyone found "incapable or unjust" [164]). She has failed in the first function of the pedagogue, which is to impose certain restraints; and her failure, coupled with the fact that Irene has now met the Queen, means that Lootie's influence is henceforth on the wane. But it is high time that Lootie's tutelage should end, for she not only breaks the king's law but the "royal law according to the scripture,

The Downstretched Hand: Individual Development in

Thou shalt love thy neighbour as thyself" (James 2:8-9). This causes her to fail to respect the sacrosanctity, in terms of both morality and fairy tale, of a promise. Irene knows that "a princess must *not* break her word" (*PG* 61)—and in MacDonald's lexicon the words "prince" or "princess" can apply to any child (see, e.g., 22, 254, 255). But Lootie's "very foolish notions concerning the dignity of a princess" (254) not only thwart Irene's efforts to make friends with the miners' children but cause Lootie herself to think that Curdie is as much of a danger to the princess as the goblins are. As Freud says, "the prohibition . . . shifts about . . . and extends to any new aims which the forbidden impulse may adopt" (*Totem and Taboo*, 30)—and Irene's promise to kiss Curdie (a promise which symbolises a great bond between them and opens the possibility of their eventual union) is just such an aim as far as Lootie, to whom a miner is almost on a par with a goblin, is concerned.

There is pathos in Lootie's increasing bewilderment about her charge, for "she loved her dearly" (*PG* 34)—as dearly, that is, as she can love. The irony of her situation is that, because she refuses contact with the unconscious, she is particularly vulnerable to its promptings—"darkened, yet fancying herself light," to borrow a phrase from Jane Austen's *Mansfield Park*[13]—and therefore she can occasionally act in a manner directly opposed to her conscious aims. Not only does she indulge Irene's desire to go "just a little farther and a little farther" out on the mountainside, but, on the Friday night when Irene has been told at all costs to seek the Queen, Lootie allows a goblin creature into the nursery by opening the window before she fetches the princess's tea—and then takes longer to bring it than she (consciously) intends.

To be fair to Lootie, she is also exposed to the promptings of her 'higher' unconscious. This brings her closer to Queen Irene than any sighting in the workroom could do, for she is influenced by the Queen through the medium of Irene. It is no coincidence that when Lootie admires the princess's ring she fixes on the image of the "fiery rose" (163)—an unconscious echo of the "rose-fire" of Queen Irene's bedroom (153)—and Irene's return from her flight up the mountain to escape the creature in her room elicits the same reaction from grandmother and nurse: the Queen "sprung from her chair . . . caught the child to her bosom, and kissing the tear-stained face over and over, sat down with her in her lap" (147). Lootie, "running to her . . . caught her in her arms and covered her with kisses" (160). "My precious darling princess!" she says for the first and only time, echoing Queen Irene's remark (a first for her): "You darling!" (147) And presently the word is echoed again as "the whole household, headed by the housekeeper, burst into the nursery to exult over their darling" (162).

But love without faith or understanding (as is indicated by her failure to realise that Irene is incapable of any kind of duplicity) is necessarily limited, and Lootie's resemblance to Queen Irene never becomes more than slight. Since she cannot integrate the conscious and unconscious levels of her personality she can only come completely under the Queen's sway when she is asleep: "How the nurse came to sleep through [the noise of animals fighting], was a mystery, but I suspect the old lady had something to do with it," says the narrator on the night when Irene goes to Curdie's rescue (196). Lootie can never be what Mrs. Peterson already is, an earthly version of Queen Irene who keeps "a little heaven" for Curdie and his father to return to "out of the low and rather dreary earth in which they worked" (123)—a clear parallel with what Irene finds in the tower: "Oh, what a lovely haven to reach from the darkness and fear through which she had come!" [144]). And "I doubt if the princess was very much happier even in the arms of her huge great-grandmother than Peter and Curdie were in the arms of Mrs. Peterson," says the narrator ([123]-124). In *The Princess and Curdie* MacDonald underlines Mrs. Peterson's similarity to the Queen—their hands feel exactly alike to the fire-sensitised Curdie (*PC* 108)—whereas Lootie, alone among the principal characters in *The Princess and the Goblin*, is never mentioned in the later book.

It is in every sense fitting that Curdie Peterson, whose name indicates apostolic descent—"thou art Peter, and upon this rock I will build my church," says Jesus to the disciple who has recognised his identity (Matthew 16:18)[14]—should unofficially replace Lootie as Irene's guardian; a guardian who, ironically, not only comes to owe Irene his life but eventually, when the promise of the kiss is honoured, becomes her peer. "I have surnamed thee, though thou hast not known me," says God through Isaiah; and as this immediately follows the words "I have even called thee by thy name," we have here the meeting of "I have called thee by *thy name*" (Curdie) and "every one that is called by *my name*" (Irene, whose name means "peace" and who is called after Jesus, the Prince of Peace [15]). The princess and the miner complement each other from the first, like the heights and depths which they respectively explore; Irene's eyes are "like two bits of night-sky, each with a star dissolved in the blue" (*PG* 9), while Curdie's are "as dark as the mines in which he worked, and as sparkling as the crystals in their rocks" (51).

The Downstretched Hand: Individual Development in

If Curdie's descent from Peter Peterson aligns him with the metaphorical rock of religious significance, it also underlines both his connection with and his essential difference from the goblins he has to combat. Curdie is the son of a rock; Helfer, son of Glump, whose cave Curdie penetrates to gain entrance to the goblin kingdom, is described by his father as being "as strong as a mountain" (73). But the less than affectionate relationship between this father-son pair, in contrast to the love between Curdie and Peter, is indicated by Helfer's expressed wish to come into his inheritance: "Here, Helfer, I'll help you up with your chest," says his father. "I wish it *was* my chest, father," responds his disgruntled son—to which Glump merely replies: "Your turn will come in good time enough!" (84). And had Curdie's capacity for faith been more developed at this point, he might have been prepared for seeing nothing extraordinary in Queen Irene's bedroom by his puzzling experience of the Glump family's cave: "To his surprise, he could discover nothing to distinguish it from an ordinary cave in the rock.... The goblins had talked of coming back for the rest of their household gear: he saw nothing that would have made him suspect a family had taken shelter there for a single night" (84-85).[16]

"Every other night or so" for months (170) Curdie explores the subterranean realm of the goblins (a Thesean labyrinth if ever there was one) to try and discover their nefarious plans against the people above ground (90-91, 93-94). But only when he is lost after his guiding string (the counterpart of Irene's thread) is moved by some goblin creatures does Curdie come upon the goblin royal family (an episode which is a travesty of Irene's being lost in the tower and then finding the Queen) and discover the goblins' principal plan—to capture the princess as a wife for their prince. "Hideous inhabitants of dark caves clearly invite a Freudian interpretation," says Tony Tanner,[17] and there are obviously sadistic sexual overtones in the projected marriage—"it *will* be nice to make her cry," says the goblin prince as he contemplates having plastic surgery performed on the toes of his intended (*PG* 176). But, as Jung points out in *Symbols of Transformation*, sexual symbolism often symbolises something else,[18] and "hideous inhabitants of dark caves" also suggest death in its most demonic aspect.[19] In the first chapter there is a resemblance between the cobs retreating into "subterranean caverns" (*PG* 11) and the fallen angels descending into hell, and the king's meeting with the other goblins in the great hall has a savour of Satan's assembly in Milton's *Paradise Lost*. Curdie, however, correctly identifies the goblin who most threatens Irene—the true Minotaur in this labyrinth—not as the prince or even the king but as the goblin queen; and he can hardly fail to sense in her a negative archetype of female power, since she not only worsts him in single combat but imprisons him in a hole (183).

The death which the goblins represent is the destruction of individuality, i.e. possession by the instinctual drives of the unconscious (and in the case of the goblin queen this gives rise to a masculine aggressiveness which ties in with that found, in *The Princess and Curdie,* in most of the women of the kingdom; though the queen's spouse describes her as "the best of housekeepers" [*PG* 187] she has few other feminine attributes). Curdie is Irene's most effective protector on the natural (as opposed to the supernatural) level, not only because he is "much farther on than Lootie" (227) but because his gifts for poetry and singing demonstrate his victory in what Jung terms "the fight against the paralysing grip of the unconscious [which] calls forth man's creative powers" ("The Dual Mother," *SoT* par. 523). He contrasts strongly with the goblins, whose hatred of poetry is a sign of their debasement.[20] Their very voices reflect the quality of their words, for the members of Glump's family speak "just as if they had bottle-brushes—each at least one—in their throats" (*PG* 83), and it is significant that, in a book in which so much attention is paid to truth, the first goblin words we hear are "Lies! lies! lies!"—preceded by "a burst of coarse tittering" (44). Most striking of all, the goblin prince proposed as Irene's bridegroom is called Harelip. Even his two-toed foot (the cloven hoof of the devil, and a mutation of his mother's ungoblinlike toes) is less important symbolically than the deformed mouth which (with uncharacteristic insensitivity) MacDonald uses to throw the eloquence and singing voice of Curdie, Irene's true partner, into sharp relief.[21]

Curdie is wrong to impute the goblins' dislike of songs to simple jealousy or resentment of insult. His rhymes strike deeper than he knows, for poet and prophet are associated in MacDonald's mind and occasionally Curdie's songs tell truths which he does not know himself;[22] after pulling off the goblin queen's granite shoe, "he saw to his astonishment that what he had sung in ignorance, to annoy the queen, was actually true: she had six horrible toes" (212). Sometimes, too, his songs tell truths which none of the goblins can bear to hear. When he says: "You're all so very dirty! . . . . You're all so thick and snorty! . . . . Beast and man so mixty!" it is not merely their personal vanity which is offended; and worse still, when he adds: "All your cheeks so slaty! . . . . All your [heads] so flinty!" (181);[23] they are reminded that in descending not to the level of beasts but *below* it to the inanimate—i.e. surrendering to the unconscious—they are on the slippery slope to nonentity.[24]

Critics who believe in the protective power of the imagination sometimes adduce faith as an addition or alternative. Roderick McGillis, for example, speaks of Queen Irene's "lamp of poetry (or faith),"[25] and Robert Lee Wolff describes the princess's thread both as "the thread of poesy" and as "the thread of faith or love" (*The Golden Key*, 166). Yet the creative imagination, however important, is not of itself effective against the spiritual danger which the goblins represent. Through Curdie, MacDonald warns us against putting too much trust in it, or for that matter in common sense; the guiding string, his means of returning from the labyrinth, is only as good as what it is fastened to (so indeed is Irene's thread, but it is 'fastened' to the Queen). Curdie's attempts to discover and circumvent the goblins' plans reflect, in so far as they relate to Irene, the tendency of unenlightened but well-meaning people to take precautions against the wrong danger. For what menaces Irene the most at this point is not the malevolence of the goblins but her own recurring doubt of the existence of the Queen—doubt that crystallises into disbelief when she discovers her king-papa's ignorance of Queen Irene's presence in the tower and cries: "Then it must be all a dream" (*PG* 105).

The king's own relationship with the unconscious is ambivalent. He is the author of the original law that forbade the princess's being out after dark; the law, in other words, that, for fear of the anarchic power of the unconscious, tried to keep her in the realm of consciousness. But it is not clear how the king knows that the law has been broken: "I cannot tell you how he had come to know. I am sure Curdie had not told him. Someone about the palace must have seen them, after all," says the narrator (107), with a deliberate vagueness which may insinuate that the king's own unconscious is at work, followed by a suggestion of Lootie-like rationalisation. On his next visit the king is disturbed by the report of goblin creatures in the garden, but he is reassured by "the presence of the ring on [Irene's] finger"—he knows, though Lootie does not, that it was not there before. And before he leaves, "Irene saw him go up the old stair; and he did not come down again till they were just ready to start; and she thought with herself that he had been up to see the old lady" (166).

Irene's earlier dismissal of the Queen as a dream creation was a prelude to seeing her again—not immediately, for many months intervene, but in the following chapter. Her next venture up the stair has been prepared for by her own desires; she "often and often wished that her huge great grandmother had not been a dream." But it is triggered by an accident reminiscent of the Sleeping Beauty;[26] while playing with some of the housekeeper's "queer ancient ornaments" (110) she runs the pin of an old-fashioned brooch into her thumb, causing serious inflammation (note that the wounding agent cannot be a spindle!) This incident marks an epoch in Irene's life. But instead of falling asleep for a hundred years she becomes, in the deepest sense, more fully awake, for to-night she discovers the genuineness of the vision. While dreams (unless they have been sent to the dreamer) are self-generated and change nothing[27]—"there was the pain always in every dream" (111)—when she gets up and climbs the tower, Queen Irene heals the wound.

The experience of being healed constitutes a crucial step in the growth of Irene's faith (as it does later in Curdie's). The first time Irene climbs the stairs, her grandmother fetches "a little silver basin and a soft white towel" (24) to wash her tearstained face, presumably from the bedroom which thus, from the beginning, impinges on the world of everyday reality which the workroom represents. The basin grows in size; at the second meeting between Irene and the Queen it becomes a large silver basin in which Queen Irene washes her granddaughter's feet. Both the washing of the face and the washing of the feet derive from the same passage of St. John's Gospel, in which Jesus "poureth water into a basin, and began to wash the disciples' feet, and to wipe them with the towel wherewith he was girded" (13:5). And in the course of their third encounter the Queen shows Irene the fullest development of the basin in the shape of "a large oval tub of silver, shining brilliantly in the light of the wonderful lamp" (*PG* 149)—a tub in which the princess will be bathed after bringing Curdie out from under the mountain, and in which she will symbolically experience the spiritual death of baptism: "[S]he sank in the cool clear water.... When she opened her eyes, she saw nothing but a strange lovely blue *over* and beneath and all about her" (230; italics mine—no breathing necessary!) This bath will bring a symbolic resurrection in its train, healing Irene's bruises and making her feel "as if she had been made over again" (231-232).[28]

Something at least equally significant takes place on Irene's second visit to the Queen. When they go into the bedroom Queen Irene fetches a "curious silver casket" containing ointment with which she anoints her granddaughter's hand (118-119)—and it not only heals her thumb but helps fit her, later on, to feel the thread (just as Curdie can feel it after the Queen has anointed his wound with the same

The Downstretched Hand: Individual Development in

ointment [268]). This suggests the symbolic anointing of which St. John speaks in his first Epistle:

> The anointing which ye have received of him abideth in you, and ye need not that any man teach you: but as the same anointing teacheth you of all things, and is truth, and is no lie, and even as it hath taught you, ye shall abide in him. (1 John 2:27)[29]

The translation from workroom to bedroom during Irene's second visit to her grandmother is important and permanent, signifying that the princess, after her initiation of struggle, suffering and doubt, is ready to penetrate deeply into the realm of the supernatural. The bedroom is where the Queen keeps her crown, that great mandala which contains every colour of the spectrum; and, now that Irene's faith in the vision has grown, her grandmother speaks more openly of her own powers. Their Christlike nature becomes increasingly apparent: "I will give you one reason . . . why you couldn't find me [last time]," she says. "I didn't want you to find me" (*PG* 114-115). This is later reinforced by the remark that "nobody could find the room except I pleased" (121), a clear echo of "[n]o man can come to me, except the Father which hath sent me draw him" (John 6:44).

Not until Irene goes into the bedroom does she begin to grasp the mystery surrounding her great-great-grandmother. This room is the domain of the supernatural and a place where the very nature of reality is questioned. Queen Irene insists on the empirical truth of the vision: "If that light were to go out, you would *fancy yourself* lying in a bare garret, on a heap of old straw, and would not see one of the pleasant things *round about you all the time*" (121; italics mine). Unlike Lewis Carroll, who, at the end of *Alice's Adventures in Wonderland*, writes of the transmutation of fantasy into "dull reality" (Ch. 12), MacDonald wants to show that reality is greater than it appears, and this is why the Queen works at heightening Irene's perceptions. Fittingly, her moon lamp guides the lost, not by shedding light on their paths (except, in deference to Lootie's lack of understanding, at the end), but by giving their eyes a greater power of seeing. And the wonderful lamp, the most compelling feature of Queen Irene's bedroom and completely under her control—"When I please, I can make the lamp shine through the walls—shine so strong that it melts them away from before the sight" (150)—is drawn from the pervasive imagery of light in St. John's Gospel, in which Jesus is described as "the true Light" (1:9).

Irene's first visit to the Queen's bedroom concludes with her sleeping in her grandmother's great oval bed, an event which, while reaffirming the superiority of vision over dreams—"no dream could be more lovely than what she had left behind when she fell asleep" (*PG* 122)—shows that her imagination as well as her faith has been enriched by her deepening relationship with Queen Irene. The dream, with its cosmic implications, builds on her love of nature:

> In a moment... the little princess was dreaming in the midst of the loveliest dreams—of summer seas and moonlight and mossy springs and great murmuring trees, and beds of wild flowers with such odours as she had never smelled before. (122)

So great an admirer of Coleridge as George MacDonald could hardly have described this episode without thinking of the scene in "Christabel" in which the heroine shares her bed with a lamia.[30] But, as we have seen in *At the Back of the North Wind*, MacDonald is never afraid to take negative associations and turn them into positive ones. The contrast with the superficially similar "Christabel" is a powerful element in the symbolic structure of *The Princess and the Goblin* at this point, and not less so because the child reader can only see one side of it. Coleridge's poem has obvious sexual connotations—penetration into the inner sanctum by the serpentine threat which has wormed its way in from the outside, etc.—but they essentially symbolise, through the negative archetype of the mother as lamia (not for nothing does Geraldine, the lamia, clash with the angelic spirit of Christabel's dead mother[31]), Coleridge's fear that a human being may be ultimately helpless in the face of a determined onslaught by the powers of evil. This is a view MacDonald sets himself to oppose. The whole episode in *The Princess and the Goblin,* so like "Christabel" in externals, differs radically from it in essentials. Queen Irene is at home in the tower, quite unlike Coleridge's lamia, the alien who, in the tradition of witches, gains entry to the castle through trickery. And, while the serpentine quality of Geraldine links her both with sensuality and the demonic, the Queen, associated with Jesus, is also linked with doves—those images of the Holy Spirit.[32]

Most important of all to MacDonald is the emphasis on Irene's freedom, owing to the Queen, throughout this encounter (a complete contrast to the coercion which has become second nature to the goblins). "Would you like to sleep with me?" asks her grandmother. "You won't be afraid then to go to bed with such an old woman?" (119) Later she says "Shall I take you in my arms?" (121) And when they

The Downstretched Hand

discuss Irene's approaching test—the necessity of returning in a week's time—the Queen says: "You may be sure I will do all I can to help you to come. But it will rest with yourself after all" (122). Whereas, in Coleridge's poem, contact with Geraldine imposes a spell that is "lord of [Christabel's] utterance" (1.268)—the lamia's body is "[a] sight to dream of, not to tell!" (1.253)—in *The Princess and the Goblin* it is Irene's own increasing maturity that keeps her "thoughtfully silent" (*PG* 135) after this episode and makes her "betray nothing, whatever efforts Lootie might make to get at her thoughts" (135-136). This is, of course, in obedience to her grandmother's earlier charge to say nothing more to Lootie about her (116), but it marks quite a change from the child who could hardly wait to tell her nurse about her "beautiful mother of grandmothers" (31). The contrast which MacDonald is making is not only between good and evil but between the external trickery of magic and the inner transformation worked by love. For evil and magic (beneficent or otherwise) have this in common—they are both essentially manipulative; while love, though its effects are less immediate and spectacular, works changes the more profound because they leave the individual free: "You may if you will" (121).

As a result of this episode in *The Princess and the Goblin*, Irene develops increased trust in the Queen. "I will both lay me down in peace, and sleep: for thou, LORD, only makest me dwell in safety," might be Princess Irene's watchword as well as King David's (Psalm 4:8), and it is no wonder that she says, when the Queen "[holds] her close to her bosom," "I didn't know anything in the whole world could be so comfortable" (*PG* 121) —a far cry from "that bosom old . . . that bosom cold" which Christabel finds in Geraldine (ll 457, 458). After their fourth meeting, Irene "often thought of her grandmother during the day, and often dreamed about her at night" (*PG* 253-254)—in other words, Queen Irene's influence is beginning to pervade her little granddaughter on both the conscious and unconscious levels. This is the best possible preparation for the trial in which Irene finds herself symbolically abandoned to her own unconscious in all its darkness.

Endnotes to Chapter 6 on page 275

CHAPTER 7

"And great shall be the peace of thy children" (Isaiah 54:13)
Mission Accomplished

"Unto the upright there ariseth light in the darkness"
(Psalm 112, v. 4)

Though Irene wakes next morning in her own bed, the question that is raised is not whether she has really been away from it but whether she will ever again be away from what the Queen's bed symbolises. When she says "I should like to lie here for ever," the old lady responds "You may if you will," and the "if you will" has to be determined by a test of faith; Irene must return to the tower on "this night week" (a Friday, like the day of Jesus's crucifixion [121]), and the Queen tells her that "[t]he only question is whether you will believe I am anywhere—whether you will believe I am anything but a dream" (122). For the development of faith is gradual and Irene's is not yet definitively confirmed: "Even now," we find after this meeting, "she could not feel quite sure that she had not been dreaming. Could it really be that an old lady lived up in the top of the house, with pigeons and a spinning-wheel, and a lamp that never went out?" (135)

The last words of *Lilith* are a quotation from Novalis—"Our life is no dream, but it should and will perhaps become one" (*L* 359)—words which Raeper describes as one of MacDonald's favourite sayings (*George MacDonald*, 153). But in *The Princess and the Goblin* Irene's key task (since nothing can be achieved without it) is to believe in the empirical reality of the Queen, and dreams are therefore adduced as illusory; "she often and often wished that her huge great grandmother had not been a dream" (*PG* 110), "not quite sure that she was not dreaming" (113), "I thought you were a dream" (114), "you would have found me sooner if you hadn't come to think I was a dream" (114), Lootie "would rub her eyes . . . and then say it had been all a dream" (115). At one point Irene does join dream and reality: "'If she is a dream,' she said to herself, 'then I am the likelier to find her, if I am dreaming'"—and "as if she had known every step of the way, she walked straight to the door at the foot of the narrow stair that led to the tower" (113). Her unconscious has, at any rate, become active, although she cannot as yet credit its validity or the source of its impulses. Although the Queen heals her inflamed hand during this

The Downstretched Hand: Individual Development in

second encounter, she finds, "That Night Week," that "even now she could not feel quite sure that she had not been dreaming," i.e. that the experience had been genuine; but she is still determined to "try to find the tower in which she had either seen or dreamed her grandmother" (135).

Irene fails the Queen's test, and for a very simple reason; she is taken by surprise. Running from the goblin creature she thinks is pursuing her, Irene dare not go up the stairs, "*which, after all, might lead to no tower!*" (137; MacDonald's italics). So she does the worst possible thing and runs out onto the mountain in the pitch dark—but then, as MacDonald points out, "that is the way fear serves us: it always sides with the thing we are afraid of." Eventually she falls by the roadside, "unable even to scream" and "half-dead with terror" (138), and, after she has picked herself up, sits dejectedly on a stone; "nobody but one who had done something wrong could have been more miserable" (139). But, as the prophet Micah says, "when I fall, I shall arise; when I sit in darkness, the LORD shall be a light unto me" (7:8). As soon as Irene realises her error—"She saw now that she ought to have run up the stairs at once" (*PG* 139)—she is given another chance; she sees the Queen's lamp shining straight through the walls of the tower and is guided back to the house. And the lamp gives courage and comfort as well as vision, for "[t]he name of the LORD is a strong tower: the righteous runneth into it, and is safe" (Proverbs 18:10).

After one last terrible moment of doubt when the door opens onto an empty room—"Irene had to fancy for a moment that the person she came to find was nowhere at all" (*PG* 143)—she opens the door to the Queen's bedroom and discovers her grandmother, not only at her youngest and most beautiful, but at her most forgiving and welcoming. It is the forgiveness that confirms Irene's faith in the Queen, for it proves that she is greater than Irene herself; the princess does not find it easy to forgive her own shortcomings, but, as St John's first Epistle puts it, "if our heart condemn us, God is greater than our heart, and knoweth all things" (1 John 3:20). "You were taken by surprise, my child, and are not so likely to do it again," says Queen Irene: "It is when people do wrong things wilfully that they are the more likely to do them again"—and she concludes with the simple invitation "Come" (*PG* 147).[1] This does not stop Irene realising that "I can't always do myself as I should like. And I don't always try" (158-159)—a clear echo of St Paul's lament in Romans 7:19 that "the good that I would I do not: but the evil which I would not, that I do."

Now, as always, Queen Irene's revelations are linked to her

granddaughter's capacity to see and believe. The lamp which, on the previous occasion, "made everything visible in the room, though not so clearly that the princess could tell what many of the things were" (*PG* 117), no longer obscures any details—or Irene's developing faith makes it possible to see them. For the first time she realises that what she has previously taken for a bouquet of roses is "a fire which burned in the shapes of the loveliest and reddest roses, glowing gorgeously between the heads and wings of two cherubs of shining silver" (145). The fire, with its attendant cherubs, is strongly reminiscent of the burning coals of purification guarded by seraphim in Isaiah 6:5-7,[2] and this purifying function is suggested when a rose burns away the mudstains Irene has left on her grandmother's dress; but when Irene asks for the same cleansing treatment, the Queen says that "it is too hot for you yet. It would set *your* frock in a flame" (*PG* 148).[3]

Nevertheless, the fire-roses seem as junior to Isaiah's live coals as the cherubim who guard them are to the prophet's seraphim, and this is consistent with MacDonald's scaling-down of the sense of danger for children. But the fire is important, for, as is indicated by the cherubim who guard it, it is the fire of knowledge (the cherubim, who represent knowledge, ranking second in the ninefold hierarchy of angels to the seraphim, who represent love).[4] This is confirmed by what Curdie, who has as yet no supernatural faith, sees when Irene brings him into the room to be introduced to her grandmother, for, though the vision shrinks to dimensions that can be grasped by the unbelieving mind, it cannot be untrue to itself. The Queen's voice becomes "the cooing of a lot of pigeons" (225); the moon lamp, a ray of sunlight; the bed with its beautiful hangings, a heap of musty straw; the bottomless silver bath, a tub; and the fire of roses, a withered apple—the fruit of the tree of knowledge of good and evil,[5] withered because knowledge without faith is dead. This is probably why there is no visible suggestion of the Queen: "She *might* have had some old woman there at least to pass for her precious grandmother!" Curdie says to his mother afterwards (236).

Irene's second visit to her grandmother's bedroom marks an important step forward both in her spiritual development and in her growth to psychological maturity—which must, indeed, go together if her personal potential is to be realised. As she internalises the Queen's values she becomes, not the Queen, but the unique individual she is meant to be. And Queen Irene's comments indicate that the wholeness and maturity she embodies are attainable by everyone: "Nothing pleases me better than to see *anyone* sit in my chair," she

The Downstretched Hand: Individual Development in

says. "I am only too glad to stand so long as *anyone* will sit in it" (156; italics mine). She treasures the development of mature individuality—and in this third encounter Irene begins to show some independence of her grandmother. Since, at this point, "there was no fear in her," it is possible for "a great quietness [to grow] in her heart" even when Queen Irene leaves the room (151). This experience of peace prepares the princess for her solitary journey under the mountain. And the Queen's lamp gives Irene an extraordinary power of seeing, which, though it lasts only for a moment, will contribute to her growing trust in her grandmother:

> She had been gazing at the lovely lamp for some minutes fixedly: turning her eyes, she found the wall had vanished, for she was looking out on the dark cloudy night. But though she heard the wind blowing, none of it blew upon her. In a moment more, the clouds themselves parted, or rather vanished like the wall, and she looked straight into the starry herds, flashing gloriously in the dark blue. It was but for a moment. The clouds gathered again and shut out the stars; the wall gathered again and shut out the clouds; and there stood the lady beside her with the loveliest smile on her face, and a shimmering ball in her hand, about the size of a pigeon's egg. (151)

Irene once asked her grandmother for an egg—and now she has got one! There could not be a better preparation for receiving the gifts of the thread and the ring, gifts that constitute both a reminder that her development is still guided (she can be sure that the Queen is at the other end of the thread) and a recognition of her own increasing maturity (the ring is the crown writ small). The fire-opal in Irene's ring (it would be a *fire*-opal, of course!) is only less pretty than the jewels in her grandmother's crown: "The stone in your ring is of the same sort—only not so good," the Queen explains. "It has only red [like the fire-roses], but mine have all colours" (153). The ring is the focus of attention here, and it is a very important link between the everyday world and the mystery surrounding Queen Irene; not only the enlightened king-papa, but the distinctly unenlightened Lootie can see it.[6] But the thread is even more mysterious. Originally spun from spiders' webs—"My pigeons bring it me from over the great sea. There is only one forest where the spiders live who make this particular kind—the finest and strongest of any" (116-117)—it can only be seen, and especially can only be felt, by those who are growing in supernatural faith.[7] The gifts of ring and thread symbolically and literally connect Queen Irene and her granddaughter, a bond which is reinforced both by Irene's claiming her grandmother's home as her own—"I'm so glad, grandmother, you didn't say—*go home*—for this is my home. Mayn't I call this my home?" "You may, my child. And I trust you will always think it your home," says the Queen (157)[8]—and by the princess's intuitive understanding that this is not a question of place, but of what Curdie's mother, Mrs. Peterson, later calls one's "inside house" (289).

The ring and the thread are given just when Irene is about to be called on to give unqualified obedience to her grandmother, for, however Queen Irene may have indulged her earlier lapse in running out onto the mountain instead of up the stairs, once Princess Irene has received the gifts she "must not doubt the thread" (155). At first this is not difficult for her. When one morning she awakens to "a hideous noise . . . of creatures snarling and hissing and racketing about," the resources of her unconscious are instantly available to her conscious mind: "The moment she came to herself, she *remembered something she had never thought of again*—what her grandmother told her to do when she was frightened" (194; italics mine). She accordingly takes off her ring and puts it under her pillow—and "she fancied she felt a finger and thumb take it gently from under her palm: 'It must be my grandmother!' she said to herself" (194). The thread "was leading her she knew not whither" (196-197)—right away from the tower stair, out onto the mountain and into countryside she had never seen before—"but she had never in her life been out before sunrise,[9] and everything was so fresh and cool and lively and full of something coming, that she felt too happy to be afraid of anything" (197). Eventually, however, the thread leads her to a rock on which the first rays of the sun alight—but a stream issues from the rock and the thread goes into the hole from which it comes. At this prospect "[a] shudder ran through her from head to foot," but "[s]he did not hesitate" and went in (198)

From this point onwards Irene's mission becomes frightening—all the more so because she does not know what her journey under the mountain is for.[10] She perseveres, not out of blind obedience, or that kind of faith which Mark Twain's Tom Sawyer defines as "believing what you know ain't so," but because her faith is firmly grounded on her personal knowledge of the Queen:

> As she went farther and farther into the darkness of the great hollow mountain, she kept thinking more and more about her grandmother, and all that she had said to her, and how kind

> she had been, and how beautiful she was, and all about her lovely room, and the fire of roses, and the great lamp that sent its light through stone walls. And she became more and more sure that the thread could not have gone there of itself, and that her grand-mother must have sent it. (199-200)

The rhythm of the first sentence expresses anxiety, but it is an anxiety that is resisted. When she does give up it is impossible to go back; but this indicates, not the overwhelming authority of the Queen, but the fact that there is no escape from death except through the tomb itself—a route Irene accordingly takes.

The cave in which Curdie is imprisoned, sealed as it is with a huge rock, suggests the tomb of Jesus. But Curdie is closer to Lazarus than to Christ,[11] for, after rolling away the great stone with Irene's help, he is symbolically resurrected into the life he has just left—a life of natural goodness without supernatural faith. Far from not doubting the thread, the obligation laid upon the princess, he is unable either to feel it or, later, to see it shining in the sun, and he follows Irene *faute de mieux*.

For Irene it is different, though she 'dies' in a symbolic crucifixion at least as terrifying as the symbolic death and burial of her friend. When the thread disappears into a pile of stones she experiences total abandonment: "It had gone where she could no longer follow it—had brought her into a horrible cavern, and there left her! She was forsaken indeed!" (201) And "My God, my God, why hast thou forsaken me?" says Jesus.[12] Some elements of the crucifixion are certainly suggested as Irene works away, "with aching back, and bleeding fingers and hands" (*PG* 205), to liberate Curdie (in the Arthur Hughes illustration, the stone Irene is holding is actually a skull [204]).

"I have counted nine bruises on you," says her grandmother later (229),[13] and, as Isaiah foretold of the suffering servant, "he was bruised for our iniquities: the chastisement of our peace was upon him" (Is. 53:5). But after her symbolic resurrection into eternity through immersion in the Queen's bottomless silver bath, with its baptismal overtones of death and rebirth,[14] Irene "felt as if she had been made over again. Every bruise and all weariness were gone, and her hands were soft and whole as ever" (*PG* 231-232). This, with its echo of the risen Jesus in Revelation—"I make all things new" (Rev. 21:5)—is resurrection; and the spotless white nightgown (Irene's own) which the Queen afterwards draws out of the fire for Irene to wear (*PG* 231) indicates that the fire is no longer "too hot for you" (148).

Irene fulfils that part of the Messianic task which has been appointed for her—"to bring out the prisoners from the prison, and them that sit in darkness out of the prison house." But then she tries to go beyond her immediate mandate and "open the blind eyes" (Isaiah 42:7) by taking Curdie up to her grandmother's room—and here she fails. When Irene realises that her friend cannot see the Queen—and when he leaves in dudgeon, thinking she has made fun of him—her first heartbroken cry is the eternal question: "What does it all mean?"(*PG* 227) But since the answer is greater than the question, and must be lived by the questioner, the Queen replies to it in the narrowest sense: "It means, my love, that I did not mean to show myself." She makes it clear that there can be no short cut to faith—"Curdie is not yet able to believe some things"—and in any case, "[s]eeing is not believing—it is only seeing" (227). But there is still comfort—"I will take care of what Curdie thinks of you in the end" (226)—and Irene's great advance towards maturity culminates in reassurances by the Queen: "Do not be afraid, my child" (230); "Don't trouble yourself about it;" "I took care of all that." Most soothing of all is the affirmation of her complete trustworthiness—"I told you to let [Curdie] go, *and therefore I was bound to look after him*" (232; italics mine).

In the course of the book Queen Irene transmits to her granddaughter the two fundamental principles of Christianity; love of God (through the Queen's divine associations) and love for other people. "I must be fair—for if I'm not fair to other people, I'm not worth being understood myself," cries Irene (228). Just as love may entail accepting the pain of not being believed or understood, so faith may entail accepting the pain of not understanding. The price paid for refusal to accept this suffering is the lack of growth exemplified in Lootie, whose drive to find a quick, facile explanation for the incomprehensible prevents her ever discovering the truth. Her reaction to Irene's account of her first meeting with the Queen is to term it a matter of make-believe, a story (i.e. lie) or a dream (33), and even though she has presumably known the princess since babyhood she never gets beyond this level of interpretation. "How *could* you get under the clothes like that, and make us all fancy you were lost! And keep it up all day too!" she says on finding Irene in bed after rescuing Curdie (249). Lootie soon realises how much the princess has matured—i.e. that she is now beyond her control—but she rationalises this into conformity with her own limited vision: "She kept foolishly whispering to the servants . . . sometimes that the princess was not right in her mind, sometimes that she was too good to live, and other nonsense of the same sort" (254).[15]

The Downstretched Hand: Individual Development in

Although her "nonsense" does not hurt Irene it is harmful to Lootie herself. The challenge of Irene's rapid advance to maturity is too much for her, demoralised as she has already been both by the king's reproaches (in "a talk that made her cry" [108]) and by the subsequent disappearances of her charge, and she shrinks from incipient mother to redundant pedagogue. Ironically it is she, fundamentally well-intentioned and affectionate as she is, who comes closest to being kidnapped by Prince Harelip, for those without faith are helpless against the powers of evil—especially when they are confronted by the inner shadows they have always striven to ignore; in Lootie's case her fear of sexuality and her fear of death. Although her unconscious has picked up glimmerings of the Queen in the tower, this beginning of enlightenment is overwhelmed in Lootie by the predominant darkness of the unconscious, which, though it enables her dimly to sense the sexual danger to Irene from the goblins—and more strongly to sense the danger of death—can only contribute to the confusion of her conscious mind. Her objection to Princess Irene's promise to kiss Curdie springs both from mere snobbish disdain of a miner boy and from the dim perception that a kiss, even the kiss of a child, may have sensual implications; but she is unable to discriminate between acceptable and unacceptable modes of sexual expression—between union with Curdie and union, the prospect of which she unconsciously senses, with a goblin: "Formerly the goblins were her only fear: now she had to protect her charge from Curdie as well" (62). Lootie must be superseded as the guardian of the law, for the lack of discernment closely related to her lack of faith means that she can oppose nothing more to evil than her limited ideas of safety and respectability.

Faith, as Irene demonstrates throughout the book, demands the courage to wait; but this waiting does not necessarily result in an elucidation of the mystery. Indeed, though Irene grasps the psychological truths the Queen wants to inculcate—for instance, the necessity of accepting other people with all their limitations—other mysteries deepen as she matures. The strangeness of the Queen's instructing the princess, after their first meeting, to "tell [Lootie] all about it exactly" (29), is as nothing compared with the strangeness of her instructions when she gives Irene the ring. Here MacDonald confronts us with a fascinating inconsistency—and not the least interesting aspect of it is that, while Irene demands an explanation of her grandmother's behaviour in the former instance, she seems unaware of the inconsistency now.

The episode starts naturally enough, with one of the anxious questions Irene frequently asks when she foresees the difficulty of integrating the mystical into the everyday world: "What am I to say when Lootie asks me where I got it?" And when the Queen replies with a smile, "*You* will ask *her* where you got it," one feels that she is at least not speaking out of character—an impression reinforced when, in answer to Irene's remark that "I can't pretend not to know," she gives one of her customary reassurances: "Of course not. But don't trouble yourself about it. You will see when the time comes" (153). Yet in the very next chapter Irene appears both to know what she does not know and not to know what she does know. "Who gave me the ring, Lootie?" she says. *"I know I've had it a long time*, but where did I get it? *I don't remember."* Lest we be tempted to treat this as a temporary lapse of memory or truthfulness, she asks her king-papa the same question in the very next chapter: "Will you tell me where I got this pretty ring? *I can't remember"* (164, 166; italics mine).

Has Irene simply changed her mind and decided to pretend after all? The question is a crucial one, and one that MacDonald forces us to confront through his emphasis on truth throughout the book. Curdie is deemed ungenerous and wrong to doubt the princess's word because he cannot see the grandmother to whom she introduces him, and this perplexity culminates in a chapter almost entirely devoted to a discussion of Irene's truthfulness: "If she were to lie I should begin to doubt my own word," says Curdie's mother (240). And in the next chapter Irene takes so serious a view of Lootie's charge that she is telling "stories" (249) as to be ready to send for her father: "If she thinks I tell lies," says the princess, rejecting Lootie's euphemism, "she had better either say so to my papa, or go away" (251).

Has the Queen, then, made Irene forget how she got the ring? If so, it runs counter to everything we have learned about Queen Irene so far, for she has always wanted to illuminate, not to obscure—and according to Jung's "The Symbolism of the Mandala," the fact that the jewel is given at a specific time and in a specific place indicates a rapid approach to reality, not a retreat from it.[16] That Queen Irene has great power over the mind is recognised by the princess when she says, on learning that her faith is to be tested, not "I hope I shan't forget," but "Oh! please, don't let me forget!" And the Queen's response is immediate: "You shall not forget" (122). But it is difficult to imagine her brainwashing her granddaughter simply to spare her an argument with Lootie—especially since she precipitated her into just such an argument after their first meeting.

This raises a third possibility; that Irene has always worn the ring,

The Downstretched Hand: Individual Development in

but has become aware of it in a different way since her encounter with her grandmother. But the giving of the ring is described in meticulous detail. First the Queen gives her a ball of thread, and Irene exclaims:

> "How pretty it is! What am I to do with it, please?"
>
> "That I will now explain to you," answered the lady, turning from her, and going to her cabinet.
>
> She came back with a small ring in her hand. Then she took the ball from Irene's, and did something with the two—Irene could not tell what.
>
> "Give me your hand," she said.
>
> Irene held up her right hand.
>
> "Yes, that is the hand I want," said the lady, and put the ring on the forefinger of it.
>
> "What a beautiful ring!" said Irene. "What is the stone called?"
>
> "It is a fire-opal."
>
> "Please, am I to keep it?"
>
> "Always."   (152-153)

Unless "always," in George MacDonald's lexicon, works backwards as well as forwards, we are being forced to face a huge inconsistency.[17] And suspension of disbelief, at least for children and the childlike, must be consistent; isolated episodes that cannot be taken at face value would not satisfy them. To doubt the veracity of MacDonald's account here would be to cast doubt on the whole book—and as MacDonald's primary aim is to promote the development of faith it would be singularly illogical to undermine the credibility of a narrator whose reliability he has taken pains to establish from the beginning. Besides, such a reading of the episode is untenable in face of the visiting king's reaction to the ring. Not only does he recognise it as having belonged to Irene's queen-mamma, who has "gone where all those rings are made" (166), but he realises that it has only just come into his daughter's possession—just when goblin-creatures have been seen in the garden! "I presume [he] would have taken Irene with him that very day, but for what the presence of the ring on her finger assured him of," says the narrator. And "[a]bout an hour before he left, Irene saw him go up the old stair" (166). If further confirmation be needed, it must be pointed out that MacDonald, who said of *The Princess and the Goblin* two months before its serial completion, "*I know it is as good work of the kind as I can do, and I think will be the most complete thing I have done*,"[18] revised the work when it was transformed from serial into book and would hardly have been oblivious to so glaring an inconsistency.

What, then, is the answer? There is no answer, but there is a solution: "Don't trouble yourself about it," says the Queen (*PG* 153). This does not mean that the question is unimportant; MacDonald takes great pains to underline the strangeness of the episode. But what really matters is that Irene, once a spectator of the mystery, has become part of it; and, through her, what was confined to the tower and the night has invaded the everyday world.

The mystery is something that goes far deeper than the integration of conscious and unconscious, however important this is to the mature personality. MacDonald discriminates very carefully between spiritual and imaginary experience, and between the various levels of the latter. Play belongs to immaturity, and on the day on which her faith is to be tested Irene plays with her dolls' house for the last time (136); after that, the "inside house" (289) is more absorbing. Dreams, unless sent to the dreamer, are essentially distinct from and inferior to visions because they come from within; the Queen warns Irene that she will fail the test if she thinks her grandmother is only a dream (122), and Curdie's dream of rising to fight the goblins when they eventually invade the house is unavailing against the reality that he is still in bed (268). As MacDonald puts it in *Lilith*, "When a man dreams his own dream, he is the sport of his dream;" but dream and vision meet when Queen Irene comes to heal Curdie's leg, for "when Another gives it him, that Other is able to fulfil it" (*Lilith*, 358). In *The Princess and the Goblin* the ultimate reality is in the domain of vision— and it consists in the mystery which surrounds the Queen.

The condition for the existence of this mystery is death. MacDonald avoids any direct mention of death in relation to the Queen, but the fact of it is inescapable. Queen Irene can lead her great-great-granddaughter to spiritual rebirth because she herself has died and now exists in eternity, something never specified but clearly to be inferred from the fact that she is a great deal more than a hundred years old (*PG* 27, 158) and that her flesh, though requiring to be fed with pigeons' eggs, transcends the limitations of mortal bodies; she has a flexible age range, tremendous powers of projection (she can direct the thread through the mountain) and simultaneous perception almost, though not quite, reaching to omniscience (she is not sure what is happening to Irene under the mountain and therefore gets anxious [222-223], but she is aware of Curdie's eating supper at home even while she sits with the princess in the tower [232]). She is also physically invulnerable; not only does she clean her dress with the burning rose which would have set Irene's frock ablaze (148)[19] but she repeatedly puts her hand into the fire—as, for example, when she retrieves the ball of thread from it (154, 229)—and, in contrast to Curdie's agonising experience in *The Princess and Curdie* (*PC* 93-94), she appears to feel no pain at all. Small wonder that, at the end of the book, Irene is sure her grandmother will be in no danger from the floods: "I believe she could walk through that water and it wouldn't wet her a bit," says the princess (*PG* 303).[20]

Death is also the condition of the darker mystery associated, albeit indirectly, with the goblin queen. Since the other goblins are toeless and shoeless it is worth considering why the queen has "A horrid set /Of sprouting toes" (191)—six per foot—and how she could have concealed this deformity before she married the goblin king and claimed the right to wear shoes as a royal prerogative; since her predecessor had worn shoes, she "would not be inferior to her" (74).[21] These details only make sense if the goblin queen is the resurrected form of the goblin king's first wife, the woman "from upstairs" (74-75) who died in giving birth to Harelip—"The king worshipped her very footmarks" (75)—and who represents a lost possibility of self that the goblin queen, destined for a second death after which there would be no resurrection (see Revelation 2:11, 20:6, 14, 15), is now obliged to repudiate. When she speaks disparagingly to her spouse of his late wife, there is an interesting ambiguity in his response. The goblin queen resents Harelip's projected marriage to a princess of the sun people:

> "I don't see why you should think it such a grand affair!" said his stepmother, tossing her head backward.
>
> "You must remember, my spouse," interposed his majesty, as if making excuse for his son, "he has got the same blood in him. His mother—"
>
> "Don't talk to me of his mother! You positively encourage his unnatural fancies. Whatever belongs to that mother, ought to be cut out of him."
>
> "You forget yourself, my dear!" said the king. (175)

Or is it "You forget *yourself*, my dear?" And the goblin queen *has* forgotten herself, as the ancestors of the goblins forgot themselves long before. Unlike Queen Irene, she is resurrected only eventually to meet, in the flood, the "second death" of Revelation (20:14).

The disappearance of a woman "from upstairs" (75) is never

mentioned in the book, presumably because, in view of the goblins' known hostility to the 'sun-people,' she has long been given up for dead—"I was afraid they were going to tear [me] to pieces," says Mrs. Peterson of her own encounter with the goblins (238-239). But it may well have contributed to the general climate of fear underlying the prohibition against the princess's ever being out after dark—though the great danger which menaces Princess Irene is of a different sort. The goblin queen is a terrible testimony that psychic and spiritual death is possible—terrible because like, on one level, the great Queen of whom she is a travesty, she represents a possible development of Irene. The sexual connotations of her surplus flesh and of her sleeping with the king under an animal skin are themselves symbolic—of a surrender to the instinctual side of the self, that is, to possession by the unconscious, which is a more far-reaching danger to Irene even than the projected marriage to Harelip (though that would be part of it). For the key question in the book is not that of the traditional fairy tale—"Will she find the right husband?"—but "What will she become?" Although she would not be nameless like her mother-in-law—a sign of lack of individuality—if Irene were to descend to the goblin kingdom, her name, and with it her character, would become a travesty of itself; for, as the goblin chancellor says, "a peace, all to the advantage of the goblin kingdom, [would] be established for a generation at least" (93).

The shadow of death hangs over the book from the very first chapter, with its tomb-like goblin caves and fear of the dark. And though death is ultimately seen in a positive light it is never shown to be anything but solemn, as we find when Irene asks her father where the ring comes from:

"It was your queen-mamma's once," he said.

"And why isn't it hers now?" asked Irene.

"She does not want it now," said the king, looking grave.

"Why doesn't she want it now?"

"Because she's gone where all those rings are made."

"And when shall I see her?" asked the princess.

"Not for some time yet," answered the king, and the tears came into his eyes. (165-166)

This is one of those points where readers may understand more than the heroine—and if they do not, the narrator, like the Queen, is not going to labour the point.

Even Queen Irene, who has overcome death, smiles "a little

The Downstretched Hand: Individual Development in

sadly" (148) when she tells Irene she is not yet ready to be cleaned by a rose from the fire, and Irene's death experience causes her grandmother painful anxiety (222-223). But if there were no death there would be no transcendence of the natural world in a fairy tale which is concerned more with spiritual than with psychological values, as is clear even apart from the mysterious Queen in the tower. Peter Peterson, Curdie's father, not only builds his hut on the rock which his name suggests (the house in which Irene lives is also built on a rock, but there is a large vein of sand underneath it)[22] but goes to see the vicar when Curdie makes his first incursion into goblin territory. And Mrs. Peterson, who has actually seen "the light [that] shineth in darkness" (John 1:5)—one of the Queen's pigeons once flew down a ray from "a large globe of silvery light" (*PG* 239) to rescue her from a group of goblins and their creatures—"made and kept a little heaven in that poor cottage on the high hill-side" (122). But, though the heavenly spirits know her—"in the sight of the angels, her hands were . . . beautiful" (123)—she is limited by the fact that she has not died. The myth of the labyrinth obtains, for her as for the Queen, but, although she can give Curdie a ball of string to help him find his way inside the mountain, and disentangle it while he sleeps—"I can't think how you do it, mother," says Curdie (126)—unlike the Queen, she can neither hold it nor direct it when he is under the mountain. In the same way, Mrs. Peterson can imbue Curdie with a conviction of her goodness and wisdom, and of the value of right conduct, without inspiring in him any transcendent faith. Only the Queen, directly or indirectly, can do this, for she has made the definitive passage to eternity.

If the condition of the mystery surrounding Queen Irene is death, its essence is love. Although Irene is only one of the Queen's "children" (158), Queen Irene loves her and works for her as if she were the only person in existence.[23] And Irene responds to the Queen's love by making what Erich Fromm describes as the necessary transition from subjectivity to objectivity, from narcissistic view of the world with herself as centre to realistic acceptance of herself and those around her:[24] "We love [God], because he first loved us," says St. John in his first Epistle (1 John 4:19), and this love extends to others too. Although she is disappointed that Curdie can neither see the Queen nor be convinced by her own faith, Irene refrains from reproaches and questions him at length to try and understand his point of view (*PG* 224-225). The same maturity informs her treatment of the angry Lootie, who accuses her, after her day in the goblin kingdom, of hiding under the bedclothes, for Irene takes herself out of Lootie's charge without inflicting the further pain of removing herself from her care.

The main sphere of action in *The Princess and the Goblin* is the inner activity of growing in faith and love. Other activity generally turns out to be futile, at least as far as its conscious objective is concerned; Curdie the miner, who night after night risks life and limb to spy on the goblins, has to be rescued by the princess and ultimately is not the one who saves her—"I wasn't good enough to be allowed to help you: I didn't believe you. Your grandmother took care of you without me," he says ruefully (284).[25] And the fact that Queen Irene not only organises the rescue of Curdie but ultimately saves her granddaughter without so much as mentioning the goblins from start to finish shows how little power evil has in the face of love and faith (in the absence of which the goblins, for their part, are unaware of Queen Irene, though they sense her power and therefore find her white pigeon terrifying [239]). The princess does, of course, see some of the goblins and their creatures, but she does not know of Harelip's designs on her until the threat is over. The plot, so far as she is concerned, is in striking conformity with St. Paul's famous injunction to think of "whatsoever things are true, whatsoever things are honest, whatsoever things are just, whatsoever things are pure, whatsoever things are lovely, whatsoever things are of good report" (Phil. 4:8), while his next instruction virtually sums up her relationship with her grandmother: "Those things, which ye have both learned, and received, and heard, and seen in me, do: and the God of peace shall be with you" (Phil. 4:9).

This is not to suggest that Irene's growth in faith has been anything but difficult. And what has primacy in *The Princess and the Goblin* is not "faith" the noun, with its suggestion of something meted out by God to passive recipients, but the verb "to believe," with its connotations of struggle and personal investment. "This is the work of God, that ye believe on him whom he hath sent," says Jesus (John 6:29), and in this as in other respects the influence of St. John's Gospel is pervasive, for, while the noun "faith" is never mentioned in this Gospel,[26] the verb "believe" occurs in all its varieties.[27] When Curdie returns home after not only being rescued from the goblins but making a bewildering visit to the Queen's tower bedroom with Irene, he goes through a debriefing which shows just what hard work believing can be: "I can't believe it," he says of Irene's description of Queen and chamber (*PG* 235), but with his mother's assistance he reaches the point when he can at least suspend disbelief—the precondition for future enlightenment.

The Downstretched Hand: Individual Development in

The special role of Curdie is that one sees in him the growth of a faith that does not originate, like Irene's, as "a gift born with you" (*PG* 150)—and even in Irene's case the Queen comments: "I doubt if you would have believed it all yourself if you hadn't seen some of it" (223). Curdie sounds just like Lootie when he says "[t]hat's all nonsense . . . I don't know what you mean" (214); the difference is that he is open to the conviction of spiritual truth, not only because, unlike Lootie, he can discern personal sincerity—"You would have thought she really meant and believed that she saw every one of the things she talked about," he tells his parents (236)—but because he has the courage to live with an unresolved mystery of a kind particularly trying to his pragmatic nature.

Curdie's courage has, indeed, never been in doubt: "He's a good boy, and a brave boy, and he has been very kind to us," Irene says to Lootie after the rescue on the mountain (60), and this judgment is echoed by her grandmother after the princess has turned the tables and rescued her friend: "He is a good boy, Curdie, and a brave boy" (223). That MacDonald attaches special importance to courage is clear from his choice of "Corage, God mend al" (a mediaevally-spelt anagram of his own name) as the family motto and of "Casa Corragio" as the name of the Italian villa of his later years. And if Curdie's plans are sometimes ineffectual, his courage never is: "If you're not afraid of them, they're afraid of you," he says of the goblins (52). But natural courage, though estimable, is not courage of the highest kind. Irene's courage is what Carl Jung calls the "treasure hard to attain" that she unearths when she descends into "the region of danger" and rescues Curdie.[28] The Queen nevertheless sees to it that Curdie's apparently wasted efforts to protect the princess bear fruit: "She sent you to help my people, anyhow," says Irene (*PG* 284),[29] and he proves also to be the instrument of the goblins' destruction.

Curdie's goodness is just as important as his courage, or more so; both queen and princess specify his goodness first. Courage without goodness may make such characters as Satan in Milton's *Paradise Lost* seem fascinating, but MacDonald, who wrote that "all wickedness tends to destroy individuality,"[30] has no intention of romanticising evil by a conjunction of qualities seldom or never found in real life. This— and his desire not to frighten child readers—is why the monarch of the "dismal regions" in *The Princess and the Goblin* (185), a travesty of Milton's Satan, is made to appear not merely grotesque but ridiculous. In Curdie's case MacDonald is concerned to portray a junior version of the just or righteous man, that is, the good man who has the courage to put his goodness into effect—and Curdie does his best to oppose the forces of evil. As the author of Hebrews says, however, "the just shall live by faith" (Heb. 10:38), and neither Curdie's courage nor his goodness can be fully effectual without it. Ronald MacDonald speaks of "brave Curdie, who can delve and fight, but must be taught to climb."[31] But illumination eventually begins to come from his own subconscious, which, under the pressure of traumatic experiences and serious questioning, is now beginning to move into consciousness:

> " . . you needn't be afraid, you know [he says to Irene]. Your grandmother takes care of you."
>
> "Ah! you do believe in my grandmother then? I'm so glad! She made me think you would some day."
>
> All at once Curdie remembered his dream, and was silent, thinking. (PG 283)

And Curdie, who has always had an instinctive sympathy for unbelief—"I'm sure nobody who met us would believe a word we said to them," he says after being rescued from the goblins (225)—now knows he will have to repent: "I wasn't good enough to be allowed to help you: I didn't believe you," he tells Irene (284).

The symbolic union of their qualities is anticipated by their changing places, which shows that each to some degree now possesses the characteristics of the other (Curdie is developing faith and Irene has developed great courage). So, just before the denouement, Curdie sleeps in one of the empty rooms in the great house and Irene is guided by the Queen's thread to his parents' cottage—"your mother has been so kind to me—just like my own grandmother!" (282) she tells him—and sleeps in his bed, from which "she caught sight of her grandmother's lamp shining far away beneath" (290). But it is in the kiss that their symbolic union is realised—"righteousness and peace have kissed each other" (Psalm 85:10)—and the kiss contains the promise of a deeper union in what MacDonald was planning as the sequel, for the last sentence of the book reads: "The rest of the history of *The Princess and Curdie* must be kept for another volume" (*PG* 308).

Union, however, does not mean parity. Curdie needs Irene more than she needs him, for she is the one who raises in his mind the painful questions that prepare him for the dawn of faith. Though considerable attention is paid to his adventures, the main focus of the book is on Irene's spiritual development and the psychological maturity that accompanies it—the rebirth which is so important in MacDonald's works.[31] In this respect one of the most encouraging things about Queen Irene is that, even though she has passed the boundary of physical death, she is still growing (something that the princess absorbs unconsciously). Her supernatural vision has not yet made her omniscient or even delivered her wholly from fear, as is clear especially from her anxiety on Irene's behalf when the princess goes under the mountain: "I've been waiting for you, and indeed getting a little anxious about you, and *beginning to think whether I had better not go and fetch you myself*," she cries on her granddaughter's return (222-223; italics mine)—so Irene and the reader know that her safety has always been assured. Irene finds it hard to accept that the Queen's certainty is ever challenged—"I don't think you are ever afraid of anything"—but the Queen's occasional opacity of vision centres on Irene herself:

> "I confess I have sometimes been afraid about my children—sometimes about you, Irene."
>
> "Oh, I'm so sorry, grandmother!—To-night, I suppose, you mean."
>
> "Yes—a little to-night; but a good deal when you had all but made up your mind that I was a dream, and no real great-great-grandmother."

But Queen Irene has also said, "[p]erhaps by the time I am two thousand years of age [i.e. more Christlike], I shall . . . never be afraid of anything" (158). In the course of her relationship with her granddaughter she moves symbolically from death to resurrection, from old age and black clothes to youth and white, until after the 'death' of Irene they are both clad in white garments (223, 231); both, in a sense, reborn.

At one time or other spiritual rebirth must make the transition into eternity, the heaven of which even the "haven" (144) of Queen Irene's bedchamber is only a shadowy image. *The Princess and the Goblin* bears out Jesus's own definition of eternal life: "[T]his is life eternal, that they might know thee the only true God, and Jesus Christ, whom thou hast sent" (John 17:3). What happens in *The Princess and the Goblin* is that MacDonald takes the description of the Messiah from the beginning of St. John's Gospel and infuses into it the parallel description from the first chapter of St. John's first Epistle. The importance of the opening verses of St. John's Gospel to the symbolism of the book is clear:

> In the beginning was the Word, and the Word was with God, and the Word was God.

> The same was in the beginning with God.
> In him was life; and the life was the light of men.
> And the light shineth in darkness; and the darkness comprehended it not.
> That was the true Light, which lighteth every man that cometh into the world.
> He was in the world, and the world was made by him, and the world knew him not.
> He came unto his own, and his own received him not.
> But as many as received him, to them gave he power to become the sons of God, even to them that believe on his name:
> Which were born, not of blood, nor of the will of the flesh, nor of the will of man, but of God.
> And the Word was made flesh, and dwelt among us, (and we beheld his glory, the glory as of the only begotten of the Father,) full of grace and truth.
> (John 1:1-2, 4-5, 9-14)

It would be difficult to surpass the solemn beauty of these words, in which the Messiah is transformed from concept into person. But even verse fourteen, which deals with personal experience, is so suffused with awe that the intimacy of St. John's relationship with Jesus is not conveyed as it is in the excited and emphatic account at the beginning of the Epistle:

> That which was from the beginning, which we have heard, which we have seen with our eyes, which we have looked upon, and our hands have handled, of the Word of life;
>
> (For the life was manifested, and we have seen it, and bear witness, and shew unto you that eternal life, which was with the Father, and was manifested unto us;)
>
> That which we have seen and heard declare we unto you, that ye also may have fellowship with us: and truly our fellowship is with the Father, and with his Son Jesus Christ.
>
> This then is the message which we have heard of him, and declare unto you, that God is light, and in him is no darkness at all. (1 John 1:1-3, 5)

In this passage we find all the emotional intensity of Irene's vividly experienced spiritual transformation. And those around the princess are influenced too, in differing degrees—whether by the change in her behaviour in the course of the book, or by being saved from the goblins and then from the flood—and they in their turn will influence the miners and their families who shelter them. "The people that walked

The Downstretched Hand

in darkness have seen a great light" (Isaiah 9:2), and when the servants and Curdie and his parents walk up the mountain at the end of the book, even Lootie, who has been obstinate in her unbelief, can see "a light, of which all but [she] understood the origin," shining on their path—though "when they looked round they could see nothing of the silvery globe" (*PG* 307). Irene, her father and their retinue ride away "into the starry night" (306), but those who remain behind—and not only Curdie, who has grown so much—are in the situation outlined by Isaiah: "[T]hey that dwell in the land of the shadow of death, upon them hath the light shined" (Is. 9:2).

G.K. Chesterton testifies that *The Princess and the Goblin* "has made a difference to my whole existence."[32] And so profound an effect is understandable since, in the course of the book, God's intention "that ye may know and believe me, and understand that I am he" (Isaiah 43:10) is responded to by his child's desire: "That I may know him, and the power of his resurrection, and the fellowship of his sufferings, being made conformable unto his death" (Philippians 3:10). It matters little that Queen Irene cannot be precisely identified with Jesus, since, as she has died, St. John's words about our transformation on the second coming of Christ are already coming true for her: "[W]hen he shall appear, we shall be like him; for we shall see him as he is" (1 John 3:2). And the same change has begun to take place in Princess Irene, who, although completely credible as an individual character, also stands for "every one that is called by my name" (Is. 43:7). She becomes not simply an older Irene, a more powerful Irene or an Irene who has changed direction, but a new creation—"she felt as if she had been made over again" (*PG* 231-232); someone who, having lost herself, has found her true self; a person who is continually "born, not of blood, nor of the will of the flesh, nor of the will of man, but of God" (John 1:13).

Endnotes to Chapter 7 on page 280

"And now, king-papa, " the princess went on, "I must tell you another thing. One night long ago Curdie drove the goblins away and brought Lootie and me safe from the mountain. And I promised him a kiss when we got home, but Lootie wouldn't let me give it him. I don't want you to scold Lootie, but I want you to tell her that a princess *must* do as she promises."

"Indeed she must, my child – except it be wrong," said the king. "There, give Curdie a kiss."

And as he spoke he held her towards him.

The princess reached down, threw her arms round Curdie's neck and kissed him on the mouth saying, –

"There, Curdie! There's the kiss I promised you!"

>Chapter 30, "The King and the Kiss"
>illustration by Arthur Hughes

PART III

THE PRINCESS AND CURDIE

by
GEORGE MACDONALD
with illustrations by
DOROTHY P. LATHROP

NEW YORK
THE MACMILLAN COMPANY
1927

'Give Curdie a paw, Lina,' said the princess.

The creature rose, and, lifting a long foreleg, held up a great doglike paw to Curdie. He took it gently. But what a shudder, as of terrified delight, ran through him, when, instead of the paw of a dog, such as it seemed to his eyes, he clasped in his great mining fist the soft, neat little hand of a child! He took it in both of his, and held it as if he could not let it go. The green eyes stared at him with their yellow light, and the mouth was turned up toward him with its constant half grin; but here was the child's hand! If he could but pull the child out of the beast! His eyes sought the princess. She was watching him with evident satisfaction.

'Ma'am, here is a child's hand!' said Curdie.

Chapter 8, "Curdie's Mission"
illustration by Dorothy P. Lathrop

CHAPTER 8

Home and Away
The Mountain and the Miner

"In the gulf of our unknown being God works behind our consciousness" ("Man's Difficulty Concerning Prayer," in *Unspoken Sermons*, Second Series, 255)

At the beginning of *The Princess and Curdie* George MacDonald says he will recount as much as is necessary of the events that transpired in *The Princess and the Goblin* "to show the tops of the roots of my tree" (15)—and it is well that he sets himself to establish an organic connection, for the reader who comes to *The Princess and Curdie* anticipating the promised sequel may be disconcerted to find the second book totally different in tone and mood from the first. This, although the serialised version of *The Princess and the Goblin* in *Good Words for the Young* ends with a plea by the child readers that "Mr. Editor" (George MacDonald) will tell them more about the Princess and Curdie, and he already has the plot in mind. He replies:

> Some day, perhaps, I may tell you the further history of both of them; how Curdie came to visit Irene's grandmother, and what she did for him; and how the princess and he met again after they were older—and how—But there! I don't mean to go any further at present.[1]

"To turn from *Goblin* to *Curdie* . . . is to move from the simple to the complex, from the safety of spiritual victory to the urgency of unending battle for spiritual survival. *Curdie* is a darker, more foreboding work," says John Pennington.[2] The difference between the two *Princess* books is greater than can be accounted for by the fact that, although in fictional time only one year has elapsed, *The Princess and Curdie* was not serialised until 1877[3] or published in book form until 1882. In the interval MacDonald's focus has shifted away from Irene and towards the old princess, who is now the "Princess" of the title; Curdie's eventual recognition of the old princess as Queen Irene is just as much of a consummation in the book as is his marriage to Princess Irene—or rather more so, since Irene is not present at the beginning.

There is a switch from the emphasis on obedience in *The Princess and the Goblin* to an emphasis on initiative in *The Princess and Curdie*. True, Curdie takes the initiative frequently in the earlier book, but

The Downstretched Hand: Individual Development in

it lands him in a goblin hole awaiting death; he is only rescued by Princess Irene's obedience to the Queen's guiding thread. What ultimately validates Curdie's capacity for taking initiatives is his growing faith—just as faith validates Irene's obedience. The closing chapters of *The Princess and the Goblin* see the dawn of faith in Curdie, but by the beginning of *The Princess and Curdie* it has receded; as Stephen Prickett says, "[h]e has eventually to find his own way to the grandmother, and even the Princess cannot help him here."[4]

The ambiance of *The Princess and Curdie* is bleaker than that of *The Princess and the Goblin*. But it nevertheless has a claim to being a children's book, for in it the son is sought by the father—the ultimate reassurance, and the reverse of what a child reader would find a threatening situation in the earlier, adult novel *Robert Falconer*, where the whole plot turns on the search for a weak father by a strong son. *The Princess and Curdie* has a framework of fatherhood, as opposed to that of (grand)motherhood in *The Princess and the Goblin*; Peter appears close to the beginning and the end in supportive roles, and this helps reduce the element of fear for the child reader. But sin and atonement are the themes of *The Princess and Curdie*, and the evil once distanced onto and made faintly ridiculous in the goblins now surfaces among men, as Curdie realises when he travels through hostile villages on his way to Gwyntystorm: "When they got so rude as nearly to make him angry, he would treat them as he used to treat the goblins, and sing his own songs to keep out their foolish noises" (115). "Mr Editor's" remark, in 1871, that *"If you once get rid of the goblins there is no fear of the princess or of Curdie" (GWY* 420; MacDonald's italics) is symbolically apt in relation to *The Princess and the Goblin*, but would oversimplify the darkening situation in *The Princess and Curdie*.

Yet the title, the locale and the *dramatis personae* of *The Princess and Curdie* make it clear that MacDonald intends a connection with *The Princess and the Goblin*, though the much reduced role of Princess Irene is one of the factors which make it not quite the sequel that a reader might expect. She does not need her thread any more, and it is never mentioned—but her ring, a major symbol of connection with Queen Irene (and her own mother) has disappeared too.[5] Yet the effects of Irene's psychological and spiritual growth in the earlier book on those around her—not only on Curdie but on Lootie, the servants and the guards—are of key importance in preparing the ground for the subsequent exploration of spiritual issues in the wider community. There is a sea-change in Irene after she (apparently) fails the test she has been set in *The Princess and the Goblin* and runs out onto the mountain instead of going up the tower, and it forces everyone to think and act differently. When she re-enters the building after being guided back by her grandmother's light, "the whole household" is "hither and thither over the house, hunting for her. A few seconds after she reached the stair of the tower, *they had even begun to search the neglected rooms*" (*PG* 142; italics mine). Afterwards Lootie tells her: "We've all been crying our eyes out, and searching the house from top to bottom for you." "Not quite from the top," thinks Irene, and the narrator adds "not quite to the bottom" (160). It is symbolically fitting that they never quite get there, as they are blind to both the higher and the lower regions of the unconscious; but there is a progression. Later, after Irene rescues Curdie from the goblins, "the people were [again] here and there and everywhere searching for the princess" (221). And, though they never see the Queen, they do find the princess in a very important sense when she takes herself out of Lootie's charge and says she will send for her father: "Everyone stared at these words. Up to this moment, they had all regarded her as little more than a baby" (250). But in *The Princess and Curdie* it is Curdie who takes over the principal responsibilities, so as far as Irene is concerned it may simply be a case of "job done."

Curdie is no longer a child; he is described as having been, at the end of *The Princess and the Goblin*, "approaching thirteen years of age," which is traditionally the threshold of manhood; and "[a]bout a year before this story began, a series of very remarkable events had just ended" (*PC* 15)—that is, he must be getting on for fourteen. And while Diamond, in *At the Back of the North Wind*, can talk about dying (*ABNW* 134)—a significant advance towards maturity—Curdie is the only protagonist in the three major fantasies who kills. In *The Princess and Curdie* sin surfaces first of all in Curdie himself; soon after he shoots the Queen's pigeon (how fitting that birds later attack him!) "[a]n evil something began to move in his heart" (*PC* 27-28). The symbolic importance of shooting the bird is huge, for the cruelty of the act separates Curdie from nature. From "[becoming] so one with the bird that he seemed to feel both its bill and its feathers ... and his heart swelled with the pleasure of its involuntary sympathy" (23-24), he becomes, as he realises, one who " had done the thing that was contrary to gladness: he was a destroyer!" (26)[6]

The far-reaching implications of Curdie's act are soon brought home to him: "Was the whole world going to make a work about a pigeon—a white pigeon?" Yes, it was! The world, or rather his perception of it, was changing in response to the change in him:

The Downstretched Hand: Individual Development in

> The sun went down. Great clouds gathered over the west, and shortened the twilight. The wind gave a howl, and then lay down again. The clouds gathered thicker. Then came a rumbling. He thought it was thunder. It was a rock that fell inside the mountain. A goat ran past him down the hill, followed by a dog sent to fetch him home. He thought they were goblin creatures, and trembled. He used to despise them. (*PC* 27)

As is well known, the incident derives originally from the shooting of the albatross in Coleridge's poem "The Rime of the Ancient Mariner" (*Lyrical Ballads*, 1798). William Raeper points out that MacDonald lectured on the "Ancient Mariner" many times and even describes him as "obsessed with the poem" which often features in his work (*George MacDonald*, 112). In his earliest novel, *David Elginbrod* (1863), David gives a convincing explication of the meaning of the ballad (*DE* 22), and an incident very similar to the shooting of the albatross occurs "off-stage," and is discussed in great detail, in MacDonald's *Wilfrid Cumbermede* (179-181), a novel published in 1872 and presumably in the process of gestation when he was writing *At the Back of the North Wind* and *The Princess and the Goblin*. To paraphrase part of Jung's discussion of the relationship between alchemy and religion—alchemy is "rather like an undercurrent to the Christianity that ruled on the surface" and "is to this surface as the dream is to consciousness"[7]—*Wilfrid Cumbermede* functions in part as a kind of undercurrent to the three major children's fantasies, but one into which negative possibilities and unresolved doubts are dumped. The ice cave in *Wilfrid Cumbermede*, unlike that in *At the Back of the North Wind*, has the power to make its visitors look at each other with a sense of horror; when Charley Osborne shoots a bird it actually dies; Charley experiences guilt but no sense of forgiveness for his destructive action and is unable to transform his longing for the existence of God into faith or to overcome his insecurity in relationships. In the end he commits suicide, a subject to which a whole chapter (entitled "A Talk About Suicide") is given—and that's *before* Charley kills himself. In Coleridge's poem and in both *Wilfrid Cumbermede* and *The Princess and Curdie* the wanton killing of a bird is regarded as a crime against nature,[8] but in "The Rime of the Ancient Mariner" and *The Princess and Curdie* "the paradox is recognized that a guilty act may be the prelude to profound spiritual discovery and knowledge."[9] Curdie has to repent before he is fit to be the instrument of salvation for the king and of punishment and reformation for the kingdom; but in his case the severity of retribution which faces the Ancient Mariner is not in question, for—thanks to the contrition which leads him to seek the old princess—the pigeon does not die and Curdie grows so quickly in self-knowledge during his encounter with Irene's great-great-grandmother that she is able to exclaim "I am so glad you shot my bird!" (*PC* 41)

The survival and healing of the pigeon are instrumental in keeping *The Princess and Curdie* within the realm of the children's book, or at least of a book "for the childlike,"[10] since Curdie's guilt is rapidly expiated; had it been otherwise he might have lost the sympathy of child readers and the focus of the book might have been too exclusively on his own personal development, important though that is, and too little on what is happening in the community at large. Furthermore, the old princess downplays the bleak fact of the near-killing not only by rejoicing at Curdie's consequent enlightenment but by refusing his offer to let her burn his bow and arrows on the grounds that "plenty of bad things . . .want killing" (42). A butcher's dog does indeed meet his fate at Curdie's hands (148), as did a goblin creature in *The Princess and the Goblin* (*PG* 246), but it is noteworthy that he never kills a human being—even during the battle at the end of the book the killing (justified this time) is done by the fully-grown adults, the king and the colonel of the guard, and no killing by Curdie or his beasts—or indeed the Queen's pigeons, whose mission is to sew confusion—is actually specified (*PC* 306-310). But though still in the realm of the childlike, the ethos of this book is very different from that of *The Princess and the Goblin* (or that of *At the Back of the North Wind*). Curdie's role as leader is part and parcel of this different ethos, in which there is a great deal of emphasis on the community, or the collective, and in which justice and judgment—key factors in relationships between the individual and the community and within the community itself[11]—are stressed. Not for nothing is the old princess nicknamed "Miss Judgment" at one point (238), with an attempt at a pun on the part of the coarse speaker but not on that of the author. Revelation, not St. John's Gospel, is now the major biblical influence, and if *The Princess and Curdie* does not take the apocalyptic vision to the point later reached in *Lilith*, dubbed by Greville MacDonald the "Revelation of St. George" (*GMHW* 548), it nonetheless has a definitely apocalyptic quality.

The theme of *The Princess and Curdie*, like those of *At the Back of the North Wind* and *The Princess and the Goblin*, is pre-eminently spiritual. But the first section—up to Curdie's departure for Gwyntystorm—attaches special importance to situating humanity in the context of the natural world,[12] while the emphasis in the rest of

The Downstretched Hand: Individual Development in

the book is on situating the individual in the context of the nation. All three elements—nature, the community and the individual—are shown to be symbolically and actually connected in *The Princess and Curdie*. The divine, though of paramount importance, is less obvious, and this is the single most important reason for the comparatively bleak ambiance of the book. If we put Bruno Bettelheim's test question—"To decide whether a story is a fairy tale or something entirely different, one might ask whether it could rightly be called a love-gift to a child"[13]—*The Princess and Curdie* would probably not rate as a fairy tale.[14] And, as befits the hero myth to which the book much more closely approximates, Curdie is either thrown back on his own resources or receives only indirect help from the old princess through the servant whom she sends to accompany him; gone is the protective intimacy with a great, loving figure which distinguishes *At the Back of the North Wind* and *The Princess and the Goblin*.

The brief opening paragraph of *The Princess and Curdie* both sets the hero in the context of nature and indicates the importance (whatever his early failings may prove to be) of his firm spiritual foundation—he is the son of Peter, whose name means 'rock,' and their cottage is built on a mountain, i.e. a rock, like that of the wise man in Matthew 7:24 and Luke 6:48. Curdie and his father are miners: "Their business was to bring to light hidden things; they sought silver in the rock and found it, and carried it out" (*PC* 13). The allusion is to the description of the miner and the mountain in the Book of Job: "Surely there is a vein for the silver, and a place for gold where they fine it. . . . the thing that is hid bringeth he forth to light" (Job 28:1, 11)[15]—and to 1 Corinthians 4:5, where St. Paul (evidently thinking of the Job passage) says that the Lord "both will bring to light the hidden things of darkness, and will make manifest the counsels of the hearts."

MacDonald's representative mountain soon recedes into the background, from which it later emerges in an almost unrecognisable form until, at the end of the book, it falls down. This should not be too surprising. *The Princess and Curdie* is set in a far broader sweep of the same terrain as *The Princess and the Goblin*, the entire setting of which is one mountain. Unquestionably, however, the mountain, where silver is mined, dominates the beginning of the later book.[16] The effectiveness of MacDonald's description derives from his skill in encouraging the reader to engage imaginatively with the passage, partly through a series of paradoxes beginning with his opinion that mountains are "beautiful terrors" (*PC* 9) but mostly through the juxtaposition of the familiar with the strange. The mountain is, on the one hand, alien to human, and indeed to warm-blooded life:

> Think of the terrible precipices down which the traveller may fall and be lost, and the frightful gulfs of blue air cracked in the glaciers, and the dark profound lakes, covered like little arctic oceans with floating lumps of ice. All this outside the mountain! But the inside, who shall tell what lies there? Caverns of awfullest solitude.... perhaps a brook, with eyeless fish in it, running, running ceaseless, cold and babbling .... Then there are caverns full of water, numbing cold, fiercely hot .... (11-12)

But, on the other hand, the use of anthropomorphic imagery places the whole of human life in the context of universal nature:

> From some [caverns] the water cannot get out, and from others it runs in channels as the blood in the body: little veins bring it down from the ice above into the great caverns of the mountain's heart, whence the arteries let it out again, gushing in pipes and clefts and ducts of all shapes and kinds, through and through its bulk, until it springs new-born to the light, and rushes down the mountain side in torrents, and down the valleys in rivers—down, down, rejoicing, to the mighty lungs of the world, that is the sea ... (12)

Since it is a symbol of self as well as non-self, the mountain has something to say about the inner nature of man; and the bringing of things hidden in the mountain to light, the avowed occupation of Curdie and Peter, symbolises the bringing of the unconscious into consciousness. This can be a frightening business for both reader and characters, for the unconscious harbours not only "precious stones" (12) but "frightful gulfs" (11) and the prospect of exploring it often arouses internal resistance. But the unconscious cannot be suppressed without great psychological cost. At the beginning of the book Curdie is mining as before, but he has now "rather shrunk from thinking about" the mystery encountered in *The Princess and the Goblin* (20) and in consequence he is "gradually changing into a commonplace man" (22).[17] Suppressing or ignoring the unconscious can even lend it a threatening aspect, [18] which is why, when the other miners (who do not believe in anything they cannot see) unconsciously sense the presence of the old princess, they start talking of her as "an old hating witch" (56-57); had Curdie, after shooting the pigeon, obeyed his original impulse to "throw the bird from him and whistle" (28), his psyche would have deteriorated to the same point.

If enlightenment is not sought, some degree of possession by the

The Downstretched Hand: Individual Development in

unconscious will ensue. The result will be either the "commonplace man" into whom Curdie is turning as he becomes "more and more a miner, and less and less a man of the upper world where the wind blew" (22), or, when possession is more advanced, men degenerating into beasts. Enlightenment must be sought; but it must be undertaken with divine guidance if the traveller is not to "fall and be lost" down one of the "terrible precipices" of his inner being (11). Just as Job's miner could not find understanding (self-knowledge) or wisdom (knowledge of one's right relationship with the world) within the mountain, so no-one can, by his own efforts, find them within the self of which the mountain is, on one level, an archetypal symbol. The conclusion of Job's description makes this plain, for neither man nor any part of the universe of which he provides an overview can supply the answer:

> But where shall wisdom be found? and where is the place of understanding?
>
> Man knoweth not the price thereof; neither is it found in the land of the living.
>
> The depth saith, It is not in me: and the sea saith, It is not with me.
>
> It cannot be gotten for gold, neither shall silver be weighed for the price thereof. . . .
>
> Whence then cometh wisdom? and where is the place of understanding?
>
> Seeing it is hid from the eyes of all living, and kept close from the fowls of the air.
>
> (Job 28:12-15, 20-21).

The answer is that "God understandeth the way thereof, and he knoweth the place thereof" (28:23); and one had better have the benefit of his protection as well as his knowledge, for the search for enlightenment is perilous—which is why Job says "[d]estruction and death say, We have heard the fame thereof with our ears" (28:22).

The fifth and sixth chapters of *The Princess and Curdie*, in which Curdie and Peter meet the old princess under the mountain, are faithful not only to Job's words about the miner—"the thing that is hid bringeth he forth to light" (Job 28:11)—but to the spirit of the prophet Daniel's complementary words about God: "He revealeth the deep and secret things: he knoweth what is in the darkness, and the light dwelleth with him" (Dan. 2:22). Probably MacDonald is thinking of those very words when Curdie calls the old princess "the mother of all the light that dwells in the stones of the earth" (*PC* 75), but the expression "Mother of Light" (70) comes from "the Father of lights" in the Epistle of James (1:17).[19]

The old princess is associated with the divine in *The Princess and Curdie*, as she is in *The Princess and the Goblin*—but in an entirely different way. In *The Princess and the Goblin* she comes across as intensely, even supremely a person, and she is also, as befits the divine association, the pivot on which the whole book turns. But in *The Princess and Curdie* neither of these things is true. Her "right name" of Queen Irene is not even given her until the last chapter (*PC* 318), and, although she plays an important part at the end of the book, and a far more important part throughout than one might suspect, her presence is primarily felt in the first section—felt in a way which is almost bewildering in its variety and overwhelming in its emphasis. She is now a less personal, in fact a highly symbolic character of great scope and complexity, for not only does she have divine overtones but she is also connected with universal nature, animate and inanimate, in a much more deliberate way than was Queen Irene in *The Princess and the Goblin;* she is, in part, a type of the Great or Earth Mother. The second time Curdie sees her in the tower, she is "seated in an ancient chair, the legs of which were crusted with gems, but the upper part like a nest of daisies and moss and green grass" (92-93)—a microcosm of the inside and the outside of the mountain in its more positive aspects. But "the Earth Mother is always chtonic," Jung tells us in *The Archetypes and the Collective Unconscious,*[20] an observation which is amply borne out in *The Princess and Curdie* when the hero and his father, exploring the inside of the mountain, see "a dark, dark and yet luminous face . . . looking at them with living eyes. And Curdie felt a great awe swell up in his heart . . ." (*PC* 65).

For under-the-earth wear the Queen, now appearing about twenty-five years old, chooses a pale green gown, a crown dominated by a great emerald, and slippers which were "one mass of gleaming emeralds, of various shades of green, all mingling lovelily like the waving of grass in the wind and sun" (67)—in other words, the symbolic associations of the chair are reproduced in a different form.[21] And the emerald does more than suggest the colour of grass, though nothing could be more emblematic of universal nature. Jung, in *Mysterium Coniunctionis,* says that green is the colour attributed to the Holy Spirit as the creative principle.[22] According to ancient legend, too, emeralds had the power of repelling demons;[23] if MacDonald knew this (which is quite likely in view of his love of jewellery) the fact that a thief would think he saw the old princess as "the demon of the mine, all in green flames" (*PC* 77)[24] would be a characteristic paradox. It is no accident that the old princess gives Peter, the rock, an emerald pulled out of the floor of the cavern (that is, the deepest place) as a newsbearer about the state of his son, who is to be her messenger (and this is the nearest thing to a magical object in the book).

When the old princess leaves Peter and Curdie alone in the dark cavern—"all was the blackness of darkness up to their very hearts and everywhere around them" (71)[25]—they are in what Jung describes as the initial state, "*nigredo* or blackness ... a quality of the *prima materia*," which can, through purification, lead to "the silver or moon condition, which still has to be raised to the sun condition"[26]—a process realised in *The Princess and Curdie* partly through the fact that the silver miners eventually become gold miners. And in *The Archetypes and the Collective Unconscious* Jung says that the Earth Mother is occasionally related to the moon.[27] In the case of the old princess this is mainly through her wonderful moon lamp (a strong, though short-lived point of connection with *The Princess and the Goblin*) and "The Mistress of the Silver Moon" is the title of the third chapter. Here she at first presents so fragile an appearance that she is identified as the Great or Earth Mother only by tenderness for one of her creatures—"The old lady put out her old hands and took [the wounded pigeon], and held it to her bosom, and rocked it, murmuring over it as if it were a sick baby" (*PC* 37). This initial fragility is hard to reconcile with the figure of powerful religious symbolism who, as soon as she gets up, appears—"when or how it came about, Curdie could not tell"—

> a tall, strong woman—plainly very old, but as grand as she was old, and only *rather* severe-looking. ... Her hair was very white, but it hung about her head in great plenty, and shone like silver in the moonlight. Straight as a pillar she stood before the astonished boy, and the wounded bird had now spread out both its wings across her bosom, like some great mystical ornament of frosted silver. (45)

Her physical resemblance to the Queen in *The Princess and the Goblin* in this passage is a superficial matter of her tall stature and white hair, for Queen Irene was never severe-looking and would not have made the startling transformation MacDonald has just described. Throughout *The Princess and Curdie* her role is quite different, on the psychological level, from the role she plays in *The Princess and the Goblin*, and the reason for the change is partly to be found in Curdie. For whereas in *The Princess and the Goblin* Queen Irene represents, on one level, what Jung would call the self—the total personality, conscious and unconscious, never completely knowable by the conscious self and therefore inherently numinous[28]—the old princess in *The Princess and Curdie*, in addition to her divine associations, on one level represents Curdie's anima, which, as Jung explains, "usually contains all those common human qualities which the conscious attitude lacks."[29]

What Curdie is doing at the beginning of the book—what we eventually find the whole country has been doing—is suppressing the "mother," or the unconscious of which the mother is a symbol.[30] It is Curdie's mother who often leads the conversation in the Petersons' cottage to the old princess and this presents him with difficulties, particularly in relation to what Irene and his mother have told him about the events of the year before:

> [A]s Curdie grew older, he doubted more and more whether Irene had not been talking of some dream she had taken for reality.... At the same time there was his mother's testimony: what was he to do with that? His mother, through whom he had learned everything, could hardly be imagined by her own dutiful son to have mistaken a dream for a fact of the waking world.

And how does he come to terms with this conundrum? "[H]e rather shrunk from thinking about it, and the less he thought about it, the less he was inclined to believe it when he did think about it...." (*PC* 20).

By and large the anima in a man represents the feminine qualities,[31] together with the unconscious that the feminine symbolises in its turn. And when Curdie's individuation process is started off (or rather restarted) by becoming conscious of his own shadow through the wanton shooting of the pigeon,[32] there is a tremendous outburst of the repressed anima; not only the spiritual level of the unconscious which up to now has been represented largely by Mrs. Peterson, but the Earth Mother, who is connected both with the non-individuated, instinctual level of the unconscious and with the source of consciousness itself: "The place of magic transformation and rebirth [the great cavern in this instance], together with the underworld and its inhabitants, are presided over by the mother," says Jung.[33]

All these aspects of the anima are combined pre-eminently in the old princess, and once again there is a stunning coincidence between MacDonald's practice and Jung's theory. Jung describes the characteristics of the anima as follows:

The Downstretched Hand: Individual Development in

> The anima is bipolar and can therefore appear positive one moment and negative the next; now young, now old; now mother, now maiden; now a good fairy, now a witch . . . the anima also has "occult" connections with "mysteries," with the world of darkness in general, and for that reason she often has a religious tinge. (*Archetypes*, par. 356)

The old princess has rather more than a "religious tinge." She fills the hearts of Peter and Curdie with "reverent delight" (*PC* 72); and Curdie, in exclaiming over her apparent contradictions, affirms her role as the anima:

> "And now I see you dark, and clothed in green, and the mother of all the light that dwells in the stones of the earth! And up there they call you Old Mother Wotherwop! And the Princess Irene told me you were her great-great-grandmother! And you spin the spider-threads, and take care of a whole people of pigeons; and you are worn to a pale shadow with old age; and are as young as anybody can be, not to be too young; and as strong, I do believe, as I am." (75)

And Jung has more to say about the qualities of the anima: "Whenever she emerges with some degree of clarity, she always has a peculiar relationship to *time:* as a rule she is more or less immortal, because outside time."[34] "You may ask me as many [questions] as you please . . . . Only I may take a few thousand years to answer some of them," says the old princess: "But that's nothing. Of all things time is the cheapest" (*PC* 74)[35]—which supports Ursula le Guin's dictum that the world of legend and fantasy is "outside time,"[36] but which also means that the old princess is eternal.

If the old princess is eternal, so is Queen Irene in *The Princess and the Goblin*, who affirms her likeness to Christ by specifying that she is approaching two thousand years of age (*PG* 158). The difference is that the particular association of the old princess in *The Princess and Curdie* is not with Jesus but with the Holy Spirit. This is why her spinning wheel makes music like "an Aeolian harp blown upon by the wind that bloweth where it listeth" (*PC* 90), for Jesus describes the operations of the Spirit in precisely these terms: "The wind bloweth where it listeth, and thou hearest the sound thereof, but canst not tell whence it cometh, and whither it goeth: so is every one that is born of the spirit" (John 3:8). Even the old princess's power of knowing everything, one of the ways in which she most closely resembles the original Queen Irene, is based on her association with the wind that "bloweth where it listeth," for instead of staying in the tower, like the

Queen, the old princess is constantly on the move—in her own words, "I am always about" (*PC* 73). Even unenlightened people can feel her influence: "Did it occur to you to think how it was [the miners] fell to talking about me?" she asks Curdie and Peter. "It was because I came to them; I was beside them all the time they were talking about me" (79-80).

Least emphasised of the Holy Spirit's roles in *The Princess and Curdie* is that of comforter, though Curdie and Peter certainly see the old princess in this way when she eventually returns to the cavern. But the inspirational quality of the Spirit for personalities growing into consciousness, far more important in the context of this book, is clearly affirmed; "you must be ready to let my idea, which sets you working, set your idea right," she tells Curdie (105). Her connection with the "Spirit of truth" (John 16:13) is also clear—"'Did I not tell you the truth when I sat at my wheel?' said the old lady. . . .'I can do no more than tell you the truth now'" (*PC* 45)—though, as she later points out, the essence of the truth is very hard to seize: "It would want thousands more [shapes] to speak the truth [about me] . . . and then they could not" (76).[37]

Most striking, however, is the fact that, to all intents and purposes, the old princess has no name. Her first name—that personal identifier—is not mentioned until the final chapter, and then only once; until then she is referred to as "the grand old princess," "the great old princess," "the beautiful princess," "the great old young beautiful princess," and often simply as "the princess," "the lady," "the old lady" or (most frequently) "the old princess"[38]—it would be inconceivable to refer to her as 'the old princess Irene.' "Non habet nomen proprium," says St. Thomas Aquinas of the third person of the Trinity,[39] and when Curdie, at the end of his first meeting with the princess, turns to ask "'Please, ma'am,'—'what am I to call you?' he was going to say"—he gets his greatest shock so far; for "when he turned to speak, he saw nobody" (*PC* 46). This is in striking contrast with Irene's first meeting with her grandmother in *The Princess and the Goblin*, when one of the Queen's first questions is "Do you know my name, child?" (*PG* 24). It also contrasts with the symbolic significance of Queen Irene's name throughout the earlier book. In *The Princess and the Goblin* it would be unimaginable to have a chapter entitled "What *is* in a Name?", at least if it were to reach the point arrived at in the following discussion: "I could give you twenty names more to call me, Curdie, and not one of them would be a false one. What does it matter how many names if the person is one?" (*PC* 76) This seems light years away from the

The Downstretched Hand: Individual Development in

original Queen Irene, for whom the name is linked with the crucial issue of "who I am" (*PG* 25). On the simplest level, of course, there can be no doubt as to who the old princess in *The Princess and Curdie* is, for in the old hall of the goblins' palace Curdie recognises her as "the old princess, Irene's great-great-grandmother" (*PC* 67). But she responds to Curdie's question, "Are you the Lady of the Silver Moon?" with the somewhat enigmatic reply: "Yes, Curdie; you may call me that if you like. What it means is true" (74). Not until the last chapter does she come into her own as "Queen Irene—that was the right name of the old princess" (318). At that point she resumes the psychological properties of the self[30] and also her specific association with Jesus.

The chapter entitled "What *is* in a Name?" is the point where the great difference between the two *Princess* books can be most clearly and perhaps most disturbingly sensed. It is partly a matter of the other question discussed by Curdie and the old princess, the question of appearance, and this is what will be most obvious to child readers. In *The Princess and the Goblin* Queen Irene does not change shape at all—not always even her dress—and she undergoes only one radical transformation, from old age to youth (and back again in Curdie's dream)—a change which, however amazing, has a logic and sequence of its own. This gives an impression of stability which is reinforced by the meaning of her name, "peace." But the pace and variety of external change in the old lady in *The Princess and Curdie*—at one point Curdie cannot tell whether she is "an old woman as thin as a skeleton leaf, or a glorious lady as young as perfection" (89)—make it a challenge to growing faith to accept her assertion of her fundamentally unvarying nature.

The continual transformation of the old princess's appearance is reinforced by the alteration that takes place in the tower rooms; they begin, in *The Princess and the Goblin* fashion, as a three-room conformation round a landing at the top of a stair, but the workroom fuses with what can only be called a huge throne room on Curdie's second visit, when, after listening to the music of spinning wheel and queen and gazing at the queen "for some time" (92), he is able to see the room in a different way. And the moon lamp is at once more conspicuous and less significant than it was in *The Princess and the Goblin*, though it does guide Curdie to the tower. It has to be said, however, that in *The Princess and Curdie* a moon (a different one!) shines in through the window of the workroom even on a moonless night:

George MacDonald's Major Fantasies for Children

"Why don't you come in, Curdie?" said the voice [of the old princess]."Did you never see moonlight before?"

"Never without a moon," answered Curdie, in a trembling tone, but gathering courage.

"Certainly not," returned the voice, which was thin and quavering: "*I* never saw moonlight without a moon."

"But there's no moon outside," said Curdie.

"Ah! but you're inside now," said the voice.... (34)[41]

On Curdie's first visit to the tower it becomes apparent before he goes through the door of the workroom that things have changed. In *The Princess and the Goblin* the humming of the spinning wheel lets Irene know if her grandmother is working; in *The Princess and Curdie* the wheel doesn't just hum, it sings. So, too, for that matter, does Mrs. Peterson's: "It was [her] spinning wheel that first taught [Curdie] to make verses, and to sing, and to think whether all was right inside him; or at least it had helped him in all these things" (33). His mother, in other words—for wheel and woman are linked in both cases—is the original source of his imaginative and moral powers; in still other words, the unconscious of which the mother is the symbol is the ultimate source of consciousness, which is marked by creativity and the power to make aesthetic and moral judgements. But real enlightenment depends on the old princess, and by the same token "as the bird of paradise to other birds was the song of [the old princess's] wheel to the song of his mother's" (33). On Curdie's next visit to the tower, the wheel serves as a line of demarcation between what used to be an ordinary workroom and a place of marvels: "Come now, Curdie, to this side of my wheel, and you will find me," says the old princess, and he does find her—"fairer than when he saw her last, a little younger still, and dressed not in green and emeralds, but in pale blue, with a coronet of silver set with pearls, and slippers covered with opals, that gleamed every colour of the rainbow" (91-92).

The wheel is more than the threshold to another vision, marvellous though this is—and although it becomes a part of the vision itself as "a great wheel of fire" (88).[42] But the spiders' thread has no guiding role in this book and is not emphasised, though the wheel has spidery associations at first: "Oh, it was such a thin, delicate thing—reminding him of a spider's web in a hedge!" (35).[43] The music of its spinning is important, producing first of all a trance-like state in which Curdie is able to achieve a measure of contact with the darker aspects of his own character which results in a burst of insight. He

The Downstretched Hand: Individual Development in

expresses it in a series of verbs indicating a new awareness: "I know now, ma'am; I understand now. . . . I see now. . . . And now I see . . . . And now I think of it. . . . And now I see too. . . . And I know. . . ." (40-41), and he thanks the old princess for "spinning it into me with your wheel" (40)—though it is her gentle invitation to confess which makes "a light . . . break in upon his mind" (39). While she is talking Curdie sinks into "a sort of reverie, in which he hardly knew whether it was the old lady or his own heart that spoke" (39)—and certainly the lady's invitation at this point, like God's purpose in respect of Nebuchadnezzar in the Book of Daniel, is "that thou mightest know the thoughts of thy heart" (Dan. 2:30). [44]

This "growth of individual being," to quote *David Elginbrod* (*DE* 419), is followed during Curdie's second visit to the tower by a shift in emphasis from truths about the self to spiritual mysteries, about which the unconscious is the medium of eventual understanding: "Shall I tell you again what I told my wheel, and my wheel told you, and you have just told me *without knowing it?*" asks the old princess (*PC* 90; italics mine), and she goes on to sing, to the accompaniment of the wheel, about the central mystery of the book—the central mystery of all three books and of nearly all MacDonald's writings:

> The stars are spinning their threads,
>   And the clouds are the dust that flies,
> And the suns are weaving them up
>   For the time when the sleepers shall rise.
>
> The ocean in music rolls,
>   And gems are turning to eyes,
> And the trees are gathering souls
>   For the time when the sleepers shall rise.
>
> The weepers are learning to smile,
>   And laughter to glean the sighs;
> Burn and bury the care and guile,
>   For the day when the sleepers shall rise.
>
> Oh, the dews and the moths and the daisy-red,
>   The larks and the glimmers and flows!
> The lilies and sparrows and daily bread,
>   And the something that nobody knows! (90-91)

Queen Irene's song in *The Princess and the Goblin*—"a strange sweet song, of which [Irene] could distinguish every word; but of the sense she had only a feeling—no understanding" (*PG* 231)—has an influence (a lasting one) only on the unconscious level. But the old princess's song in *The Princess and Curdie*, to use a contemporary phrase, 'touches all the bases.' It situates the world (comprehensively though compactly described in terms of animal, vegetable, mineral and weather) in a universal context of stars and suns; it prophesies, through its descriptions of gems turning to eyes, trees gathering souls and sleepers rising, the attainment of the highest degree of integration of the unconscious with the conscious mind, i.e. full individuation; and throughout, and most important, it sings of the resurrection, a spiritual fulfilment which transcends all the rest—"the something that nobody knows."[45] But this is something Curdie cannot fully grasp until the end of the book.

Throughout *The Princess and the Goblin* Queen Irene is a source of immediate reassurance to her little granddaughter, who is, after all, a child in a sense in which Curdie, a member of the work force on equal terms with men, is not. When Irene comes to the tower room after a temporary fall from grace, it is "a lovely haven to reach from the darkness and fear through which she had come!" (*PG* 144)—and that's because of the Queen. But when Curdie, after his much more serious fall from grace at the beginning of *The Princess and Curdie*, is about to leave the tower room and turns to speak once more to the old princess, the situation is virtually reversed. In *The Princess and the Goblin* Irene has to contend with the fear of finding nobody in the room, which is bad enough in all conscience: "Every little girl knows how dreadful it is to find a room empty where she thought somebody was; but Irene had to fancy for a moment that the person she came to find was nowhere at all" (*PG* 143). But Curdie's situation is worse, for, on turning to speak, "he saw nobody" where he has just seen somebody. He does not know whether the old princess is still there or not, for "the moonlight had vanished, and the room was utterly dark." As a result, "[a] great fear, such as he had never before known, came upon him, and almost overwhelmed him" (*PC* 46).

For the key to this contrast we must look beyond the difference in age, circumstances and psychological development between the protagonists of the two books and consult again the end of Job's description of the mine under the mountain, leading as it does to the question: "Whence then cometh wisdom? and where is the place of understanding?" For in the final and culminating verse of the chapter God gives the answer to man: "The fear of the Lord, that is wisdom; and to depart from evil is understanding" (Job 28: 20, 28). Curdie has turned his back on evil, but—as "our consciousness is infinitely

The Downstretched Hand

less than we"[46]—he does not realise how much darkness is still within him. By the time he departs for Gwyntystorm, however, he has been convinced of the trustworthiness and power of the old princess—in other words, if Alexander Cruden's definition be right, he has been well and truly initiated into the fear of the Lord, which means "that reverence for God which leads to obedience because of one's realization of his power, as well as of his love to man;"[47] and Curdie's great trial of putting his hand in the fire "needs only trust and obedience" (*PC* 93). What MacDonald has to do now is to make Curdie's conviction convincing to the reader; to make each one of them feel, as Curdie does, not only that "wisdom and knowledge shall be the stability of thy times" but that "the fear of the LORD is his treasure" (Isaiah 33:6).

Endnotes to Chapter 8 on page 285

CHAPTER 9
The Shadow

"We are a shadow and a shining, we" (*The Diary of an Old Soul*, 117)
"I never seem to understand any thing till I understand its shadow" (*Donal Grant*, 38).

When *The Princess and Curdie* begins a fictional year has passed between *The Princess and the Goblin* and its 'sequel,' and MacDonald takes the chance to expedite his hero's growth to maturity, if the fact that "he grew at this time faster in body than in mind" can pass under such a denomination; MacDonald adds that this growth is attended by "the usual consequence, that he was getting rather stupid—one of the chief signs of which was that he believed less and less of things he had never seen" (*PC* 21). The enlightenment Curdie attains by the end of *The Princess and the Goblin* has faded—indeed, the narrator seems to have forgotten quite how great it was—and he has become capable of doing "the thing that was contrary to gladness" and of being "a destroyer" (26). But Curdie hasn't finished developing yet and MacDonald underlines the spiritual implications of personal change: "There is this difference between the growth of some human beings and that of others: in the one case it is a continuous dying, in the other a continuous resurrection" (22). With regard to Curdie the time has come to settle the question.

"Perhaps the fullest exploration of the moral law in fantasy," says Stephen Prickett of *The Princess and Curdie*,[1] and this exploration starts with Curdie, though it does not end with him. What he does that is psychologically decisive, quite simply because it cannot be separated from the moral law, is to make what Blake would call a transition from innocence to experience. Later Curdie realises that "I was always doing wrong, and the wrong had soaked all through me" (*PC* 40)— something never true of either Diamond or Irene—and his dialogue with the old princess turns into a confessional experience, which he in turn (true to his mission to the nation) later demands of the delinquent servants in the king's palace (256-258). "Even when God deals with a nation as a nation, it is only as by this dealing the individual is aroused to a sense of his own wrong, that he can understand how the nation has sinned, or can turn himself to work a change," says MacDonald in *The Miracles of our Lord* (304). The specific sin that brings Curdie to the tower, or place of perspective (a salient feature of hero myth), is the wanton shooting of the Queen's pigeon, and this has two features which adumbrate some of the major concerns of the book; first, it is a sin against nature, and secondly, it is an act of violence.

Though in both *The Princess and the Goblin* and *The Princess and Curdie* MacDonald applauds, on moral grounds, Curdie's original decision to stay with his parents instead of accompanying the king to court, it is clear that psychologically he was not ready to leave; his "I can't get on very well without you" (*PG* 305) is no mere form of words. By staying with his parents he may have been saved from incurring a greater degree of corruption than he actually does, or perhaps it would be truer to say that he has been saved from being weakened to the point where he would be ineffectual and unable to carry out the mission assigned him by the old princess. Curdie needs to undergo the equivalent of Frobenius's "night sea journey" through travelling to Gwyntystorm,[2] something which Diamond undergoes in *At the Back of the North Wind* but which in *The Princess and Curdie* is not an essentially passive, though profound experience but a series of demanding trials. This would not have been possible under the protection of the king—nor, indeed, would Curdie have developed a constructive and trusting relationship with Lina, the helper given him by the old princess, who is essential to his mission to the nation as a whole. His 'might-have-been' is one of the pages in the royal palace (Curdie notes how like his dress is to his own [180])[3] of whom the old princess, in the guise of a housemaid, says that she doesn't take him to be a bad fellow (252)[4]—but who, though he offers courageous support, does not possess the quality of leadership which is absolutely necessary to the accomplishment of Curdie's mission.

In part MacDonald's exploration of moral law in *The Princess and Curdie* takes the form of a commentary on Wordsworth's poem "Michael,"[5] with Curdie as a Luke who does not leave for the city until he has been adequately prepared to deal with its temptations—and, perhaps, with Peter as a Michael who follows his son to the city to help him instead of pining by an unfinished sheepfold (to be fair, one has to remember that Wordsworth's Michael is eighty-four years old). There are many suggestive resemblances between poem and book— the triangular family unit, the engagement of father and son in the same work, the lamp which, though differently sited, gives out so much light that Michael's cottage, built like the Petersons' on "rising ground" (l.132), is known as "THE EVENING STAR" (l.139),[6] and Luke's dawn departure for the city. There is even a single tree, though it is near the cottage rather than in the middle of a "desolate heath" (*PC* 115).⁷ The end of the poem, too, resembles the end of *The Princess and Curdie*, for the fate of the cottage in "Michael" has the same bleak finality as the downfall of Gwyntystorm:

> The Cottage which was named the EVENING STAR
> Is gone—the ploughshare has been through the ground
> On which it stood . . . .
> . . . . and the remains
> Of the unfinished Sheep-fold may be seen
> Beside the boisterous brook of Greenhead Ghyll.
> (ll. 476-478, 480-482)

Wordsworth's poem actually begins with an anticipation of its bleak ending: "It is in truth an utter solitude" (l.13), he says of the area, and the only monument to the sheepfold is "a straggling heap of unhewn stones" (l.17)—perhaps comparable to the "great silence" after the demise of Gwyntystorm and to the "stone-obstructed rapid of the river" (*PC* 320). And Michael's defeat is as comprehensive as the destruction of the city. Until he was forty he had had to toil to free half his "patrimonial fields" from debt (l.224), eventually reincurred from another source—and Luke's failure to retrieve the situation means that all his father's efforts have been futile and he loses both land and son; eventually "the estate/ Was sold, and went into a stranger's hand" (ll.474-75).

But MacDonald, great as is his love of Wordsworth, is saying that Michael has got his priorities wrong.⁸ What is important is taking notice of "bees and butterflies, moths and dragon-flies, the flowers and the brooks and the clouds" (*PC* 22)—that is, loving nature for its own sake—and this is a moral and spiritual matter transcending emotional attachment or aesthetic appreciation, for all these things are "the things of our father" which we must be true children of God to appreciate.⁹ Sad though Michael's situation is, there is a great deal of selfishness in his love for Luke; he prefaces his son's departure by taking him to the sheepfold and laying on him a monumental guilt trip which culminates in an unduly ambitious assertion of influence:

> . . . . should evil men
> Be thy companions, think of me, my Son,
> And of this moment; hither turn thy thoughts
> And God will strengthen thee . . . (ll.405-408)

Curdie follows almost exactly this mental procedure when he is thrown into a cellar in Gwyntystorm (*PC* 157-158), but he originates it himself and there is of course no sense of guilt involved:

The Downstretched Hand: Individual Development in

> [H]e began to think about his father and mother in their little cottage home, high in the clear air of the open mountain-side, and the thought, instead of making his dungeon gloomier by the contrast, made a light in his soul that destroyed the power of darkness and captivity. (160)

And in *The Princess and Curdie* the lady of the emeralds, associated with the Holy Spirit as she is, has already made it clear that her claims are paramount: "'Peter,' said the lady . . . 'you will have to give up Curdie for a little while'" (77).

Some elements of "Michael" are reversed in *The Princess and Curdie*. Luke's laying of the first stone of the sheepfold is virtually the opposite of the Queen's pulling the great emerald, embedded in the rock, out of the cavern floor (*PC* 75-76); and Luke's neighbours who, "as he passed their doors, /Came forth with wishes and with farewell prayers" (ll.428-429), contrast strongly with the ill-mannered strangers Curdie meets on his travels. Most important, of course, is the focus in *The Princess and Curdie* on the son and not on the father, whose role is subordinate, though still significant; only in this book does the father 'keep tabs on' and eventually seek the son, and at the instigation of the mother—a level of protectiveness which reminds one that, though Curdie reaches man's estate, this is essentially a book for children. "Michael," on the other hand, is basically a study of the father in this situation; Luke's city episode is reduced to a brevity which, while effective in its context, makes it little more than a footnote to the poem—and he has no Lina to help him. But after Curdie leaves for Gwyntystorm he is exposed, not to worldly temptations, like Luke, but to danger, physical, psychological and spiritual, all of which has to be braved in order for him to carry out his mission to king and nation—and, ironically, after succumbing to temptation at the outset and then repenting of what he has done. Furthermore, Curdie has the extra complication of uncertainty about what he is meant to do—"I go without a notion whether I am to walk this way or that, or what I am to do when I get I don't know where" (*PC* 104)[10]—and he must undertake a voyage (in more ways than one) of discovery.

He has, however, the advantage of a source of physical energy that is both positive and powerful, as befits one who not only enjoys rude health but is on the threshold of manhood; for "the horse signifies a quantum of energy that stands at man's disposal," says Carl Jung in *Symbols of Transformation* ("The Sacrifice," par. 658)—and Curdie is to some extent his own horse. His name is just different enough from the Scottish Gaelic word *cuddie* or *cuddy* for the connection not to be too obvious (or not obvious at all). This word, which means a donkey, horse or ass—presumably 'horse' is the animal intended—would sound very like "Curdie" if pronounced with a Scottish accent (Sir Walter Scott, in *Old Mortality*, does much the same thing in the case of Cuddie Headrigg the ploughman, with the confirmatory bonus that his surname means "the turning area for a plough").[11] And Curdie really needs an abundant supply of energy, for no train, no boat, no North Wind will carry him anywhere and he has vast distances to traverse. Furthermore, Curdie's inner horse not only represents his "animal vitality" ("The Sacrifice," par. 616) but the telescoping of what Jung describes as "the hero and his horse [symbolizing] the idea of man and the subordinate sphere of animal instinct"[12]—a source of psychic energy. Whereas Diamond, in *At the Back of the North Wind*, needs Horse Diamond to symbolise the instinctual drives which he must integrate into a mature personality, Curdie needs no such separation of powers in this sphere, for his inner horse is so thoroughly integrated into his personality that he later refuses the king's offer of a mount for the battle—"I must be near my beasts" (*PC* 300).

Once Curdie sets out on his journey his bow and arrows, the original weapons of offence, are not seen again; he takes with him only a stick and the trusty mattock he has used in the mines.[13] But the violence he encounters gradually gains momentum. Even before he leaves, the conversation of the other miners reveals for the most part a misdirected sense of the menace in the environment. A prey to unconscious impulses, they attribute malice to the old princess of whose presence they are dimly aware; she is "an old hating witch" (56-57) who can at best be made to seem less threatening by ridicule, and hence the nickname "old Mother Wotherwop" (56). Their fear generates superstition, and mistaking good for evil influences means that the miners are not likely to be of much use in a battle against what St. Paul would describe as "spiritual wickedness in high places" (Ephesians 6:12). But although unenlightened they are fundamentally well-meaning and harmless, and things are very different when Curdie actually leaves home.

The nearer he gets to Gwyntystorm, the more aggressively Curdie is treated by people who, like the inhabitants of the city (and of Bulika in *Lilith*), act directly counter to the spirit of the biblical injunction to welcome the stranger (Matthew 25:35 et al). Even the children are rude, and one little boy throws a stone at him—a gesture all too appropriate, for Gwyntystorm, the name of which suggests violence and cold,[14] is a symbolic representation of Jerusalem, the city that, as

The Downstretched Hand: Individual Development in

Jesus says, "killest the prophets, and stonest them that are sent unto thee" (Luke 13:34).[15] But the stone-throwing child falls, and Curdie, by returning him kindly to his mother and incurring her blessing (*PC* 115), makes the first move to restore the harmonious balance in the kingdom, where masculine strength has degenerated into aggression and feminine gentleness has been contaminated by the prevailing harshness.[16] In Gwyntystorm itself his act finds its counterpart in the little girl, Barbara, who toddles out to meet Curdie and Lina and takes them back to her grandmother's house.

Throughout Curdie's journey to the city there is a tremendous struggle between the integration of consciousness and the unconscious, both personal and collective, and the darker forces of the unconscious which resist enlightenment—the latter symbolised largely by nature in its negative aspects. Curdie's own growth into consciousness is anticipated at the point of his leaving his parents' home, for "[j]ust as he crossed the threshold the sun showed the first segment of his disc above the horizon" (*PC* 113). It is of course a chicken-and-egg situation, for if significant development had not already taken place Curdie would not have been able to leave at all. The separation is rendered easier by Curdie's having already absorbed some of the attributes of his father, as is indicated not only by his surname, Peterson, and their common occupation of mining the rock, but by the episode in which they meet the "Mother of Light" under the mountain (65-66; 70)—and in which it is crucial that they both be present (70-71).[17]

Having made rather a mess of the labyrinth experience in *The Princess and the Goblin* (the heroine has to step in and rescue him from the Minotaur—but that's all right; he's not the hero), Curdie must come well out of the desert experience in *The Princess and Curdie* if he is to accomplish the work (whatever it may be) that the old princess is sending him to do. And just as it did after he killed the pigeon, nature wears an alien and disturbing aspect. The "great desolate heath" (115) is in fact taboo, especially after dark:

> Nobody lived there, though many had tried to build in it. Some died very soon. Some rushed out of it. Those who stayed longest went raving mad, and died a terrible death. Such as walked straight on, and did not spend a night there, got through well, and were nothing the worse. But those who slept even a single night in it were sure to meet with something they could never forget, and which often left a mark everybody could read. (115-116)

This is the terrain of the unconscious, which is fraught with psychic dangers—even that of getting through well and being none the worse, which means, since contact with the unconscious has been avoided (they "did not spend a night there") that the character will continue to be superficial. There is a suggestion here of the earlier scene on the mountainside after Curdie shoots the Queen's pigeon (27), when all nature seemed to turn against Curdie (27)—but the undercurrents of the present scene are much more sinister. As we saw in *The Princess and the Goblin*, the essence of all taboo is the fear of demons (see Freud, *Totem and Taboo*, 58), in this case representing the negative qualities of the unconscious; and the growth on the spiritual level produced by Curdie's confession and self-enlightenment in the old princess's tower is not secure until the instinctual drives of his unconscious have been encountered and mastered. Curdie is still in the process of doing this and has so far done little more than unleash them, which is why the old princess tells him that "[i]t is very dangerous to do things you don't know about" (38)—and she might well have added, 'things you don't know about are dangerous.'[18]

The idea of a tree has been quietly implanted in the reader's mind from the very first chapter, which summarises the remarkable events of *The Princess and the Goblin;* MacDonald says: "I will narrate as much of them as will serve to show the tops of the roots of my tree" (15). And when Curdie is crossing the desolate heath, the most prominent feature of the landscape is an "ancient hawthorn" (115), the only tree for miles and a degenerate specimen—which adds a wry point to the fact that it is also, like the mountain, a symbol of the self:[19] "[I]t looked . . . like a human being dried up and distorted with age and suffering, with cares instead of loves, and things instead of thoughts" (117). The tree is the shadow of the old princess,[20] and "might have been enough for a warning" (117)[21]—as might the sunset, which is described in terms of "the deathbed of the sun, dying in fever and ague" (118). But Curdie's unconscious is still only beginning to come into consciousness and is experiencing a backlash from his own shadow, which rejects enlightenment; he does not sense any danger, so he lies down under the tree and prepares to sleep.

At this moment the servant promised by the old princess (104) arrives from the direction of the sun, "moving about like a fly over his burning face. It looked as if it were coming out of his hot furnace-heart" (118)[22]—and it is in fact Lina, the mysterious helper described by Jung as appearing in "the fiery agony of the furnace."[23] As her name suggests, she is also connected with Luna, the moon, which represents the unconscious.[24] When Curdie first meets her, soon after

The Downstretched Hand: Individual Development in

shooting the white pigeon, he hardly takes any notice of her; but she assures his unchecked passage up to see the Mistress of the Silver Moon (*PC* 86) and for the first time he also sees "the Silver Moon itself" (92). On the level of archetype there is a strong connection between Diana, the moon, and "her hunting animal the dog, who represents her dark side"[25]—and amid Lina's jumble of animal qualities, the canine predominate. But she is also connected with the sun, which represents consciousness; moreover, as Jung says, the moon itself is not wholly unconscious.[26] Her name not only suggests "luna" but "lion," the golden beast, and perhaps the "fierce lion" of Job 28:8 who has not passed by the mysterious path in the mountain, i.e. the exploration of the unconscious—although during the course of the book Lina grows into consciousness precisely through such an exploration, appearing to understand more and more of what Curdie says to her and eventually beginning to emit light from her eyes (*PC* 163, 167). If Lina's name suggests 'lion' it is a feminised version of the word, which is perhaps why MacDonald continues the link through the image of an unambiguously female great cat; she "went round and round [Curdie], purring like a tigress, and rubbing herself against his legs" (148). Curdie later tells Irene that he thinks "Lina is a woman, and that she was naughty, but is now growing good" (204).

The motif of fire which runs throughout *The Princess and Curdie* begins with the old princess's rose fire in the dove tower (first encountered, of course, in *The Princess and the Goblin*). This is the fire in which Curdie's hands are sensitised[27] so that he can read character—if people change internally it is because of what they do, so "the change always comes first in their hands" (*PC* 98). Lina's paw, the first 'hand' that he reads, discloses "the soft, neat little hand of a child" (102), so that even though she does not possess Curdie's full confidence from the beginning—he is uneasy when she is behind him (120) and "did not altogether *like* Lina" (121-122)—her paw and her provenance give him something to build on. And Lina seems not only to have passed the test of the rose fire. Connected both with the unconscious becoming conscious (the moon) and with consciousness (the sun) and the shadow thrown off by consciousness (the sun was "very large and very red and very dull . . . a dusty fog was spread all over him" [118]),[28] it is fitting that Lina should be what Jung calls a psychopomp, "a mediator between the conscious and the unconscious and a personification of the latter."[29] For Curdie, in spite of his experience of his own shadow and the 'baptism of fire' which helps him discern the inner nature of others, is inexperienced enough to be caught off his guard when danger assumes an unexpected form and to need protection: "Only heroes who have the animals and the anima on their side have a chance to survive," says Marie-Louise von Franz; "the hero in decisive moments does not do much. It is the animals and the anima who take over the action." Lina, who encapsulates the whole lot, proves able to do just that (which is just as well, since for the hero himself to do something about destructive situations "increases the dark power, giving it more libido"[30]). And Lina proves so ready to risk her life to save his, and so consistently helpful, that Curdie becomes "not merely very fond but very trustful of her" (*PC* 126).

The immediate threat comes to Curdie from a most unexpected quarter—a large flock of singing birds, which, especially in view of the lesson of respect for all things natural which he has so recently learned (through the medium of a bird, too!) he is inclined to like. But if the tree is the shadow of the old princess, the "wicked birds" (124) are the shadows of her white pigeons,[31] unleashed by Curdie's having given way to a violent impulse and bent on avenging the harming of the first bird; as Jung says, the slaying of a wild animal is an offence against the Great Mother ("The Dual Mother," *SoT* par. 503), and the instinctual forces which she represents know nothing of contrition or forgiveness. The birds, oblivious to the Queen's ultimate healing of the pigeon, intend to kill, and this symbolises the destruction of all possibility of individuation and achievement; just as the old princess sends Curdie on a great mission, her shadow wants to thwart it.[32] First the birds try to dance round Curdie and the tree in what Jung fortuitously describes as a "vicious circle" which will imprison and paralyse him.[33] Thanks to Lina, who is lying on the other side of the tree, they can only form a vicious semi-circle. This is why, although Curdie's conscious mind is becoming disempowered by their hypnotic singing and dancing, his unconscious is becoming more active: "All the time he had kept doubting every now and then whether they could really be birds, and the sleepier he got, the more he imagined them something else" (*PC* 122-123).[34] This is never explained—but the possibilities of the unconscious have been opened to the reader.

Just as he falls asleep the birds attack, and Curdie is saved only because Lina, who is alert to danger from the unconscious, draws them off and ultimately defeats them. Curdie "gladly wondered" afterwards why "the wicked birds had not at once attacked his eyes" (124), but they can only attack through the unconscious of which they are themselves projections and have to wait until Curdie's eyes are closed before beginning their assault. In this way they would leave

The Downstretched Hand: Individual Development in

an "I," or conscious ego, which, since it was disembodied, would be unable to integrate with its own unconscious and yet, paradoxically, would never be able to escape from the dark sphere of unconscious influence represented by the tree.

The disaster that would have ensued would have meant isolation, not individuation[35] for Curdie, and the end of all possibility of fulfilling his potential, but it would also have had ramifications on a national scale; it would have been a premature crucifixion, Curdie being, so to speak, nailed to the tree without having done what he was meant to do. What in fact happens is that a considerable degree of personality integration takes place, and this is only the prelude to more. Curdie's unaided consciousness proving totally ineffectual in the dark, he blunders back to the old hawthorn tree where the pain of his wounds at least prevents his sleeping on the heath—if indeed there were any further risk to be run by doing so. And from this point he begins to develop an increasingly close relationship with Lina, who, in the attack by the birds, not only saves his life but incurs wounds much more severe than his own. The projected destructive impulses of his own non-individuated unconscious are put to flight by her defensive strength; what falls to Curdie in the fight and its aftermath is first the passive, then the nurturing role associated with female stereotypes. The stick his father cut for him in the wood (113) has served only as a subliminal suggestion that trees and woods are to be important on Curdie's journey, and we never hear of it again. But the goatskin wallet supplied by his mother is ideal as material for the collar which Curdie sews to cover Lina's weakest spot—her bare, ugly and by now pitifully wounded neck: "He found there was just enough, and the hair so similar in colour to Lina's, that no one could suspect it of having grown somewhere else" (125). Lina fights for Curdie and he sews for her; in other words, masculine strength can be tender and feminine protectiveness can be strong.

The night episode on the heath could have led to possession; as Jung says of Hiawatha's battle in the forest, if the hero had lost he would have been killed and possessed by a demon ("The Dual Mother," *SoT* par. 523). As it is, the whole tendency of the episode in *The Princess and Curdie* is to promote the bringing of the unconscious into consciousness. One might apply here what Jung says of other birds in "The Personification of the Opposites": "The birds are personified contents of the unconscious which, once they are made conscious, cannot become unconscious again" (*MC* 180 n.308). And they do *not* become unconscious again. Even in their quality of shadows of the old princess's pigeons, the "wicked birds" (124), their evil propensities once defeated, become a source of strength which enables the pigeons to appear in the culminating battle as agents of legitimate force—"the white-winged army of heaven" (*PC* 311).[36] At that point the pigeons recharge their strength by circling round the head of the old princess, now in the form of a housemaid, just as their shadows had tried to encircle her shadow in the shape of the old hawthorn tree. The word "strange" is almost as much in evidence here as it was during the episode on the heath:

> It seemed to [Irene] right strange that the pigeons, every one as it came to the rear, and fetched a compass to gather force for the re-attack, should make the head of her attendant on the red horse the goal around which it turned; so that about them was an unintermittent flapping and flashing of wings, and a curving, sweeping torrent of the side-poised wheeling bodies of birds. Strange also it seemed that the maid should be constantly waving her arm towards the battle. And the time of the motion of her arm so fitted with the rushes of birds, that it looked as if the birds obeyed her gesture, and she were casting living javelins by the thousand against the enemy. (308)[37]

Curdie's bow and arrows, which the old princess had not wanted him to burn, are finally back—and they are wielded, so to speak, by the rider of the red horse which in Revelation symbolises destruction.[38] Even the earliest bird-episode of all—Curdie's shooting of the pigeon—is subsumed into the battle scene so as to give it the energy which transforms mere aggression into constructive action: "The moment a pigeon had rounded [the housemaid's] head, it went off straight as bolt from bow, and with trebled velocity" (308-309).

After the battle round the hawthorn tree Curdie and Lina journey together for seven more days—with no road to follow, although when Peter leaves for the city later in the book he "sped along the road to Gwyntystorm" (289). His psyche is of course much more fully integrated than his son's: "[W]e understand each other—you and I, Peter" (77) says "the great old young beautiful princess" under the mountain (78), after holding his hand lovingly for a moment (a significant gesture). But the son cannot experience life through the father, and so Curdie sets off, soon to be joined by Lina. Their travels take them on a day's journey through a forest, which, says Jung, has "a maternal significance" like the tree; furthermore, "the meaning of the forest coincides essentially with that of the tabooed tree."[39] But now the tabooed tree on the heath, apparently as much dead as

The Downstretched Hand

alive, has proliferated into a living forest and the darker side of the unconscious has become a source of strength.[40] When the sun goes down the unconscious becomes active again, but this time the threat is not nearly so great as before and, after her strengthening victory over the predatory birds, it is controlled by Lina with comparative ease. What prove to be forty-nine extraordinary beasts approach her one by one, completely ignoring Curdie's conscious ego;[41] the psychopomp, Lina, is needed to mediate between consciousness and the unconscious, including the collective unconscious in which Curdie also participates. After an initial conversation with Lina each of the forty-nine engages in a one-to-one combat with her which she always wins.[42] Overcome, not killed, they follow her until, when they reach open country, she sends them back into the forest, to be recalled when needed; chaotic instincts of violence and aggression, less destructive than before, have again been subjugated and will be positively used in Curdie's mission to purge the palace at Gwyntystorm of evil and to win the battle against traitors and invaders.

After Lina overcomes the forty-nine creatures, Curdie can see them, if not well, at least better than he could see the birds on the heath, which he could only imagine to be "something else" (123):

> Before [the Uglies] were all gathered . . . it had got so dark that he could see some of them only a part at a time, and every now and then . . . he would be startled by some extraordinary limb or feature, undreamed of by him before, thrusting itself out of the darkness into the range of his ken. (131)[43]

The bringing of the unconscious into consciousness, or "the range of [Curdie's] ken" (131), is necessarily a progressive affair. By the time Curdie reaches Gwyntystorm, however, his personality is at least sufficiently well integrated for him to be literally and figuratively 'out of the wood.'

Endnotes to Chapter 9 on page 290

CHAPTER 10

Gwyntystorm

"The nation cannot change save as its members change; and the few who begin the change are the elect of that nation" (MacDonald, *The Miracles of Our Lord*, 304).

"The integration of unconscious contents is an individual act of realization, of understanding, and moral evaluation. . . . Only relatively few individuals can be expected to be capable of such an achievement. . . . The maintenance and further development of civilization depend on such individuals" (Jung, "The Fight with the Shadow," in *Civilization in Transition*, par. 451).

In *The Princess and the Goblin* no-one has to worry about the state of the nation as a whole; that can be left to Irene's king-papa. What matters most is the relationship between Irene and her great-great-grandmother. But in *The Princess and Curdie* MacDonald deals not only with the psychological and spiritual enlightenment of Curdie but with the problem of getting humanity at large (as represented by the nation, symbolised in its turn by the city [1]) to re-orient itself in relation to God. Curdie's mission, as "[o]ne who is come to set things right in the king's house" (*PC* 238)—the focal point for the whole country—is to achieve this re-orientation.

In the Gwyntystorm section of *The Princess and Curdie* there is a shift in the respective roles of Curdie and Lina, for, after the adventures in heath and forest during which Lina has protected him and promoted in him a considerable degree of personality integration, the energy of Curdie's instinctual drives, both negative and positive, has been channelled into the service of his conscious aims and he is now ready to take the lead. In one sense he is brought home where he began; besides being the symbolic focus of the nation—the mother archetype in its communal aspect[2]—Gwyntystorm is the alter-ego of Curdie's home on the mountain. Built on "a great rock in the river, which dividing flowed around it" (134), the city resembles the Petersons' cottage, which, in *The Princess and the Goblin*, is protected from the storm by its foundation:

> But for a huge rock against which it was built, and which protected it both from the blasts and the waters, it must have been swept if it was not blown away; for the two torrents into

The Downstretched Hand: Individual Development in

> which this rock parted the rush of water behind it united again
> in front of the cottage. (*PG* 288)

The resemblance extends beyond the cottage to the great house, home of Irene, and in two respects the capital appears to have an advantage over the original mountain environment. While the great house in *The Princess and the Goblin* is built over a vein of sand which eventually admits the goblins into the wine cellar (*PG* 264-265), the hollow places under the palace at Gwyntystorm, though they also lead into the wine cellar, admit only Curdie and "the avengers of wickedness" (*PC* 251-252); and the "mighty rock" on which the city is founded proves full of gold rather than the silver ore mined by Curdie and his father (though we are told that "[o]f the many other precious things in their mountain they knew little or nothing"[13]). But a comparative disadvantage of Gwyntystorm is also evident, for what is a rock to a mountain?

One of the first things Curdie does on entering the city is to hew a projecting stone out of the road. This is an allusion to the "precious corner stone" mentioned in Isaiah (28:16) and cited in the first epistle of Peter (2:6), though (true to form) MacDonald does not construct an obvious parallel; the stone is simply too close to the gates. It does, however, prove to have the precious quality specified by prophet and apostle, and it is certainly "a stone of stumbling and . . . a rock of offence" (Isaiah 8:14) to the king's baker and the king's barber, the first people Curdie meets within the city walls; the baker in particular is of those who "stumble, and fall, and [are] broken" (Isaiah 8:15). Curdie's interest in the stone (apart from his original desire to help the baker) is financial; he finds confirmatory gold deposits in the rock wall of the palace cellar and is set on "[making] the king rich, and independent of his ill-conditioned subjects" (*PC* 222). But the "lovely greenish yellow" (223)[3] of the "half-crystalline white stone" (222) suggests the New Jerusalem, of which the writer of Revelation says "her light was like unto a stone most precious, even like a jasper stone, clear as crystal" (Rev. 21:11), while "the street of the city was pure gold" (Rev. 21:21). Gwyntystorm has the right foundations,[4] or at least the right potential—but she is something close to a travesty of the heavenly Jerusalem.

The baker and the barber constitute an important introduction to the citizens of Gwyntystorm, exemplifying in a small way the malaise of the city. What has occurred is a symbolic polarisation of masculine and feminine, the qualities each is generally associated with—reason, strength and drive in the case of the masculine principle, intuition, tenderness and the impulse to connect in that of the feminine[5]—and the aspects of the self that each symbolises; consciousness in the case of the masculine principle and the unconscious in that of the feminine. When the unconscious is suppressed, as is the case in Gwyntystorm, not only do the "feminine" qualities deteriorate or disappear—small wonder that, to the king's distress, the court ladies never come near Princess Irene (*PC* 228)—but the instinctual drives of the unconscious take on a negative character and its transcendent spiritual level either fades or degenerates into superstition. The upshot of the polarisation process in the city has in fact been the dominance of the masculine principle in its most destructive form; one favourable neither to fatherhood nor achievement. And the imbalance, which began, significantly, with the death of Irene's mother—"The king told [Curdie] that for some years, ever since his queen's death, he had been losing heart over the wickedness of his people" (227)—can only be redressed by Curdie, the child of a harmonious marriage and a young man who, as he grows into wholeness, learns with Lina's help to integrate the feminine aspects of his psyche.

The first thing Curdie notices on entering Gwyntystorm is the decayed condition of its defences, for the suppression of the feminine principle means the loss of masculine protectiveness and, paradoxically, a reduction in strength: "The gates . . . were dropping from their great hinges; the portcullis was eaten away with rust . . . the loopholed towers had neither floor nor roof, and their tops were fast filling up their interiors" (134-135). In the sphere of relationships the suppression of the feminine, the connecting element, has led to fragmentation; the king's baker and the king's barber, though supposedly friends, have no real liking or concern for each other—and, like the rest of the populace, no sense of loyalty to the king whose livery they wear. This fragmentation promotes selfishness which, coupled with the aggressive impulses of the suppressed unconscious, leads to many forms of violence—physical aggression, cheating, theft, treachery and "evil words" (304). And both violence and selfishness are related, on the collective level, to commerce, with its potential for competition and greed—perhaps never more clearly than when the citizens, on hearing of the approach of a great army, "instead of rushing to their defences . . . each and all flew first to their treasures, burying them in their cellars and gardens, and hiding them behind stones in their chimneys" (291).

The connection of commerce with violence may seem strange to modern minds, and the inhabitants of Gwyntystorm would have

The Downstretched Hand: Individual Development in

scorned it: "Commerce and self-interest, they said, had got the better of violence" (135). But there is an echo here, as in *At the Back of the North Wind*, of the prophet Ezekiel: "By the multitude of thy merchandise they have filled the midst of thee with violence, and thou hast sinned," Ezekiel tells the prince of Tyrus (Ezek. 28:16), apparently referring to the city, which is an extension of the prince himself and suffers a fate similar to that of Gwyntystorm: "I shall make thee a desolate city, like the cities that are not inhabited.... I will make thee a terror, and thou shalt be no more: though thou be sought for, yet shalt thou never be found again," Ezekiel prophesies in God's name (28:20, 21).

The most obvious form of violence in Gwyntystorm is misdirected physical force, as Curdie finds when Lina is attacked by the butchers' dogs; the vicious animals and their fierce, knife-wielding masters, who form a semi-circle which complements the earlier semi-circle of the birds round the ancient hawthorn on the heath, are such personal shadow projections of Curdie and Lina as to pose a direct challenge. The newcomers kill the first two dogs that reach them—the first time Curdie has been able to fight his own shadow and the first time he has fought for Lina. And his earlier exclamation: "Oh, Lina! if the princess would but burn you in her fire of roses!" (*PC* 127) is darkly echoed by the prophetic remark of one of the butchers, enraged by the death of his mastiff: "Your brute shall be burnt alive for it." Prophetic in his turn, Curdie replies "Not yet" (145).

The aggressive masculinity of Gwyntystorm is so dominant that most women and even children are tainted by it. Much later, when the king and his followers ride out to battle, we find that "[m]any were the eyes unfriendly of women that had stared at them from door and window as they passed through the city; and low laughter and mockery and evil words from the lips of children had rippled about their ears" (303-304). But the few good inhabitants of the city are for the most part women or girls. The baker's wife (who, like Curdie and Lina, had come to the city as a stranger) passes the acid test, for women, of not being repelled by Lina's ugliness—as do Princess Irene and the housemaid who, unrecognised as the old princess, lays her hand on Lina's head: "Now I know you are a true woman," says Curdie (226). And if the hostility of the king's baker and the king's barber manifests itself in heartless indifference even to each other, they have feminine counterparts in Derba and Barbara, a grandmother and granddaughter with important symbolic roles to play. Derba—prefigured by the baker's wife, an honest and kindly woman who sells Curdie some of the best bread (142)—is not only the counterpart of the baker but bread personified, since her name is an obvious anagram of the word. Her little grandchild Barbara is the counterpart of the barber;[6] though she does not touch the king's hair she plays with his crown (283), and the word "crown" also suggests the top of the head. The baker and the barber are in effect the shadows of Derba and Barbara, but in the corrupted state of Gwyntystorm the shadows are to the fore.

There is no symmetry in the correspondence of the two pairs, since the baker and the barber are merely friends (as friendship goes in Gwyntystorm) while Derba and Barbara are blood relations. What is in question is not allegory but symbolism, which works on many different levels. Derba's house, for example, is analogous to the biblical Bethlehem ("the house of bread"), and not simply because "bread" lives in it. It suggests the stable in which Jesus was born, for it not only has a thatched roof and at one point shelters a stable boy but accommodates Curdie and Lina when they are turned away from the inn (with a vengeance, as people throw things at them from the windows [147]).[7] And Derba is linked to the old princess, not only because she is a grandmother (a position of special honour and significance in MacDonald's work), but because she is a figure who is regarded by the populace in much the same light as the Old Mother Wotherwop of the miners' earlier gossip—"the people called her a witch, and would have done her many an ill turn if they had not been afraid of her" (148). Her symbolic association with the old princess is reinforced because, like the door of Queen Irene's tower, the door of her own cottage is open at opportune moments[8]—and much more because she is eventually charged with preparing the king's food, which brings her "bread" to life.

If the sacramental symbolism of Derba is clear, it finds no parallel in Barbara; but the child has nonetheless a spiritually significant role to play. Reversing the earlier incident in which Curdie restores a boy who has been throwing stones at him to his mother, she comes out, takes the stranger by the hand and guides him to her grandmother's house. And although Barbara, in spite of being a child in the "house of bread," is not a Christ-figure, her spiritual function extends beyond the welcoming of the outcasts. She is the king's Barbara in a far more real sense than her counterpart is the king's barber (138-139, 161), and her name has a dimension his does not— possibly deriving from Cockney rhyming slang, with which MacDonald, in his frequent dealings with the poor of London, must have been familiar. It is quite likely that 'barber's pole,' which would probably have been shortened to 'barber's,' means 'soul' [9]—or even that MacDonald, as is consistent

The Downstretched Hand: Individual Development in

with rhyming slang, thought this up himself; for "the moment [the king's] eyes fell upon little Barbara . . . his soul came into them with a rush" (283).[10]

But much must happen before Derba, Barbara and the old princess are installed in the palace, and it is Curdie, whose masculinity has been tempered by feminine influences until its aggression has turned into strength, who must be the primary agent of salvation. In order to prevent Derba's house being burned down the morning after he arrives in Gwyntystorm, Curdie gives himself up to the soldiers and is imprisoned in a cellar to await his appearance before the magistrate. But he eventually escapes, with Lina's help, and reaches the wine cellar under the palace. To do this he must brave the danger of crossing a chasm at the bottom of which is an underground river; and falling into the water, apart from its obvious inconvenience, symbolises being overpowered by the paralysing grip of the unconscious[11]—completely taboo in that, although the unconscious must be progressively integrated into consciousness, it must not be allowed to overwhelm the conscious mind.

The palace, the focal point of the nation, is the source of the corruption which has contaminated Gwyntystorm and the outlying regions. Nearly all the servants are tainted. In *The Princess and the Goblin* the butler delays the invading goblins by getting them drunk in the wine cellar; the butler in *The Princess and Curdie* ranks with the foremost villains as a traitor who poisons his master's wine. In the great hall Curdie finds three servants asleep in armchairs and looking "like fools dreaming themselves kings" (*PC* 181); it transpires that six of the chief officers of the court are dreaming themselves kings indeed—an unpleasant truth that the sick king has wasted much of his energy in trying to evade (228). Corruption extends all the way down; even the dogs and cats sleep in the kitchen while the rats run about the floor (180), in contrast to "my Tom and Mrs. Housekeeper's Bob," who, as the cook says in *The Princess and the Goblin*, "will put to flight any number of rats" (*PG* 263).

The condition of the palace reflects the inadequacy of the king's servants at all levels, and Curdie finds that the lower regions of the palace, the places where food is prepared, are full of "filth and disorder . . . . It was like a hideous dream" (*PC* 180). Even the king's bedchamber, which is a pale reflection of the old princess's tower room, "dimly lighted by a silver lamp that hung from the ceiling" (183), is neglected by the servants (242). And the king is ill in the "great bed, surrounded with dark heavy curtains" (183), while Princess

Irene, without her ring, has no supernatural help to give; indeed, in a reversal of their roles in *The Princess and the Goblin*, it is she who needs Curdie's help to open her eyes to the evil around her.

The king, like most of the characters in this section of the book, is designated only by his role (Dr. Kelman's name simply indicates what he does). This means, among other things, that the self has all but succumbed to what Jung, in "The Myth of the Hero," calls the greatest danger threatened by a confrontation with the unconscious, namely "the disintegration of the personality into its functional components, i.e. the separate functions of consciousness, the complexes, hereditary units, etc." (*Psychology and Alchemy*, par. 439). Only the king's stubbornly holding onto his crown, the symbol of consciousness, has prevented the ultimate disintegration—though what the conspirators really want, in more ways than one, is his will (see *PC* 217). So the king's councillors, possessed by their own desire for power, plot against their lawful ruler and are mutually distrustful—the lord chamberlain, for example, "began to doubt the doctor's fidelity to the conspiracy" (217). This state of affairs is reflected in the general population: "No man pretended to love his neighbour,[12] but everyone said he knew that peace and quiet behaviour was the best thing for himself" (134).

The results, in the palace especially, are disastrous, for "such was the state to which a year of wicked rule had reduced the moral condition of the court, that in it all [Curdie] found but three with human hands" (271). The king himself has long been aware of evil influences within the community at large: "The main cause of his illness was the despondency with which the degeneration of his people affected him," and he knows that "[t]he whole country was discontented . . . and there were signs of gathering storm outside as well as inside his borders" (228). To most of the citizens of Gwyntystorm, the epicentre of fragmentation, the king is merely a figurehead: "What was a king for if he would not take care of his people's heads!" complains the baker after he has hurt his own (136). That the sovereign means no more to his people—"it dawned upon [Curdie] . . . that he had never heard the least expression of love to him" (188)—is an important sign of their degeneration; as Curdie tells Irene, "lying and selfishness and inhospitality and dishonesty [are] everywhere; and to crown all, they speak with disrespect of the good king, and not a man of them knows he is ill" (200). This is strange indeed, considering that the entire male workforce of the kingdom below the rank of courtier wears the king's livery, the symbol of collective unity and also of the integrity of the self of which the king, in his turn, is the symbolic head.[13]

The Downstretched Hand: Individual Development in

There is a definite link between the king and the miner, who is now answering the invitation which the king gave him at the end of *The Princess and the Goblin*. During the city section of *The Princess and Curdie* it is apparent not only that the king needs Curdie but that Curdie needs the king to call him forth into greater consciousness. This makes excellent psychological sense, for on one level Curdie and the king are aspects of the same self—Curdie as ego and the king, described in *The Princess and the Goblin* as "the wisest man in the kingdom" (299-300), as the principal embodiment of the Wise Old Man archetype (one more reason why he is never given a name).[14] His understanding of the situation is in some ways deeper than Curdie's; when his thoughts and words seem to wander, "Curdie could not be certain that the cause of their not being intelligible to him did not lie in himself." In their quality of individual characters within the story, monarch and miner are growing closer together; the king "as it were put himself in [Curdie's] hands" (*PC* 227)—a hugely significant metaphor in the context of the book—and the trust this implies is confirmed by his later allowing Curdie (much to Irene's amazement) to take his crown away: "I stroked his hands," Curdie tells her, "and took the crown from them; and ever since he has slept quietly, and again and again smiled in his sleep" (235). This prefigures the king's subsequent adoption of Curdie as his heir and future son-in-law, an occasion on which he addresses him as "my own boy" and "the king's Curdie" (315); he has already called him "my son" (298).

When Curdie first arrives at the palace, the king and the colonel of the guard (who comes to love Curdie "as if he were at once his son and his angel" [284], and in whom Curdie discovers "a good, honest human hand" [272]) are the only ones in bed; by the morning of the battle they are the only high-ranking men at court to be on their feet. But much must be done before this desirable reversal is achieved, and Curdie must be the doer—even the old princess putting herself under his authority in the form of the housemaid. The king, as an individual character, has a psyche so disordered that neither his conscious nor his unconscious self can function properly; hence the paradoxical statement that "[h]e could not sleep, and had terrible dreams" (228). This undesirable state of affairs is promoted by the royal physician, Dr. Kelman, who always comes at midnight to rouse the king and gives him poisoned wine that makes sleep difficult. The king's unconscious, dominant at night, tries to warn him about Dr. Kelman: "Every night, an evil demon in the shape of his physician came and poured poison down his throat. He knew it to be poison, he said, somehow, although it tasted like wine" (229). But his struggle to repress the perception of evil wastes his psychic energy and confuses him still further, so that by the time Curdie sees him the king is finding it virtually impossible to distinguish between conscious and unconscious—"[h]e went wandering in a maze of sorrows, some of which were purely imaginary, while others were truer than he understood" (228).

Curdie, for his part, only goes to bed once in the book, and that is before his mission starts. He gets plenty of sleep, however, for he and Lina watch and wake alternately when they are spending a day in the cellar (219); the last time is on the night before the battle, when he has "an old mantle of the king's thrown over him" (293)—another intimation that he is (literally) beginning to take on the mantle of kingship. And since he has been through the labyrinth of the unconscious, in the shape of the heath and the wood, and has, through Lina, conquered the beasts it contains, he is qualified to use the humans within the beasts to control the beasts within the humans; in other words, elements from the unconscious which have come into consciousness have more energy than elements which have remained unconscious.

In the case of the servants the conquest of the beast within is a relatively simple, though highly unpleasant operation which consists first in a call to repentance and then in punishment and expulsion by the Uglies. The more the unconscious is ignored, especially when it contains elements that properly belong to consciousness but have been repressed—"He will not let either his own conscience or my messenger [the housemaid] speak to him," says Curdie of the butler (256)—the more dangerous it becomes;[15] and the Uglies, "animal forms wilder and more grotesque than ever ramped in nightmare dream" (247), owe much to the "locusts . . . [w]ith power, as the scorpions of the earth have power" in Revelation (9:3ff) which, themselves the descendants of creatures sent in Old Testament plagues, are instruments of vengeance;[16] there is even a scorpion among the Uglies.

The servants, as is fitting, are treated far less severely than the courtiers whose responsibility it is to oversee them, and at first the punishments inflicted in *The Princess and Curdie* are indignities rather than torments—being "soused in the stinking water that had boiled greens . . . smeared with rancid dripping" etc. (263)—but they are unpleasant enough in all conscience; and I say "conscience" advisedly, because the objective is not only to purge the palace of the unworthy servants but to make the servants conscious of their darker selves. The women, here as elsewhere more in touch with the unconscious than are men, "ran hither and thither throughout the hall, *pursued each by her own horror*, and snapped at by every other in passing" (261; italics mine). The men at first try to deny the reality of the experience, but the mutilation of the footman, who loses a finger when trying to tease the tapir, impels everyone to run into the kitchen. At this point the beasts do indeed behave like the locusts of Revelation:

> [The servants] were flung about in all directions; their clothes were torn from them; they were pinched and scratched any and everywhere . . . the scorpion kept grabbing at their legs with his huge pincers; a three-foot centipede kept screwing up their bodies, nipping as he went; varied as numerous were their woes. (262-263)

Compare this with the voices of the goblin creatures in *The Princess and the Goblin:*

> The noises they made, although not loud, were as uncouth and varied as their forms, and could be described neither as grunts nor squeaks nor roars nor howls nor barks nor yells nor screams nor croaks nor hisses nor mews nor shrieks, but only as something like all of them mingled in one horrible dissonance. (*PG* 130-131) [17]

But this is a noise-only matter, and the humour never far below the surface in *The Princess and the Goblin* reduces the frightfulness of the creatures; in *The Princess and Curdie* this humour is entirely lacking, and the rather sadistic punishment of the servants hardly makes its way to the reader's feelings. The scene of retribution in the sculleries is particularly unappealing: "I dare not tell all that was done to them," says MacDonald (263), and one feels that he has told quite enough— even allowing for the fact that literary critics have generally reached a ripeness of years when, as G.K.Chesterton opines, enough guilt has accrued to make justice less attractive than mercy.[18] Children of an age to want to see evil punished[19] are unlikely to be reading the book, and the older reader's sense of justice may well be offended by the fact that the "inexorable avengers" (263) testify in their flesh to their own corruption.

At last the servants (except the butler, who is reserved for a worse fate) are expelled from the palace and "left, some standing, some lying, some crawling, to the farther buffeting of the waterspouts and whirlwinds ranging every street of the city" (263). So the injunction reported by Matthew is fulfilled: "Cast ye the unprofitable servant into outer darkness: there shall be weeping and gnashing of teeth" (Matthew 25:30). Other members of the household are also expelled—

"Out of their beds in their night-clothing, out of their rooms, gorgeous chambers or garret nooks, the creatures hunted them" (*PC* 271). Of the servants, only the page who literally and figuratively stands by the housemaid can stay to fight in the final battle. Even the three anonymous sleepers with human hands are simply allowed to dress themselves and leave—presumably because, even though they are not negative projections of the unconscious, they have not actually become conscious and therefore cannot be sources of energy.

The chief conspirators, however, require a different treatment from that meted out to the rest of the household. While the negative components of the Wise Old Man archetype—the "magician, deceiver, corrupter, and tempter"[20]—have achieved a spurious unity through conspiracy, they can aim only at dominance; they have no idea how to govern, and the foolishness of their original intention to "pick a quarrel with the most powerful of their neighbours" (*PC* 266) is surpassed by the eventual treachery of the lord chancellor, one of their "tools" (265), in inviting one of these neighbours to take over the kingdom.

It is both appropriate and paradoxical that the king, once he has begun to surrender to despondency, should be poisoned by a snake in the form of his physician, for the snake is associated both with venom and with healing and transformation.[21] In the present case a function of consciousness, in the shape of the physician, has been possessed by a destructive drive from the unconscious—"the man hated the king, and delighted in doing him wrong" (231). The aptly-named Dr. Kelman is an alter ego of legserpent, but without the wings that suggest that Ugly's gradual ascent into consciousness. In this case Curdie's gift for testing hands, which first made him detect in the physician "the belly of a creeping thing" (192), becomes superfluous, for when "[t]he light fell upon his face from above . . . [Curdie] saw the snake in it plainly visible" (230-231). The doctor is just about to prick the king with his lancet, "an involuntary hiss of hate between his closed teeth" (231), when Curdie orders Lina to attack—and it says much about Dr. Kelman's abuse of his function that he meets the same fate as the butchers in having one leg crushed by Lina's jaws.[22]

One might expect the physician to hate his natural antagonist, the vulture concealed within the body of the lord chamberlain—a character who already regards him with distrust (217). But it falls to legserpent to execute justice upon his traditional foe. Wrapping himself around both bed and councillor, he begins to hiss in his face; and the chamberlain

The Downstretched Hand: Individual Development in

> woke in terror unspeakable, and would have started up; but the moment he moved, the legserpent drew his coils closer, and closer still, and drew and drew until the quaking traitor heard the joints of his bedstead grinding and gnarring. Presently he persuaded himself that it was only a horrid nightmare, and began to struggle with all his strength to throw it off. Thereupon the legserpent gave his hooked nose such a bite, that his teeth met through it—but it was hardly thicker than the bowl of a spoon; and then the vulture knew that he was in the grasp of his enemy the snake, and yielded. (267-268)

Finally legserpent twists the silver bed so that the lord chamberlain is "shut in a silver cage out of which it was impossible for him to find a way" (268)—rather like the description of Babylon in Revelation as "a cage of every unclean and hateful bird" (Rev. 18:2).

Each conspirator except the doctor, whose crushed leg is guarantee enough that he cannot escape, is guarded by one of the "avengers of wickedness" (*PC* 251-252). Clubhead watches beside the butler, who is tied hand and foot under the cask of poisoned wine; Lina—and her prisoner's conscience—guards the secretary, who "sank fainting into a chair" (267); the tapir is charged with the surveillance of the master of the horse, whom he keeps in bed by pecking his legs with his proboscis, and the attorney-general is secured in his chair by a large spider, "which, having made an excellent supper, was full of webbing" (269). Even the gluttonous magistrate outside the palace is not forgotten; having been "pulled from his bed in the dark, by beings of which he could see nothing but the flaming eyes, and treated to a bath of the turtle soup that had been left simmering by the side of the kitchen fire" (279), he is "put . . . again into his bed, where he soon learned how a mummy must feel in its cerements" (280).

This last punishment has obvious connotations of death, and the whole episode means much more, symbolically, than simple retribution. The inferior functions of the personality which the plotters in *The Princess and Curdie* represent, however, are not destroyed but brought into harmony with the total self—using the energy of those elements of the unconscious already brought under the control of the conscious mind. A stanza from MacDonald's poem *The Diary of an Old Soul* shows the opposite side of the same coin, employing startlingly similar images to acknowledge the ever-present need to struggle against the negative impulses of the unconscious:

> With every morn my life afresh must break
> The crust of self, gathered about me fresh,

George MacDonald's Major Fantasies for Children

> That thy wind-spirit may rush in and shake
> The darkness out of me, and rend the mesh
> The spider-devils spin out of the flesh—
> Eager to net the soul before it wake
> That it may slumberous lie, and listen to the snake.
> (October, stanza 10, 277)

In *The Princess and Curdie* the symbolic power of projection is used to the full, and the "evil men" are seen in opposition to the "good beasts" (*PC* 314). They must undergo the symbolic death of realising this before they can eventually be reformed under the tutelage of Queen Irene; in order to know, for example, that that he is "in the grasp of his enemy the snake" (268), the lord chamberlain must first realise that he is a vulture—something intimated to the reader on the character's first appearance:

> He was a lean, long, yellow man, with a small head, bald over the top, and tufted at the back and about the ears. He had a very thin, prominent, hooked nose, and a quantity of loose skin under his chin and about the throat.... His eyes were very small, sharp, and glittering, and looked as black as jet. (213)

In the case of the attorney-general the moment of self-recognition is particularly striking, for it is ironic that, while his role is to oversee the administration of justice, he should exemplify the corruption which is rampant in the palace: "He had been trying the effect of a diamond star which he had that morning taken from the jewel room" (269), a theft of the same order as a servant's theft of a brooch from a writing table (239-240), though on a grander scale. Before being bound by the spider, he "sat in a chair asleep before a great mirror;" ready, in other words, for the vision which would correct his illusion of possessing the extraordinary qualities symbolised by the stolen jewel. On awaking,

> he fancied himself paralysed; every limb, every finger even, was motionless: coils and coils of broad spider-ribbon bandaged his members to his body, and all to the chair. In the glass he saw himself wound about, under and over and around, with slavery infinite. (269) [23]

Revelation is not succeeded by repentance—though that will presumably come in the wood under Queen Irene's guidance. But the first step is the realisation of what the still lower functions of the personality represented by menservants asleep in armchairs could not perceive—that he has been a fool dreaming himself a king (181).

The Downstretched Hand: Individual Development in

Since the king, his courtiers and his servants represent aspects of the nation as well as aspects of the individual psyche, the expulsion of the conspirators is a symbolic purging of the sins of the community at large. The form it takes is an imaginative rendering of the ritual practised on the Day of Atonement, as prescribed in Leviticus. Two goats were to be selected, one of which was to be offered as a sacrifice to God—a role which, in *The Princess and Curdie*, devolves upon Lina, who actually wears a goatskin band around her neck and who is burned alive in the Queen's fire of roses. The second goat—collectively represented in MacDonald's book by the seven beasts on which the conspirators are bound—is treated by the high priest in Leviticus as a scapegoat for the sins of the people:

> And Aaron shall lay both his hands upon the head of the live goat, and confess over him all the iniquities of the children of Israel, and all their transgressions in all their sins, putting them upon the head of the goat, and shall send him away by the hand of a fit man into the wilderness

> And the goat shall bear upon him all their iniquities unto a land not inhabited: and he shall let go the goat in the wilderness. (Leviticus 6:21, 22)

In *The Princess and Curdie*, the "unveiling terror" which makes each of the seven plotters look like "the villain he was" (*PC* 314) replaces the confession of iniquity—and according to ancient tradition there were seven deadly sins.

The function of the high priest in Leviticus is taken over by the king in *The Princess and Curdie,* though (as is usual in MacDonald) with a New Testament update, for he is not only priest but sacrificial victim. In contrast to the symbolic death faced by the conspirators the night before the battle, the king is given new life: "I wake from a troubled dream," he tells Curdie. "A glorious torture has ended it, and I live" (298). He has been a "living sacrifice" on a "table-altar" (295) in a room resembling the holy place of Leviticus, even to the burning coals of fire on the altar (Lev. 16:12), for he "lay all within the fire" of roses (*PC* 294).

On one level this strengthens and purifies him for the battle. The colonel of the guard, in whom Curdie has found "a good, honest, human hand" (252), is another aspect of the wise old man archetype. He, like the king, has been ill in bed and is revitalised—"He knew it not, but the old princess had passed through his room in the night" (298)—and he can take his place astride his black horse[24] while the king prepares to "go to the battle, and conquer" (300) astride his "white steed, with the stones flashing on his helmet" (302-303); like the white horse in Revelation, of whose rider it is said: "A crown was given unto him: and he went forth conquering, and to conquer" (Rev. 6:2). The "horse that was red" which symbolises destruction (Rev. 6:4) also appears, in this case ridden by the old princess in the guise of a housemaid—and her pigeons play the ultimately decisive role in defeating the enemy. As the battle is not the ultimate conflict of Armageddon, however, there is no equivalent of the "pale horse" which represents death in Revelation (6:8); Irene's white pony is a reminder that she is not much beyond childhood.

If there is no Armageddon, there is nonetheless a judgement, and the king—who stands, significantly, on "the steps of the ancient cross" (*PC* 313)—is both priest and judge. Curdie is associated with him in his priestly function; not only do both bind the plotters on the backs of the beasts, but before the battle Curdie shares the messianic associations of the king—and of the old princess, who, when the king is the victim, performs the priestly role of offering the sacrifice. The link is forged, not because Curdie watches what happens (as he also does when Lina burrows into the rose fire) but through the imagery used. "She was large and strong as a Titaness" (295), says MacDonald towards the end of the chapter entitled "The Sacrifice." It concludes with the words "[Curdie] sank into a dreamless sleep" (296); and the very first sentence of the next chapter reads: "He woke like a giant refreshed with wine" (297)—quoted verbatim from Psalm 78 as rendered in the Anglican *Book of Common Prayer*: "So the Lord awaked as one out of sleep: and like a giant refreshed with wine" (v. 66).

Being burnt is a powerful motif in *The Princess and Curdie*, from Curdie's plunging his hands into the fire of roses early in the book (93-95) to the complete consuming of Lina in the final chapter (319). "Your brute shall be burnt alive," say the butchers (145), and later they plan to extend this treatment to Curdie as well (278). Like the unjust magistrate who also proclaims that Lina is to be roasted alive (154), they see only the destructive side of burning. But its function is actually to purify, redeem and (in Curdie's case) sensitise, for he in particular must develop in the context of the community and therefore, in the present emergency, needs to fast-forward his understanding of others. If those who have been possessed by lower, non-individuating instincts—the seven sleeping retainers in the hall, whose hands Curdie experiences as two ox hooves, three pig's trotters, one hoof of donkey or pony and a dog's paw, "seemed . . . to have eaten and drunk so much

The Downstretched Hand: Individual Development in

that they might be burned alive without waking" (179)—the implied future redemption of the seven conspirators, whose shadows they are (yes, things have got so bad that there are shadows of shadows) may eventually integrate them into consciousness.

But the destructive power of fire—that is, to kill—is associated with those who are not actually burned themselves; those who are, benefit. Curdie's hands are sensitised and the king is brought into consciousness—"I wake from a troubled dream"—by the "glorious torture" (298) of the Queen's rose fire in which he has been immersed. Lina is, in one sense, destroyed by the fire which she enters willingly on the Queen's command and which consumes her: "There went up a black smoke and a dust, and Lina was never more seen in the palace" (319). Yet, as so often in MacDonald, a curse is turned into a blessing. "[S]he shall be utterly burned with fire," says the author of Revelation of Babylon (18:8), but Lina, who looked as though she were "coming out of [the sun's] hot furnace-heart" when originally running across the heath (*PC* 118), has evidently longed for the redemptive process earlier foreseen by Curdie—"Oh, Lina! If the princess would but burn you in her fire of roses!" (*PC* 127)—and which is finally completed.

The general purgation in *The Princess and Curdie*, however, is not complete. Before the battle, all the dwellers in the city were united in enmity to the palace: "It swarmed with evil spirits, they said; whereas the evil spirits were in the city, unsuspected" (290-291). And after the battle only the status quo has changed. The citizens of Gwyntystorm are subdued, not penitent; they have not been brought out of unconsciousness—and since, as Jung says, "unconsciousness makes no difference between good and evil,"[25] all they can say of their country's victory is "We must submit . . . or the king and *his demons* will destroy us" (*PC* 312; italics mine). Indeed, "there was lamentation in Gwyntystorm, for no one could comfort himself, and no one had any to comfort him" (313)—words reminiscent of the lamentations of Jeremiah after the sack of Jerusalem: "[A]mong all her lovers she hath none to comfort her;" "Zion spreadeth forth her hands, and there is none to comfort her;" "there is none to comfort me" (Lamentations 1:2, 17, 21). And the citizens of Gwyntystorm mourn as though it had been defeated, in much the same way as the kings, merchants and shipmasters mourn the fall of Babylon, which has become "the habitation of devils" (Rev.18:2). "Alas for their city! their grandly respectable city! their loftily reasonable city!" lament the people of Gwyntystorm (*PC* 277)[26] in a condensed echo of the mourners in Revelation: "Alas, alas that great city Babylon, that mighty city!";

"Alas, alas, that great city, that was clothed in fine linen, and purple, and scarlet, and decked with gold, and precious stones, and pearls!"; "Alas, alas, that great city, wherein were made rich all that had ships in the sea by reason of her costliness!" (Rev.18:10, 16, 19).

In fairy tale tradition, Curdie is promoted to Prince Conrad[27] and eventually marries Princess Irene. But there remains a discord between individual and community which detracts even from the symbolic completeness of the married pair, for George MacDonald makes it plain that although there is a 'happy' there is no 'ever after'—not in this world, at least. The concordance of masculine with feminine in Curdie's marriage to Irene fails, as their childlessness indicates, to provide symbolic completeness. On the highest level it is the old princess, and not Princess Irene, with whom Curdie cooperates in *The Princess and Curdie*, sometimes without knowing it—and how odd it is that the boy who has had no difficulty in recognising the "great old young beautiful princess" (*PC* 78) in the person of an old countrywoman (81) should be unaccountably blind to her when she assumes the form of a housemaid. During the final battle it is Peter who realises her true identity—as is confirmed when the maid says: "Ah, friend Peter! . . . thou hast come as I told thee!" (310)—just as St. Peter in the New Testament realises the true identity of Jesus:

> Jesus . . . asked his disciples, saying, Whom do men say that I the Son of man am?
>
> And they said, Some say that thou art John the Baptist; some, Elias; and others, Jeremias, or one of the prophets.
>
> He saith unto them, But whom say ye that I am?
>
> And Simon Peter answered and said, Thou art the Christ, the Son of the living God.
>
> (Matthew 16:13-16)

In St. Matthew's Gospel, St. Peter's insight is given a tremendous affirmation by Jesus—"Blessed art thou, Simon Bar-Jona: for flesh and blood hath not revealed it unto thee, but my Father which is in heaven" (16:17)—and symbolically this has also happened to Curdie's father, whose recognition of Queen Irene, with her divine associations, shows the highest development of consciousness. It is not surprising that later, mining at the back of the king's wine cellar (an interesting locus in both the *Princess* books), he should discover "a cavern all crusted with gems" (*PC* 318)—i.e. still more treasures of the unconscious to be brought into consciousness, and this time without any danger of undermining the city. No wonder that when they first meet, in

The Downstretched Hand: Individual Development in

the great cavern under the mountain, the old princess takes Peter's hand, holds it lovingly and says "we understand each other—you and I, Peter" (77).

But Curdie fails to recognise Queen Irene even in the moment of victory; when his father says "there I was, in the nick of time to save the two princesses!" his son replies: "The *two* princesses, father! The one on the great red horse was the housemaid" (313). This, of the person who not only "looked at him steadily for a moment" and then "looked him once more in the face" on their first meeting in the palace (226, 227), but whose hand he actually takes (246)—without associating it with that of the old princess! (104) Puzzling indeed. When Curdie first sees the housemaid she is weeping by a fire (224), but perhaps his failure to remember that the old princess was doing this when he last saw her (95) is not strange. What is more surprising is that he should fail to connect princess and housemaid when he sees the old princess, whom, at this juncture, he "saw and knew," heaping burning roses on the king, "a living sacrifice" (295), on the night before the battle—even though he had actually asked the king to let the housemaid take his place by the bed while he slept in the corridor. But though, the next morning, "the housemaid sat where he had left her" (297), it does not occur to Curdie that she and the old princess are one—nor does he give any thought (except in its immediate aftermath [81]) to her warning, before he leaves for Gwyntystorm that "[y]ou shall see me again—in very different circumstances ... and ... it *may* be in a very different shape" (79).

Were Irene not a comparatively minor figure in this book, her own non-recognition of Queen Irene, which is even more puzzling, might excuse his. Even stranger is the fact that the Queen and Irene, as Bonnie Gaarden points out in *The Christian Goddess*, have no one-to-one contact at all (151)—until the battle, that is, when the old princess stops Irene's retreating pony and they watch the conflict side by side. Even now they do not speak; but it is extraordinary that Irene can watch the old princess, at the moment of greatest danger, waving a "dense cloud" of pigeons towards the battle (*PC* 307)—something that seems to her "right strange"—without realising who is apparently "casting live javelins ... against the enemy" (308). Yet some time before Curdie's arrival she had been reassured about his safety because "one of my grandmother's pigeons with its white wing flashed a message to me through the window ... and then I knew my Curdie wasn't eaten by the goblins, for my grandmother wouldn't have taken care of him one time to let him be eaten the next" (190). She recognises the pigeon, but not the old princess! Ringless and threadless though she is, Irene's memory is faithful to her grandmother—but her power of immediate perception has been lost.

In St. Luke's Gospel the disciples recognise the risen Jesus when he breaks bread—"their eyes were opened, and they knew him" (24:31)—and in *The Princess and Curdie* this is transferred to the pouring of the wine at supper. The revelation is general, but the focus is on Curdie's moment of recognition:

> As she poured out for Curdie red wine that foamed in the cup... she looked him in the eyes. And Curdie started, and sprang from his seat, and dropped on his knees, and burst into tears. And the maid said with a smile, such as none but one could smile,--
>
> "Did I not tell you, Curdie, that it might be you would not know me when next you saw me?" (*PC* 316)

The washing of the disciples' feet as described in John's account of the Last Supper—"he poureth water into a bason, and began to wash the disciples' feet, and to wipe them with the towel wherewith he was girded" (John 13:5)—becomes a simpler service, and John's and Luke's accounts of service and recognition are telescoped into one: "Then the king would have yielded her his royal chair. But she made them all sit down, and with her own hands placed at the table seats for Derba and the page. Then in ruby crown and royal purple she served them all" (*PC* 316). [28]

Masculine and feminine influences in the nation are brought into harmony when Curdie recognises Queen Irene, and it is between the Queen and Curdie (now married to Irene and raised to the status of "Prince Conrad" [315]) that the *coniunctio*, the union of opposites which symbolises the wholeness brought about by the individuation process,[29] takes place. This has been some time in preparation, starting with the sacrificial fire in which the king was purified and which was witnessed by Curdie—connected with the old princess even then by proximate imagery, for, while "[s]he was large and strong as a Titaness" (295), he woke afterwards "like a giant" (297). At some point after the revelation of Queen Irene's identity and Curdie's marriage to Irene there is another such fire. This time Curdie, not Irene, goes to the "uppermost rooms" (318) to find the Queen, presumably drawn by his 'higher' unconscious to arrive at the operative moment; the Queen—in what magically proves to be the very room in which, long before, "[Curdie's] touch had been glorified by her fire"—is putting

The Downstretched Hand: Individual Development in

the final touches to "a huge heap of [blazing] red and white roses." Lina burrows into them while Curdie looks on (319), and, as Jung says, "the *coniunctio* of the 'royal' pair is represented by the sacrificial fire burning between them."[30] And Curdie, for his part, does not need Lina any more—or has assumed her helpful qualities.

MacDonald's desire to turn negatives into positives is also exemplified here, for he is alluding to an ominous but apposite passage from the Book of Daniel: "I beheld even till the beast was slain, and his body destroyed, and given to the burning flame" (Dan. 7:11). Curdie has at one point told Irene that he believes Lina to be a woman who "was naughty, but is now growing good" (*PC* 204)—and, as a psychopomp, she is also close enough to the unconscious to combat its darker impulses when they threaten someone who aims for enlightenment (as when she fights off the mysterious birds which menace Curdie on the heath) and to reveal them to the unenlightened, as, it is suggested, she does to some of the delinquents at court: "Lina slid through the servants like a shapeless terror through a guilty mind" (209-210). By the time she enters the sacrificial fire, not only alive but eager, she is ready to lose even the memory of her earlier imperfections—and so the defeat and destruction of Daniel's beast becomes, in her case, the ultimate purification of transcendence. Just as Lina (luna) once appeared to come out of the sun, so now she returns to it. The silver or moon condition is raised to the sun condition: "The *rubedo* . . . follows direct from the *albedo* as the result of raising the heat of the fire to its highest intensity," says Jung.[31] This is just what Queen Irene does in this, the third and last purifying fire in the book.

The *coniunctio* is not completely balanced, as the Queen is active and powerful while Curdie is a spectator, but it is a major point of departure for the continuing individuation which Curdie will presumably undergo—and for the dispersal of the "faint mist as of unfulfilment" which overshadows the Queen's own joy at the moment of celebration (*PC* 316).

Gwyntystorm does not become the New Jerusalem. While the eighteenth chapter of Revelation, which has such an important bearing on *The Princess and Curdie*, prophesies the ruin of Babylon, the nineteenth acclaims the triumph of justice, the marriage of the lamb and the glorious appearing of the "KING OF KINGS, AND LORD OF LORDS" (Rev.19:16); but in *The Princess and Curdie*, the New Jerusalem is not ultimately dominant in this world. After the victory over the invaders Irene and Curdie are married, and all looks set fair for as 'happy ever after' a prognosis as is feasible in a kingdom where "[t]he nation was victorious, but the people were conquered" (*PC* 313). Queen Irene, Peter, Joan and many upright people move to the city or its environs and try to transform it, but the need to bring in people from outside to form "a new and upright court" (317) is in itself an admission of incipient failure. The disjunction between the collective and individual levels of the book is never fully resolved, as is underlined by the intriguing fact that the deterioration and eventual destruction of Gwyntystorm are to some extent brought about by the allies themselves. It is Curdie who, when he discovers gold in the rock of Gwyntystorm, initiates the idea that this wealth should be mined: "As soon as he had got the king free of rogues and villains, he would have all the best and most honest miners, with his father at the head of them, to work this rock for the king" (223). Peter and the king (who appoints him general of all his mines [315]) fully concur with this plan, which for some time benefits Gwyntystorm but which, after their deaths, degenerates into a greedy exploitation that leads to the collapse of the pillars of rock supporting the city.

Because myths and fairy tales are felt to be timeless (or set in an unspecified era of the past) it is tempting to overlook MacDonald's awareness of contemporary events and the impact that they have on him; but he is very capable of siting them in myth. It is probable that the amazing, widely publicised and long-running story of the California gold rush (from 1848 until approximately 1858) played its part in the denouement of *The Princess and Curdie*. James Wilson Marshall, a carpenter, was the first to spot what he believed to be grains of gold in the soil of California—at first, loose gold and gold nuggets could be picked off the ground[32]—and even so Curdie spots gold in the surface rock of Gwyntystorm (*PC* 222). MacDonald, who abominated the pursuit of riches for their own sake, would think the unbridled greed to which gold mining gives rise after Curdie's day an all too probable development, as it had been in America. The chaotic lawlessness that characterised California before and for some time after it became part of the United States (soon after the beginning of the gold rush) has a parallel in the chaotic state of Gwyntystorm in the later stages of the king's illness; even the lynchings that occurred in California find an echo in the fate proposed for Curdie and Lina by the citizens of Gwyntystorm. We have all heard of the "miner, forty-niner"[33] who lived "in a cavern, in a canyon"—and though there were not many Clementines about in California at the time, since the swift and enormous inrush of population was mostly masculine, this suits with the aggressively masculine character of Gwyntystorm

The Downstretched Hand: Individual Development in

and the nation before the king's victory. The cavern and the canyon, not to say the miner in the song, are fortuitous—and the eventual diminution in the supply of Californian gold may have had something to say to MacDonald too. He must have heard about the gold rush, especially during his eight months' tour of America in 1872-73, and his failure actually to refer to it proves nothing; as William Raeper remarks, MacDonald's American experiences were never mentioned in his work (even his later years in Italy only figured in the first few pages of *A Rough Shaking*),[34] but they must have impressed him deeply. And "The Wreck of the Golden Mary," a story by Charles Dickens and Wilkie Collins about a ship carrying people to California to participate in the gold rush,[35] presumably made an impression too. The denouement of *The Princess and Curdie* is not an allegory of the gold rush, but it probably owes a great deal to that long-running and very public event.

The fall of Gwyntystorm is also strongly reminiscent of Samson's destruction of the great house of the Philistines in the sixteenth chapter of Judges.

> And Samson took hold of the two middle pillars upon which the house stood, and on which it was borne up. . . . And he bowed himself with all his might; and the house fell upon the lords, and upon all the people that were therein. (Judges 16:29, 30)

The catastrophe in *The Princess and Curdie*, though it is not brought about deliberately, is described with no less impact. The later, greedy king

> caused the miners to reduce the pillars which Peter and they that followed him had left standing to bear the city. . . . One day at noon, when life was at its highest, the whole city fell with a roaring crash. The cries of men and the shrieks of women went up with its dust, and then there was a great silence. (*PC* 320)

Just so the avengers summoned by the Lord to punish Tyrus—that same monarch to whom Mr. Coleman, in *At the Back of the North Wind*, bears an unfortunate resemblance—"shall break down thy walls, and destroy thy pleasant houses: and they shall lay thy stones and thy timber and thy dust in the mist of the water" (Ezekiel 26: 12).[36]

The implied taboo which has been in force ever since Curdie crossed the chasm between the dungeon and the king's wine cellar—'Don't fall into the water'—receives the ultimate violation, and the city, which has never satisfactorily resolved the imbalance between masculine and feminine, dissociated consciousness and repressed (and therefore threatening) unconscious, is finally overwhelmed. The price of failure is loss of identity, and it is expressed in a way which owes as much to the Old Testament as to Revelation; the ninth psalm, for example, says: "Thou hast destroyed the wicked, thou hast put out their name for ever and ever. . . . and thou hast destroyed cities, their memorial is perished with them" (Ps. 9:5,6). Gwyntystorm comes to just such an end:

> Where the mighty rock once towered, crowded with homes and crowned with a palace, now rushes and raves a stone-obstructed rapid of the river. All around spreads a wilderness of wild deer, and the very name of Gwyntystorm has ceased from the lips of men. (*PC* 320)

If this does not detract from the truth that gains of considerable value are made by individuals in *The Princess and Curdie*, there remains the inescapable fact that the victory of good over evil is, at least within the time frame of the book, only partial. The ending owes much to Ezekiel's prophecy of the retribution awaiting Jerusalem for its sins; in Ezekiel 14:21 the prophet, in a strong anticipation of Revelation, goes through each of the "four sore judgments," or punishments, that will be inflicted (note especially the "noisome beast") and in each case says that even if Noah, Daniel and Job were there, "they should deliver but their own souls by their righteousness" (14:14); even their sons and daughters would not be saved (14:16, 18, 20). This is reflected in the selective salvation which marks the end of *The Princess and Curdie*, but MacDonald, as befits the author of a book for the childlike (if this one fully merits that description), is somewhat more lenient than Ezekiel. The eventual redemption both of the Uglies and of the conspirators themselves is strongly intimated: "Barbara, who seemed to know of [the Queen] sometimes when nobody else had a notion whither she had gone, said she was with the dear old Uglies in the wood;" and "Curdie thought that perhaps her business might be with others there as well" (318). He himself exhibits a striking growth to maturity, and saves king and nation—but not for much more than his lifetime. Princess Irene and Curdie get married—but they have no children. Good people come to live in Gwyntystorm—but they die out, or their descendants are corrupted. The end of the book is dominated by the decline and ultimate annihilation of the city, which, in a fairy story as in hero myth, the king's victory and the royal marriage would symbolically have redeemed; there is, in fact, an amazing split

The Downstretched Hand: Individual Development in

between personal and universal symbolism here. No wonder that, at the victory banquet, Queen Irene's joy is "overshadowed by a faint mist as of unfulfilment" (316). MacDonald's creed is that true personal fulfilment is only to be found in eternity, and one senses that it will eventually follow; as the Queen herself has died and been resurrected her descendants may be expected to follow the same path, and this must be open to everyone. But all that is described on the universal level at the end of *The Princess and Curdie* is the ultimate death which is loss of identity, as symbolised by destruction, emptiness and—most of all—by the loss of the city's name.

Bruno Bettelheim, distinguishing between myth and fairy tale, says of myth that "at its end there is neither recovery nor consolation; there is no resolution of conflict, and thus no happy ending" (*The Uses of Enchantment,* 1).[37] When one reflects that the destruction of Gwyntystorm was unwittingly initiated, at least in part, by the 'good guys,' the overall impression left by the book becomes depressing. If the neglect of the city's defences is the fault of the citizens (134-135); if, like the inhabitants of Bulika in *Lilith,* they hate strangers and the poor (see *Lilith* Ch. XX111); if the citizens rush to betray their king and country to the enemy (see, e.g., *PC* 291); it is Curdie, Peter and the miners he imports who set in train the eventual collapse of Gwyntystorm. Both fairy tale and hero myth promote the triumph of good over evil by dealing with a single crisis, victory in which implies a permanent resolution; but MacDonald's sombre take on the matter in *The Princess and Curdie* is that there is no final victory in this life, and may well raise the question 'What was it all for?'

The answer is given, insofar as it is given anywhere, in George MacDonald's final fantasy, *Lilith.* Gwyntystorm foreshadows Bulika, the capital city in *Lilith,* a place which is much darker than its predecessor. The woman who, like the kindly baker's wife in Gwyntystorm, was originally a stranger to the city, tricks Vane by offering him shelter (like Derba) but then shutting him out once he has escorted her safely home (*Lilith* 172-173); he obtains bread only because someone throws it at him in mistake for a stone (168)[38]—and then can only eat it because he retreats outside the gates; and the monarch, far from being a weakened and sinned-against king, is herself the chief source of evil in the city and fills it with fear. Bulika is full of death and the threat of death, something which, until the sombre and long-deferred ending, only happens in *The Princess and Curdie* in the accepted context of a battle (and then not to the defenders). But in the original manuscript of *Lilith,* Vane, once diverted from his journey to heaven and returned to his own house, concludes by saying that "a comforter was given me, and the name of my comforter is Hope." [39] In the penultimate sentence of the book proper, he says: "I wait; asleep or awake, I wait" (*L* 359).[40]

Something of the bleak ending of *The Princess and Curdie* and the prevailing darkness of *Lilith* surely comes from the tragedies that befell the MacDonald family in the later years of the nineteenth century. *The Princess and Curdie* was written and serially published in 1877, against the background of their daughter Mary's death in April after an illness of a few years' duration—the first of their children to die. Later the picture darkened even more; Maurice died in 1879, Lilia's engagement was broken off in 1880, Grace died in 1884 and their grandchild Octavia in 1891, the year in which the MacDonalds' eldest daughter, Lilia, also died. "'What is it all for?' I should constantly be saying with Tolstoi, but for the hope of the glory of God," says MacDonald to Louisa in a letter dated July 1891.[41] But in October of that year he writes "we must remember that we are only in a sort of passing vision here, and that the real life lies beyond us . . ."[42] The tutor, looking at Diamond's body at the end of *At the Back of the North Wind*, says: "They thought he was dead. I knew that he had gone to the back of the north wind" (*ABNW* 378); and this is expanded at the end of *Lilith*, where there is a compelling account of the protagonist's joyful ascent to the heavenly kingdom—until a hand gently pushes him through a little door and he finds himself back in his library (*L* 356). In the final chapter, "The 'Endless Ending,'" Mr. Vane says: "When I wake at last into that life which, as a mother her child, carries this life in its bosom, I shall know that I wake, and shall doubt no more" (*L* 359).

While George MacDonald was writing *At the Back of the North Wind* he was presumably not thinking about *The Princess and Curdie;* he may not have been thinking about *The Princess and the Goblin* until the story of Diamond was in its later stages. But by the end of *The Princess and Curdie* there is in some sense a rounding-off of the three major fantasies, all of which end with the departure of the protagonist or protagonists on the next stage of their journey to full individuation and fulfilment. *At the Back of the North Wind* begins with The Wilderness, a compacted form of the Eden from which the Colemans are expelled and the wilderness of care into which they and their innocent dependants are precipitated. *The Princess and Curdie* ends with a desolate wilderness betokening the loss of personal (for many) and collective identity—and the previous departure of the

The Downstretched Hand

'good guys,' presumably into the transcendence of heaven, does not soften the sombre tone of the ending; nothing, indeed, could be more sombre than the loss and complete forgetting of a name, associated as that is with loss of identity. But in spite of everything there is a subliminal note of hope. Although a "stone-obstructed rapid of the river" now "rushes and raves" (*PC* 320) where Gwyntystorm once stood—an image of chaos—the "wilderness of wild deer" suggests that the wilderness, though empty, is not barren. It is an image of possession by the dark side of the unconscious, but there is still a spark of life there which intimates, however faintly, the possibility of hope for the future. We may yet begin again where we have ended—and, like Mossy and Tangle in "The Golden Key," finish by "going up to the country whence the shadows fell" (*The Light Princess and Other Fairy Tales*, 215).

"It is a strange thing that however long I may have been about a book, I am always compelled to finish it in a hurry," says MacDonald in a letter dated August 1880—but he adds immediately that "that does not mean carelessly."[43] This in no way alters the fact that the ending of *The Princess and Curdie* is an enigma.

Endnotes to Chapter 10 on page 298

Down swooped the birds upon the invaders; right in the face of man and horse they flew with swift-beating wings, blinding eyes and confounding brain. Horses reared and plunged and wheeled. All was at once in confusion. The men made frantic efforts to seize their tormentors, but not one could they touch; and they outdoubled them in numbers. Between every wild clutch came a peck of beak and a buffet of pinion in the face. Generally the bird would, with sharp-clapping wings, dart its whole body, with the swiftness of an arrow, against its singled mark, yet so as to glance aloft the same instant, and descend skimming: much as the thin stone, shot with horizontal cast of arm, having touched and torn the surface of the lake, ascends to skim, touch, and tear again. It was a storm in which the wind was birds, and the sea men.

   Ch 33, "The Battle"
   illustration by Dorothy P. Lathrop

"Come in," said the voice of the princess.

Curdie opened the door – but, to his astonishment, saw no room there. Could he have opened a wrong door? There was the great sky, and the stars, and beneath he could see nothing - only darkness. But what was that in the sky, straight in front of him? A great wheel of fire, turning and turning, and flashing out blue lights!

Chapter 8, "Curdie's Mission"
illustration by James Allen

CONCLUSION

"Out of my dark self, into the light of my consciousness" (*Lilith* 357).

"Everything which we cannot understand is a closed book of larger knowledge and blessedness, whose clasps the blessed perplexity urges us to open" ("The Voice of Job," *USS* 2, 353).

Once upon a time I had an article on George MacDonald rejected (to my intense annoyance) because the assessor felt that, as Jung postdated MacDonald, I could not have been justified in drawing on his theories. Yet, as David Holbrook says in his introduction to the Everyman edition of *Phantastes:* "We applaud our century for the surrealists, who are supposed to have opened up the landscape of the 'other world' of the unconscious. But fantasists like George MacDonald sat down to explore that world with an astonishing conviction and confidence . . ."[1] And fantasists were not alone in doing this. MacDonald was by no means the first writer to refer to the unconscious, at least by implication; if Charles Dickens, for example, writes of the dawn of individual consciousness in Pip at the beginning of *Great Expectations* (1861),[2] Jane Austen describes the possible disjunction between consciousness and the unconscious in her unfinished novel *Sanditon* as long ago as 1817, in the person of Mr. Parker: "All that he understood of himself, he readily told . . . and where he might be himself in the dark, his conversation was still giving information, to such of the Heywoods as could observe"[3]—a passage which could hardly conform more closely to Jung's dictum that "unconscious phenomena . . . manifest themselves in an individual's behaviour. An attentive observer can detect them without difficulty, while the observed person remains quite unaware of the fact that he is betraying his most secret thoughts or even things he has never thought consciously."[4] MacDonald, in "The Butcher's Bills" (1882), takes it further: "[T]here is that in every human mind which no man's neighbour, nay, no man himself, can understand" (*Stephen Archer and Other Tales*, 163).

But MacDonald is most interested in the integration of the unconscious with consciousness in the individual—something described strikingly in a passage about Euphra in *David Elginbrod* when she casts off the control which the mesmerist Von Funkelstein ('a fake stone') has exercised over her through her unconscious: "Hence

The Downstretched Hand: Individual Development in

her two lives were blended into one life; and she was no more two, but one. This indicated a mighty growth of individual being" (*DE* 419).[5] Such growth can be a life-long process: "You are but beginning to become an individual," the raven tells Mr. Vane in *Lilith* (*L* 30). And it is a process to which both author and reader can contribute. "The best thing you can do for your fellow, next to rousing his conscience, is—not to give him things to think about, but to wake things up that are in him; or say, to make him think things for himself," says MacDonald in "The Fantastic Imagination" (*Orts* 319)—as good a definition of bringing the unconscious into consciousness as one could find. And MacDonald believes in extending consciousness itself, as we see in the case of Arthur Manson, in *There and Back*, who, under the tutelage of Mr. Wingfold, the parson, develops "ten times his former consciousness; his life was ten times the size it was before" (*TB* 360-361).[6]

"I may define 'self' as the totality of the conscious and unconscious psyche, but this totality transcends our vision; it is a veritable *lapis invisibilitatis*," says Jung,[7] and George MacDonald takes this even further; it is worth reiterating that, while Jung defines the individuation process as the integration of the unconscious into consciousness,[8] which he describes as "the problem . . . of becoming whole,"[9] George MacDonald holds that individuation, which he sees in the same terms, is only a means to "the final end [of] oneness [with God]—an impossibility without it."[10] And God is involved in the individuation process from first to last; when Mr. Vane, in *Lilith*, speaks of his experiences as possibly having been a dream which came "[o]ut of my dark self, into the light of my consciousness," Hope replies that "the dark of thy own unconscious self" must have been inspired with a dream by God (*L* 357, 358).

A striking feature of George MacDonald's fantasies is the effect that they can have on readers, and this is due, in part, to their reaching parts of the unconscious that other works (and other writers) do not always reach. Not all readers experience the life-changing conversion of spirit famously undergone by C.S. Lewis after reading *Phantastes*: "A few hours later I knew that I had crossed a great frontier," he writes in the preface to his *George MacDonald: An Anthology*. After describing his consequent escape from the "darker and more evil forms" of Romanticism, he says that at first he

> was only aware that if this new world was strange, it was also homely and humble; that if this was a dream, it was a dream in which one at least felt strangely vigilant; that the whole book

George MacDonald's Major Fantasies for Children

had about it a sort of cool, morning innocence, and also, quite unmistakably, a certain quality of Death, *good* Death. What it actually did to me was to convert, even to baptize (that was where the Death came in) my imagination.[11]

G.K. Chesterton was at least as profoundly changed by reading *The Princess and the Goblin*, as I've already noted, and it is reasonable to assume that other people have been influenced to a greater or lesser degree by MacDonald's works. He himself was very much alive to the potential of literature to transform the reader, and it is worth remembering that the rationale of *Adela Cathcart* (1864), a precursor of the popular modern book club, is therapeutic story-telling.

When lecturing on children's literature I occasionally came across students who found the beginning of *The Princess and the Goblin* frightening; probably the same students who found *Alice's Adventures in Wonderland* frightening, and for the same reason—that they could sense the underlying preoccupation with death in both works. A much more peaceful, though powerful approach to death is found in *At the Back of the North Wind*, the story of a young boy who makes friends with death, dies, and enters eternity. The experience of an undergraduate who had recently been touched by a family tragedy bears this out. A week before their wedding her brother and his fiancée were driving round a corner when they suddenly came upon a line of stationary traffic. The last vehicle had poles lashed to its roof; they smashed through the windscreen of her brother's car, killing him outright and sending his fiancée to hospital. She proved to be brain-dead, but her father, who could not accept the situation, would not allow the ventilator to be switched off. Day after day my student sat with her brother's fiancée, reading the text we were studying at the time—*At the Back of the North Wind*. "There is such peace in that book," she said.

George MacDonald's works—and not only the fantasies—also raise questions, of differing levels of seriousness, in some readers' minds. One that teases me is, why does he never mention Jane Austen? I can well imagine that her novels would not strike a sympathetic chord with MacDonald, for although she is, like him, a profoundly religious writer, her approach is entirely different and he might have found it heavy going to penetrate the sophistication, the social setting and so forth —especially as he considered 'society' to be a promoter of the superficial and worthless. In *Weighed and Wanting* (1882), for example, Hester Raymount's vocation—to be with and at the service of the poor—is threatened by the prospect of marriage to Lord Gartley, who expects her to abandon what he considers her idiosyncratic pursuits in order to undertake the less onerous duties of a lady in society; and in *Castle Warlock*, published in the same year, MacDonald goes so far as to say that the "all-pervading, ill-odoured phantom called Society, is but the ghost of a false God" (*CW* 357). Since he was an extremely courteous person MacDonald would never have lent himself to the gratuitous disparagement of another author,[12] though he was prepared to voice disapproval privately where he felt it was really called for—in the case of Thackeray, for example ("that awful *Vanity Fair*" [*GMHW* 393])—but I had begun to wonder if he had ever read any of Jane Austen's works; if he would have thought reading a novel of the "By a Lady" type a waste of his time and energy; when the answer presented itself in *Weighed and Wanting* aforesaid. What should appear, in the discussion between Major Marvel and Hester of her relationship with Lord Gartley, and especially the later discussion between Miss Vavasor (Lord Gartley's aunt) and Hester of her engagement to him, but a clear, though inverted echo of the encounter between Elizabeth Bennet and Lady Catherine de Bourgh, in *Pride and Prejudice*, about Elizabeth's possible engagement to Darcy![13] I suspect, however, that one sample was enough, and that *Pride and Prejudice* was the only Jane Austen novel MacDonald ever read; had he got as far as *Mansfield Park* he might have felt differently.[14]

More important questions need to be asked, though not necessarily answered, about the enigmas that sometimes present themselves in MacDonald's fantasies. As a rule George MacDonald is both consistent and profound; but where a discrepancy occurs the profundity does not necessarily diminish. Occasionally there appear to be simple glitches in proofreading, as when Cripple Jim is at one point denominated "Joe" in *At the Back of the North Wind* (255). But a discrepancy sometimes indicates that MacDonald is inviting the reader to consider, or even to participate in, a mystery, as in the case of Princess Irene's ring in *The Princess and the Goblin* (not even mentioned in *The Princess and Curdie*). A mystery at least as great (though few readers notice it on the conscious level) is Queen Irene's total silence, throughout the book, on the subject of the goblins—and the total silence of the goblins about the Queen. And many other unanswered questions—ranging from possible oversights to intriguing puzzles to numinous mysteries—are raised in the three books under discussion. Some of them should simply be left unanswered; it would be as inappropriate to inquire too minutely into Irene's education[15] as to ask who feeds the goldfish at Mole End in Kenneth Grahame's *The Wind in the Willows* when Mole has left. But the "very large birds" who attempt to dance round Curdie and the "dreary old hawthorn tree" in *The Princess and Curdie* (121, 117) rouse questions in Curdie's own mind: "All the time he had kept doubting every now and then whether they could really be birds, and the sleepier he got, the more he imagined them something else" (122-123)—a mystery perhaps more explicable, or at least more explorable to the reader than to Curdie, though no answer is ever given.[16] And why, in *The Princess and the Goblin*, does Peter not search for Curdie when he is missing under the mountain for two nights and the intervening day? It's true that before Curdie's first solitary night in the mine—with his father's permission (*PG* 68)—Peter says he won't stay with his son because he wants to visit the parson (69), which probably indicates a sense of the need for spiritual guidance in an atmosphere of increasing menace (though Curdie has not told him about his encounter with goblins and their creatures on the mountain the evening before, nor that the goblins came up to the cottage during the night [65]). But paternal concern would surely prompt an eventual search.

Greater questions—questions about the meaning of life—can be asked and, if not always answered, at least accommodated in a nonthreatening way in the comparative simplicity of a children's book, which need not deal, for example, with such often fraught areas of adult life as romantic relationships or sexual immorality. "Why is why?" Diamond murmurs over and over to himself one night when he is falling asleep (*ABNW* 176); but in *At the Back of the North Wind* questions about the meaning of life are approached with trust. In the adult novel *Malcolm* (1875), on the other hand, the mad laird Stephen Stewart, with his experience of living with deformity and of being rejected by and terrified of his mother, is tormented by the same mystery. His frequent saying, almost a refrain, of "I dinna ken whaur I cam frae," with its initial elaboration of "I dinna ken whaur ye cam frae. I dinna ken whaur onybody comes frae" (*M* 8), echoes Jesus's condemnation of those who are to be cast into hell—"I know you not whence ye are."[17] And this and the laird's bewilderment, as even on his death bed he says "I kenna whaur I'm gaein' till" (*M* 404), encapsulates two of the fundamental questions of human life—'Who am I?' and 'What does it all mean?'

The laird—definitely one of the childlike for whom MacDonald declares that he writes ("The Fantastic Imagination," *Orts* 317)—occasionally goes to the village school and sits with the children in the hope of finding the answer; and for him the promise of an answer to his final question—"Wull I ever ken whaur I cam frae?" (*M* 404)—comes

The Downstretched Hand: Individual Development in

in his last moment, when he sees "the bonny man!"—Jesus (405). The same question is asked in *At the Back of the North Wind*. "Where did you come from, baby dear?" sings Diamond to his new baby sister. But in the context of a children's book, and from a background of loving security, he can express her answer: "God thought about me, and so I grew" (*ABNW* 324). "'You never made that song, Diamond,'" said his mother (325); and the implication (though not Martha's meaning) is that it comes from the ultimate mystery—God himself.

In *At the Back of the North Wind* George MacDonald is teaching the child reader about death—a reality far more immediately present to children of his own time than to children of to-day, but of course of universal relevance. The whole book is focused on death, from the title onwards; not too obviously, for MacDonald does not want the child reader to approach the subject with fear, so the meaning of the title becomes progressively apparent. The goal of the book is the transcendent world of eternity, which, though always immanent, must ultimately be reached by dying—and MacDonald's aim is to engender, through Diamond, the trust that enables death to be approached with peace. Except for the mystery of God himself there is no greater mystery than death, and hence the importance of the little mysteries which teach the need to live with unanswered questions—but which also keep possibility open. They are the antechambers of eternity, just as the blue cave in the iceberg[18] which carries Diamond on the final part of his journey to the North Pole is the antechamber of the ice ridge which surrounds the country at North Wind's back: "He could see the side of the blue cave through [North Wind's] very heart" (*ABNW* 108). And North Wind encourages him: "Just go straight on, and you will come all right [i.e. all will be well with you]. You'll find me on the doorstep" (109). Death must ultimately be experienced alone; no family member, no friend, no witness, no author can accompany the dying person when the moment comes, and nothing can make the transition from death to eternity less than awe-inspiring. But MacDonald makes it appear exactly that: awe-inspiring and not terrifying.

The *Princess* books also treat of the mystery of death, and in both there are what might be called preliminary mysteries which resonate with the unconscious. One such, in both *Princess* books, is the relationship between Curdie and his father, the symbolic, as well as the psychological importance of which is indicated from Curdie's first appearance when, asked who he is, he responds not by giving his name but by saying "I'm Peter's son" (*PG* 52). The enigma becomes more apparent in *The Princess and Curdie*. Except that Peter gives Curdie fatherly advice from time to time, their relationship approximates to that described by Bruno Bettelheim in what he calls "the oldest fairy tale," originally found in an Egyptian papyrus dating from 1250 B.C. and, though largely forgotten, surviving in many versions. This is a tale of two brothers—a stay-at-home brother and an adventurous brother who eventually needs to be rescued by his peer; "one typical feature of these stories is that some magic life token, which symbolizes the identity of the two, indicates to one when the other is in serious danger, and this sets the rescue going," says Bettelheim.[19]

In *The Princess and Curdie* the relationship is vertical rather than horizontal, but it works in the same way. Here the "magic life token"— exceptional in MacDonald—is the emerald which the "Mother of Light" (*PC* 70) pulls out of the cavern floor to give to Peter as a sign of his son's changing fortunes; if not an identification, it implies a strong connection between them. And not long afterwards Peter, after feeling Curdie's fire-taught hands, refuses to allow his own to be felt. Would there not be equal contact in either case? The mystery extends to the hands of the king, for, though Curdie strokes them, they do not give rise to any thoughts about the king's nature. In fact, Curdie, Peter and the king all have, in a sense, the same hands—a case of "I and my Father are one" (John 10:30). It may be, too, that the nameless page who repents and comes over to the king's side does not have his hands felt because they are fundamentally the same as Curdie's, only weaker; Curdie accepts him on the housemaid's fairly lukewarm recommendation—"there is one of the pages I don't take to be a bad fellow" (*PC* 252).[20] The absence of a name probably does not have quite the same meaning here as it does in the case of Diamond's baby brother, in *At the Back of the North Wind*, who, as "the duck of diamonds" (*ABNW* 164), is essentially going to take Diamond's place, for the unnamed page always trails behind Curdie. As he represents the limited development Curdie would have attained if he had made the 'wrong' decision and left with the king at the end of *The Princess and the Goblin*, his subsequent regeneration—he stands up for the housemaid against the other servants (*PC* 255-256) and conducts a one-man intelligence service for the defenders (292)— and his promotion (still unnamed) to knighthood, are dependent on Curdie's achievements. The one thing the page cannot do is lead—and leadership is essential for the protagonist.

The moral superiority of Curdie's decision, at the end of *The Princess and the Goblin*, to stay with his parents rather than to go with the king seems on the face of it extremely doubtful, in spite of Princess Irene's strong endorsement—"That's right, Curdie!"—followed, as it is, by the king's own approval: "I too think you are right, Curdie" (*PG* 304). Why should the king, set on putting the ablest and best into office and removing anyone incapable or unjust (164), give him an invitation which it would be wrong to accept? In fact it demonstrates that, although MacDonald writes for the childlike rather than for children, *The Princess and the Goblin* is on one level very much a children's book (after all, it did start life in a children's journal and, in the serialised version, children actually talk to the editor, i.e. the author). Irene and Curdie mature considerably in the course of it, but in the end they have to do what is still appropriate; revert to their status as children and remain with their respective parents. "I can't get on very well without you," says Curdie to Peter and Joan (305), and he is not just being polite.

It is, however, a position with hazards of its own for Curdie. At the beginning of *The Princess and Curdie* he is in danger of succumbing to a regression which is the prelude to a false maturity: "He was gradually changing into a commonplace man" (*PC* 22).[21] Had Curdie gone with the king, he would have had Irene's companionship and would not have degenerated in this way; but on the other hand he would not have shot the Queen's pigeon, experienced forgiveness, been attacked by his unconscious demons or been given Lina and the Uglies to help him in his mission—in other words he would not have brought so much of his unconscious into consciousness and therefore would have been a shallower and less integrated person.

Some symbolic developments in *The Princess and Curdie* are not followed up, or not followed up consistently. In the dark cellar-dungeon in Gwyntystorm Curdie notices that Lina's eyes have started to emit light (162-165, esp. 163). This is a definite sign of her rise into consciousness, and it is very convenient for the purpose of digging a hole in the dark and, later, facilitating the passage of the Uglies across the chasm between dungeon and wine cellar. But not much is made of the change thereafter. Although Lina is with him, Curdie still has to light his "very little bit" of candle to examine their stolen pie in the dark cellar (177). And when they go up the stairs and into the hall he is very conscious of the lack of light (178-179); in the sculleries he again lights a candle, "but only to see ugly sights" (180). But Lina, however great her symbolic value, is essentially a minor character (if such she may be called) and MacDonald may simply be making the occasional slip. What is much more important (and much stranger) is that although Curdie actually takes the housemaid's hand (246) he does not realise that she is the old princess—she whose hand was the first he ever felt and which had been "just the same to his fire-taught touch as it was to his eyes" (104). He tests the housemaid by getting her to look Lina in the face without crying out: "Now I know you are a true woman," he says (226). MacDonald has prepared us for this to some extent: "Those who know me *well*, know me whatever new dress or shape or name I may be in; and by and by you will have learned to do so too," the old princess tells Curdie much earlier when they are in the cavern (78), and Curdie still has a lot of growing to do; but it is still strange.

Diamond, in *At the Back of the North Wind*, lacks Curdie's shadow side (not completely conquered after the old princess gives him absolution for having shot her bird). MacDonald, however, does not find goodness at all unrealistic: "[W]hatever the demand of the age, I insist that that which *ought* to be presented to its beholding is the common good uncommonly developed, and that not because of its rarity, but because it is truer to humanity," he writes in *Sir Gibbie* (*SG* 49), and he describes Gibbie Galbraith, when a child, as "a rarity, but a rarity in the right direction, and therefore a being with whom humanity has the greater need to be made acquainted" (48).[22] His dumb hero is called a "divine idiot" (288), a term more or less equivalent to "God's baby" but which can only be used by the narrator, just as "God's baby," in *At the Back of the North Wind*, can only be said by other characters.[23] The shadow in Gibbie's case is erroneously attributed to him by ignorant gossip, for he is for some time referred to as a "broonie" or "brownie" (113, 127 et al)[24]—and, because of the animal skins he has been in the habit of wearing, as a "beast loon" or "beast boy" (174, 196 et al). In a sense he conflates (though innocently) the images of a goblin and a goblin creature, linking this book, on the level of imagery, with *The Princess and the Goblin*.[25] The real shadow Gibbie bears is the shadow of the evil of others, focussed at one point, when he has been unjustly beaten, in "a great cross marked in two cruel stripes on his back" (141). Another character to whom a hole in the wall is important at one stage of his life (89, 102)—and he is the only one to go in and out through a catflap (85, 89, 101)—Gibbie is a 're-echoing' of Diamond for adult readers.[26] Although, unlike Diamond, he reaches adulthood and marriage and comes into his title and estate, he is set apart by his dumbness, as Diamond is by being thought "silly." There is, however, a major miracle in Gibbie's case—one which confirms his sanctity.

The Downstretched Hand: Individual Development in

Looking down at the flood that at one point threatens to overwhelm his adopted home, "'O Jesus Christ!' he cried" (*SG* 225). This does not, however, betoken the cure of the character once described as a "live silence" (297). Donal Grant's earlier comment that "the cratur's as dumb's a worum" remains true thereafter (150), and the stupendous aberration passes almost unnoticed.

There is a composite echo of Diamond (with a shadow component) in Mark Raymount and Moxy Franks, two characters in *Weighed and Wanting*. Mark, the son of the house, lives upstairs; Moxy, son of the wretched family of acrobats hiding in the cellar, represents Mark's shadow[27]—not evil (though Moxy's professional title is "the Serpent of the Prairies" [*WW* 420])—but fear: "Mother, don't put me in a hole," "Mother, don't let them put me in a hole," "Don't put me in the hole," Moxy says several times when he is dying of smallpox (422-424), and he is not immediately reassured when one of his brothers reminds him that "Jesus Christ was put in the hole . . . . but he didn't mind it much, and soon got out again" (423). Ultimately, however, Moxy says "Mother . . . you *may* put me in the hole" (433), which MacDonald describes as "that conquest over the fear of death . . . with which the child-spirit passed into wide spaces" (445). Mark Raymount dies too—he dies upstairs and Moxy downstairs—but his resemblance to Diamond is more obvious. Martha, in *At the Back of the North Wind*, says that Diamond has "been at his old trick of walking in his sleep" (*ABNW* 322); he feels at one point as if he "could almost fly," thinks of "those precious dreams he had so often had, in which he floated about on the air at will" (358), and is described at various points as "God's baby." Mark's surname of Raymount, in *Weighed and Wanting*, is a compound of "Raymond" and "The Mound" in *At the Back of the North Wind;* he walks in his sleep (*WW* 537-538), says "I feel so light sometimes, I think I could fly" (549) and is described as "a Christ-child, if ever child might bear the name" (604). "I am going to your father and my father—to our great father," he tells Mr. Raymount when he is dying (608), and the risen Jesus said "I ascend unto my Father, and your Father; and to my God, and your God" (John 20:17).[28]

In *The Princess and Curdie* there is no such declaration of faith. But in MacDonald's fantasies there is always a departure for an unknown but trusted future where, presumably, the answer to all questions will be found—what Colin Manlove describes as "a sense of approaching promise" (*Christian Fantasy*, 175), best summed up in *Robert Falconer* (1868): "We were going on into the universe—home to the house of our Father" (*RF* 555). This is the whole drift of *At the Back of the North*

George MacDonald's Major Fantasies for Children

Wind. So great is the immanence of resurrection throughout that the very first sentence speaks of the ultimate world of the spirit: "I have been asked to tell you about the back of the North Wind," says the narrator [1]. In *The Princess and the Goblin* the heroine goes to the intermediate stage of her earthly father's house, though one senses a huge drive to ultimate transcendence through the agency of the Queen. The difference in *The Princess and Curdie* is that, although the principal characters transcend this world, the reader is left contemplating what remains behind.

MacDonald has brought more "hidden things" to light than most of us, but not everything important is brought to the light of consciousness, or not immediately. Roderick McGillis speaks of the "instructive ambiguity" of the *Princess* books,[29] and although it is certainly true, as William Raeper says, that his symbols "begin a process which acts on the unconscious mind of the reader" (*George MacDonald*, 202*)*, this process may take a long time to reach his conscious mind—if it ever does. The symbolic and thematic overspill which often occurs between MacDonald's books, and especially between those close to each other in date of composition, is particularly compelling.[30] It is not surprising that the semi-autobiographical *Ranald Bannerman's Boyhood*, which appeared just after *At the Back of the North Wind*, incorporates some of the images both of its predecessor and of its close successor, *The Princess and the Goblin* (in doing which it reveals the blurring of realism and fantasy which is often a feature of MacDonald's work). The cradle harnessed to two broken chairs which Diamond drives at the beginning of *At the Back of the North Wind* stems from a conscious memory on the author's part; when MacDonald was six a brother, John MacKay, died in infancy, and it seems probable that the empty cradle in *At the Back of the North Wind* is a symbolic reflection of this loss—none the less important because it is unlikely to make much impact on the conscious level. MacDonald cannot be more specific about the death of a baby because the plot builds up to the carefully prepared climax of Diamond's own death, but the subliminal suggestion that a baby has died plays a part in this preparation. The account in *Ranald Bannerman's Boyhood* echoes the loss of MacDonald's little brother more directly: "Not only were mother and baby gone, but the cradle was gone too," says Ranald of the moment when he realises that his little brother is dead (*RBB* 16). In the fantasies, the loss is divided in two—the baby has died in *At the Back of the North Wind* and the mother in *The Princess and the Goblin*.

The Downstretched Hand: Individual Development in

Robert Falconer, very close to *At the Back of the North Wind* and *The Princess and the Goblin* in date of composition—it was published in book form in 1868—contains many images and situations which foreshadow these fantasies. I've already mentioned the two horses, Red Rorie and Black Geordie, the first of a veritable equine procession in MacDonald's books; and "[t]he great iron steamer" which eventually carries Robert and his father to a watery grave (*RF* 566)—itself foreshadowed within the book by the image of the rising sun as a "ship of glory" (227) and, at one point, by the recurring mental image of a boat with no-one on board, waiting to bear [Robert] out on "the sea of the unknown" (229)—reappears in *At the Back of the North Wind* as the ship sunk by North Wind on the night of the great storm, also foreshadowed by the sinking of the Ning-po in *Guild Court*. The high incidence of ship-sinkings, particularly in MacDonald's early works, stems in all probability from a recent maritime disaster—for public events resonated with George MacDonald as well as personal ones, as is consistent with his belief that individuality develops in a universal context. In 1854 the steamship SS Arctic, on a return journey from Liverpool to New York, was rammed by another ship in foggy conditions off the Canadian coast and sank with the loss of about 350 people, including every woman and child on board. The news, sent by telegraph, soon filled newspapers on both sides of the Atlantic, and the calamity, which remained in the public consciousness for decades, had a similar impact to that of the sinking of the Titanic in 1912. [31]

Robert Falconer and *At the Back of the North Wind* were not alone among MacDonald's early books in echoing this tragedy,[32] probably deepened for MacDonald by his own love of the sea; in his first novel, *David Elginbrod* (1863), a sinking ship already appears as a figure of speech—"the old ship gone down in the quiet ocean of Time" (*DE* 451)—but there is no actual shipwreck, as there is in *Guild Court* (1868), where it is a tragic plot-changer, and in *Robert Falconer*, where it is the culmination of Robert's completed life-search. These last, however, are not children's books and so there is no escaping boat, carrying someone with a part still to play in the story, as there is in *At the Back of the North Wind* (99)—a positive feature which is also found in *Alec Forbes of Howglen* (1865), not a children's book but one in which the detailed account ends with the hero's attainment of full manhood. Here fears of the loss of the *Sea Horse*, together with Alec's return and his description of what had happened, are all compacted into the last few chapters—but foreshadowed throughout the book,[33] especially by Alec's and his friend Curlie's boat-building and by the drowning of

Kate Fraser in the sea of which she has always had an obsessive fear. The shipwreck in *Alec Forbes of Howglen* echoes the icy conditions of the disaster of 1854 and prefigures Diamond's penetration into the land enclosed by the ice ridge at North Wind's back, though in a more threatening fashion—for Alec, after a great iceberg has wrecked the *Sea Horse*, eventually finds himself alone in a snowy waste with a real prospect of death. His earlier discovery of Annie Anderson, asleep and almost dead of cold in his snow hut, foreshadows this in its turn (*AFH* 79)—and Margaret, in *David Elginbrod*, becomes trapped in the snow and would have slept the sleep of death but for being rescued by Hugh Sutherland (*DE* 85).

The Princess and the Goblin, too, is foreshadowed in earlier books. *David Elginbrod*, for example, boasts two rings—one diamond and one crystal—which were mysteriously stolen; the diamond ring had belonged to Hugh Sutherland's father, the crystal ring (of sinister significance) had once belonged to the ill-omened and long-deceased Lady Euphrasia. The slightly later *Guild Court* (1868) features a rose diamond ring that Lucy Burton has inherited from her mother; but in this adult novel (for if the children's fantasies are not intended solely for children, some of the novels are not intended for children at all), the ring becomes for a while the focus of guilt and disloyalty (though not hers). And Irene's thread, in *The Princess and the Goblin*, is also prefigured; not only by the metaphorical "spider's thread" envisioned by Robert Falconer in the novel of that title (*RF* 399), but by the more daunting image of the "invisible cable" with which, in *Guild Court*, Mrs. Worboise holds her son Thomas (*GC* 13)—and the "cable of Love" which connects Thomas with Lucy's heart (240).

Perhaps the most important foreshadowing of *The Princess and the Goblin* is the value attached to peace in *Robert Falconer*, focused especially in Robert's meditations in the Alps (*RF* 396-97) and, in *The Princess and the Goblin*, embodied in the name 'Irene.' Mary St. John, the Falconers' next-door neighbour, is in some ways a prelude to the Queen. She offers piano lessons to Robert (a "rough diamond" in his boyhood [198]), and, to reach her, he goes "upstairs to the mysterious door" that connects the two houses, but approaches the "wondrous door" three times before he dares to go through and ascend a further stair to "the paradise of Miss St. John's room" (197), also described as "the chamber of enchantment" (201) in the chapter entitled "The Gates of Paradise." The sacred association of her name,[34] plus an age difference of ten years, suggest the reverence inherent in Robert's "worshipping regard" of Mary St. John—"He no more dreamed of

The Downstretched Hand: Individual Development in

marrying Miss St. John than of marrying his forbidden grandmother" (331). His actual grandmother, however (a total contrast to what we find in *The Princess and the Goblin*), opposes any music other than psalms to such an extent that she not only burns Robert's violin but, when she guesses that he is finding musical solace with Miss St. John, she investigates the "door of bliss" and has it walled up (201)—thus turning it, from Robert's side, into "the living tomb of his [dead] mother's vicar on earth" (201).

Sometimes it is possible, like Mrs. Peterson in *The Princess and the Goblin*, to disentangle the thread—that is, to find what underlies certain images and situations; but the ending of *The Princess and Curdie* is particularly puzzling. As I've noted, I believe that the widely publicised Californian gold rush of the late 1840s, which to MacDonald would have seemed very negative in character, played its part in the denouement. But although the violence and still more the apparent hopelessness of the ending may be a shock, MacDonald does not spring it upon the reader totally without preparation. For one thing the whole tone of the book is different from that of the two earlier fantasies: "Crossing over into *The Princess and Curdie* is like entering into another country," as William Raeper says (*George MacDonald*, 329). There is no mentor or reassuring adult friend (Diamond has three, not counting his parents—though the tutor is perhaps more of a witness—and Irene has the all-powerful assistance of the Queen). In *The Princess and Curdie* the old princess will not even give precise guidance (*PC* 104-105). She sends help in the shape of Lina, but Curdie has to be his own mentor, as he has to be his own horse, and the reassurance so palpable in *At the Back of the North Wind* and *The Princess and the Goblin* is stripped away. The rift between king and people never really heals, and the king (acting on Curdie's advice!) has worsened it by giving up on loyalty, which involves warm community relationships, and seeking independence, which can end in isolation—and which ultimately precipitates the destruction of the city. In the final chapters, just when the reader is accustomed to expect the victory of good over evil, there is disappointment; the victory, which should be both personal and collective, is only on the personal level of the king and his followers. "The nation was victorious, but the people were conquered," says MacDonald after the battle (*PC* 313), and the split in the collective sphere betokens future disaster. Furthermore, the eventual death of Irene and Curdie, without children to succeed them, puts the story at the dark end of the spectrum of myth.

Yet although MacDonald seems almost to despair of this world in *The Princess and Curdie*, he cannot let it go. This shows when he later "echoes" and develops Barbara, Derba's granddaughter, in his novel *There and Back* (1891)—a title which in itself suggests his belief in the circular trend of developments in this life,[35] and therefore in the persistence of hope. The heroine, another Barbara, is very popular; "everybody liked Barbara," he says, and so does he (*TB* 81).[36] Her background—she comes from New Zealand[37]—means that she is refreshingly free of the petty restrictions of social convention. Furthermore, "[s]he seemed to regard every one as of her own family. People were her property—hers to love! . . . She wanted to know what people thought and felt and imagined. . . . She seemed to understand what the animals were thinking, and what the flowers were feeling" (81), and at one point she says "I think I *am* happiness" (252). The openness, curiosity and affectionate nature of little Barbara in *The Princess and Curdie* (with a touch of Irene in *The Princess and the Goblin*) are extended, for this Barbara is growing up; but the connection is not lost. Maintained by her childlike appearance—"so small that she looked fragile" (82), with "almost baby-like cheeks" and "grace, more child-like than womanly" (108), "the little colonial girl" (216) is as rare and special as the child whose namesake she seems to be. At one point MacDonald is almost fatuous in his enthusiasm; Lady Ann (the arch-villain of the piece) "saw a sudden radiance light up the face of Barbara, and change its expression, from that of a lady rightfully angry and a little scornful, to that of a child-angel" (220). Barbara is perhaps best summed up, in MacDonald's view, by what he says of her when she first appears: "So small and so bright, the little lady looked a very diamond of life" (45).[38]

But this was for the future. The bleak ending of *The Princess and Curdie* remains a mystery which must be confronted (I wholeheartedly sympathise with Margery Fisher's indignation that one abridged version has simply omitted the offending finale).[39] The book straddles the genres of hero myth and fairy story, and, as Bruno Bettelheim tells us, the ending in myth is nearly always tragic[40]—but this does not help to elucidate its meaning. What is sure is that the book is about the collective and not just the individual; Curdie's mission, as he eventually discovers, is not only to save the king's life but to make the reform of the nation possible. In *The Miracles of Our Lord*, MacDonald says: "The nation cannot change save as its members change; and the few who begin that change are the elect of that nation."[41] Curdie begins, though he cannot complete that change, and he is one of the elect; but not until his eventual recognition of the old princess at the royal banquet—this time when she pours wine for him and looks him in the eyes (316)—does he realise his own potential as fully as is possible in this world. The revelation acknowledges the divine associations of the old princess, for it echoes the revelation of the risen Jesus to the disciples at Emmaus: "[H]e was known of them in breaking of bread" (Luke 24:35), an echo of the Last Supper (see, e.g., Luke 22:17-18). The Queen comes into her own; but even now "[her] joy [is] overshadowed by a faint mist as of unfulfilment" (*PC* 316)—that is, the story is incomplete.

On the collective level the city represents those instinctual drives of human nature which make against individuation—represented by what the prophet Jeremiah would describe as "brutish" men (Jer.10:8 et al). He proclaims God's word against Babylon: "I will make drunk her princes, and her wise men, her captains, and her rulers, and her mighty men; and they shall sleep a perpetual sleep, and not wake" (Jer. 51:57). Perpetual sleep is not in question in Gwyntystorm, for the future redemption of the conspirators is hinted at—but there is a lot of sleeping in its most incapacitating sense before the end of the book, and this symbolises a lack of enlightenment. Without enlightenment there can be no individuation, without individuation there can be no love, and without love there can be no collective integration, or community—so the city is destroyed. But Queen Irene is not destroyed; Derba and Barbara are not destroyed; the king, Curdie and Irene are not destroyed; nor are Peter and Joan, the page, Sir Bronzebeard, the Uglies, or any citizens with honest human hands, whether already living in Gwyntystorm or brought in from the outside—or even the conspirators, who Curdie implies are visited by Queen Irene in the wood as are "the dear old Uglies" (Barbara's description, 318).

And if there is hope for the conspirators there is hope for everyone: "MacDonald's world," says Bonnie Gaarden, "is full of individuals who are just beginning on journeys toward perfection that might take millennia" (*The Christian Goddess*, 160). In *The Princess and Curdie* MacDonald does not give the powerful and beautiful description to be found in *Robert Falconer* of what the irresistible fire of God's love will do for sinners in hell, where they will be brought to see for themselves those truths they have been trying all their lives to evade (*RF* 447-448). The blank left at the end of *The Princess and Curdie* is far more forbidding than the death that closes *Robert Falconer*, as if the author has given up on his creation, or God on his world.[42] But the menace of extinction which is implied in the final paragraph is mitigated by the fact that all the characters known to the reader have already left the city. They have died—but death has already been transcended in Queen Irene; and, as MacDonald says in *The Hope of the Gospel*: "When we are true children, if not the world, then the universe will be our home" ("Jesus in the World," *HG* 52). And at the end of the Book of Ezekiel, to which there are many allusions in *The Princess and Curdie* (and some in the earlier fantasies), the prophecies of the destruction of Israel, Jerusalem, King Tyrus etc. conclude with the promised restoration of the city, the name of which, we are told in the final verse of the book, will be "The LORD is there" (Ezek. 48:35).

Although the environs of Gwyntystorm become "a wilderness of wild deer" (*PC* 320), we have already seen that a wilderness can be a beginning which it is possible eventually to outgrow, as happens in the case of Diamond in *At the Back of the North Wind*—though the Colemans' estate is a wilderness more in name than in fact; the sort of contrived wilderness one finds in *The Flight of the Shadow* (1891), itself an echo of a fashion for such wildernesses going back to the previous century: "Miss Bennet, there seemed to be a prettyish kind of a little wilderness on one side of your lawn," says Lady Catherine de Bourgh in *Pride and Prejudice* (1813).[43] And MacDonald goes out of his way to express his sense of the possibilities of this fashion. Not only is the wilderness in *The Flight of the Shadow* (the name of the narrator, significantly, is Mrs. Day) introduced by a passage reminiscent of the beginning of Diamond's dream of the stars in *At the Back of the North Wind*—"the roses, both wild and tame, that grew together in the wilderness!" says the narrator (*FS* 80)[44]—but Mrs. Day's uncle had made the wilderness himself according to the plan laid out by Lord St. Albans in his essay "On Gardens" (81), a passage which MacDonald quotes at length (81-82) and of which Mrs. Day says: "The passage concerning the wilderness, gave me, and still gives me so much delight, that I will transplant it like a rose-bush into this wilderness of mine [the book], hoping it will give like pleasure to my reader" (81).

The wilderness of wild deer in *The Princess and Curdie* is made of sterner stuff; not a horticultural conceit, but a terrain which owes nothing to human input and is uncontrolled—much more, in short, like an ending. Yet there is a connection and a progression. Diamond's dream, in *At the Back of the North Wind* (some time after the chapter headed "Diamond Makes A Beginning," in which he starts to engage in a practical way with the world) begins with "the old garden" (*ABNW* 232), but soon changes into unknown territory full of roses—and there is a "thin rosy vapour which hung over all the wilderness." Diamond

The Downstretched Hand: Individual Development in

"wandered on and on, wondering when it would come to an end" (233); and though this one ends in the region of the stars (a place of beginnings at this point), it is a stage in that evolution of the unknown which, in another context, could become truly wild. But this, in its turn, can symbolise enormous possibility. Mr. Christopher, in *Weighed and Wanting*, says: "God's beginnings do not *look* like his endings, but they *are* like" (*WW* 426)—and the reverse may be the case. If the end of *The Princess and Curdie* seems disappointingly definite, with none of the 'happily ever after' feeling that would have characterised a fairy tale, Richard Tuke (later Lestrange), in *There and Back*, has the opposite experience as a reader. He begins his acquaintance with Coleridge by reading "Christabel"—"and never again had he been so keenly aware of disappointment as when he came to the end . . . and found that it was not there" (*TB* 121). He next turns to *The Rime of the Ancient Mariner*, and is delighted by a poem the end of which revisits the beginning in such a way as to make a complete circle comprehending huge inner development (though it has to be said that the mariner is condemned to travel the world repeating his story at intervals).

The last chapter of *The Princess and Curdie* is uncompromisingly entitled "The End," which implies finality, whereas the last chapter of *Lilith*—another challenging work—is entitled "The 'Endless Ending,'" which implies continuation (the very last word of *Lilith A*, the original manuscript of *Lilith*, is "Hope" [539]).[45] But, as Roderick McGillis observes:

> On the final page of *The Princess and Curdie* MacDonald writes, 'The End', but the reader catches the irony: the end is a beginning. Just as the book begins with a lyric expression of the world's geological beginnings . . . it comes full circle to an expression of yet another beginning. The wilderness of wild deer and the raving river of the book's final paragraph are, in the age of Darwin, a sign of renewal, of new beginnings. Creation begins anew in an unpeopled world. The possibilities of hope fill this as yet untainted wild. MacDonald's imagination is apocalyptic; the conclusion of *The Princess and Curdie* is what MacDonald calls in his sermon, 'The Consuming Fire', a 'partial' revelation. In a universe of infinite meaning, created by an infinite God, all revelations must be partial, encouragements to keep us on the look-out for further revelations.[46]

What we have in *The Princess and Curdie* is indeed a partial revelation—the Last Judgement without the Second Coming. The only recourse is to do what Anodos does in *Phantastes* and Mr. Vane in *Lilith*—what

George MacDonald's Major Fantasies for Children

George MacDonald did in the last five years of his life when, after a stroke, he simply stopped talking—and that is to wait. "I can't feel quite sure yet," says Diamond on the question of whether North Wind exists in her own right or is a creation of his own brain. "You must wait a while for that," North Wind replies (*ABNW* 365). Even Queen Irene, in *The Princess and the Goblin,* has to wait: "I've been waiting for you, and indeed getting a little anxious about you," she says when Irene returns from rescuing Curdie *(PG 222).*

But there is always a sense of hope in the waiting in George MacDonald: "That you would not understand if I were to try ever so much to make you—not yet—not yet," says Queen Irene in answer to one of Irene's questions (*PG* 150), and the adult reader is subjected to the same discipline of waiting—often for answers to questions—as the child. An answer, in any case, may not be a pat solution: "You have not half got to the bottom of the answers I have already given you," the old princess tells Curdie at one point (*PC* 102-103). But she also says: "You may ask me as many [questions] as you please . . . . Only I may take a few thousand years to answer some of them" (74); that is, 'you will die first.' Understanding must be gained by living the answers to one's own questions—and by accepting that full understanding will only be attained in a visionary future.

"[C]ome out of the darkness of your exile; come into the light of your home," God invites man.[47] The strain of waiting for the light is certainly greater in *The Princess and Curdie* than in the earlier fantasies, since there is no overall resolution here and so the darkness of exile is more apparent. In *At the Back of the North Wind* the reader, like Diamond himself, has been brought to trust in the unknown future behind North Wind's back, and *The Princess and the Goblin* ends with a cheerful anticipation of Irene's and Curdie's future adventures. But the fundamental hope in all three fantasies is suggested in a dialogue between the child readers and the editor at the end of the serialised version of *The Princess and the Goblin:*

> *"Then you're leaving the story unfinished, Mr. Editor!"*
>
> *"Not more unfinished than a story ought to be, I hope. If you ever knew a story finished, all I can say is, I* never *did. Somehow stories won't finish. I think I know why, but I won't say that either now."* [48]

Endnotes to Conclusion on page 305

The pigeon gave a flutter, and spread out one of its red-spotted wings across the old woman's bosom.

"I will mend the little angel," she said, "and in a week or two it will be flying again. So you may ease your heart about the pigeon."

"Oh, thank you! thank you!" cried Curdie.. "I don't know how to thank you."

"Then I will tell you. There is only one way I care for. Do better, and grow better, and be better."

Chapter 3, "The Mistress of the Silver Moon"
illustration by James Allen

ENDNOTES

ENDNOTES TO INTRODUCTION

1. In 1863. They greeted it with enthusiastic approval, especially on the part of MacDonald's son Greville. See Greville MacDonald, *George MacDonald and His Wife* (Johannesen, 2005; from 2nd ed., London, 1924), 342. It is possible that MacDonald's choice of central symbol in "The Golden Key," which appeared in *Dealings with the Fairies* in 1867, was inspired by the golden key in *Alice*.

2. *An Expression of Character: The Letters of George MacDonald*, ed. Glenn Edward Sadler (Grand Rapids, Michigan, 1994), 288.

3. In *A Dish of Orts* (1892), 317. There are, however, gradations of the childlike. *At the Back of the North Wind*, *The Princess and the Goblin* and to a lesser extent *The Princess and Curdie* contain elements which are specifically geared to children, and the serial publication of all three was in a children's journal, *Good Words for the Young*, which had changed its title to *Good Things* by the time *The Princess and Curdie* appeared from January to June, 1877; *At the Back of the North Wind* was serialised from November 1868 until October 1870 and *The Princess and the Goblin* from November 1870 until June 1871.

4. MacDonald's first fantasy, *Phantastes* (1858), is subtitled *A Faerie Romance for Men and Women*, and he described it to his father as "a sort of fairy tale for grown people" (Sadler, 126). But, as Gillian Avery says regarding both *Phantastes* and *Lilith* (his last fantasy, published in 1895), "[h]is greatest work lies in the simpler fantasies for children" ("The Return of the Fairies," in "British and Irish fairy tales," *The Oxford Companion to Fairy Tales*, ed. Jack Zipes. 2nd ed. [Oxford, 2015], 82).

5. "A Sketch of Individual Development" (1880), reprinted in *A Dish of Orts* (1893) and reproduced by Johannesen (1996); 72.

6. Taylor, G.P. *The Shadowmancer* (London, 2003). In fact, many readers (especially Muslims) have responded enthusiastically to the "eternal images of faith" with which Graham Taylor (an Anglican vicar) wished to deal. "I didn't set out to write a Christian book and it's not a Christian book," he says on the *Shadowmancer* website page under BBC York (2004).

That's all right then!

7. Cit. in Greville MacDonald, *George MacDonald and His Wife*, 375. One Victorian fault-finder was George McCrie, who, in *The Religion of Our Literature* (London, 1875), complains that "the great design of all his works [is] to disseminate his religious opinions, which are dangerous and unsound" (295). The date of publication makes McCrie's view particularly interesting as he does not exempt the children's fantasies from this judgement (assuming that he thought them worth reading). For an extensive sampling of contemporary reviews of *The Princess and the Goblin* and *The Princess and Curdie* see Roderick McGillis, introduction to *George MacDonald: The Princess and the Goblin and The Princess and Curdie* (Oxford, 1990), x-xi.

8. One has to bear in mind that his Calvinistic background, followed by theological training and a few years as a Congregational minister, accustomed him to preach. Being squeezed out of his benefice for what some thought to be heresy, including an interest in German theology and the suggestions of a state of probation for heathens in the next world (*GMHW* 180) and of the possibility of eternal life for animals [*GMHW* 177-178], would indicate that no preaching of his would be hidebound by convention. Gillian Avery asserts that MacDonald was born into a milieu that had "the deepest possible distrust of the imagination" ("George MacDonald and the Victorian Fairy Tale," in *The Gold Thread: Essays on George MacDonald*, ed. William Raeper [1990], 126); yet, as Colin Manlove puts it in "MacDonald and Kingsley: A Victorian Contrast," these authors are "arguably [the] only two significant writers of Christian fantasy in the Victorian period" [*The Gold Thread*, 140]). MacDonald dislikes and rejects the view that certain kinds of literature—predominantly fantasy and fairy tale— are fundamentally incompatible with religious faith, or at least with religious observance. Mrs. Cathcart, in *Adela Cathcart* (1864), is set up as a straw woman to embody this attitude; one of her many negative comments is that fairy tales, if suitable for children at all, should not be read at "sacred times" such as Christmas (*AC* 55, 56). MacDonald is reacting against an increasingly old-fashioned attitude;

Jack Zipes, in the introduction to *The Oxford Companion to Fairy Tales* (Oxford, 2015), says that by the 1830s "the fairy tale had become acceptable for young readers . . . . adults themselves became more tolerant of fantasy literature and realized that it would not pervert the minds of their children" (xxviii). MacDonald is not, however, against the rejection of individual books if the reason seems to him good enough, and in "My Uncle Peter" there is an approved book-burning; the narrator's uncle puts a book on the fire and then begins reading a chapter of the New Testament "as if for an antidote to the book he had destroyed"—a volume by Sterne (*AC* 281-282). A somewhat gentler treatment is accorded to Thackeray's *Vanity Fair*, which MacDonald simply describes in a letter to Louisa as "that awful *Vanity Fair*" (*GMHW* 393); and he trusts that *The Portent* "will not be classed with what are commonly called *sensational novels*" (dedication to the 1864 edition; his italics)—no doubt fearing that the Gothic elements of the story may be thought to take it into a genre which he dislikes. Stephen Prickett, in "Adults in Allegory Land: Kingsley and MacDonald," says: "With Kingsley and MacDonald we find the possibilities of fantasy as an art form consciously explored and openly discussed for the first time" (*Victorian Fantasy*, 2nd ed. [Waco, Texas, 2005], 159).

9. See Tolkien, "On Fairy-Stories" in *Tree and Leaf* (reprinted in *The Tolkien Reader*, New York, 1966 [for 1964]) on the Primary and Secondary Worlds (47ff). W.H. Auden would class *At the Back of the North Wind* as a combination of the categories of "Feigned Histories" (the Primary part) and fairy tales (the Secondary part); see his afterword to the Bodley Head edition of *The Golden Key* (London, 1967), 82 (originally published in 1867 in *Dealings With the Fairies* [later retitled *The Light Princess and Other Fairy Stories*]).

10. See "On Fairy-Stories," 40.

11. *At the Back of the North Wind* (1871); 13, 91, Ch. V11, 323, 201, 136, 191. Originally serialised in *Good Words for the Young*, Nov. 1868—Oct.1870.

12. Ravenna Helson, in "The Psychological Origins of Fantasy for Children in Mid-Victorian England," describes

Diamond as "the first divine child in children's fantasy" (*Children's Literature: The Great Excluded* [later entitled *Children's Literature*], 3 [1974]; 74). In "Sitting on the Doorstep: MacDonald's Aesthetic Fantasy Worlds and the Divine Child-Figure," Ally Crockford posits that, "[i]n its union with the spiritual, the child-figure offers a bridge between divinity and humanity" and "represents *a union of humanity and divinity,* if one that can only ever be defined by its unrealisable potential" (*Rethinking George MacDonald: Contexts and Contemporaries,* ed. Christopher MacLachlan, John Patrick Padziora & Ginger Stelle [Glasgow, 2013], 154).

13. Stephen Prickett, in his preface to the Broadview Press edition of *At the Back of the North Wind* (several countries, 2011), says that "of all MacDonald's children's books it is by far the most grimly realistic in its portrait of social injustice, poverty, and disease" (12), while the editors, Roderick McGillis and John Pennington, describe it in the introduction as "the only one of his children's books to combine Victorian realism with Romantic fantasy" (27). The allusion to suicide is grim in a children's book, even by the standards of Victorian realism, yet the topic, a recurring issue throughout his works, was certainly on MacDonald's mind when he was writing it. He refers to suicide humorously in only the second sentence of *At the Back of the North Wind*: "An old Greek writer mentions a people who lived [at the back of the north wind], and were so comfortable that they could not bear it any longer, and drowned themselves" [1]. In *Guild Court: A London Story* (1868), Thomas Worboise says "I think I must have killed myself before now, if it hadn't been for [my rescuers]" (*GC* 329). In *Wilfrid Cumbermede,* a novel published in 1872, soon after *At the Back of the North Wind* and not long after the serialised version of *The Princess and the Goblin,* there is a detailed treatment of the subject, including a whole chapter entitled "A Talk About Suicide" and the suicide of one of the main characters, Charley Osborne (*WC* [346]-360, 443-445). As early as *Adela Cathcart* (1864) an account of a suicide and its consequences is interpolated into the story "The Cruel Painter" (392-393). Kate Fraser, in *Alec*

Forbes of Howglen (1865), apparently drowns herself in the sea (*AFH* 364-65), and in *Robert Falconer* (1868; serialised in *The Argosy* in 1866-67) the protagonist finally spots his long-sought father when he (Robert) is persuading a desperate woman not to drown herself. In this chapter, "The Suicide" (*RF* 491-512), he talks of the most appalling aspects of suicide (503-505); in a later discussion of the topic his attitude is more robust (547-551). MacDonald's treatment of the topic in *Robert Falconer* is especially important to the present study because the book, in serial form, preceded *At the Back of the North Wind* by little more than a year, and in view of his habits of composition the latter book must have been much on his mind. Between the two *Princess* books Juliet Meredith, in *Paul Faber, Surgeon* (1879), contemplates killing herself, and is even thought to have done so (*PFS* 251-252; 268-269, 271). MacDonald's very first fantasy, *Phantastes*, includes the attempted suicide of the narrator, Anodos: "I will not be tortured to death," he cries when left desolate on a wintry shore: "I will meet it half-way" (*Ph* 222). But, although he plunges into the "heaving abyss" and "sank far into the waters, and sought not to return" (222-223), he is rescued by the sea itself; even a boat is provided. This works well symbolically—but no thanks to him. The subject of suicide recurs in many of MacDonald's later books, from a shockingly casual mention in *Weighed and Wanting* (1882)—"[V]avasor's elder brother would have had [the earldom], but he killed himself before it fell due" (*WW* 316)—to Isy's attempt to drown herself in his last novel, *Salted With Fire* (1897). She is prevented from doing so by a man who, to deter her from future attempts, threatens her with being hanged! (*SF* 68). There is no mention of suicide in the *Princess* books.

14. *The Princess and the Goblin*, 69. Michael Mendelson says that the book belongs to a hybrid fictional genre, the mythic fairy tale, the pattern of which can be traced back to German writers, e.g. Goethe and Novalis (a major influence on MacDonald, who published a translation of "Twelve of the Spiritual Songs of Novalis" for private circulation in 1851). See Mendelson, "The Fairy Tales of George MacDonald and the Evolution of a Genre," in *For*

the Childlike: George MacDonald's Fantasies for Children, ed. Roderick McGillis (Metuchen, N.J., & London, 1992), 41. Maureen Duffy, in *The Erotic World of Faery* (London, Sydney, Auckland, Toronto, 1972), describes MacDonald's fantasies as "nineteenth-century supernatural parables" (292).

15. G.K. Chesterton, introduction to *GMHW*, 9. Interestingly, in August 2013 he was recommended for beatification, an essential prelude to canonisation; discussion of his suitability for this distinction is (I believe) still ongoing.

16. "Toads, Tongues and Roses," a review by Marina Warner in the *Times Literary Supplement*, Nov. 16th 2012, 11. MacDonald is not exercised about purity of genre.

17. Something which in any case MacDonald dislikes; see the chapter in which the narrator talks about the goings-on in the pulpits of Gwyntystorm on "Religion Day" (*The Princess and Curdie*, 274ff) and, more importantly, the passage in *Robert Falconer* in which Falconer says of his 'church': "We count any belief *in* [Jesus]—the smallest—better than any belief about him—the greatest" (*RF* 468). More simply still, MacDonald says in *A Dish of Orts* (1893): "Love aright, and you will come to think aright" (293).

18. Miss Coleman plays an introductory part in this; long before Joseph starts teaching him to read, Diamond, seeing North Wind assume the forms of different animals on the return journey from the country at her back, "knew all the creatures from a picture book that Miss Coleman had given him" (*ABNW* 124). As the whole journey proves to have been a dream, it may be opined that Miss Coleman's gift had special significance.

19. Arthur Hughes was very close to the family; his nephew was engaged to MacDonald's daughter Mary until she died of tuberculosis in 1878.

20. See William Raeper, *George MacDonald* (Tring, Herts., 1987), 326. MacDonald begins one letter to Irene "My great Goblin" (September 20th 1872; Sadler, 197). It is interesting to note that Kelpie, Malcolm's beloved but fiery mare in *The Marquis of Lossie* (1877), eventually becomes much more gentle after giving birth to a foal—who grows

into "a magnificent horse" and is named "Goblin" (*MQL* 383-384).

21. In *Robert Falconer*, written fairly soon after his European tour, there is an interesting discussion of Robert's feelings about church spires (*RF* 388-390). It is ironic that G.K. Chesterton, who admires MacDonald so much, singles out an attraction to heights as places for prayer as being morally and spiritually dangerous (see "The Hammer of God," in "The Innocence of Father Brown," *The Father Brown Stories* [London, 1929], 222-223).

22. Through the skylight of his cabin—and see *ABNW* 105-107, where North Wind blows off the hatch and lifts Diamond out of a storeroom.

23. "The Imagination: Its Functions and Its Culture," in *A Dish of Orts*, 21.

24. And sometimes with a very interesting twist. Poppie, in *Guild Court*, a character who bears a strong resemblance to Nanny, in *At the Back of the North Wind*, follows Lucy Burton and Thomas Worboise to the wax works (presumably Madam Tussaud's), and when (to MacDonald's strong disapproval) they go into the Chamber of Horrors, Poppie seeks warmth by "[lying] down with the dead"—under the cover over the Duke of Wellington (*GC* 61). This foreshadows the House of Death in *Lilith*, where the children each choose to share a couch with one of the dead. In *Storied Revelations: Parables, Imagination and George MacDonald's Christian Fiction* (Eugene, Oregon, 2013), Gisela Kreglinger discusses MacDonald's sense of the need to 're-echo' scriptural symbols which have grown too familiar and have therefore lost their function of revealing truths; she suggests that his understanding of poetry is very close to his understanding of scripture (146-148). This also applies to his understanding of prose, for, as MacDonald says in "The Imagination: Its Functions and Its Culture," "every new embodiment of a known truth must be a new and wider revelation" (*Orts* 22)—and characters and situations can be the means of "new and wider revelation" as well as symbols.

25. *Book News* cxxvii (March 1893), 304; cit. in Raeper, *George*

MacDonald, 403n. This appears to have been his only interview.

26. The semi-autobiographical *Ranald Bannerman's Boyhood* was serialised in *Good Words for the Young* from November 1869 until October 1870, overlapping the second half of *At the Back of the North Wind*, which also concluded in October 1870. The serialisation of *The Princess and the Goblin* began in November 1870 in the same periodical. As Daniel Gabelman tells us, *The Miracles of Our Lord* was originally serialised in the *Sunday Magazine* from October 1869 to September 1870 (see "'Divine Alchemy': *The Miracles of Our Lord* in its Context," in *Rethinking George MacDonald: Contexts and Contemporaries*, ed. Christopher MacLachlan et al. [Glasgow, 2013], 23).

27. An artist friend decorated the ceiling of MacDonald's study in The Retreat, Hastings, with stars and a moon against a dark blue background (*GMHW* 386). The family moved there in 1867.

28. *GMHW*, 412. G.K. Chesterton would certainly have endorsed this view (but for the "of the kind"). In his introduction to *George MacDonald and His Wife* he says: "All George MacDonald's other stories, interesting and suggestive in their several ways, seem to be illustrations and even disguises of that one" (*GMHW* 11).

29. "Of all my father's works, this remains the 'best seller'," says Greville MacDonald (*GMHW* 361), and in recent years it is certainly *At the Back of the North Wind* which has attracted the most attention. Not only has this book given part of its name to the journal of the George MacDonald Society (*North Wind: A Journal of George MacDonald Studies*) but it has inspired both a collection of essays (*Behind the Back of the North Wind: Critical Essays on George MacDonald's Classic Children's Book*, ed. John Pennington and Roderick McGillis [Hamden, CT, 2011]), and the 2011 Broadview edition of *At the Back of the North Wind* cited above.

30. See *GMHW* 72-73. In *Lilith*, published almost forty years later (London, 1895, reproduced by Johannesen in 1994 from the 1896 edition), it becomes a point of entry and departure for his spiritual adventures, as is underlined by

the first chapter's being entitled "The Library." Michael Burt points out the significance of Anodos's lengthy and intense experience of reading in the library of the Fairy Palace in *Phantastes* ("Books in *Phantastes*," in *"Phantastes and the Development of the Imagination," North Wind: A Journal of George MacDonald Studies*, 35 [2016], 100). And see, e.g., William Gray's "George MacDonald's Marvellous Medicine" in *Fantasy, Myth and the Measure of Truth: Tales of Pullman, Lewis, Tolkien, MacDonald and Hoffmann* (Basingstoke, 2010), 35.

31. A tradition which still survives. In a powerful and beautifully written modern example of hero myth, Richard Adams' *Watership Down*, the doe Vilthuril, at the end of the book, tells the rabbit kittens a story which encapsulates the adventures of the rabbits in symbolic form: " 'I seem to know this story,' whispered Hazel [the Chief Rabbit], 'but I can't remember where I've heard it.' " And the link between story and life is maintained in the final [pre-epilogue] sentence: "Underground, the story continued" (*Watership Down* [New York: Macmillan, 1972], 422, 424).

32. In *The Hope of the Gospel* (1892), 25. This edition published by Johannesen in 1995 with *The Miracles of Our Lord* (1870).

33. "Man's Difficulty Concerning Prayer," *Unspoken Sermons, Series Two* (originally published in 1885), in *Unspoken Sermons, Series 1, 11, 111* (Johannesen 1997), 255.

34. Ursula le Guin, "The Child and the Shadow," in *The Language of the Night: Essays on Fantasy and Science Fiction*, ed. Susan Wood (New York, 1979), 62.

35. "Myth and Archetype in Science Fiction," in *The Language of the Night*, 79.

36. Carl Jung, "The Psychology of Christian Alchemical Symbolism," in *Aion: Researches into the Phenomenology of the Self* (Vol. 9 ii of *The Collected Works of C.G. Jung*, trans. R.F.C. Hull, ed. Sir Herbert Read, Michael Fordham, Gerhard Adler. 2nd ed. [London 1968; from 1959]), par. 280. All future references to Jung's works will be designated by volume title and paragraph number and by volume number in the case of first references.

37. Richard Reis, in *George MacDonald* (New York, 1972), is one of the earlier critics to refer to Jung's theories in connection with MacDonald's archetypal characters and the archetype of the shadow (116-117). Edmund Cusick, in "MacDonald and Jung," in *The Gold Thread: Essays on George MacDonald*, ed. William Raeper (Edinburgh, 1990), discusses the applicability of Jungian theory to MacDonald's work in general and reviews some of the critics who have taken a psychological and particularly a Jungian approach to it (57-58, 59-61). William Raeper discusses the applicability of Jungian theory to MacDonald's work in a chapter on *Phantastes* (*George MacDonald*, esp. 150-151, 153, 154). See also Ravenna Helson, "The Psychological Origins of Fantasy for Children in Mid-Victorian England," in *Children's Literature: The Great Excluded*, 3 (1974), 66-76, and Joseph Sigman, "The Diamond in the Ashes: A Jungian Reading of the 'Princess' Books," in *For the Childlike: George MacDonald's Fantasies for Children*, ed. Roderick McGillis, 183-194 (Sigman also gives a Jungian perspective on *Phantastes;* see "Death's Ecstasies: Transformation and Rebirth in George MacDonald's *Phantastes*," in *English Studies in Canada*, 11, No. 2 [1976], 203-226). Katharine Bubel is also interested in Jungian theory; see "Knowing God 'Other-wise': The Wise Old Woman Archetype in George MacDonald's *The Princess and the Goblin, The Princess and Curdie* and 'The Golden Key'," in *North Wind: A Journal of George MacDonald Studies*, 25 (2006), 1-17; and see Bonnie Gaarden's study, *The Christian Goddess: Archetype and Theology in the Fantasies of George MacDonald* (Lanham, Maryland, 2011), esp. 11-13, 74-75. William Gray, in "George MacDonald, Julia Kristeva and the Black Sun," is much less inclined to believe in the applicability of Jungian theory to MacDonald's work, though he admits that his attitude has mellowed since the first appearance of this essay (in *Death and Fantasy: Essays on Philip Pullman, C.S. Lewis, George MacDonald and R.L. Stevenson* [Newcastle, 2008], 9, 9n). 2008], 9, 9n). In his essay "George MacDonald's Marvellous Medicine," in *Fantasy, Myth and the Measure of Truth*, Gray says that MacDonald's work "lies right on the cusp between the Romantic understanding of the unconscious and the psychoanalytical

interpretation developed by Freud and Jung" (Basingstoke and New York, 2010; 59). In *"Phantastes:* All Mirrors are Magic Mirrors," Jonathan Litten states his intention "to show where [MacDonald's and Jung's] ideas on the imagination and the unconscious converge" (*North Wind*, 35 [2016], 105).

38. *Ranald Bannerman's Boyhood*, 150-159. Even in *Wilfrid Cumbermede*, the grimmest of MacDonald's novels from this period, the chapter headed "The Darkest Hour" is followed by a chapter headed "The Dawn."

39. "The Remission of Sins," in *The Hope of the Gospel*, 41.

40. See, e.g., "The Battle for Deliverance from the Mother," in *Symbols of Transformation* (Vol. 5, 2nd ed., of the *Collected Works*), par. 459: "The task [of keeping the libido, or active energy, in a state of progression] consists in integrating the unconscious, in bringing together 'conscious' and 'unconscious.' I have called this the individuation process." Jung considers the individuation process "the central problem of modern psychology" ("Flying Saucers: A Modern Myth," in *Civilization in Transition* [Vol. 10, 2nd ed., of the *Collected Works*], par. 809.

41. "Life," in *Unspoken Sermons, Second Series*, 298. The sentence in full reads: "Hence the final end of the separation [from God the creator] is not individuality; that is but a means to it; the final end is oneness—an impossibility without it."

42. "Escape Routes," in *The Language of the Night*, 205.

43. "The Butcher's Bills," in *Stephen Archer and Other Tales*, 164, 163 (originally published in 1882 as *The Gifts of the Child Christ, and Other Tales*). No wonder Mr. Dempster also has a "miserably stunted consciousness" (181).

44. "A Sermon," in *A Dish of Orts*, 287.

45. *A Book of Strife, in the Form of the Diary of an Old Soul;* March, 209.

46. "A Sketch of Individual Development," *Orts* 72.

47. "Miracles of Healing Solicited by the Sufferers," in *The Miracles of Our Lord*, 304.

48. See Carl Jung, "The Relations between the Ego and the

Unconscious," in *Two Essays on Analytical Psychology* (Vol. 7, 2nd ed., of the *Collected Works* [Princeton, 1966]): "As the individual is not just a single, separate being, but by his very existence presupposes a collective relationship, it follows that the process of individuation must lead to more intense and broader collective relationships and not to isolation" (par. 241n.). It is, however, "imperative to make a clear distinction between personal contents and those of the collective psyche" (par. 241). William Raeper defines the collective unconscious as "the psychic reservoir of the whole of mankind" (*George MacDonald*, 151).

49. Colin Manlove notes that MacDonald was familiar with alchemy from his reading of Paracelsus and particularly of Jacob Boehme; see "A Reading of *At the Back of the North Wind*" in *Behind the Back of the North Wind: Critical Essays on George MacDonald's Classic Children's Book*, 162, 173n4. Aren Roukema explores MacDonald's use of alchemical symbolism in *Phantastes* and cites Greville MacDonald's description of a conversation in which his father said that the "river of life" in *Lilith* was made up of the four elements of mediaeval alchemy—water, air, earth and fire (see "The Shadow of Anodos: Alchemical Symbolism in *Phantastes*," in *North Wind* 31 [2012], 52). Catherine Persyn constructs a detailed and persuasive exposition of the importance of alchemy in *At the Back of the North Wind*; see "'In My End is My Beginning': The *fin-negans* Motif in George MacDonald's *At the Back of the North Wind*" (*Mythlore* 24, Winter-Spring 2006, 53-69). In "'Divine Alchemy;' *The Miracles of Our Lord* in its Context," Daniel Gabelman emphasises MacDonald's own use of the phrase "divine alchemy" in *The Miracles of Our Lord* (see *Rethinking George MacDonald: Contexts and Contemporaries*, esp. 29).

50. "Introduction to the Religious and Psychological Problems of Alchemy," *Psychology and Alchemy* (Vol. 12, 2nd ed., of the *Collected Works*), par. 43.

51. *George MacDonald: Scotland's Beloved Storyteller* (Minneapolis, Minnesota, 1987), 309.

52. John Pridmore, "Talking of God and Talking of Fairies: Discourses of Spiritual Development in the Works of

George MacDonald and in the Curriculum," in *North Wind* 22 (2003), 2 (from an essay in the *International Journal of Children's Spirituality*, 7, No. 1 [2002], 35).

53. Dickens did something very similar in the first chapter of *Great Expectations*, which appeared in *All the Year Round* in 1860-61 and in book form in 1861, and which MacDonald must have read—though given the prevalence of the idea in his work (even North Wind says "ever since I knew I had hair" [*ABNW* 77])—it is likely that he was struck by the coincidence of idea rather than inspired to emulate it. The idea persists throughout his work: "[S]oon after, I came to know that I was myself" we find in the original manuscript of *Lilith* (*Lilith* 367).

54. Kirstin Jeffrey Johnson instances "the primacy of Light over darkness" as one of Isaiah's themes ("Curdie's Intertextual Dialogue: Engaging Maurice, Arnold, and Isaiah," in *George MacDonald: Literary Heritage and Heirs*, ed. Roderick McGillis (Wayne, Pennsylvania, 2008), 157.

55. See the introduction to "The Revelation to John," *The Jewish Annotated New Testament*, ed. Amy-Jill Levine and Marc Zvi Brettler (Oxford, 2011), 464.

56. Joel Rosenberg, "The Closing Chapters of 2 Samuel" in "1 and 2 Samuel" (*The Literary Guide to the Bible*, ed. Robert Alter and Frank Kermode [London, 1987], 139-140). It may be noted that in each of the three battles against the Philistines outlined in the closing verses of Ch.21, a son (and in one case the brother) of Goliath, the giant earlier killed by David, is killed by David's army. The last son "had on every hand six fingers, and on every foot six toes" (2 Sam. 21:20)—shades of the goblin queen in *The Princess and the Goblin* (*PG* 212).

57. The divine associations of North Wind, the intermediary, owe much to ideas concerning the "primal wind" in the Old Testament; "breath of God," "spirit of God" and "mighty wind" are not differentiated there, says Theodore Gaster (*Myth, Legend, and Custom in the Old Testament* [New York, 1969]), 4. Ulrich Knoepflmacher ascribes to North Wind a pagan divinity; she is an "expanding goddess," i.e. she expands Diamond's limits, he says in "Sundering Women

from Boys" (*Ventures into Childland: Victorians, Fairy Tales, and Femininity* [Chicago and London, 1998], 290).

58. *Summa theologica*, 1, xxxvi, art.1 (cit. in Jung's "A Psychological Approach to the Trinity," in *Psychology and Religion: West and East*, Vol. 11, 2nd ed., of the *Collected Works* [London and Henley, 1969], par.276, n.8). In *The Princess and the Goblin*, on the other hand, the importance of Queen Irene's name is emphasised in her first conversation with Princess Irene.

59. As the final instalment of *At the Back of the North Wind* was succeeded the next month by the first instalment of *The Princess and the Goblin*, there was presumably a 'creative overlap' between the two books. And MacDonald is open to the idea of what one might term the evolving trilogy, as we find in the case of *Annals of a Quiet Neighbourhood* (1867), *The Seaboard Parish* (1868) and *The Vicar's Daughter* (1872). Wynnie Percivale, the narrator of the last book, is talked into writing it by her father and her husband—and especially by Mr. S., the publisher of the first two, who feels "the necessity for another story to complete the *trilogy*, as he called it," which suggests that the third book was an afterthought (2). In *An Expression of Character: The Letters of George MacDonald*, MacDonald writes rather tentatively on the subject to his publisher: "I should be glad to have a copy or two of [*The Vicar's Daughter*] to give away. I am sorry it had got parted from the other preceding two, "The Annals," and "Seaboard Parish," with which it formed a trilogy, so to say . . ." (Sadler, 366).

60. Greville MacDonald speaks of his father's "avowing himself confirmed more strongly than ever, if this were possible, in his Trinitarian faith" after a friendly discussion with a famous Unitarian preacher (*GMHW* 453). Ronald MacDonald, in "George MacDonald: A Personal Note," writes: "I remember very well his saying that the Unitarians were among the most instant to get him to preach; and that he always stipulated for liberty to maintain the doctrine of the Trinity" (*View From a Northern Window*, ed. F. Watson. London, 1911), 69. See also Kerry Dearborn, *Baptized Imagination: The Theology of George MacDonald* (Aldershot, Hampshire, 2006), 84-85 and elsewhere.

61. See MacDonald's Preface to *Orts* (1893), n.p. G.K. Chesterton, on the other hand, in a column entitled "George MacDonald and His Work" in the *Daily News*, London (1901), says that "Dr. MacDonald's tales of real life are allegories, or disguised versions, of his fairy tales" (see "Appreciations," 305-314, in *The Gospel in George MacDonald: Selections from His Novels, Fairy Tales, and Spiritual Writings*, ed. Marianne Wright [New York, England and Australia, 2016], 306).

62. Carl Jung, "The Fish in Alchemy," in *Aion*, par. 216.

63. Max Luthi, *Once Upon a Time: On the Nature of Fairy Tales* (Bloomington and London, 1976 [for 1970]), 156.

64. "The Raising of the Dead," in *The Miracles of Our Lord*, 396.

65. "Miracles of Healing Unsolicited," *Miracles* 282; from "the Father of lights" in the General Epistle of James, 1:17, a phrase cited in many of MacDonald's works, among them *Annals of a Quiet Neighbourhood* (1867)—"Everything good comes from the Father of lights" (260); *Robert Falconer* (1868)—"the holy will of the Father of Lights" (228); "The History of Photogen and Nycteris: A Day and Night Marchen," in *Stephen Archer and Other Tales* (1883)—"At last the sun shot up into the air, like a bird from the hand of the Father of Lights" (142); *There and Back* (1891)—"the lower winds and sidelong rays of art, all from the father of lights, crept in, able now to work for his perfect will" (277); and *Weighed and Wanting* (1882), where it is cited most notably by Mark Raymount, "a Christ-child, if ever child might bear the name" (604), on his death-bed, reaffirming the biblical dictum that "[e]very good as well as every perfect gift is from the father of lights" from his own experience: "Oh, he is such a good father of lights!" (600). The phrase is cited even more memorably in *Malcolm*, first published between the two *Princess* books in 1875, in which some of the most striking instances of bringing light out of darkness are to be found. The blind piper, Duncan MacPhail, paradoxically exercises a "ministry of light" by cleaning almost all the lamps in Portlossie (*M* 77) and becomes "a priest in the temple of Light" (78). The mad laird, Stephen Stewart, utters great cries to the "Father o' lichts"

(187), especially during a sermon preached in a "dark cave" on the seashore (185). He brings Mr. MacLeod's sermon to an abrupt end when the preacher is warning of the wrath to come: "*'Father o' lichts!'* once more burst ringing out, like the sudden cry of a trumpet in the night" (189).

ENDNOTES TO CHAPTER 1

1. Carl Jung defines the mandala as "the psychological expression of the totality of the self" ("A Study in the Process of Individuation," in *The Archetypes and the Collective Unconscious*, Vol. 9 i, 2nd ed., of the *Collected Works*, par. 542).

2. In "Sorrow the Pledge of Joy" in *The Hope of the Gospel*, 97. In *At the Back of the North Wind* MacDonald says that "to know a person's name is not always to know the person's self" (9)—but on the symbolic level this may mean that one does not always realise how fully the name expresses the person's self, or, as in Diamond's case, that the self has not yet fully grown into the name.

3. Carl Jung, "Individual Dream Symbolism in Relation to Alchemy," in *Psychology and Alchemy*, par. 263.

4. "The Inheritance," in *Unspoken Sermons Series Three* (1889), 612.

5. "He was the family's own Diamond," says William Raeper in *George MacDonald* (345). He notes (*GM* 326) that Maurice also inspired Mark Raymount in *Weighed and Wanting* (1882). Kathy Triggs, in *The Stars and the Stillness: A Portrait of George MacDonald* (Cambridge, 1986), cites a review of one of MacDonald's lectures which appeared in the *Pittsburgh Methodist Recorder* in February 1873 and which included the information that Louisa MacDonald had identified Maurice as "the lad who suggested . . . by his quaint sayings, that weird writing, 'On the Back of the North Wind'" (122). Maurice (b. 1864) was less than five years old when *At the Back of the North Wind* began serial publication in *Good Words for the Young* in November 1868.

6. See also Robert Trexler, "Dombey and Grandson: Parallels Between *At the Back of the North Wind* and *Dombey and*

Son," in *North Wind: A Journal of George MacDonald Studies*, 29 (2010), esp. 71-74, where he compares Ch. 8 in *Dombey and Son* with Ch. 13 in *At the Back of the North Wind*. MacDonald's sense of the inspirational quality of Dickens is spelt out in "The Butcher's Bills," when he says of the Dempsters, an unsatisfactory couple in an unsatisfactory marriage: "If only they would have read Dickens together! Who knows what might have come of it!" (*Stephen Archer and Other Tales*, 1883 [originally *The Gifts of the Child Christ and Other Tales*], 165).

7. Tolkien, "On Fairy-Stories," in *Tree and Leaf* (*The Tolkien Reader*, 52 et al). Tolkien also talks about the "Secondary World" of fantasy.

8. See "The Great Exhibition," on line in *Wikipedia, the free encyclopedia*. Deirdre David, who, in her introduction to *The Cambridge Companion to the Victorian Novel* (2nd ed., Cambridge, 2012), describes the Crystal Palace as a "huge glass conservatory" because of the live elm trees inside it, says that "this shimmering palace was divided into four areas displaying raw materials, machinery, manufacturing, and fine arts. In a sense, [it] provided visual and textual knowledge about how the world worked" (6).

9. Lewis Carroll was a delighted visitor: "[H]is eye was immediately drawn to some of the 'ingenious pieces of mechanism 'on display . . . The whole exhibition, he declared, was 'a sort of fairyland,'" says Robert Douglas-Fairhurst in *The Story of Alice: Lewis Carroll and the Secret History of Wonderland* (London, 2015), 58. One exhibit was an alarm clock bed, designed to toss its occupant onto the floor in the morning; this was the brainchild of Theophilus Carter, possibly the original of the Mad Hatter (see Martin Gardner, *The Annotated Alice: Alice's Adventures in Wonderland and Through the Looking-Glass*. Revised ed. [Harmondsworth, Middlesex, 1972], 93). Charlotte Bronte was delighted too, as Clement Shorter records in *The Brontes' Life and Letters:* "It is a wonderful place. . . . Whatever human industry has created you find there, from the great compartments filled with railway engines and boilers, with mill machinery in full work . . . [to] the most gorgeous work of the goldsmith and silversmith, and the carefully

guarded caskets full of real diamonds and pearls" (see http://www.mytimemachine.co.uk/greatexhibition.htm). Charles Dickens was less enthusiastic: "He forced himself to visit the Exhibition, found it a muddle and [said] he had always had an instinctive feeling against it," says Claire Tomalin (*Charles Dickens: A Life*. London and elsewhere, 2011, 233). But an article in *Household Words* (which he "conducted," but in which authorship was not acknowledged) begins: "Nothing which has occurred for years has been more calculated to gratify the pride of an Englishman than the Great Exhibition" ("A Pilgrimage to the Great Exhibition from Abroad," *Household Words* 3. 321, in *Dickens Journals Online*). Another article, "The Great Exhibition and the Little One," spoke of "the extraordinary display of enginry and machinery" and of what "sturdy old England" had to say, through the Exhibition, about what continental nations with their revolutions could achieve "by works of peace, by studious observation and by steady persevering resolution" (*Household Words*, 357).

10. See Greville MacDonald, *GMHW* 218, and William Raeper, *George MacDonald*, 83, 86.

11. As MacDonald's grandfather, an uncle and his beloved and revered father had at various times run a linen-weaving factory, a thread factory, a bleachworks and meal mills (Raeper, 18-23), MacDonald would have found no fault with the Crystal Palace Exhibition for being, as *Wikipedia* puts it, "a celebration of modern industrial technology and design" ("The Great Exhibition," 1). He had nothing against business unless it was greedy or dishonest (Greville MacDonald says that he began to take a more negative view of industrialism from the mid1860s onwards, influenced in all probability by John Ruskin; but "[m]y father's unqualified optimism kept strong within him the faith that . . . the ignominies of man's industrial progress [might] yet prove to be comprehended within the creative Will" [*GMHW* 329]). MacDonald would not have thought the Exhibition vainglorious on the score of Empire; it was the first of several World's Fair exhibitions of culture and industry and twenty-eight countries exhibited. He would have been unlikely to disapprove on that score in any

case, since at one point he even envisaged the possibility of a "re-conquest" of Ireland (Sadler, *The Letters of George MacDonald*, 318). In its second incarnation in another part of London (from 1854) the Crystal Palace was an important cultural centre, hosting exhibits ranging from ancient history to dinosaurs as well as concerts and other public entertainments. And the MacDonald family interest continued; as Kirstin Jeffrey Johnson tells us, some of the MacDonald daughters belonged to the Handel Choir of the Crystal Palace ("Curdie's Intertextual Dialogue: Engaging Maurice, Arnold, and Isaiah," in *George MacDonald: Literary Heritage and Heirs*, ed. Roderick McGillis; ref. archived letters in note 9, 173).

12. Sadler, *The Letters of George MacDonald*, 51.

13. *George MacDonald and His Wife*, 543. A passage in *Castle Warlock* (1882) makes clear MacDonald's preference for diamonds above all other jewels: "All the gems were there—sapphires, emeralds, and rubies; but they were scarce to be noted in the glorious mass of ever new-born, ever dying colour that gushed from the fountain of the light-dividing diamonds" (*CW* 342). As for symbolism: "Your honesty, my son, is a diamond in my heart," the dying laird tells Cosmo (289).

14. See his introduction to the Oxford World's Classics edition of *The Moonstone* (Oxford, 1999), xxiii. Sutherland says that the national press began its 'explosive' coverage especially after 1855, with the abolition of the last of the "taxes on knowledge." Taxes on newspaper advertisements were abolished in 1853 and stamp duty in 1855; see *The Oxford History of England: The Age of Reform 1815-1870*, by Sir Llewellyn Woodward (2nd ed., Oxford, 1962). The new rail services and the speed of steam printing presses were also major factors in the expansion of the press (Sutherland xxiii).

15. Cit. in John Sutherland's edition of *The Moonstone*, [liii]. *The Moonstone* was originally published in weekly instalments in *All the Year Round* from January-August 1868 and in volume form in July of that year. *At the Back of the North Wind* began its run in *Good Words for the Young* in Nov.

1868. I doubt, however, that Collins' novel inspired the choice of a name for MacDonald's protagonist; it reflects the fascination of the Koh-i-Noor, general at the time, which persists even to this day. A 1983 episode of the BBC series *Bergerac* revolves largely round an enormously valuable diamond, about which an auctioneer feels obliged to say that it has never belonged to an Indian maharajah and is not accursed. More recently, *The Daily Telegraph* has described the efforts of a Pakistani lawyer to have the Koh-i-Noor repatriated to his country (part of which used to belong to India). According to the article, the lawyer has made it a lifetime cause and has written 786 letters on the subject to the Queen and Pakistani officials (Mohammad Zubair Khan and Philip Sherwell: "New battle over jewel in Empire's crown as Pakistan stakes a claim," February 9th 2016). In a *Telegraph* article of April 19th 2016, however, India's solicitor-general is reported as having told a judge that in the opinion of the culture ministry the diamond need not be returned; it had been given to the East India Company in 1849 by the successors of Maharajah Ranjit Singh as compensation for helping them in the Sikh wars (the All India Human Rights & Social Justice Front disagreed, feeling that the Koh-i-Noor is "the essence of the country"). This diamond features in David Pickering's *Dictionary of Superstitions* (London, 1995), in which possession of the jewel is said to be unlucky.

16. Alison Milbank speaks of his (and Kingsley's) "defamiliarising both this world and the life to come" ("Imagining the Afterlife: The Fantasies of Charles Kingsley and George MacDonald," from *Dante and the Victorians*, repr. in *Behind the Back of the North Wind: Critical Essays on George MacDonald's Classic Children's Book*, ed. John Pennington and Roderick McGillis, 91).

17. Diamond the horse is the literary progenitor of Strawberry, the London cab horse in C.S. Lewis's *The Magician's Nephew*, whose name also owes something to Mr. Raymond's horse, Ruby. As a jewel, Horse Diamond's name (given him because of the white lozenge on his forehead, see *ABNW* 290) harmonises with Ruby's—and though not an angel-horse like him, his literary descendant becomes a flying

horse ("Fledge") in Narnia.

18. See Carl Jung, "The Psychic Nature of the Alchemical Work," in *Psychology and Alchemy*, par. 396: "The soul . . . rules the mind and this rules the body." In "The Battle for Deliverance from the Mother" (*Symbols of Transformation*, par. 460), he says of the hero that "the totality of his being . . . is rooted in his animal nature and reaches out beyond the merely human to the divine." Fernando Soto, in a discussion of the derivation and significance of Diamond's name, makes a fascinating case for Spenser's *Faerie Queen* as a source of it; he points out that in Book 4, Cantos 2 and 3, Spenser tells the story of the three sons of Agape, Priamond, Diamond and Triamond, whose individual strengths are complementary. Soto also notes that Ch. 20 of *Phantastes*, in which elements of their story appear, begins with an epigraph from *The Faerie Queen* ("Cosmos and Diamonds: Names and Connoting in MacDonald's Work," in *North Wind: A Journal of George MacDonald Studies*, 20 [2001], 34-37.

19. Perhaps drawing on a pre-birth memory—in contradistinction to his later birth into a preview of death by going through North Wind in the ice cave (112). "The Cave and the Rock are . . . ancient symbols of motherhood: Lazarus emerging from a cave or 'little house' is easily seen as a new-birth symbol," says Gilbert Cope in *Symbolism in the Bible and the Church* (London, 1959), 103. See also Jung, *Alchemical Studies* (Vol. 13, 2nd ed., of the *Collected Works*), par. 156.

20. See Cope, 36: "As a mother encloses her young, so the cradle confines the baby." Cope adds that a boat is also one of the main symbols of a feminine 'container' which provides safety—and North Wind, in one of her most maternal moments, tells Diamond before his sea voyage to the North Pole: "The yacht shall be my cradle, and you shall be my baby" (*ABNW* 105).

21. In *Symbols of Transformation* Jung says that in the context of the visions he is analysing "the hero and his horse seem to symbolize the idea of man and the subordinate sphere of animal instinct" ("The Battle for Deliverance

from the Mother," par. 421). See also *The Archetypes and the Collective Unconscious*, where Jung comments as follows on a patient's dream: "The sky-woman is the positive, the bear the negative aspect of the 'supraordinate personality' [the total self], which extends the conscious human being upwards into the celestial and downwards into the animal regions" ("The Psychological Aspects of the Kore," par. 341). In "Symbols of the Mother and of Rebirth" (*Symbols of Transformation*, par. 334), he observes that "to be born of the Spirit means to be born of the fructifying breath of the wind," and also that in St. John's Gospel, Ch. 3, the same Greek word is used for "Spirit" and "wind" (see vv. 5-8).

22. Which MacDonald doesn't want to do, though he comes close; Diamond's parents are not Joseph and Mary (the mother of Jesus) but Joseph and Martha. The name "Martha" sounds like "mother," but it does not suggest that there has been a divine birth—and the biblical Martha, sister of another Mary, is the worrier of the family (see St. Luke's Gospel, 10:38-42), a role to which Diamond's mother may lay some claim. Gillian Avery describes him as "a Christ-like child" ("George MacDonald," in *The Oxford Companion to Fairy Tales*, 373).

23. And see Jung, "A Psychological Approach to the Trinity" in *Psychology and Religion: West and East*, par. 267: "We are no more than the stable in which the Lord is born."

24. While Diamond was driving Horse Diamond in his father's cab, Lucy Burton, in *Guild Court* (published in 1868 and previously serialised in *Good Words*) was commuting to work as a music teacher six days a week on the underground railway which, built on a cut-and-cover system, opened in London in 1863—the first in the world (see Paul Atterbury's *Wonder Book of Trains* [Newton Abbot & Cincinnati, 2012], 95). Work had begun on it in 1854 (see "Chronology" in *The Cambridge Companion to the Victorian Novel*, xiii).

25. Sigmund Freud, "Taboo and Social Ambivalence," in *Totem and Taboo* (Vol. X111 of *The Standard Edition of the Complete Psychological Works of Sigmund Freud*, ed. James Strachey, Anna Freud, Alix Strachey and Alan Tyson:

London and Toronto, 1955), 56.

26. "I do not write for children, but for the childlike, whether of five, or fifty, or seventy-five," says MacDonald in "The Fantastic Imagination" (*Orts*, 317).

27. MacDonald made Wordsworth's line "The Child is father of the Man" the motto of *Good Things for the Young*, the journal in which *At the Back of the North Wind* and *The Princess and the Goblin* were published, when he was editor (see the Broadview 2011 edition of *At the Back of the North Wind*, 149 n1).

28. The divine association is clear; see, e.g., "The Salt and the Light of the World," in *The Hope of the Gospel*, 162-175. Jesus applies these words to his disciples: "Ye are the salt of the earth. . . . Ye are the light of the world" (Matthew 5:13, 14), and in John 8:12 and 9:5 he says "I am the light of the world." As MacDonald puts it, "God alone is the light, and our light is the shining of his will in our lives" (*HG* 166). Stephen Prickett, in his preface to the Broadview 2011 edition of *At the Back of the North Wind*, says that "Raymond" also has a Teutonic meaning of "protecting hands" (12). Mr. Raymond's name takes another form in *Weighed and Wanting* (1882), where Mr. Raymount, another incarnation of George MacDonald, is a professional writer whose son, Mark, is very much in the Diamond tradition. In one of MacDonald's last novels, *The Flight of the Shadow* (1891), the narrator is Mrs. Belorba Day—another variation on "the light of the world."

29. See Jung, "The Personification of the Opposites," in *Mysterium Coniunctionis* (Vol. 14, 2nd ed., of the *Collected Works*), par. 188: "The appearance of Diana necessarily brings with it her hunting animal the dog, who represents her dark side." The dog in Nanny's dream does not appear until the moon has been darkened by clouds: "When the moon shines in her fullness the 'rabid dog,' the danger that threatens the divine child, is chased away," says Jung (par. 154). What Nanny does is to shut the door of the summer house in the dog's face, but it comes to the same thing—and the dream dog corresponds to Jung's 'rabid dog,' for it comes into the dream garden "yelping and bounding" so

that Nanny "thought if he caught sight of me, I was in for a biting first, and the police after" (*ABNW* 297).

30. See, e.g., "The Personification of the Opposites," *Mysterium Coniunctionis* par. 127, where Jung speaks of "the primary pair of opposites, consciousness and unconsciousness, whose symbols are Sol and Luna." The moon also symbolises "the principle of the feminine psyche" (par. 221). Jung notes that the moon-goddess appears in children's dreams and cites the dream of a little girl going through a difficult time ("The Psychological Aspects of the Kore," *Archetypes*, par. 344).

31. Mandalas are often circular or globular, which gives the moon some claim to be one. And see "The Symbolism of the Mandala," in *Psychology and Alchemy*, par. 247: "I may define 'self' as the totality of the conscious and unconscious psyche, but this totality transcends our vision; it is a veritable *lapis invisibilitatis*."

32. In *Robert Falconer*, serially published a year before *At the Back of the North Wind*, there are two significant horses in corresponding colours, Black Geordie and Reid Rorie. In *Paul Faber, Surgeon* the surgeon owns a red horse, Ruber, and a black horse, Niger. Ruber is definitely the dominant one, and the reader meets him before he meets the hero: "Just in front of [the rector and his wife], in the air, over a high hedge, scarce touching the topmost twigs with his hoofs, appeared a great red horse" which the rector momentarily took for the mount of Death in Revelation (*RF* 2). Horse Diamond in *At the Back of the North Wind* is presumably black, though MacDonald does not say so—and Arthur Hughes, as Coleman Parsons points out, makes him black in the August 1870 number of *Good Words for the Young*; see "The Progenitors of Black Beauty in Humanitarian Literature," *Notes and Queries* April 19th 1947, 156.

33. See Jung, "The Structure and Dynamics of the Self," in *Aion*, par. 351: "Psychologically . . . three—if the context indicates that it refers to the self—should be understood as a defective quaternity or as a stepping-stone towards it. The complement of the quaternity is unity." In *Psychology and Religion* he says: "If the Trinity is understood as a

process ... then, by the addition of the Fourth, this process would culminate in a condition of absolute totality" ("A Psychological Approach to the Trinity," par. 290).

34. "A Psychological Approach to the Trinity," par. 292.

35. Symbolically the ruby is very well suited to symbolise an aspect of the self, since, as a carbuncle (which used to mean any kind of red precious stone) it too can be the *lapis;* see Jung, "Alchemical Symbolism in the History of Religion," *Psychology and Alchemy,* par. 552 n.86.

36. Cf. Luke 2:49: "Wist ye not that I must be about my Father's business?"

37. Surely a foreshadowing of *The Princess and the Goblin;* why should there be a lamp *inside* the moon?

38. On the occasional association of bees with the Great Mother archetype, see Jung, "The Psychological Aspects of the Kore," *Archetypes,* par. 312 n., and Gilbert Cope, "Archetypes of Male and Female," in *Symbolism in the Bible and the Church,* 157-158: "[T]here was often an association between the Great Mother and the Queen Bee of the honey hive." Cope's bees, however, have to do with fertility rather than storms. When Diamond is pondering his experiences at the end of the book he refers to Nanny's dream, not just as her dream about the moon but as the dream about "the moon and the bees" (*ABNW* 365).

39. "The Lapis-Christ Parallel," *Psychology and Alchemy,* par. 449. Jung refers in part to the casting of Shadrach, Meshach and Abednego into the "burning fiery furnace" where they were joined by a fourth; "and the form of the fourth is like the Son of God" (Daniel 3:6 et al., 25).

40. In "On Fairy-Stories" Tolkien says that "the desire to converse with other living things" is the basis of "the talking of beasts and creatures in fairy-tales, *and especially the magical understanding of their proper speech*" (66; italics mine). This is found in "The Golden Key" (1867), in which Mossy and Tangle, walking through the forest, find "endless amusement from the talk of the animals;" but "[t]hey soon learned enough of their language to ask them necessary questions," which is not the case in *At the Back*

of the North Wind (see *The Light Princess and Other Fairy Tales*, Johannesen, 192). There certainly are elements of the fairy tale in *At the Back of the North Wind*—but of course, if one accepts Leslie Fiedler's dictum that "[i]n the fairy tale, bliss and misery are not equated with Christian Salvation, Hell and Heaven—but with Getting Married and Being Eaten," *At the Back of the North Wind* would be utterly beyond the pale of faerie anyway (Introduction to *Beyond the Looking Glass: Extraordinary Works of Fairy Tale and Fantasy*, ed. Jonathan Cott [New York, 1973], xiv). Curdie, in *The Princess and the Goblin*, is faced with the prospect of being eaten (see *PG* 186-189), and even Diamond, at the very beginning of *At the Back of the North Wind*, wonders whether "if the wind should blow the house down, and he were to fall through into the manger, old Diamond mightn't eat him up before he knew him in his nightgown" (*ABNW* 3)].

41. The lion, eagle and bull are the emblems of the evangelists Mark, John and Luke respectively, according to St. Jerome's attribution. We are never told how Ruby, a mount for angels to ride on (320), comes to be working for Mr. Raymond in the first place.

42. Perhaps a reference to Jack Sprat and his wife; versions of this rhyme had been in existence since the seventeenth century (see Humphrey Carpenter and Mari Prichard, *The Oxford Companion to Children's Literature* [Oxford and New York, 1984], 276).

43. Lending itself is rather problematic, since the lack of ownership of what is lent opens the way to negative possibilities including misconstruction. Oddly, North Wind, who admits to having been the moon lady in Nanny's dream (365) and who in that capacity expresses the fear that Nanny has stolen the ruby ring (307), knows perfectly well that Nanny was lent the ring by Mrs. Raymond. "[I]t's your papa's ring that they've stolen," says Hugh Sutherland to his pupil in *David Elginbrod*. "He lent it to me, and what if he should not believe me?" (278) In *Robert Falconer* (1867) the horses Black Geordie and Red Rorie are "borrowed" by Robert and Shargar in an attempt to rescue Mysie Lindsay from the clutches of their owner

(367f.); he might have thought the term a euphemism.

44. Catherine Persyn, in "And All About the Courtly Stable / Bright-Harnessed Angels Sit": Eschatological Elements in *At the Back of the North Wind*," points out that Diamond's baby sister is born during Ruby's 'probationary' period with the family, and comments: "There is an interesting symmetry that must be pointed out between the twin phrases 'as if the red beast had brought ill luck with him' (309-310) / 'as if she [the baby] had brought plenty with her' (311)—the latter inviting one not to take the former at its face value" (*North Wind*, 20 [2001], 16).

45. Jung, *Mysterium Coniunctionis*, pars. 200, 664 and elsewhere.

46. "Concerning Mandala Symbolism," *Archetypes*, par. 660.

47. "The Self," *Aion*, par. 45. And see Ursula K. Le Guin: "[W]hen you have followed the animal instincts far enough, they must be sacrificed, so that the true self, the whole person, may step forth from the body of the animal, reborn" ("The Language of the Night," in *The Language of the Night*, 57).

48. "Religious Ideas in Alchemy," *Psychology and Alchemy*, par. 334.

49. In *The Seaboard Parish*, which appeared in 1868, just before the serialisation of *At the Back of the North Wind* began, MacDonald describes the baby found abandoned in the vicarage garden as "God's baby" (59)—in this case in the sense of God's gift.

50. In *David Elginbrod* the tutor, Hugh Sutherland, is the protagonist, and he makes a nest in an oak-tree for his pupil (153-154) and often sits in it himself: "It had become almost a habit with Hugh to ascend the oak-tree in the evening, and sit alone, sometimes for hours, in the nest he had built for Harry" (285).

51. Nanny's name suggests her eventual role. Interestingly, in the episode of *At the Back of the North Wind* published on July 1st 1870 in *Good Words for the Young*, her name is given as "Nannie," which is much more like a name or nickname; see the comparison between the serial version and the first edition of *ABNW* in the Broadview 2011 edition of *At the Back of the North Wind*, 37.

52. The *Concise Oxford Dictionary* gives "ducky diamond" as a synonym for "darling." The term 'diamond' comes from London slang and is still in fairly common use, particularly in the expression "Diamond Geezer," or 'a really great guy' (heard recently on the BBC). Not long ago a washing machine repairman called me a diamond for offering him a cup of tea! The word 'duck' or 'ducks' has long been a friendly, if informal mode of address in cockney English and in some parts of the country outside London (the Scottish equivalent is 'hen'). The term "duck o' diamonds" has always been a great compliment—unless used sarcastically.

53. *The Oxford Dictionary of English Etymology*, ed. C.T. Onions (Oxford 1966).

54. Cit. in Jung, "Religious Ideas in Alchemy," *Psychology and Alchemy*, par. 378. See also 1 Peter 2:4, in which Jesus is compared to a "living stone."

55. In "The Imagination: Its Functions and Its Culture," MacDonald refers to heaven as the "crystal shrine" of religion (*Orts*, 30).

56. First published by Jane Taylor in *Rhymes for the Nursery* in 1806 and obviously known long before. By about 1860 it had been set to music and about ten years later it formed the basis of a pantomime (see *The Oxford Companion to Children's Literature*, 547). MacDonald was always alive to this image; in *David Elginbrod* he says that "the stars were sparkling overhead like diamonds that had been drinking the light of the sun all day" (*DE* 314).

57. See Jung, "The Psychological Aspects of the Kore," *Archetypes*, par. 343: "From ancient times any relationship to the stars has always symbolized eternity. The soul comes 'from the stars' and returns to the stellar regions." This could hardly be closer to Diamond's two-layered dream of the stars and his subsequent desire to return to them: "I can see the first star peeping out of the sky. I should like to get up into the sky. Don't you think I shall, some day?" (*ABNW 344*). MacDonald was a great lover of Dante (see *ABNW* 113-115, where he writes about "Durante's" experience of visiting the country at North Wind's back); the last line of

each of the three parts of the *Divina Commedia*—*Inferno*, *Purgatorio* and *Paradiso*—refers to the stars.

58. "Concerning Mandala Symbolism," *Archetypes*, par. 637. And, as Catherine Persyn notes, "Diamond . . . has become his own name" ("'In My End is My Beginning': The *fin-negans* Motif in George MacDonald's *At the Back of the North Wind*," *Mythlore* 24 [2006], 64). See "The New Name," in *Unspoken Sermons Series 1:* "[I]t is only when the man has become his name that God gives him the stone with his name upon it, for then first can he understand what his name signifies" (72).

59. Interestingly, *The Miracles of Our Lord* was originally serialised in the *Sunday Magazine* from October 1869 to September 1870 (see Daniel Gabelman, "'Divine Alchemy': *The Miracles of Our Lord* in its Context," in *Rethinking George MacDonald: Contexts and Contemporaries*, ed. MacLachlan, Pazdziora and Stelle [Glasgow 2013], 23). *At the Back of the North Wind* was serialised in *Good Words for the Young* at roughly the same time (November 1868-October 1870; see the Broadview 2011 edition of *At the Back of the North Wind*, 35-38). The essays "The Raising of the Dead," "The Resurrection" and "The Transfiguration"—which MacDonald sees as "a foretaste of the resurrection" (*Miracles*, 436)—must have been much in MacDonald's mind when he was writing *At the Back of the North Wind*.

ENDNOTES TO CHAPTER 2

1. See Roderick McGillis, "Outworn Liberal Humanism: George MacDonald and 'The Right Relation to the Whole,'" in *Behind the Back of the North Wind* (Hamden, CT, 2011), 82.

2. Kirstin Jeffrey Johnson, in "Curdie's Intertextual Dialogue," in *George MacDonald: Literary Heritage and Heirs*, ed. Roderick McGillis, asserts the importance of considering MacDonald's work "contextually" (153ff); her focus is on the literary, theological and biblical context of *The Princess and Curdie*. Fernando Soto, in "The Two-World Consciousness of *North Wind*: Unity and Dichotomy in

MacDonald's Fairy Tale," in *Behind the Back of the North Wind*, situates *At the Back of the North Wind* in the context of Greek mythology (128-147). MacDonald himself is very much aware of the importance of contexts, both 'outside' and (in *At the Back of the North Wind* especially) 'inside' the book, i.e. in the depiction of Diamond's character.

3. See, e.g., Robert Lee Wolff, *The Golden Key: A Study of the Fiction of George MacDonald* (New Haven, CT, 1961), 148, 160; Colin Manlove, *Modern Fantasy: Five Studies* (Cambridge, 1975), 79-80, and "A Reading of *At the Back of the North Wind*" in *Behind the Back of the North Wind*, where he points out that Diamond is a "dia-mond or two-world soul" (172); Fernando Soto, "The Two-World Consciousness of *North Wind:* Unity and Dichotomy in MacDonald's Fairy Tale," in *Behind the Back of the North Wind*, 128-147. Stephen Prickett, in *Victorian Fantasy*, says: "We cannot fully reconcile the two realms" (167); Naomi J. Wood says that "the work divides into two halves, two worlds, two modes" ("Suffer the Children: The Problem of the Loving Father in *At the Back of the North Wind*," in *Behind the Back of the North Wind*, 64) and Roderick McGillis, in "Language and Secret Knowledge in *At the Back of the North Wind*," says that "[t]he centre of serenity . . . is clearly evident both in the noumenal world of fantasy and in the phenomenal world of London" (*For the Childlike: George MacDonald's Fantasies for Children*, 147). Greville MacDonald was probably the first to write of the "two-world consciousness" of *At the Back of the North Wind* (*GMHW* 361).

4. Ronald MacDonald, "George MacDonald: A Personal Note," in *View From a Northern Window*, 103. He adds that "[b]ecause [MacDonald's] religion was his life, he could no more divide the religious from the secular than a fish separate swimming from water" (112).

5. *Pace* Rolland Hein, who says: "[A]s long as *At the Back of the North Wind* maintains a semi-fantastic setting, it . . . is charming and convincing; but at the point at which it seeks to demonstrate its theme in the real world of London coachmen, it fails to sustain one's acceptance" (*The Harmony Within: The Spiritual Vision of George MacDonald* [Grand

Rapids, Michigan, 1982], 51-52). Ulrich Knoepflmacher describes the book as having a "meandering quality" and as "a narrative that challenges our habitual notions of structure"—a challenge to which the looser format of serial publication afforded scope ("Erasing Borders: MacDonald's *At the Back of the North Wind*," in *Ventures into Childland*, 229).

6. Sir Llewellyn Woodward, *The Age of Reform, 1815-70;* 42. MacDonald himself first travelled to Huntly by train in 1855; the train ran right past his family home to the nearby station (see Raeper, *George MacDonald,* 126-127). The beginning of the railway era had a tremendously energising effect. Not only did it greatly increase the possibilities of travel but it brought change in other areas; it has even been credited with helping to inspire the Impressionist Movement through the new-found freedom it afforded (Hannah Furness, Arts Correspondent of the *Daily Telegraph,* quotes Philip Hook, author and senior international specialist at Sotheby's, to this effect [*DT* Jan. 26th 2015). John Ruskin, in *The Ethics of the Dust* (1866), is less enthusiastic, but cannot deny the impact of the railways: "I heard an orator, and a good one too, at the Working Men's College ... make a great point in a description of our railroads; saying, with grandly conducted emphasis, 'They have made man greater, and the world less.' His working audience were mightily pleased ..." (22). Charles Dickens, whose character, Paul Dombey, in *Dombey and Son* (first published serially between 1846 and 1848) probably influenced the characterisation of Diamond, is very interested in railway travel (not always in its most felicitous aspects; the villainous James Carker is cut to pieces by a train). Dickens himself was involved, on Sept. 2nd 1865, in a serious train crash on the South Eastern Railway (the line, though not the route that Diamond would have used) in which some passengers lost their lives and which nearly cost him part of the manuscript of *Our Mutual Friend,* as he discloses in the postscript to that novel. One of his favourite dogs died in another railway accident later that year (see *The Charles Dickens Encyclopedia,* ed. Michael and Mollie Hardwick [London, 1973], 364).

7. *The Age of Reform*, 47-49.

8. When Diamond drives his father's cab in Bloomsbury we see the blending of old and new; his very first fare is a man in a hurry to catch a train, and Diamond takes him to King's Cross—a railway station opened in 1852 to replace a smaller one built just before the Great Exhibition of 1851. When he gives a free ride to the man who saves him from the roughs in Wapping (210), and who turns out to be Miss Coleman's former intended, they initially start off for Charing Cross, a railway station only opened in 1864 (see "Eleanor Cross" in *Wikipedia*).

9. The *Concise Oxford Dictionary* says that coal is sometimes referred to as "black diamond." Stephen Prickett notes that diamond is a form of carbon, the same element as graphite, a type of coal (preface to the Broadview 2011 edition of *At the Back of the North Wind*, 10). See also Lisa Makman's article, "Child's Work Is Child's Play: The Value of George MacDonald's Diamond," in which she discusses the connection between coal, diamonds and coal mining (*Behind the Back of the North Wind*, 110). She also points out that Hugh Macmillan, in the December 1868 issue of *Good Words for the Young*, published an article entitled "A Lump of Coal" in which he explained the origins of coal in terms of a precious treasure associated with the magic of childhood (122; the serialisation of *At the Back of the North Wind* began in October). John Ruskin, in *The Ethics of the Dust* (originally ten lectures on the elements of crystallization delivered at a girls' school), says that diamonds and charcoal are closely related (*Dust*, 10; N.B. he also mentions the Crystal Palace, 22-23). MacDonald was presumably familiar with *The Ethics of the Dust*, for the phrase "valley of diamonds" occurs in his essay "The Government of Nature" in *The Miracles of Our Lord* (1870), 417: Ruskin's first lecture is entitled "The Valley of Diamonds." Interest in geology was widespread in Victorian times, particularly following Charles Lyell's publications on the subject in the 1830s. Charles Kingsley, whose "Madam How and Lady Why, or, First Lessons in Earth Lore for Children" appeared in early issues of *Good Words for the Young*, also wrote an essay about coal—"The Coal in the Fire," in *Town Geology*, 1872—in which he

says: "We may consider the coal upon the fire as the middle term of a series, of which the first is live wood, and the last diamond" (7). MacDonald read geological works from as early as 1845, says Gisela Kreglinger in *Storied Revelations* (114), and he had studied chemistry, among other things, at King's College, Aberdeen.

10. 'Speculation' is the key word here. MacDonald tells us that "no man can make haste to be rich without going against the will of God, in which it is the one frightful thing to be successful" (*ABNW* 247)—and the man who was so set against gambling that he would not allow anyone who had so much as set foot in Monte Carlo to visit the Casa Corragio (Raeper, 354) disapproved strongly of the behaviour of Miss Coleman's unsatisfactory suitor, Mr. Evans: "[I]t was in a measure through his influence that [Mr. Coleman] entered upon those speculations which ruined him" (*ABNW* 246).

11. This is something that really registers with MacDonald. In *David Elginbrod* (1863) he says that the impoverished Hugh Sutherland "rarely made use of a crossing on a muddy day, without finding a half-penny somewhere about him for the sweeper. He would rather walk through oceans of mud, than cross at the natural place when he had no coppers" (315-316).

12. See Jung, *Psychology and Alchemy*, pars. 425, 426ff.

13. "Hoxton, where [Mr. Coleman] would be unknown" (*ABNW* 130).

14. "I will smite the winter house with the summer house; and the houses of ivory shall perish, and the great houses shall have an end, saith the LORD" (Amos 3:15). This is the only reference to a summer house (presumably a second home) in the Bible.

15. Though MacDonald is aware of the limitations of money, he is far from seeing it as an evil thing: "Money was the token of service rendered, and like all symbols must be treated reverently," says Greville MacDonald of his father's attitude to it (*GMHW* 346), and, in a letter to Mrs. A. J. Scott, MacDonald claims "a sense of the sacredness of money and . . . a conviction that it is only the vulgar mind

that regards it as an unclean thing—because in secret it worships it" (cit. in *GMHW*, 440). It is interesting to note that Curdie, in *The Princess and Curdie*, obliged to go into the empty baker's shop when the palace is virtually under siege and take a loaf of bread for the king, leaves the price of it on the counter (208). In *At the Back of the North Wind* Diamond is aware of the practical necessity of earning a living and his scrupulousness in working out the correct fare for an old gentleman has already demonstrated his responsible and businesslike attitude to money (224).

16. Paul Dombey, in Dickens' *Dombey and Son* (1848), has a somewhat similar discussion with his father (who is similarly wrongfooted). "What's money after all?" Paul asks his father. "I mean, Papa, what can it do?" . . . . "Money, Paul, can do anything." . . . . "'If it's a good thing, and can do anything,' said the little fellow, thoughtfully . . . 'I wonder why it didn't save me my Mama.' He didn't ask the question of his father this time. Perhaps he had seen, with a child's quickness, that it had already made his father uncomfortable" (Ch. V111).

17. To give but two examples from work of the same period, the ring Queen Irene gives to Princess Irene, in *The Princess and the Goblin*, is in fact her mother's ring, as her king-papa attests (*The Princess and the Goblin*, 165). In the earlier *Guild Court* (1868), Lucy Burton's ring ("a good-sized rose-diamond" [365]) is "her mother's jewel" (309) and an important factor in the plot; while in the still earlier *David Elginbrod* (1863) it is Hugh's father's diamond ring which is stolen by Von Funkelstein (the 'false stone') together with a much less valuable crystal ring which is an heirloom with mysterious associations (278-279).

18. MacDonald uses the same metaphor in relation to Mr. Dempster in "The Butcher's Bills": "Dempster . . . was not yet a clinker out of which all the life was burned" (*Stephen Archer and Other Tales*, 153).

19. In the course of his visionary ascent to heaven in the penultimate chapter of *Lilith*, Mr. Vane says of the stones that fashioned the gate of the celestial city: "[A]mong them I saw the prototypes of all the gems I had loved on earth—

far more beautiful than they, for these were living stones" (*L* 355). But then, "nothing in this kingdom was dead; nothing was mere; nothing only a thing" (356).

20. *The Interpreter's Dictionary of the Bible: An Illustrated Encyclopedia*, ed. Buttrick, George Arthur and others (New York, 1962), 11, 904. See also *The Jewish Annotated New Testament*, ed. Levine and Brettler, which discusses the symbolic value of the number twelve in the context of Judaism; "the structure of John's eschatological Jerusalem", in particular, "reflects the twelve-fold perfection of Israel" (note on Revelation Ch. 6, 475).

21. St. Thomas is recalling a saying of Aristotle. Cit. in Jung, "Christ, a Symbol of the Self" (*Aion*, par. 92).

22. See Jung, "The Personification of the Opposites," in which he cites St. Hilary as saying that "salt contains in itself the element of water and fire" and Picinellus as saying: "Two elements which stir up an implacable enmity between themselves are found in wondrous alliance in salt. For salt is wholly fire and wholly water." Jung also says that "the most outstanding properties of salt are bitterness and wisdom" (*Mysterium Coniunctionis*, pars. 326, 330).

23. "*At The Back of the North Wind* is no less than a rewriting of the *Purgatorio* for children," says Humphrey Carpenter in *Secret Gardens: A Study of the Golden Age of Children's Literature* (Boston, 1985, 82), referring particularly to Diamond's visionary experience of the land at North Wind's back. Early in the chapter entitled, like the book, "At the Back of the North Wind," MacDonald writes at some length about "Durante" (*ABNW* 114). Several critics have discussed Dante's influence on MacDonald; for a detailed study in relation to *At the Back of the North Wind* see John Patrick Padziora and Joshua Richards, "The Dantean Tradition in George MacDonald's *At the Back of the North Wind*," *SEVEN: An Anglo-American Literary Review* 29 (2012), esp. 63-78.

24. Cit. in Jung, "Symbols of the Mother and of Rebirth," in *Symbols of Transformation*, par. 308. Diamond is certainly not the "sun-god" of whom Frobenius speaks, but he is a "solar figure" both symbolically (because a diamond

contains light) and psychologically (because he is coming into consciousness). Metaphorically he is, like the sun-god, "shut up in the mother's womb"—or as nearly as makes no matter--because, as North Wind puts it, "[t]he yacht shall be my cradle, and you shall be my baby" (*ABNW* 105).

25. See Cope, *Symbolism in the Bible and the Church*, 93, 94.

26. Compare the children in C. S. Lewis's *The Chronicles of Narnia*, who find that *no* time has elapsed when they return from Narnia to this world. The whole episode of Diamond's supposed visit to the land at North Wind's back is somewhat reminiscent of St. Paul's experience (obliquely referred to) of having been caught up into the third heaven, "whether in the body, I cannot tell; or whether out of the body, I cannot tell" (2 Corinthians 12:2ff). Ulrich Knoepflmacher describes it as limbo and—in a chapter fortuitously entitled "Erasing Borders"—as "a borderland between life and death" (*Ventures into Childland*, 241, 249).

27. MacDonald's trip to Norway on the *Blue Bell* (during which he suffered agonies from an abscessed knee) began on June 10th 1869 and ended on July 1st; the instalments of *At the Back of the North Wind* had been appearing monthly and it may be supposed that the July 1st instalment—Ch. VI, "Out in the Storm" in the eventual book—was already with the printer before he left. No episode appeared on August 1st, as he was presumably recuperating, but in the November issue, Part 11 in the serialised version, Chapter 1 is entitled (like Ch. 1X in the book), "How Diamond got to the Back of the North Wind." Martha greeted her sick son in the December 1869 issue of *Good Words for the Young*. See "Comparison of the Serial Version and First Edition of *At the Back of the North Wind*" in *At the Back of the North Wind*, ed. Roderick McGillis and John Pennington, 35, 36.

28. *Symbolism in the Bible and in the Church*, 94.

29. Though it has been prepared for earlier in childhood. Left alone in a cathedral while North Wind sinks a ship, "he thought he could sing. . . . at home he used to sing, to tunes of his own, all the nursery rhymes he knew. So he began to try *Hey diddle diddle*, but it wouldn't do. Then he tried *Little Boy Blue*, but it was no better. Neither would *Sing a Song of*

Sixpence sing itself at all. Then he tried *Poor old Cockytoo*, but he wouldn't do. They all sounded so silly! And he had never thought them silly before" (85-86).

30. Paradise Row was in what was then a run-down area; John Ruskin purchased property there for Octavia Hill's slum reform movement (see the Broadview 2011 edition of *At the Back of the North Wind*, 171 n1). An ironic address, though a real place, it is first found in *If I Had a Father*, a drama written soon after *Phantastes* but not published until it was included in *Stephen Archer and Other Tales* (1882). The address occurs in the context of a father, Thomas, looking for his daughter (*SAOT* 273, 275)—very different from the situation in *At the Back of the North Wind*. But there is a strong correspondence in family irregularity (Nanny's being the family in question in the latter book). Bill, a street urchin interrogated by the father, Thomas, says he lives in the church cellar with an aunt ("haunt") who "feeds musty, and smells strong" (274).

31. Bill, in *If I Had a Father*, comments that Thomas is probably his daughter's natural enemy: "Ain't it yer father as bumps yer 'ed, an' cusses ye, an' lets ye see him eat?" (*SAOT* 276), and "fathers ain't nice i' this 'ere part 'o the continent" (291). By the end of the play, however, Bill is more positive: "Shouldn't mind much if I had a father o' my own arter all!" (353).

32. After which they do (Cripple Jim, like Nanny, never returns to the mother who has injured and starved him—and he had left his original haunts even before moving to The Mound [334]). At one point, when Diamond is singing in the garden at The Mound, "Nanny and Jim sat a little way off, one hemming a pocket-handkerchief, and the other reading a story to her" (349). There is no indication of how or when Cripple Jim learned to read.

33. Colin Manlove, in "A Reading of *At the Back of the North Wind*," says that London "is peopled with alchemical symbolism in the names Mr. Coleman, Old Sal, Diamond, and Ruby" (*Behind the Back of the North Wind*, 158). Old Sal the cellar-dweller ('sal' is often used for salt in alchemy) is of key importance, although she is neither seen (except

in Arthur Hughes' illustration) nor heard, and she has kindred—possibly descendants—in Ursula Le Guin's *The Tombs of Atuan* (1972), the second of the *Earthsea* books, in which the menacing Nameless Ones of earth, foes to individual consciousness and freedom, are inseparably linked with their subterranean element (and further removed from individuality than Old Sal, for no-one ever sees them, even 'off-stage' like Nanny and other characters in *At the Back of the North Wind*). Ursula Le Guin is familiar with MacDonald's work, as is clear from her having written the introduction to the Puffin Classics edition of *The Princess and the Goblin* (ed. of 2010), v-vi.

34. Little Christmas, a crossing-sweeper in "My Uncle Peter" (*Adela Cathcart* [1864], 289-294), is a forerunner of Nanny, as is Poppie in *Guild Court* (1868). Nanny also owes something to Nancy Kennedy, in *Robert Falconer* (1867-68), a girl sold to an inveterate drinker, Widow Walker, with a view to becoming a prostitute. Nelly, in the same work, already seems to be a prostitute at the behest of an unpleasant elderly woman who refers to her as her child (461-463); she perhaps represents what Nanny, in *At the Back of the North Wind*, might have become—what, seen from a realistic perspective, she probably would have become had she not been rescued; Old Sal's apparently capricious habit of shutting her out from time to time may be a more sinister exercise of power than it appears ('you have nowhere and nothing without me'). Nanny, however, embodies a much fuller development of certain aspects of Nancy and Nelly—and in any case MacDonald would never have mentioned the prospect of prostitution in view of his primary readership of children. Maggy, in Dickens's *Little Dorrit* (1855-57), may also have helped shape Nanny; certainly they both experience hospital as paradise (probably the reference in both cases is to the Great Ormond Street Hospital for Sick Children). Robert Lee Wolff points out Nanny's debt to Jo the crossing-sweeper in *Bleak House*, which was published in 1853 (see *The Golden Key*, 157); and it is interesting to note that in an uncorrected slip in both the serial and book versions of *At the Back of the North Wind*, the crossing-sweeper Cripple Jim is referred to at

one point as Joe (255). In the Broadview 2011 edition of *At the Back of the North Wind* there is an extract from a chapter of Henry Mayhew's *London Labour and the London Poor* (1852) in which he describes the conditions of crossing-sweepers in general and of one in particular ("Crossing-Sweepers," Appendix C, 345-347).

35. She is admitted to the fever ward in hospital; and see Broadview *ABNW*, 188 n5.

36. Jean Webb, "Realism, Fantasy and a Critique of Nineteenth Century Society in George MacDonald's *At the Back of the North Wind*," in *"A Noble Unrest": Contemporary Essays on the Work of George MacDonald*, ed. Jean Webb (Newcastle, 2007), 17.

37. Poppie, in *Guild Court* (1868), is tormented by boys who throw dirt at her when she is sweeping her crossing. This is how she reacts: "I looks up at St. Pauls's, and I says, 'Please, Jesus Christ, help me to give it 'em.' And then I flies at 'em with my broom, and I knocks one of 'em down" (*GC* 267). In this book Poppie (not his mother) lames the boy—a cart goes over his leg—and she gives him all her "ha'pence." In *At the Back of the North Wind* these elements are rearranged and extended into a relationship between boy and girl.

38. The Book of Deuteronomy also speaks of "the precious things of the earth," and MacDonald is surely echoing these words. They are part of a litany of blessings proclaimed by Moses before his death:

> Blessed of the LORD be [Joseph's] land, for the precious things of heaven, for the dew, and for the deep that coucheth beneath,
>
> And for the precious fruits brought forth by the sun, and for the precious things put forth by the moon,
>
> And for the chief things of the ancient mountains, and for the precious things of the lasting hills,
>
> And for the precious things of the earth and fullness thereof
>
> (33:13-16)

ENDNOTES TO CHAPTER 3

1. See, e.g., Amos 2:9: "Yet destroyed I the Amorite before them, whose height was like the height of the cedars, and he was strong as the oaks; yet I destroyed his fruit from above, and his roots from beneath."
2. Presumably a country retreat.
3. See, e.g., Jeremiah 29:17, 18; 42:17; Ezekiel 14:21.
4. MacDonald loves Coleridge's poetry so much that, had he not specifically referred to the Bible here, it would be tempting to see an allusion to "Kubla Khan"--"A damsel with a dulcimer/ In a vision once I saw"—especially as Coleridge also speaks of "those caves of ice!" The poem would, of course, have been out of Diamond's reach at this point, but it surely resonates with the author.
5. J. Lindblom: *Prophecy in Ancient Israel* (Oxford, 1962), 6.
6. This resembles a passage in the earlier *David Elginbrod* (1863): "He . . . dreamed that he was a little child, lost in a snowstorm; and that, just as the snow had reached above his head, and he was beginning to be smothered, a great hand caught hold of him by the arm and lifted him out" (314).
7. This passage also resembles some verses from Ezekiel in which the prophet is overcome by "the appearance of the likeness of the glory of the LORD. / And when I saw it, I fell upon my face, and I heard a voice of one that spake. / And he said unto me, Son of man, stand upon thy feet, and I will speak unto thee" (Ezek. 1:28 and 2:1). Later, the spirit "put forth the form of an hand, and took me by a lock of mine head; and the spirit lifted me up between the earth and the heaven" (Ezek. 8:3). Ezekiel's mission, however, is to warn evildoers to change their ways and to proclaim the future punishment of those who do not, in which he is quite unlike Diamond.
8. With a condensation of metaphor, the tree suggests not only the place where it has grown—"the wilderness"— but its owner, Mr. Coleman ("being much decayed in the middle" [90]).

9. Note the switch to specifically religious terminology.

10. Catherine Persyn describes this as a stage in the "psychanody, or ascent of the psyche to its original source" which is "the alchemical Great Work," to be completed by the deserving through a "second death" ("'In my end is my beginning': the fin-negans motif in George MacDonald's *At the Back of the North Wind*," *Mythlore* 24 [2006], 60, 58, 61). Ulrich Knoepflmacher characterises Diamond's subsequent return through North Wind as a second birth (*Ventures into Childland*, 247).

11. Daniel praises God for "[giving] wisdom unto the wise, and knowledge to them that know understanding; / He revealeth the deep and secret things; he knoweth what is in the darkness, and the light dwelleth with him" (Daniel 2:21-22).

12. The king's failure to remember the dream is understandable, for it proves not to be a revelation of Nebuchadnezzar's unconscious self but a disclosure of the present and future state of the kingdom of Babylon which has come to him from God because of his standing as king. The next time, Nebuchadnezzar manages to remember his dream—of a great tree which, Daniel tells him, represents the king himself and tells of his present might, future downfall and ultimate redemption.

13. In *Wilfrid Cumbermede* (1872) an ice-cave is also the locus of death and death-like experiences (141-142, 163-164), though it suggests "the infinite of God" in its origins (142) and in the possibility of resurrection (164).

14. See Daniel 7:1-28.

15. North Wind gives Nanny the dream of the moon because she is psychologically ready, or potentially ready for it, although her earlier habits of thought prove too strong; she soon regresses to dismissing it as "only a dream" (308) and later as nonsense (355). In *Adela Cathcart* (1864) MacDonald makes it plain that dreams can have a strong connection with the personal unconscious: "I had entered the secret places of my own hidden world by the gate of sleep, and walked about them in my dream," says John Smith (460).

16. For a detailed and fascinating discussion of the symbolic meaning of the moon, and especially of North Wind's identity as a "Lunar Goddess," see Catherine Persyn's article "A Person's Name and a Person's Self, or: Just *Who is North Wind*," *North Wind* 22 (2003), 62 et al. See also her "'In My End is My Beginning': The *fin-negans* Motif in George MacDonald's *At the Back of the North Wind*," *Mythlore* 24 (2006), esp. 60-61, 63-64.

17. *"The Psychological Aspects of the Kore,"* in *The Archetypes and the Collective Unconscious*, par. 343. MacDonald was a great lover of Dante (see *ABNW* 113-115, where he writes about "Durante's" experience of visiting the country at North Wind's back); the last line of each of the three parts of the *Divine Comedy*—*Inferno, Purgatorio* and *Paradiso*—refers to the stars.

18. There are marked resemblances between the Revelation of St. John and the later chapters of the Book of Daniel, especially Ch. 7.

19. There is a horse called Thanatos, or Death, in *The Flight of the Shadow* (1891). He is usually referred to by the English translation of his name and even, on one occasion, as "dear old Death" (*FS* 71).

20. See Lesley Willis (Smith), "Old Wine in New Bottles: Aspects of Prophecy in George MacDonald's *At the Back of the North Wind*," in *Behind the Back of the North Wind*, 35 (from *For the Childlike*).

21. The great sword given to him is "a symbol of divine chastisement" (see M. G. Easton, *The Illustrated Bible Dictionary*, revised ed. [London, 1989], 646); and a symbol of war (see, e.g., note to Rev. 6: 4 in the *Jerusalem Bible*).

22. Joseph is of course wrong. Ruby thinks he should save himself for his own master, and the worst piece of "ill luck" is the result of an act of wilful destruction—the deliberate spraining of his ankle which prevents him from working for a month. Ruby can have even more negative associations: Carl Jung, in "The Battle for Deliverance from the Mother," *Symbols of Transformation*, says that "[t]he goddess of death, Hel, rides on a three-legged horse in time of pestilence" (par. 428).

23. This necessity is not explained, but Ruby is not contradicted.
24. Coleman Parsons points out that Arthur Hughes makes Old Diamond black in the August 1870 number of *Good Words for the Young;* see "The Progenitors of Black Beauty in Humanitarian Literature," *Notes and Queries* (19 April 1947), 156.
25. See note on Rev. 6:5-6, *New Jerusalem Bible*, 2037; the balances are a symbol of famine. In *The Flight of the Shadow* (1891) there is a horse whose name means "death" and who looks very like Old Diamond at this juncture: "[O]h, how changed he seemed! His tall figure hung bent over the pommel, his neck drooped heavily. And the horse was so thin that I seemed to see, almost to feel his bones. Poor Thanatos! he looked tired to death . . ." (*FS* 260).
26. Compare *Wilfrid Cumbermede*, in which the protagonist finds his former mare Lilith—"my white Lilith" (426)—pulling a one-horse chaise: "Was it possible?—could it be my Lilith betwixt the shafts of a public cabriolet? . . . . She was badly groomed and thin, but much of her old spirit remained. I soon entered into negotiations with the driver . . . . and made her my own once more . . . . She turned her head sideways towards me with a low whinny of pleasure" (456-457). The near-apocalyptic language is lacking.
27. Subsequently Gabriel addresses him as "a man greatly beloved" and "O man greatly beloved" (Dan. 10:11, 19). The importance of understanding and considering is also emphasised: "And I heard a man's voice . . . which called, and said, Gabriel, make this man to understand the vision. . . . [Gabriel] said unto me, Understand, O son of man" (Dan. 8:16-17).
28. See Matthew 6:31, 34: "Therefore take no thought, saying, What shall we eat? or, What shall we drink? or, Wherewithal shall we be clothed? . . . . Take therefore no thought for the morrow; for the morrow shall take thought for the things of itself. Sufficient unto the day is the evil thereof." See also Luke 12:22-23, 29-30.
29. In a rare slip, North Wind specifies twice, rather than three times as many lambs—but it does not matter, for the recognition of individuality is the point. Diamond

comments that the poem seems to say "two new ones are better than one that's lost" (360), which he does not believe: "Nobody, ever so beautiful or so good, will ever make up for that one going out of sight" (361).

30. MacDonald echoes this idea in *The Diary of an Old Soul*: "Thou in my heart hast planted, gardener divine / A scion of the tree of life" (*Rampolli*, 188: January, v.21).

31. God even compares himself to a tree: "I am like a green fir tree. From me is thy fruit found" (Hosea 14:8).

32. Another woman who, like North Wind as the lady in the moon in Nanny's dream, sits with her head in her hand.

33. John Pennington says that "*North Wind* subverts closure [striven for by realistic novels] by ironically portraying death as a new and better beginning" ("Alice at the Back of the North Wind, or the Metafictions of Lewis Carroll and George MacDonald," *Behind the Back of the North Wind*, 56).

ENDNOTES TO CHAPTER 4

1. "The Voice of Job," in *Unspoken Sermons Second Series* (1885), 328-362; 328.

2. Another difference; instead of the prospect of eternity, Job gets a lifespan of 140 years and continuity through his many descendants, but for MacDonald resurrection is a perennial theme. The early novel *The Seaboard Parish* (1868) is aglow with it, and Mr. Walton preaches a sermon on the subject which occupies almost a whole chapter (409-422). In MacDonald's last novel, *Salted With Fire* (1897), there are two resurrections within the book itself; first the improbable bodily resurrection of Isy, who for two weeks is apparently dead, and secondly the far more important spiritual resurrection of James Blatherwick: "He had been dead, and was alive again!" (290; see Luke 15:24: "[M]y son was dead, and is alive again," and 15:32: "[T]hy brother was dead, and is alive again"). All these 'in-life' resurrections are preludes to the "glorious resurrection-morning" foreseen in *Lilith* (L 349).

3. Gisela Kreglinger notes that the personification of death was quite common in Victorian fiction; see *Storied Revelations*, 164. See also Melody Green, "Death and Nonsense in the Poetry of George MacDonald's *At the Back of the North Wind* and Lewis Carroll's *Alice* books" (*North Wind*, 30 [2011], esp. 40-41). Marilyn Pemberton, in "The Ultimate Rite of Passage: Death and Beyond in 'The Golden Key' and *At the Back of the North Wind*" (*North Wind*, 27 [2008]), says that "one of the North Wind's guises is that of Death itself" (42); and Gillian Avery, in "George MacDonald," describes North Wind as "a mother-figure, but also a personification of death" (*The Oxford Companion to Fairy Tales*, 373).

4. "Even fairy-stories as a whole have three faces: the Mystical towards the Supernatural; the Magical towards Nature; and the Mirror of scorn and pity towards Man," says Tolkien. "The essential face of Faerie is the middle one, the Magical. But the degree in which the others appear (if at all) is variable" ("On Fairy-Stories," in *Tree and Leaf*, 26).

5. See, e.g., David Robb, "Fiction for the Child," in *George MacDonald* (Edinburgh, 1987). He describes North Wind as "a compendium of all the many and contradictory meanings which we detect in her" (126)—including the power of nature and something like poetic inspiration. Her "overriding identification" is with death (124). (Part of "Fiction for the Child" has been republished in *Behind the Back of the North Wind*, 26-31).

6. See Carl Jung, "The Syzygy: Anima and Animus," in *Aion: Researches into the Phenomenology of the Self*, par. 33: The anima is "a psychopomp, a mediator between the conscious and the unconscious and a personification of the latter." This is what connecting the Primary and Secondary Worlds in *At the Back of the North Wind* often entails.

7. North Wind doesn't mind "re-echoing" this trigger in the dream she sends to Nanny, who has never seen the inside of The Wilderness, but who seeks refuge from the yelping dog in a little summer house with a ruby-coloured pane (297-298). The 'real' summer house at the Colemans' has a little window with coloured glass (55).

8. See, e.g., "The Battle for Deliverance from the Mother," *Symbols of Transformation*, par. 4
9. "The Psychological Aspects of the Kore," in *Archetypes*: "From ancient times any relationship to the stars has always symbolized eternity. The soul comes 'from the stars' and returns to the stellar regions" (par. 343).
10. Odd, this, since, as Jung points out in *Aion*, the left corresponds to the feminine ("Christ, a Symbol of the Self," par. 99). The masculinity of the boy-angels, not yet complemented by the femininity of the girl-angels, indicates a certain androgyny.
11. "Wordsworth's Poetry," in *A Dish of Orts*, 256. McGillis and Pennington, in the Broadview edition of *At the Back of the North Wind*, compare Diamond's dream with Wordsworth's "Ode," in which birth is a sleep and a forgetting (207n).
12. See Wordsworth's Preface to his "Ode: Intimations of Immortality from Recollections of Early Childhood," in *English Romantic Writers*, ed. David Perkins (New York, 1967), 279.
13. Colin Manlove says that MacDonald "valued the imagination because he believed it to be the dwelling-place of God in man" (*The Impulse of Fantasy Literature* [London & Basingstoke, 1983], 72). "To inquire into what God has made is the main function of the imagination," says MacDonald himself in "The Imagination: Its Functions and Its Culture" (*A Dish of Orts*, 2; this essay originally published in 1867).
14. See, e.g., Charles Kingsley's *The Water-Babies* (1863) and MacDonald's own *The Wise Woman: A Parable*, originally published as *The Lost Princess: Or the Wise Woman* (1875). Bonnie Gaarden, in *The Christian Goddess: Archetype and Theology in the Fantasies of George MacDonald*, comments: "Fairy and folktale, which surged in popularity during the Victorian era, have strong genre conventions of powerful female figures (the Wise Woman, the Fairy Godmother), but MacDonald appears to be the only Victorian writer who regularly Christianized these conventions" (2).

15. See Jung, "Psychological Aspects of the Mother Archetype," in *The Archetypes and the Collective Unconscious*, esp. par. 148—"The concept of the Great Mother . . . embraces widely varying types of mother-goddess"—and par. 156. And see Nancy Willard's "The Goddess in the Belfry: Grandmothers and Wise Women in George MacDonald's Books for Children" in *For the Childlike: George MacDonald's Fantasies for Children*, ed. Roderick McGillis, esp. 68. See also Katharine Bubel's article, "Knowing God 'Other-wise': The Wise Old Woman Archetype in George MacDonald's *The Princess and the Goblin*, *The Princess and Curdie* and 'The Golden Key'," in *North Wind*, 25 (2006). Robert Lee Wolff comments that "The Mother-God we have found incarnated in the long succession of grandmother-goddesses, earth-spirits, and wise women in the fairy-tales. In the fiction, God is effeminate" (*The Golden Key*, 374). Bonnie Gaarden, in *The Christian Goddess*, makes a detailed study of these issues.

16. "Concerning Rebirth," *Archetypes*, par. 231.

17. When North Wind takes Diamond to revisit The Wilderness a few days before his death he is disappointed by its changed appearance: "The only thing left that he cared about was the hole in the wall where his little bed had stood" (373)—and this feature rounds off his journeys with North Wind, just as it had begun them. The image of the hole in the wall occurs elsewhere; in "The Carasoyn," for example, the stolen girl talks to Colin through "a hole in the head of your bed"—and "Colin knew the knot-hole well enough" (*The Light Princess and Other Fairy Tales*, 223). The Book of Ezekiel is a possible influence here, for the prophet is shown a hole in the wall by his spirit visitant (Ezek. 8:7) and is required to dig it out and leave by it on his mission. Greville MacDonald cites a letter written in Hastings in 1858: "The house is pretty comfortable now, but the floors are very open between the boards. Through these the wind blows like knives. . . . I have pasted brown paper over the cracks," and posits that this "may have provided the germinal idea for *At the Back of the North Wind*" (*GMHW*, 288 and n.). Perhaps unfortunately, 'the hole in the wall' is now (at least in the UK) a synonym for

a cash dispenser.

18. See Cope, *Symbolism in the Bible and the Church*, on the maternal symbolism of the cradle and on the boat as a symbol of femininity (36)—and see his remarks on the wood of which cradles (and coffins) are made as one of the basic "*mater*-ials" of civilisation (171).

19. Fernando Soto, in "The Two-World Consciousness of *North Wind:* Unity and Dichotomy in MacDonald's Fairy Tales," points out that the meaning of the name 'Martha' in Aramaic is 'a lady' (*Behind the Back of the North Wind*, 146n).

20. Nanny speaks more truly than she knows when she tells Diamond, much later, that he has "a tile loose" (295 and elsewhere).

21. Cf. "We love him, because he first loved us" (The First Epistle General of John, 4:19).

22. David Robb notes that "[a]ll North Wind's visits . . . are stages by which his health is steadily undermined" (*George MacDonald*, 125). North Wind's promise that Diamond will be much better for coming out bodes well for his psychological and spiritual wellbeing, if not for his physical health.

23. The *Light Princess and Other Fairy Tales*, 49.

24. Cope cites John 3:1-8: "The wind bloweth (the spirit breatheth) where it listeth" (*Symbolism*, 101).

25. And see, e.g., Isaiah 14:15: "Yet thou shalt be brought down to hell, to the sides of the pit"; Is. 38:18: "For the grave cannot praise thee, death cannot celebrate thee; they that go down into the pit cannot hope for thy truth"; Ezekiel 26:20: "When I shall bring thee down with them that descend into the pit."

26. *The Golden Bough: A Study in Magic and Religion*, 3rd ed. (London, 1915); see x. 315ff., ii. 330 ff., x. 343, 344, i. 322, 326, 135, and especially xi. 158ff. The strength of the Old Testament hero Samson, in Judges, is also in his hair; though he is definitely not a witch, it is clear that the idea has been around for centuries.

27. "All the strength of [*At the Back of the North Wind's*] teaching is allusive—an appeal to the imaginative seeing of a truth rather than a claim for its passive acceptance on the score of authority," says Greville MacDonald (*George MacDonald and His Wife*, 362). For Diamond the learning process works in the same way.

28. See, e.g., "The Dual Mother," in *Symbols of Transformation*, par. 503, esp: "The animal is a representative of the unconscious, and the latter, as the matrix of consciousness, has a maternal significance. . . . All animals belong to the Great Mother." See also Bruno Bettelheim, *The Uses of Enchantment*, 76.

29. *A Book of Strife, in the Form of the Diary of an Old Soul*, in *Rampolli*, March, 208.

30. Also discussed in my "Old Wine in New Bottles: Aspects of Prophecy in George MacDonald's *At the Back of the North Wind*," in *Behind the Back of the North Wind: Critical Essays on George MacDonald's Classic Children's Book*, ed. John Pennington and Roderick McGillis (from *For the Childlike: George MacDonald's Fantasies for Children*, ed. Roderick McGillis).

31. "Conservatism in Fantasy: Ursula Le Guin," in *The Impulse of Fantasy Literature*, 31.

32. *Christian Fantasy: From 1200 to the Present*, 175.

ENDNOTES TO CHAPTER 5

1. *The Princess and the Goblin* was originally serialised in *Good Words for the Young*, 1870-71, and first published in book form by Strahan (London, 1972).

2. "On Fairy-Stories," in *Tree and Leaf*, 68.

3. *The Marquis of Lossie* (1877), 78.

4. In *The Portent*, published in 1864 (and originally serialised in the first three issues of the *Cornhill Magazine*, 1860), there are three resurrections—the resurrection of waking (28-29); the mysterious resurrection of Duncan Campbell's horse, Constancy (109-110; 120); and "the resurrection

from illness" which is "a resurrection of all nature" (101). In the serialised version of the story Duncan and Lady Alice (who marry in the later version) do not meet again until after death (see Raeper, *George MacDonald* 206). The concept of resurrection, whatever forms it took, always preoccupied MacDonald—but all were foreshadowings of the ultimate resurrection to which he looked forward.

5. St. Matthew refers to Isaiah as saying: "[t]he people which *sat* in darkness saw great light," and continues "to them which *sat* in the region and shadow of death light is sprung up" (4:16; my italics). Definitely less poetic than Isaiah's actual words; but Matthew's verse encapsulates what happens later when Irene runs out on the mountain in the dark instead of keeping her promise to visit her grandmother (*PG* 139), so that there is a suggestion of both the universal and the individual application of the lines.

6. *The Uses of Enchantment*, 98. An interesting variation of this situation, as far as *The Princess and the Goblin* goes, occurs in the story "Tattercoats," in which the daughter of an old lord (a widower) dies in childbirth; in consequence he hates his granddaughter and refuses ever to see her. The other servants, except for an old nurse who occasionally give her scraps of food and torn petticoats from the ragbag, drive her out of doors with blows and mockery; her only friend is a crippled goose herd who plays on his pipe to cheer her. Fortunately he turns out to be the king's son and there is a splendid marriage ("Tattercoats," in the Wordsworth Classics ed. of *English Fairy Tales* [Ware, Hertfordshire, 1994], 55-60).

7. Magic, as Colin Manlove says, "tries to subdue all things to the self," and he instances the One Ring in Tolkien's *The Lord of the Rings* which "makes the people who wear it desire to subdue others to their will while it subdues them to its own" (afterword to "On the Nature of Fantasy," in *The Aesthetics of Fantasy Literature and Art*, ed. Roger C. Schlobin [Notre Dame and Brighton, 1982], 32). Carl Jung thinks along the same lines ("The Fish in Alchemy," *Aion*, par. 216). Bruno Bettelheim, in "The Child's Need for Magic," takes a different view (*The Uses of Enchantment*, 45-53)—but MacDonald inclines to the former side of

the question. His short fairy tales, however, do draw on the power of magic, as Colin Manlove discusses in detail in "MacDonald's Shorter Fairy Tales: Journeys into the Mind" (*SEVEN: An Anglo-American Literary Review* 22 [2005], esp.13).

8. Opinion recorded by Greville MacDonald and cited in W.R. Irwin's *The Game of the Impossible: A Rhetoric of Fantasy* (Urbana, Chicago and London, 1976), 93. Humphrey Carpenter affirms that in *The Princess and the Goblin* MacDonald is "creating an alternative religious landscape which a child's mind could explore and which could offer spiritual nourishment" (*Secret Gardens*, 83).

9. The exception is to be found in *The Princess and Curdie*, where the emerald which the old princess pulls out of the floor in the mine (*PC* 75-76) acts as a sign of Curdie's wellbeing or otherwise when he is far away from his parents.

10. When Lootie sees the ring she has to believe that Irene has always worn it; how else could it make sense to her? (163). The king, on the other hand, when he hears that goblin creatures have been seen in the garden, "I presume would have taken Irene with him that very day *but for what the presence of the ring on her finger assured him of*"—i.e. the presence of Queen Irene (166; italics mine). Bonnie Gaarden, in *The Christian Goddess*, describes the ring as "a mandala symbol" which "represents Irene's conscious connection to the grandmother and is, itself, another symbol of her Christ-self" (127).

11. "In practically every fairy tale good and evil are given body in the form of some figures and their actions," says Bettelheim in *The Uses of Enchantment*, 8-9. "Was he good? Was he wicked?" was the question children often asked Tolkien, for, he says, "they were more concerned to get the Right side and the Wrong side clear" than to ask what Andrew Lang thought they most wanted to know: " 'Is it true?' " ("*On Fairy-Stories,*" 38n, 36).

12. *Good Words for the Young* (June 1871), 420.

13. *Good Words for the Young* (Nov 1870), 3. This may be partly a joke, as MacDonald's daughter Irene was nicknamed "Goblin"—but it's also a 'watershed warning,' along the

lines of TV announcements that 'some people may find material contained in this programme upsetting.' The goblins, with their farcical appearance, are a toned-down version of their predecessors in *Phantastes* who surprise Anodos as he wanders in an "underground country" (*P* 210): "From behind a rock a peal of harsh grating laughter, full of evil, rang through my ears, and, looking round, I saw a queer, goblin creature, with a great head and ridiculous features, just such as those described, in German histories and travels, as Kobolds." To Anodos he and his companions seem "fairy devils" (211). Robert Lee Wolff comments on the goblins in *Phantastes* and other works as manifestations of the German *Elementargeister* (*The Golden Key*, 47, 87 and elsewhere). In *Phantastes* the loving beech tree calls the menacing Ash "the goblin" (*P* 54).

14. Jung discusses "the darkness of the unconscious" in *Mysterium Coniunctionis* ("Adam and Eve," par. 646) and "the dark world of the unconscious" in *Psychology and Alchemy* ("The Prima Materia," in "Religious Ideas in Alchemy," par. 436).

15. In *Symbols of Transformation* Jung says: "The more negative the attitude of the conscious [in this case, those who administer the law] towards the unconscious, the more dangerous does the latter become" ("The Battle for Deliverance from the Mother," par. 450). "Whan God tells ye to gang into the mirk, gang!" says Tibbie Dyster to Annie Anderson in *Alec Forbes of Howglen* (1865; 125), and the Queen, through the agency of her thread, later tells Irene to do precisely this.

16. Although Jung says that "any woman with whom a relationship exists—for example, a nurse or governess or perhaps a remote ancestress" can represent aspects of the mother archetype ("Psychological Aspects of the Mother Archetype," in *Archetypes*, par. 156). Mrs. Peterson is portrayed as the ideal mother—to Curdie (*PG* 123-124). She only once gets the chance to take Irene on her knee (280) and her role is so largely symbolic that her Christian or individuating name is not given; only in *The Princess and Curdie* do we discover that this "wife and mother—two persons in one rich, happy woman"—is called Joan (*PC* 82).

17. Stephen Prickett, in *Romanticism and Religion: The Tradition of Coleridge and Wordsworth in the Victorian Church* (Cambridge,1976), suggests, with some misgivings, that Queen Irene may be an allegory of the Church (237-238), a possibility also entertained by Gwen Watkins: "If she is [in the *Princess* books] Ecclesia, then she is the Church itself, terrible as an army with banners . . ," and she adds: " I suspect that she may be Christianity itself, since she is not yet two thousand years old" ("A Theologian's Dealings with the Fairies," in *North Wind,* 7 [1988], 11, 12). Maureen Duffy, in *The Erotic World of Faery,* says that she is "divine grace or faith" (292), while John Pennington, in "Muscular Spirituality in George MacDonald's Curdie Books" (in *Muscular Christianity: Embodying the Victorian Age,* ed. Donald E. Hall [Cambridge, 2006; from 1994]), describes her as "a concrete incarnation of belief and faith" (138). Robert Lee Wolff, in *The Golden Key,* describes her as "MacDonald's own mythological creation, the grandmotherly goddess" (166); K.M. Briggs, in *The Fairies in Tradition and Literature,* says that "In *Curdie and the Goblins* [sic] . . . the fairy godmother is raised to almost angelic stature" (184); Richard Reis, in *George MacDonald,* describes her as the Freudian superego, the "Fairy Grandmother" in the attic (81); Roderick McGillis, in "George MacDonald's *Princess* Books: High Seriousness," in *Touchstones: Reflections on the Best in Children's Literature,* ed. Perry Nodelman (West Lafayette, Ind., 1985), says that she is associated with the Virgin Mary, Christ and John the Baptist, but does not elaborate on these associations (147); William Raeper, in *George MacDonald,* says that Queen Irene is "the poetic, mystic, hidden face of God" (262). Kerry Dearborn, in *Baptized Imagination: The Theology of George MacDonald* (Aldershot and Burlington, 2006), describes her as "[t]he Christ-figure in the *Princess* books" (69); Nancy Willard, in "The Goddess in the Belfry: Grandmothers and Wise Women in George MacDonald's Books for Children," in *For the Childlike,* says that "[a]s Irene, she is one of the three goddesses of Greek mythology who control the seasons" (68). Colin Manlove does not favour a divine interpretation of the Queen; in *Modern Fantasy* he goes no farther than considering her to be a

puzzle with religious overtones (87-90), and in "*The Princess and the Goblin* and *The Princess and Curdie*," in *North Wind* 26 (2007), he describes "the goblins and the grandmother" as "two sides of the imagination, and of the unconscious" (5). Kathy Triggs, in *The Stars and the Stillness*, thinks that the "Princess" in *The Princess and Curdie* is visualised as "a feminine aspect of God" (108), whereas Daniel Creed, in "Connecting Dimensions: Direction, Location, and Form in the Fantasies of George MacDonald," identifies the Queen in both *Princess* books, like "all the matrons in MacDonald's fiction," as Eve (*North Wind*, 33 [2014], 18). David Robb, in *George MacDonald*, advances a triple interpretation which covers pretty well everything except Greek mythology: "Grandmother is clearly an embodiment of the divine principle . . . she might best be regarded as representing the divine in each of us. More immediately, she can be seen as a dimension of Princess Irene . . ." (118). Katharine Bubel describes her as conforming to the archetype of the Wise Woman; see "Knowing God 'Other-wise': The Wise Old Woman Archetype in George MacDonald's *The Princess and the Goblin*, *The Princess and Curdie* and 'The Golden Key'," in *North Wind*, 25 (2006), 5ff. Deirdre Hayward asserts that she conforms to Boehme's conception of the Sophia as, among other things, "a female revelation of God" and "a divine principle of wisdom" ("The Mystical Sophia: More on the Great Grandmother in the *Princess* Books," *North Wind*, 13 [1994], 29). William Gray says that "the *Princess* books are dominated by a numinous mother figure, thousands of years old, who has an intimate if unspecified relationship with the divine" (*Fantasy, Myth and the Measure of Truth*, 53). Bonnie Gaarden describes the princess's grandmother as "Irene's Christ-self" (126, 127) but also says: "Grandmother Irene cannot be pinned down to one meaning" but has psychological, divine and poetic associations (*The Christian Goddess*, 125-126).

18. Previously discussed in my "'Born Again:' The Metamorphosis of Irene in George MacDonald's *The Princess and the Goblin*," in *Scottish Literary Journal: A Review of Studies in Scottish Language and Literature*, 12, 1 (1985). Colin Manlove says that by climbing to the attics

and meeting the Queen, Princess Irene "has found her truer self. . . . She has climbed upwards into her 'higher' imagination. This lady's name is also Irene, suggesting her identity with the princess" ("*The Princess and the Goblin* and *The Princess and Curdie*," *North Wind*, 26 [2007], 7).

19. See "Christ, a Symbol of the Self," in Jung's *Aion*, esp. par. 70: "*Christ exemplifies the archetype of the self* [Jung's italics]. He represents a totality of a divine or heavenly kind, a glorified man, a son of God *sine macula peccati*, unspotted by sin." See also "Christ as Archetype" (*Psychology and Religion*, pars. 226-233).

20. "Curdie's Intertextual Dialogue: Engaging Maurice, Arnold, and Isaiah," in *George MacDonald: Literary Heritage and Heirs*, ed. Roderick McGillis, 157.

21. In the Book of Proverbs (Ch.8) the Wisdom of God is a female figure (*Hokma* in Hebrew, *Sophia* in Greek). Jewish teachers substituted the masculine *Logos* (the Word) on the grounds that one should speak of God in masculine terms (see Philo, *De Fuga et Inventione*, in *Philo*, transl. F.H. Colson and G.H. Whitaker [London and Cambridge, Mass., 1958], V, 37). In hero myth, to which the Gospel narrative conforms in many respects, the protagonist often has an androgynous dimension. In Richard Adams's contemporary myth, *Watership Down*, the Chief Rabbit, who is not in the least effeminate, is named Hazel—and his younger brother Fiver, the smaller and more vulnerable of the two, is the one who sires rabbit kittens and "to his doe, Vilthuril, Fiver was devotedly attached" (418; an echo of Jane Austen if ever there was one!)

22. For the sake of convenience the Queen is almost always referred to as Irene's grandmother rather than as her great-great-grandmother, and the grandmother is an important (though occasionally negative) figure in many of MacDonald's books. It is noteworthy that in *The Vicar's Daughter* (coeval with *The Princess and the Goblin*) there is a character called Marion *Clare* (meaning clear, luminous or pure), a literary descendant of Mary St. John in *Robert Falconer* (both characters are based on Octavia Hill, an active Victorian philanthropist and friend of

the MacDonalds). Miss Clare's home is in an extremely dilapidated building, up several flights of stairs—"You'd better go up till you can't go no further, an' knocks yer head agin the tiles," a neighbour tells her visitors (*Daughter* 128)—and the poor among whom she lives and for whom she works give her (in spite of her youth) what she calls "the honourable name of grannie" (131).

23. And which, through its gender balance, contributes an element of androgyny to a Queen so feminine as to embody, in her changes of age, the whole range of woman's life.

24. Alexander Cruden, *Cruden's Complete Concordance to the Bible*, ed. C.H. Irwin, A.D. Adams, S.A. Waters (Guildford and London, 1977 [from 1930]), 448; and see MacDonald's essay "The New Name," in *Unspoken Sermons Series 1*, 67-78.

25. See A. Colin Day, *Collins Thesaurus of the Bible* (London, 2002), 1. Amy-Jill Levine and Marc Zvi Brettler, in *The Jewish Annotated New Testament*, specify that when Jesus says, in John 8:58, "before Abraham was, I am," the "I am" is an allusion to God's revelation to Moses at the burning bush (177; note on vv 56-58). Probably the most relevant of the special "I AMs" to *The Princess and the Goblin* is "I am the light of the world" (John 8:12).

26. That Irene MacDonald lends her name to the princess by no means undermines this view; it is most likely that the MacDonalds chose this name for their daughter *because* of its meaning.

27. This is not negated by the Queen's consumption of pigeon's eggs (28-29). The risen Jesus, to prove to his affrighted disciples that he was not a ghost—since seeing him in the flesh was not enough—asked: "Have ye here any meat?" and was presented with "a piece of a broiled fish, and of an honeycomb./And he took it, and did eat before them" (Luke 24:41-43).

28. Carl Jung shares this view. In *The Structure and Dynamics of the Psyche* (Vol. 8, 2nd ed, of the *Collected Works*), he says that "ancestor-worship ... is primarily a protection against the malice of the dead" ("The Psychological Foundations of Belief in Spirits," par. 575). Dr. John Bligh, a former

colleague at the University of Guelph with a theological background, said that *The Princess and the Goblin* is about ancestor worship. MacDonald did not (consciously) believe in this, but during a talk at the Casa Corragio he said: "Remember, we carry about with us all we have inherited from our ancestors in body and in mind" (notes taken by the Rev. W.F. Curtoys and cit. in *George MacDonald and His Wife*, 507n).

29. "In My End is My Beginning," *Mythlore* 24, 3/4 (2006), 53.

ENDNOTES TO CHAPTER 6

1. In his essay "A Sketch of Individual Development" (1880), in *A Dish of Orts*, MacDonald goes into the early stages of a child's psychological development—all seen in terms of births. He talks of a child's second birth, to self-consciousness (45); of his third birth, which springs from the consciousness of strife (46); and of his possible fourth birth—the birth in him of Will as opposed to mere Desire (47). For MacDonald the concept of rebirth carries on into maturity. In *Robert Falconer* (1868; serialised in 1867), he says that "to get [a man] to do as the Son of Man did, in ever so small a degree, was the readiest means of bringing his highest nature to the birth" (345), and this concept recurs throughout his works. Eventually it merges with the concept of resurrection.

2. The motif of losing and finding occurs frequently in MacDonald. In "The Carasoyn," for example, Colin says: "It seems the way to find some things is to lose yourself" (*The Light Princess and Other Fairy Tales*, 229).

3. See, e.g., the tower at the Court of the Terrenon in Ursula le Guin's *A Wizard of Earthsea*. It is not until he reaches this high spot, with a window in each of the four walls, that Ged is able to take stock of his own conduct. In the Gospels the tower is the cross.

4. See also Bonnie Gaarden, *The Christian Goddess*, 140.

5. Which is precisely why the Queen does not want Lootie

to see her; she does not want to reinforce her incapacity for faith (and cf. *The Hope of the Gospel*, 118: "If we had seen God face to face, but had again become impure of heart—if such a fearful thought be a possible idea—then we should no more believe that we had ever beheld him").

6. There is a connection, in MacDonald's mind, between love of nature and openness to spirituality. In 1855 he wrote to his wife from Huntly: "God, the Sky God—the Green Earth God be with you; *our own God*, as David [the psalmist] says." This, taken out of context, might be held to indicate a Pantheism which was no part of his faith—but soon afterwards he wrote of the "God of mountain lands, and snowdrops, of woman's beauty and man's strength—the God and Father of our Lord Jesus Christ" (*GMHW* 229, 240).

7. "If [his son] shall ask an egg, will [his father] offer him a scorpion?" says Jesus (Luke 11:12).

8. See again Sigmund Freud, *Totem and Taboo*, 56: "[Children] consistently assume that if two things are called by similar-sounding names this must imply the existence of some deep-lying point of agreement between them."

9. A former student, a Canadian of Scottish descent, told me that there really was a Scottish name "Lootie"—she had a relative named "Leutie." The *Scottish National Dictionary*, Vol. 6, gives "loot" or "lowt" as variations of the English "lout," and the adjective "lowttie" or "louty" as meaning slow, inactive or loutish—but these words hardly describe Lootie, although MacDonald may want her name to have negative associations. On the other hand, he may have got the name from Coleridge's "Lewti, or the Circassian Love-Chaunt," though MacDonald's Lootie and Coleridge's Lewti have little in common. We never find out Lootie's real name; possibly an indication that her individuality is limited.

10. *Pace* Thomas L. Martin, it is not the mockery (laughter) that overcomes the darkness in this case, but the lack of fear of which it is a manifestation; Curdie himself attributes it to the goblins' dislike of singing (see "God and Laughter: Overcoming the Darkness in Modern Fantasy Literature,"

in *North Wind*, 34 [2015], 6).

11. I am indebted for information about the pedagogue to Dr. John Bligh, whose course on "The Bible as Literature" I attended at the University of Guelph. See also Galatians 3:12: "The law is not of faith." The law is only of use while the taboo is in force.

12. This of course is a substitute for the real night sky. It is noteworthy that there is a better representation of it (complete with moon lamp) in Queen Irene's bedroom: "The walls were . . . blue—spangled all over with what looked like stars of silver" (118), and when Irene returns from the mountain "the blue walls and their silver stars for a moment perplexed her with the fancy that they were in reality the sky which she had left outside a minute ago . . . " (144). MacDonald is very attached to this image; in *Ranald Bannerman's Boyhood*, published, both serially and in book form, only a year before *The Princess and the Goblin*, the ceiling of Ranald's bedroom "was a ceiling indeed; for the sun, moon, and stars lived there" (*RBB* 13), and MacDonald's own study in The Retreat, Hammersmith (a house into which the family moved in 1867), was decorated by his friend, the artist Cottier, with "a dark blue ceiling with scattered stars in silver and gold, and a silver crescent moon" (*GMHW* 386).

13. Ed. John Wiltshire; in *The Cambridge Edition of the Works of Jane Austen* (Cambridge: CUP 2005), 423.

14. The Greek word 'petros' (Peter) means 'rock.' The significance of this in Curdie's case is underlined by his being the only child character in the major children's fantasies to have a surname at all—even Diamond, who is rooted in the Primary World of everyday reality, hasn't got one.

15. Isaiah 45:4; 43:1, 7 (italics mine).

16. Perhaps a substratum of possible future receptivity has been deposited.

17. Tony Tanner, "Mountains and Depths—An Approach to Nineteenth-Century Dualism," *Review of English Literature*, 3.4 (Oct. 1962), 52.

18. See, e.g., "Two Kinds of Thinking," par. 7, and "Symbols of the Mother and of Rebirth," par. 329.

19. Or evil impulses in the unconscious. Harry Armstrong, narrator of the short story "The Cruel Painter," speaks of "gnomes of terror, deep hidden in the caverns of Teufelsburst's nature" (*Adela Cathcart* [1864], 39).

20. Roderick McGillis says that they "pervert language," which is indeed the case (see his introduction to the World's Classics edition of *The Princess and the Goblin* and *The Princess and Curdie*, xix). This often has a comical or even a ridiculous effect, though it overlays a solid substratum of malice.

21. See Bettelheim, *The Uses of Enchantment*, 70 n.: "In fairy tales and dreams, physical malformation often stands for psychological misdevelopment;" and see Cordelia Sherman, "The Princess and the Wizard: The Fantasy Worlds of Ursula K. Le Guin and George MacDonald," in *For the Childlike*, ed. Roderick McGillis (from *ChLa Quarterly*, 1987): "In both Curdie books, evil is physically repellent" (198). For MacDonald, careful as he is about possible effects, especially on child readers, this seems extremely unkind—but in these instances symbolism rules.

22. And see "The Imagination: Its Functions and its Culture," in *A Dish of Orts*: "[T]he fact that there is always more in a work of art . . . than the producer himself perceived while he produced it, seems to us a strong reason for attributing to it a larger origin than the man alone—for saying at the last, that the inspiration of the Almighty shaped its ends" (25).

23. The book editions say "hands," but this appears to be a slip as the text of the serialised version reads "*heads* so flinty" and the goblins are known for their hard heads (*Good Words for the Young*, April 1871, 300; italics mine). The goblins' reaction calls to mind the words of one of the sceptical miners in *The Princess and Curdie*: "I never knew a man that wouldn't go in a rage to be called the very thing he was" (*PC 61*).

24. Here we may remember the lines from *The Diary of an Old Soul* quoted earlier: "Leave not thy son half-made in beastly

guise--/ Less than a man, with more than human cries—/ An unshaped thing in which thyself cries out!" (March, 209; v. 19).

25. Roderick McGillis, "The Fantastic Imagination: The Prose Romances of George MacDonald," (PhD diss., University of Reading 1973, 97).

26. MacDonald must have the Sleeping Beauty on his mind, for, in one of the conversations between author and reader which occur in the serialised version, "Mr. Editor" states most emphatically that *The Princess and the Goblin* is not another form of that story (*Good Words for the Young*, Nov. 1870, 3). He does, however, admit in *At the Back of the North Wind* that the story of Princess Daylight is indebted to the Sleeping Beauty (*ABNW* 257).

27. It is a different matter when a dream has been sent. Curdie's wounded leg is healed by Queen Irene, who appears to him in a dream (268)—i.e. neither will nor faith is required on his part, for his conscious mind is securely muzzled. In *The Princess and Curdie*, Peter tells his son that "if a lady comes to you in a dream . . . and tells you not to talk about her when you wake, the least you can do is hold your tongue" (*PC* 54).

28. Cf. Revelation 21:5: "Behold, I make all things new." The bath of death and rebirth figures in "The Golden Key" (1867), where Mossy and Tangle each have this baptismal experience in the bath of the Old Man of the Sea. Tangle's experience is particularly striking. When she gets out, "[a]ll the fatigue and aching of her long journey had vanished. She was as whole, and strong, and well as if she had slept for seven days"—and when she glides down the river indicated by the Old Man of the Earth, "[h]er head was under water, but that did not signify, for . . . she could not remember that she had breathed once since her bath in the cave of the Old Man of the Sea." This has been foreshadowed by her earlier immersion in the fish tank belonging to "Grandmother," although at that point she still needs to breathe: "Two or three [fish] got under her head and kept it up." Mossy has a similar experience of death and resurrection as a result of his immersion in the Old Man of the Sea's bath ("The

Golden Key," in *The Light Princess and Other Fairy Tales*, 201-202, 205, 184, 210-211).

29. The sense of 'abiding' persists when Irene sleeps in the Queen's bed: "I should like to lie here for ever," says Irene when her grandmother holds her "close to her bosom" in her beautiful bed. "You may if you will," replies the Queen (*PG* 121).

30. A female monster, often depicted with a snake's body and a woman's head and breasts. Jung says that a negative mother-imago can turn into a lamia (see "The Battle for Deliverance from the Mother," in *Symbols of Transformation*, par. 457). In *Wilfrid Cumbermede*, Wilfrid compares his mare, Lilith, to "the witch-lady in Christabel, 'beautiful exceedingly'" (426)—but Lilith the mare has a lovely disposition, quite unlike that of the wicked lady of legendary provenance who figures much later in *Lilith*.

31. Christabel is "the babe for whom she died" (l. 630), just as Irene is, presumably, the baby for whom her mother died, although MacDonald does not spell it out.

32. Bard Bracy, in Coleridge's poem, dreams that dove and snake are locked in a death struggle (ll. 541-54). When Irene, in *The Princess and the Goblin*, decides that her meeting with her grandmother has been "all a dream," i.e. with no basis in reality, there is a strange visitation: "At that moment a snow-white pigeon flew in at an open window and settled upon Irene's head" (*PG* 105). This recalls the baptism of Jesus, after which "the heavens were opened unto him, and he saw the Spirit of God descending like a dove, and lighting upon him" (Matthew 3:16; see also Mark 1:10, Luke 3:22, John 1:32).

ENDNOTES TO CHAPTER 7

1. The Queen's capacity for forgiveness is a divine quality: "Who is a God like unto thee, that pardoneth iniquity?" says Micah (7:18).

2. "Then said I, Woe is me! For I am undone; because I am a man of unclean lips, and I dwell in the midst of a people of unclean lips. . . . Then flew one of the seraphims unto

me, having a live coal in his hand, which he had taken with the tongs from off the altar . . . . And he laid it upon my mouth." The purifying function of the rose fire in *The Princess and Curdie* draws on this passage. Ch. 10 of the Book of Ezekiel also contains several references to "coals of fire from between the cherubims" (v.2, and see vv.6,7) which have a bearing on Queen Irene's fire; their function in Ezekiel, however, is punitive.

3. Because Irene has not yet 'died.'

4. See *The Shorter Oxford Dictionary*.

5. In the Garden of Eden, see Genesis 2:9: "And out of the ground made the LORD God to grow every tree that is pleasant to the sight, and good for food; the tree of life also in the midst of the garden, and the tree of knowledge of good and evil." The fruit of this tree was Eve's and then Adam's undoing.

6. In *Wilfrid Cumbermede*, published in the same year as *The Princess and the Goblin*, there is also an important ring—though this one does not connect the natural and the supernatural. Mary Osborne goes to sleep in the wrong guest bedroom without realising that Wilfrid is in the bed; when he wakes up he leaves discreetly, but a maid finds a ring there and brings it to him. Discreet still, he puts the ring on his little finger and later returns it to a bewildered Mary, earning a glance which "lies treasured . . . in the secret jewel-house of my heart" (358-359).

7. On the significance of the thread, see also Colin Manlove, *Modern Fantasy*, 88. William Raeper, in *George MacDonald*, says that it was taken and adapted from Norman Macleod's *The Golden Thread* (1861), an allegory about a boy who must follow the thread home to his father (413, n.52). Raeper uses this image in the title of his collection of essays, *The Gold Thread: Essays on George MacDonald* (Edinburgh, 1990). Nancy-Lou Patterson, in "Kore Motifs in *The Princess and the Goblin*," points out that Theseus was freed from the labyrinth by means of Ariadne's guiding thread (*For the Childlike*, 173). Joseph Sigman, in "The Diamond in the Ashes: A Jungian Reading of the 'Princess' Books," also points out a connection between Curdie's labyrinthine

experience and that of Theseus (*For the Childlike*, 185), as do other critics. The guiding, or at least the connecting thread is a universal archetype; Lord Hailsham, a Conservative politician, said in 1975: "I believe there is a golden thread which alone gives meaning to the political history of the West, from Marathon to Alamein, from Solon to Winston Churchill and after. This I chose to call the doctrine of liberty under the law" (cit. in *Lend Me Your Ears: Oxford Dictionary of Political Quotations*, 4th ed., 2010).

8. "Abide in me, and I in you," says Jesus (John 15:4), and he elaborates on this point at some length (John 15:4-10).

9. Again violating the taboo against being out in the dark—but it no longer matters.

10. "I do not think the time will ever come when we shall not have something to do, because we are told to do it without knowing why," says MacDonald in "True Christian Ministering," and he continues: "Those parents act most foolishly who wish to explain everything to their children . . . . No; teach your child to obey, and you give him the most precious lesson that can be given to a child" (*A Dish of Orts*, 1893), 307. See also Curdie's discussion with the old princess of his mission in *The Princess and Curdie*, 104-105.

11. See John 11:41-44, which describes Jesus's raising of Lazarus from the dead. Lazarus's tomb, like Curdie's prison, "was a cave, and a stone lay upon it" (John 11:38).

12. Matthew 27:46 and Mark 15:34. Jesus is quoting the first line of Psalm 22, which describes the crucifixion in some detail but culminates in an affirmation of the trustworthiness and praiseworthiness of God and a prophecy of the coming of his kingdom.

13. In *Guild Court* MacDonald describes nine as a magical number (146).

14. See, e.g., Colossians 2:12: "Buried with him in baptism, wherein also ye are risen with him through the faith of the operation of God, who hath raised him from the dead;" and Romans 6:4: "We are buried with him by baptism into death: that like as Christ was raised up from the dead by the glory of the Father, even so we also should walk in

newness of life."

15. Nanny makes similar remarks about Diamond in *At the Back of the North Wind*. In *The Princess and the Goblin* Lootie's opinion does not seem to gain any general credence.

16. "The Symbolism of the Mandala," in *Psychology and Alchemy*, par. 285.

17. There is no mention of Irene's ring in *The Princess and Curdie*.

18. *GMHW* 412; Greville MacDonald's italics. There are no italics in the letter as published in Glenn Edward Sadler's *An Expression of Character: The Letters of George MacDonald* (174).

19. "[I]t is too hot for you *yet*," says the Queen (148; my italics). But after Irene's symbolic death and resurrection in the silver bath her grandmother draws her nightgown from the fire—and instead of bursting into flames, it becomes "as white as snow" and "smells of all the roses in the world" (231).

20. Jesus walked on water during his earthly life: "And in the fourth watch of the night Jesus went unto them, walking on the sea" (Matthew 14:25). Gilbert Cope, in *Symbolism in the Bible and the Church*, says that this shows his control of the unconscious (93). The Queen—who is not Jesus—has gained a similar potential through her resurrection. Her opposite number, the goblin queen, drowns with most of her people.

21. She still has the goblins' soft feet. It is interesting to note that one of the sons of Goliath, the giant killed by David (1 Samuel 17:49), had six toes per foot—and six fingers per hand (2 Samuel 21:20). He was killed by one of David's nephews. The goblins, of course, are of diminutive stature.

22. In St. Matthew's Gospel Jesus speaks of "a foolish man, which built his house upon the sand; / And the rain descended, and the floods came, and the winds blew, and beat upon that house; and it fell: and great was the fall of it" (7:26, 27). The king's house in *The Princess and the Goblin* "appeared in danger of falling" (301), but fortunately there is a sufficient preponderance of rock to preserve it

until the miners can divert the stream. In *The Princess and Curdie* the whole city of Gwyntystorm is built on a rock—unfortunately with not merely a vein of sand, but a whole chasm beneath it. This is a symbol which recurs in MacDonald's work; in *Alec Forbes of Howglen* (1865), for instance, Tibbie Dyster's "bit hoosie's fund't upon a rock, and the rains may fa', and the wins may blaw, and the floods may ca at the hoosie, but it winna fa', it canna fa', for it's fund't upon a rock" (281). In *Sir Gibbie* (1879), Gibbie rushes to his friends' cottage and is at first appalled at not being able to see it: "From the top of the rock against which it was built, shot the whole mass of the water he had been pursuing.... When he came near, to his amazement there stood the little house unharmed, the very center of the cataract!" (225)

23. MacDonald spoke as follows to Greville of Louisa's love for her children: "You have no conception . . . how deep and passionate is your mother's love for you—for you and for your brothers and sisters, *as if you were each her only chick*" (*GMHW* 471; Greville MacDonald's italics). Of the human person's relationship with God MacDonald says: "Before him stands each, as much an individual child as if there were no-one but him" *(Miracles,* 97). Daniel Gabelman, in *Divine Carelessness*, emphasises MacDonald's description of the relationship between God and the individual as being "awful in its singleness" (148-155).

24. See Erich Fromm, *The Art of Loving*, ed. Ruth Nanda Anshen (New York, 1963), 99.

25. This complements Diamond's remark in *At the Back of the North Wind* that "I'm good enough to believe it, Ruby" (321). I am puzzled by David Robb's opinion that Curdie displays "massive competence in dealing with the goblins" (*George MacDonald*, 121). He has to be rescued from them by a little girl!

26. Except in the form "faithless" (20:27). It does occur once in his first Epistle (I John 5:4).

27. Various forms of the verb "to believe" are used far less by the other Evangelists, who use the word "faith" a few times; this word comes into its own in St. Paul's Epistles, where

variations of "believe" are also widely used (see *Cruden's Concordance*).

28. "The Symbolism of the Mandala," in *Psychology and Alchemy*, par. 438.
29. A prefiguring of his role in *The Princess and Curdie*.
30. *Alec Forbes of Howglen*, 315.
31. "George MacDonald: A Personal Note," in *View From a Northern Window*, 103.
32. Introduction to *GMHW*, 9.

ENDNOTES TO CHAPTER 8

1. *Good Words for the Young*, June 1st 1871, 420; MacDonald's italics. He took over the editorship in 1871.
2. John Pennington, "Muscular Spirituality in George MacDonald's Curdie Books," in *Muscular Christianity: Embodying the Victorian Age*, 140.
3. In *Good Things: A Picturesque Magazine for Boys and Girls*.
4. "The Two Worlds of George MacDonald," *North Wind* 2 (1983): 22.
5. MacDonald has forgotten, or deliberately overlooks, Queen Irene's answer to Irene's question on receiving the ring in *The Princess and the Goblin*—"Please, am I to keep it?"—"Always" (153).
6. MacDonald underlines this by a clear allusion to Scripture: "[A]h God! Who knows the joy of a bird, the ecstasy of a creature that has neither storehouse nor barn!" (*PC* 24), and Jesus says: "Consider the ravens . . . which neither have storehouse nor barn" (Luke 12:24; see also Matthew 6:26). In *The Hope of the Gospel* MacDonald says: "We are not complete men, we are not anything near it, and are therefore out of harmony, more or less, with everything in the house of our birth and habitation" ("Jesus in the World," *HG* 51).
7. "Introduction to the Religious and Psychological Problems of Alchemy," in *Psychology and Alchemy*, par. 26.

8. The image recurs in *There and Back* (1891). This time, however, there is an important difference. In the chapter headed "The Rime of the Ancient Mariner" (in the course of which the hero, Richard, even discusses different editions of the poem), the heroine, Barbara, finds a dying pigeon with a broken wing. Like Curdie's pigeon, "[i]t kept opening and shutting its eyes," and just as in Curdie's case "the mute appeal of the dying thing had gone to her heart" (*TB* 120). This time no guilt has been incurred. But the bird dies, which is not the case in *The Princess and Curdie*—and consolation (not immediately available to Richard and Barbara) is expressed by the narrator: "Oh, surely it is in reason that not a sparrow should fall to the ground without the Father!" (120). What the sad incident does, in Barbara's case, is make her think for the first time about what might happen after death. MacDonald gives a full interpretation of the shooting of the albatross and its implications for the ancient mariner and the rest of the crew in *David Elginbrod* (1863), 22.

9. Introduction to "The Rime of the Ancient Mariner" in *English Romantic Writers*, ed. David Perkins, 405.

10. "The Fantastic Imagination," in *A Dish of Orts*, 317. The importance of this quality for MacDonald goes beyond the question of readership: "The boy should enclose and keep, as his life, the old child at the heart of him," the narrator says of Curdie (*PC* 23), and the corollary of this is to be found in MacDonald's preface to *The Light Princess and Other Fairy Tales* (1893): "He who will be a man and will not be a child, must, he cannot help himself, become a little man, that is, a dwarf" (xii).

11. But then, as MacDonald says in "Justice," in *Unspoken Sermons, Series Three*, 514: "Love is justice."

12. "All that moves in the mind is symbolized in Nature," says MacDonald in "The Imagination: Its Functions and Its Culture" (*Orts*, 9).

13. *The Uses of Enchantment*, 27 (quoting the poem that immediately prefaces Lewis Carroll's *Alice Through the Looking Glass*).

14. G.K. Chesterton, who, as previously cited, thinks that

MacDonald's realistic novels are disguised versions of his fairy tales, specifies *The Princess and Curdie* as a "magnificent fairy tale" with an intimate relationship to *The Marquis of Lossie*: "Suddenly we realise that the two stories are the same, that one runs inside the other, and that the realistic novel is the shell and the fairy tale the kernel" ("George MacDonald and His Work," the *Daily News*, June 11th 1901; cit. in *The Gospel in George MacDonald*, ed. Marianne Wright, 306, 308).

15. For the importance of the Book of Job to MacDonald see his essay, "The Voice of Job," in *Unspoken Sermons: Second Series* (1885), 328-362.

16. See Robert Lee Wolff, *The Golden Key*, 87-91, on the importance of mines and mining to the German Romantics—notably Novalis and Hoffman, for whose influence on MacDonald in this respect see especially 88-89.

17. "I love the common with all my heart, but I hate the common-place," says John Smith, the narrator of *Adela Cathcart* (1864), 312.

18. See Jung, "The Battle for Deliverance from the Mother," in *Symbols of Transformation*, par. 450: "The more negative the attitude of the conscious towards the unconscious, the more dangerous does the latter become."

19. In *Annals of a Quiet Neighbourhood*, first published in 1867, the vicar quotes St. James practically verbatim. "Every good gift and every perfect gift is from above, and cometh down from the Father of lights," says the apostle (James 1:17), and Mr. Walton says: "Everything good comes from the Father of lights" (*AQN* 260). The most striking echoes of St. James's words in MacDonald are to be found in *Malcolm* (1875), in which the mad laird, Stephen Stewart, often says (or cries) "Father o' lichts!" –e.g. 148, 189, 232, 355 and 404 (when he is on his deathbed).

20. "The Psychological Aspects of the Kore," par. 312.

21. The throne of God in the Book of Revelation has "a rainbow round about [it], in sight like unto an emerald" (Rev. 4:3).

22. "The Personification of the Opposites," par. 137.
23. Joan Evans, in *Magical Jewels of the Middle Ages and the Renaissance, particularly in England*, cites De Boot on the demon-repellent qualities of emeralds (153).
24. Since "[g]ood people see good things; bad people, bad things" *(ABNW* 37).
25. The allusion is to the General Epistle of Jude, who describes the backsliders among the early Christian community as "wandering stars, to whom is reserved the blackness of darkness for ever" (v.13). Peter and Curdie are almost as desolate as this until the return of the Comforter in the shape of the Lady of the Emeralds (see John 14:18: "I will not leave you comfortless: I will come to you," and 14:28: "Ye have heard how I said unto you, I go away, and come again unto you").
26. "Religious Ideas in Alchemy," in *Psychology and Alchemy*, par. 334.
27. "The Psychological Aspects of the Kore," par. 312.
28. "The Symbolism of the Mandala," in *Psychology and Alchemy*, par. 247.
29. *Psychological Types*, par. 804.
30. See, e.g., Jung, "The Battle for Deliverance from the Mother," *SoT* par. 450. As he notes, "the unconscious is infinitely greater than the mother and is only symbolized by her."
31. Jung describes the anima as "The Archetype of the Feminine" ("The Dual Mother," *SoT* par. 514).
32. See Jung, "A Psychological Approach to the Trinity," in *Psychology and Religion*, par. 292: "The individuation process is invariably started off by the patient's becoming conscious of the shadow."
33. "Psychological Aspects of the Mother Archetype," in *Archetypes*, par. 158.
34. "The Psychological Aspects of the Kore," *Archetypes*, par. 356.

35. It also takes time to understand the answers. In the course of their next meeting the old princess says "You have not half got to the bottom of the answers I have already given you" (102-103).

36. See her introduction to the 2010 Puffin Classics edition of *The Princess and the Goblin*, v-vi.

37. After talking of the Comforter (the Holy Spirit), MacDonald says: "All spirit must rise victorious over form. ... No form is or can be great enough to contain the truth which is its soul; for all truth is infinite, being a thought of God" ("Miracles of Destruction," in *Miracles* [423-424]). North Wind, in *At the Back of the North Wind*, says: "I have to shape myself various ways to various people. But the heart of me is true" (*ABNW* 363)—and Diamond sees her in many shapes when he is returning from the supposed land at her back (123-134).

38. See, e.g., 27, 28, 32, 77, 78 and especially Ch. V111.

39. *Summa theologica* 1, xxxvi, art. 1; cit. in "A Psychological Approach to the Trinity," *Psychology and Religion*, par. 276 n.8.

40. "I may define 'self' as the totality of the conscious and unconscious psyche, but this totality transcends our vision; it is a veritable *lapis invisibilitatis*," says Jung in "The Symbolism of the Mandala" (*Psychology and Alchemy*, par. 247). The definition he gives in *Psychology and Religion* is perhaps easier to grasp: "The self is defined psychologically as the psychic totality of the individual" ("A Psychological Approach to the Trinity," par. 232).

41. One of the paradoxes of *The Princess and Curdie*, in which natural symbolism is of key importance, is that, as relates to the moon, nature is less natural than it was before; if this is not magic, it is an attempt to excite wonder which extends the possibilities of the universe.

42. Even the old princess's spinning wheel presents itself as a "great wheel of fire" in the (internal) sky—an image taken straight from Shakespeare's *King Lear*, though without its negative connotations: "Thou art a soul in bliss/ But I am bound upon a wheel of fire" (Act 1V scene vii l.45).

43. Forming a connection with *The Princess and the Goblin*, in which Queen Irene's thread is spun from cobwebs made by a particular kind of spider and brought across the great sea by her pigeons (*PG* 116-117). This is foreshadowed in *Robert Falconer* (1868): "With the faintest track to follow, with the clue of a spider's thread to guide him, he would have known that his business was to set out at once to find, and save his father" (*RF* 399). In *The Princess and Curdie* the spider motif is unattractively developed in relation to the old princess: "She sat crumpled together, a filmy thing that it seemed a puff would blow away, more like the body of a fly the big spider had sucked empty and left hanging in his web, than anything else I can think of" (36).

44. In *Psychology and Alchemy* Jung speaks of the anima—one function of the old princess—as "the personified unconscious" ("The Symbolism of the Mandala," par. 242 n.118) and of her function "as mediator between conscious and unconscious" (par.242 n.119), a function which she shares with the psychopomp, "the one who shows the way" ("The Initial Dreams," par. 74).

45. The poem is replete with references to the New Testament. The overall theme of the resurrection ("the time when the sleepers shall rise") is accompanied by a resurrection promise from the Beatitudes; "[t]he weepers are learning to smile/And laughter to glean the sighs" echoes Matthew 5:4: "Blessed are they that mourn, for they shall be comforted"—and the references to lilies (Matthew 6:28, Luke 12:27), sparrows (Matthew 10:29, 31; Luke 12:6,7) and daily bread (Matthew 6:11, Luke 11:3) all echo remarks made by Jesus to encourage trust in God.

46. "The Remission of Sins," in *The Hope of the Gospel*, 41.

47. Alexander Cruden, *Cruden's Concordance*, 209.

ENDNOTES TO CHAPTER 9

1. Prickett, Stephen. *Romanticism and Religion: The Tradition of Wordsworth and Coleridge in the Victorian Church*, 182.

2. Cope, *Symbolism in the Bible and the Church*, 93.

3. A strange observation in view of the fact that most of the men in the kingdom, whatever their employment, wear the king's livery.

4. Queen Irene in *The Princess and the Goblin* describes Curdie in more positive terms—"He is a good boy, Curdie, and a brave boy" (*PG* 223)—but this is before his possible deterioration to a 'might-have-been' in *The Princess and Curdie*.

5. MacDonald's admiration of Wordsworth's poetry is well known, and in "Wordsworth's Poetry," in *A Dish of Orts*, he describes one of his poems, the "Ode: Intimations of Immortality from Recollections of Early Childhood," as "that grandest ode that has ever been written" (*Orts* 256). The narrator of *Wilfrid Cumbermede* praises both Wordsworth and Coleridge as "the prophets of the new blessing" of a sense of "the spiritual influences of Nature, so largely poured on the heart and mind of my generation" ([131]).

6. MacDonald calls Hesper Redmain, in *Mary Marston* (1881), "The Evening Star" when she has been beautifully dressed for a social occasion by the eponymous heroine (190)—there is even a poem in her honour with that title (191)—and the previous chapter, in which the actual dressing is described, is entitled "The Evening Star" (184-190).

7. In the first chapter of *The Princess and Curdie* MacDonald applies the metaphor of a tree to both the *Princess* books: "I will narrate as much of [the events of the earlier book] as will serve to show the tops of the roots of my tree" (15).

8. MacDonald says in *Castle Warlock* (1882) that "[Cosmo's] love of place [the family-owned land] was in danger of becoming a disease" (*CW* 46).

9. "When we are true children . . . the universe will be our home . . . . Hence, until then, the hard struggle, the constant strife with Nature—as we call the things of our father." In "Jesus in the World," *The Hope of the Gospel*, 52.

10. Exaggerated uncertainty, as the old princess points out; she reminds him that she has told him to set out for the court, which lies to the north.

11. See the *Scots-English, English-Scots Dictionary, Collins Dictionary,* and *Old Mortality* (1816). MacDonald knew Scott's work but would not have needed to source the idea from him; probably it was MacDonald's private joke in an otherwise virtually horseless fantasy—Irene does say, in *The Princess and the Goblin,* "What a funny name!" (55) According to the *Scottish National Dictionary,* the word "Curdie" (literally meaning a small coin) is also a nickname for a boy very small for his age—but this does not seem to apply in the present case. In *Alec Forbes of Howglen* (1865) the protagonist's closest friend is nicknamed "Curly," which may also have influenced MacDonald's choice of name for Curdie Peterson.

12. "The Battle for Deliverance from the Mother," *Symbols of Transformation* par. 421.

13. The old princess tells Curdie not to destroy his bows and arrows but to practise with them every day and become a good shot, as plenty of bad things need killing (43). There is no follow-up to this as far as Curdie himself is concerned, but the bow and arrows reappear in a different context (see below).

14. The name 'Gwyntystorm' in Welsh actually means "a storm of winds" (see Colin Manlove, "*The Princess and the Goblin* and *The Princess and Curdie,*" in *North Wind,* 26 [2007], 34). It might not suggest this to child or even adult readers, however, and MacDonald presumably thought that 'winter's storm' was the association they would make (and see Freud, *Totem and Taboo,* 56).

15. In Gwyntystorm itself "a number of boys returning from school . . . began to stone the strangers" (146).

16. See also Roderick McGillis, introduction to *The Princess and the Goblin and The Princess and Curdie,* xix.

17. "Father-attributes may occasionally fall to the son himself, i.e., when it has become apparent that he is of one nature with the father" (Jung, "The Dual Mother," *SoT* par. 516). At one point Peter and Curdie appear to be 'two minds with but a single thought,' as, for example, when they are waiting for the "Mother of Light" (*PC* 70) to return to the cavern: "Each set his lamp by his knee, and watched it die.

Slowly it sank, dulled, looked lazy and stupid. But ever as it sank and dulled, the image in his mind of the Lady of Light grew stronger and clearer" (71). It is interesting, however, that when she is setting up her next meeting with Curdie, the old princess virtually sends Peter to the right-about: "Come to me in the dove-tower to-morrow night, Curdie—alone" (82).

18. See Jung, "The Philosophical Tree," in *Alchemical Studies*, par. 428: "[A]t the first meeting with the self all those negative qualities can appear which almost invariably characterize an unexpected encounter with the unconscious. The danger is that of an inundation by the unconscious, which in a bad case may take the form of a psychosis if the conscious mind is unable to assimilate, either intellectually or morally, the invasion of unconsciousness."

19. "Mountain and tree are symbols of the personality and of the self" (Jung, *Alchemical Studies*, par. 407). According to a survey conducted by the *Daily Telegraph* in July 1983, many more negative superstitions are associated with the hawthorn than with any other tree. Al de Vries, in the *Dictionary of Symbols and Imagery*, says that it was sacred to the Great (White) Goddess; in the Celtic tree-alphabet it signifies death; it is related to the moon; the Crown of Thorns [also a circle associated with a tree] is supposed to have been made from it. This *Dictionary* informs us, oddly, that hawthorn "protects against baby-snatching by bird-witches," but adds that "the reverse may have been true"—at all events, "the hawthorn must not be taken into the house, because she killed children in bird-disguises." More interesting in connection with *The Princess and Curdie*, "it is often found where deadly fights are to take place."

20. Cope says that "the Tree" is "very frequently to be seen in association with the Mother Goddess in one form or another" (*SBC* 171). Marion Lochhead, in *Renaissance of Wonder: The Fantasy Worlds of C.S. Lewis, J.R.R. Tolkien, George MacDonald, E. Nesbit and Others* (San Francisco, Cambridge, London etc., 1977), refers to Yggdrasil, the tree of Nordic mythology which is rooted in the abode of the giants, the world of the dead and the dwelling of the descendants of the gods; it recurs in modern myths and is

"the source of the tree magic, for good or evil, in George MacDonald" (110). Carl Jung identifies Yggdrasil as the "world-ash" and says that according to Nordic myth at the end of the world it becomes "the guardian mother, the tree pregnant with death and life" ("Symbols of the Mother and of Rebirth," in *Symbols of Transformation*, par. 367).

21. In the Book of Ezekiel the vine is used as a metaphor for a mother (in its turn a metaphor for the land of Israel)) who begins by being "fruitful and full of branches by reason of many waters" and ends, after falling, by being "planted in the wilderness, in a dry and thirsty ground" (Ezekiel 19:10, 13).

22. A comparable and in a sense complementary incident occurs in *Lilith:* "A spot appeared on the face of the half-risen moon. To my ears came presently the drumming of swift, soft-galloping hoofs, and in a minute or two, out of the very disc of the moon, low-thundered the terrible horse" (*L* 221). In *Lilith* the masculine horse comes out of the feminine moon instead of the feminine creature out of the masculine sun.

23. "The Lapis-Christ Parallel," *Psychology and Alchemy* par. 449. Jung and MacDonald are both thinking of the "burning fiery furnace" in the Book of Daniel (referred to in *At the Back of the North Wind* [323]). Lina is also the "magical travelling companion" mentioned in Jung's "The Symbolism of the Mandala" (*PA* par. 155). See also Beryl Rowland's *Animals with Human Faces: A Guide to Animal Symbolism* (London, 1974), 58.

24. See Jung, "The Personification of the Opposites," in *Mysterium Coniunctionis*, par. 127.

25. "The Personification of the Opposites," *MC* par. 188.

26. "The Personification of the Opposites," par. 223: "[T]he moon is not only dark but is also a giver of light and can therefore represent consciousness."

27. At the old princess's command, "Curdie . . . rushed to the fire, and thrust both his hands right into the middle of the heap of flaming roses" (93-94). Something strikingly similar occurs in *Alec Forbes of Howglen*, although in a very

different context. Alec, to protect Annie Anderson from vicious and undeserved punishment at school, charges into "Murder" Malison, the schoolmaster, and, "doubling him up, sent him with a crash into the peat fire which was glowing on the hearth. In the attempt to save himself, he thrust his hand right into it . . . "(*AFH* 48).

28. MacDonald's view of the symbolic masculinity of the sun fully accords with Jung's. In the Puffin and Wordsworth editions of *The Princess and Curdie* the sun has been changed from masculine to neuter by editors of a literal turn of mind. But the masculinity of the sun is important in the symbolic structure of this book and is emphasised in MacDonald's adult novels as well as in his books for children. To quote but a few examples from different times in MacDonald's writing career, in *Ranald Bannerman's Boyhood* (1871) the sun is referred to as "Mr. Sun" (*RB* 6) and seems to be the moon's husband (5); in *Sir Gibbie* (1879) the sun "was now far down his western arc" (*SG* 141); and in *Lilith* MacDonald, after describing the sun as the "master-minister of the human tabernacle," says "he is but a coal from the altar of the Father's never-ending sacrifice to his children" (*L* 348; 1895). The concept is frequently found in a religious context; Gilbert Cope, in *Symbolism in the Bible and the Church*, says: "The sun by day and the moon by night . . . often serve as symbols of male and female" (Cope, 197).

29. "The Syzygy: Anima and Animus," in *Aion: Researches into the Phenomenology of the Self*, par. 33. She is also Curdie's anima, namely "the personification of the inferior functions which relate a man to the collective unconscious," says Jung in *The Symbolic Life: Miscellaneous Writings* (Vol. 18 of the *Collected Works*, par. 187).

30. Marie-Louise von Franz, *Shadow and Evil in Fairy Tales* (Zurich, 1974), 234-235.

31. "Birds . . . have a special relation to the tree," says Jung ("The Philosophical Tree," in *Alchemical Studies*, par. 415).

32. The tree and the birds which try to encircle it reveal the negative side of the mother archetype—itself a symbol of the unconscious—which "may connote anything secret,

hidden, dark; the abyss, the world of the dead, anything that devours, seduces, and poisons, that is terrifying and inescapable like fate" (Jung, "The Mother Archetype," in *The Archetypes and the Collective Unconscious,* par. 158). In MacDonald's *The Golden Key* the tree itself attacks Tangle and she is rescued by the air-fish who plays a role similar to Lina's, although, ironically, as a sort of bird: "[A]s the last of the light was disappearing, [Tangle] passed under a tree with drooping branches. It propped [sic; should be 'dropped'] its branches to the ground all about her, and caught her as in a trap. She struggled to get out, but the branches pressed her closer and closer to the trunk. She was in great terror and distress, when the air-fish, swimming into the thicket of branches, began tearing at them with its beak.... Then the air-fish came from behind her [just like Lina], and swam on in front, glittering and sparkling all lovely colours; and she followed" (180).

33. "The Battle for Deliverance from the Mother," *Symbols of Transformation* par. 456.

34. Hugo Rahner, in *Greek Myths and Christian Mystery* (London, 1957), says that "[t]he sirens of Holy Scripture are nocturnal, demonic bird figures that live in the desert" (359), and "it was held—wholly in the spirit of the original [Homeric] myth—that the purpose of Scripture was ... to express the fact that these God-forsaken places had been given over to the power of the demons" (360). He quotes St. Jerome in *Cohortatio* as saying that "the Sirens are in fact symbols of Satan and his demonic host; their song ... is but an imitation of that first deceit of man which was perpetrated by the devil himself" (cit. 364). What should Curdie hear but "a sweet sound of singing" (*PC* 121)—typical of all sirens. Carl Jung comes in almost tamely in comparison; speaking of the Babylonian birds in Revelation, he says: "The birds are soul-images, by which are meant the souls of the damned and evil spirits" ("Symbols of the Mother and of Rebirth," *SoT* par. 315).

35. See Jung, "Archetypes of the Collective Unconscious," in *Archetypes:* "The contrast between desert [the "desolate heath" in *The Princess and Curdie*] and paradise [the place where fulfilment or transcendence is attained] ... signifies

isolation as contrasted with individuation, or the becoming of the self" (par. 73).

36. "As birds flying, so will the LORD of hosts defend Jerusalem," says Isaiah (31:5). Kirstin Jeffrey Johnson cites Isaiah 60:8: "Who are these that fly as a cloud, and as the doves to their windows?" ("Curdie's Intertextual Dialogue," 175 n. 17).

37. "The attribute 'strange' probably expresses, as in dreams, a peculiar emphasis or numinosity" ("Symbols of the Mother and of Rebirth," *SoT* par. 348). It is interesting to note that in the original manuscript of *Lilith A*, the first draft of *Lilith*, Mr. Raven caws loudly, "and the next instant came shooting through the dark, like a great white arrow-head, the shining pigeon his wife" (appended to *Lilith*, Johannesen, 486).

38. "And there went out another horse that was red; and power was given unto him that sat thereon to take peace from the earth, and that they should kill one another; and there was given unto him a great sword" (Revelation 6:3).

39. "The Battle for Deliverance from the Mother," *SoT* par. 420.

40. In *Phantastes* (1858) the forest actually contains the tabooed tree, the Ash—so taboo that it manifests itself as its own shadow and is aggressively masculine (*Ph* 51-53; the beech tree even calls him "the goblin" [54]). The Ash is, however, more than balanced by the beech tree, who is protective and maternal and hopes eventually to become a woman (54-60). The Maid of the Alder Tree is a further variation on a theme; a woman in front and a tree behind, her back "was a rough representation of the human frame, only hollow, as if made of decaying bark torn from a tree" (84)—and she, like the Ash, is a "walking Death" (86).

41. And see Jung, "The Dual Mother," *SoT* par. 505: "All the lions, bulls, dogs, and snakes that populate our dreams represent an undifferentiated and as yet untamed libido, which at the same time forms part of the human personality and can therefore fittingly be described as the *anthropoid psyche*."

42. The fact that Curdie never, unlike Anodos, Diamond or Tangle, understands Lina's conversations with the beasts, confirms that she is not a true animal but (on one level) part of himself—just as the Uglies are part of the shadow of the collective unconscious.

43. The same sort of thing happens in the wood in *Phantastes*, when Anodos is "haunted with the feeling that other shapes, more like my own size and mien, were moving about at a little distance on all sides of me. But as yet I could discern none of them . . ." (*Ph* 48). Eventually, for this and other reasons, the forest in *Phantastes* becomes menacing.

ENDNOTES TO CHAPTER 10

1. "The city symbolizes the totality of man, an attitude of wholeness which cannot be dissolved," says Carl Jung in *The Symbolic Life: Miscellaneous Writings*, par. 268.

2. See, e.g., Jung, "Symbols of the Mother and of Rebirth," in *Symbols of Transformation*, par. 303: "The city is a maternal symbol, a woman who harbours the inhabitants in herself like children."

3. Resembling Lina's eyes, which are "dark green, with a yellow light in them" (101).

4. See Isaiah 28:16: "Behold, I lay in Zion for a foundation a stone, a tried stone, a precious corner stone, a sure foundation."

5. See Jung, "The Personification of the Opposites," in *Mysterium Coniunctionis*, par. 224: "For purely psychological reasons I have . . . tried to equate the masculine consciousness with the concept of Logos and the feminine with that of Eros. By Logos I meant discrimination, judgment, insight, and by Eros I meant the capacity to relate." In par. 225 Jung does, however, add that instances to the contrary leap to the eye at once, but his proposition is nevertheless of value as a generalisation. Roderick McGillis says: "The feminine power so effective in *The Princess and the Goblin* gives way to the aggressiveness of masculine power in *The*

Princess and Curdie" (introduction to the World's Classics edition of *The Princess and the Goblin* and *The Princess and Curdie*, xix).

6. Barbara becomes the king's Barbara (or vice versa—"the king was now Barbara's playmate" [*PC* 283])—and the resemblance between the words "barber" and "Barbara" is surely deliberate. Commenting on the term 'barber,' Jung says: "Since olden times shaving the head has been associated with consecration, that is, with spiritual transformation or initiation. . . . This . . . goes back to the old idea that the transformed one becomes like a new-born babe . . . with a hairless head" ("Transformation Symbolism in the Mass," *Psychology and Religion* par. 348).

7. Kirstin Jeffrey Johnson points out that Derba is also the name of a town that shelters Peter and Barnabas in the fourteenth chapter of Acts; that the name means "free man" in Gaelic; and that in Middle English it means "place where the deer graze"—foreshadowing what will happen after the fall of Gwyntystorm ("Curdie's Intertextual Dialogue: Engaging Maurice, Arnold, and Isaiah," 177 n31).

8. Even to shelter some of the servants expelled from the palace (272)—and "a poor old fellow in rags and tatters" (a pale echo of Curdie) upon whom the butchers set their dogs (280).

9. Rhyming slang originated with Cockneys in the East End of London, and MacDonald would certainly have been familiar with it as he visited poor tenants of the philanthropist Octavia Hill, a friend of the MacDonalds (see, e.g., Raeper, *George MacDonald*, 265, 272). Usually there are two key words—"brown bread" = "dead," "daisy roots" = "boots," for example—but oddly enough the rhyming word is often dropped; "plates of meat" (for "feet") becomes "plates," "apples and pears" (for "stairs") becomes "apples," "loaf of bread" (for "head") becomes "loaf," "china plate" (for "mate") becomes "china," etc. Rhyming slang spread outside London and some expressions, such as "use your loaf," are in fairly general use. Expressions come and go; a "Germaine Greer" used to be a beer, but that may

have changed. It was re-energised by a TV series, *Minder*, in the 80s, and its adaptability means that there are always stirrings of life in it (Australia, for example, has a thriving branch—see John Ayto's *The Oxford Dictionary of Rhyming Slang* [Oxford and New York: 2002]). On Sept. 27th 2017 a TV presenter spoke of "going on the rock 'n roll" ("dole," or benefits). Rhyming slang is more an approach to language than a list of words and phrases.

10. MacDonald's barber, however, has a sinister quality that seems almost the opposite of "soul." When he grasps Curdie's hand, "his was the cold smooth leathery palm of a monkey" (140). Monkeys are apparently the only creatures in the whole creation which MacDonald, the animal-lover, does not like; when at the end of *Lilith* Mr. Vane, Lona and their companions traverse a live forest, full of lovely birds and squirrels, during their ascent to the heavenly city, "[n]ot one monkey of any sort could they see" (*L* 351)—this in a terrain in which even serpents grow into birds (353). Perhaps, in spite of his belief in evolution (and devolution), MacDonald had some misgivings about Darwin's *On the Origins of Species by Means of Natural Selection*, which appeared in 1859.

11. A "watery abyss" is symbolically a "region of danger" (Jung, "The Myth of the Hero," in *Psychology and Alchemy*, par. 438), and water is "the commonest symbol of the unconscious" ("Archetypes of the Collective Unconscious," *Archetypes*, par. 40).

12. In direct contravention of Jesus's command to love your neighbour as yourself (see Matthew 19:19; 22:39; Mark 12:31; Luke 10:27).

13. And see Jung, "Gnostic Symbols of the Self," in *Aion*, par. 310: "[F]or the anonymous individual of the populace, every king carries the symbol of the self."

14. The Wise Old Man is "the superior master and teacher, the archetype of the spirit, who symbolizes the pre-existent meaning hidden in the chaos of life. He is the father of the soul…" (Jung, "Archetypes of the Collective Unconscious," *Archetypes*, par. 74), and "always appears when the hero is in a hopeless and desperate situation" ("The Phenomenology

of the Spirit in Fairytales," *Archetypes,* par. 401). The times are out of joint, however, for in *The Princess and Curdie* the king's illness, which symbolises the spiritual sickness of the nation, means that the wise old man now needs the hero to rescue him from his *own* "hopeless and desperate situation." The archetype does not always represent the "helper and redeemer;" it can also be negative, says Carl Jung in "Psychology and Literature." This is not the case in *The Princess and Curdie,* but Jung goes on to say: "This image has lain buried and dormant in the unconscious since the dawn of history; it is awakened whenever the times are out of joint and a great error deflects society from the right path" ("Psychology and Literature," in *The Spirit in Man, Art and Literature* [Vol. 15 of the *Collected Works*], par. 159). Curdie's charge is to restore the Wise Old Man to his right relation to individuals and especially to the country as a whole.

15. See Jung, "The Battle for Deliverance from the Mother," *SoT,* par. 450: "The more negative the attitude of the conscious towards the unconscious, the more dangerous does the latter become."

16. Gilbert Cope, in *Symbolism in the Bible and the Church,* says that "in apocalyptic speculations the figures of a bewildering variety of monsters signify the punitive activity of God—the agents of his 'wrath'" (95).

17. Curdie (*PC* 131) suspects them to be regenerating forms of the goblin creatures from the mines in *The Princess and the Goblin.* The goblins themselves survive only as a single creature of superstition in *The Princess and Curdie*—"the cellar goblin," whose role is supposedly to protect the wine (121).

18. Bruno Bettelheim, in *The Uses of Enchantments,* cites G.K. Chesterton's remark (in *Orthodoxy* [London, 1909]) that "children are innocent and love justice, while most of us are wicked and naturally prefer mercy" (144).

19. Bettelheim says: "The child feels that all's well with the world, and that he can be secure in it, only if the wicked are punished in the end" (*Uses of Enchantment,* 147).

20. Jung, "Psychology and Literature," *The Spirit in Man, Art*

and Literature, par. 159. The magician is represented here by the doctor.

21. Cope points out that in the twenty-first chapter of the Book of Numbers snakes both kill and heal (*Symbolism in the Bible and the Church*, 183). On the positive side, Carl Jung, in *Psychology and Religion*, instances the snake's casting its skin each year as a prototype of renewal ("Transformation Symbolism in the Mass," par. 348). Lina, in process of redemption, is described as having a "head . . . something between that of a polar bear and a snake" (*PC* 101), and "legserpent," one of the Uglies she has conquered, is of the greatest utility in getting his companions across the chasm and into the king's cellar (249-250).

22. Much has been said about the symbolic or psychological significance of injury to a leg or foot in MacDonald's work (see, e.g., Raeper, *George MacDonald*, 206). The meaning may vary, but the importance and frequency of the image may well owe something to the fact that his father's left leg had been amputated the year after MacDonald was born due to "white swelling" (*GMHW* 34). As so often, MacDonald gives us the "shadow" side of the case; in *Malcolm* (1875), the Marquis of Lossie, who proves to be Malcolm's father, dies because he refuses to have his gangrenous leg amputated until it is too late (*M* 420-422).

23. In *Symbols of Transformation* Jung cites a passage from the dream-book of Jugadeva: "Whoever dreams that his body is wrapped round with bast, creepers or cords, with snake-skins, threads or webs, will certainly die" ("The Dual Mother," par. 542). The death that threatens in *The Princess and Curdie* is psychological and spiritual.

24. See Revelation 6:5, in which the rider, and by association the horse, symbolises famine (but only a general sense of destruction in *The Princess and Curdie*). The four horses of the apocalypse (including the pale horse ridden by Death, which does not figure here) were associated with agents of divine punishment: "And power was given unto them over the fourth part of the earth, to kill with sword, and with hunger, and with death, and with the beasts of the earth" (Rev. 6:8). This echoes Ezekiel's prophecy of the divine

punishment of Jerusalem, Ezekiel 14:13-21, especially its climax: "How much more [destruction there will be] when I send my four sore judgments upon Jerusalem, the sword, and the famine, and the noisome beast, and the pestilence" (14: 21).

25. "Christ, a Symbol of the Self," in *Aion*, par. 97.

26. The reference is to *The Book of Nations* (*PC* 274), which is probably, in its turn, a reference to Adam Smith's *An Inquiry into the Nature and Causes of the Wealth of Nations* (1776). The *Oxford Companion to English Literature* (4th ed; Oxford, 1967), summarises Smith's theory as follows: "His political economy is essentially individualistic; self-interest is the proper criterion of economic action. But the universal pursuit of one's own advantage contributes, in his view, to the public interest" (876-877).

27. Kirstin Jeffrey Johnson notes that the name "Conrad" is Old German for "bold counsellor" or "wise counsellor," a phrase based on Isaiah 9:6; see "Curdie's Intertextual Dialogue" 174, n.15.

28. There may also be an echo here of George Herbert's poem "Love's Feast," in which Jesus invites the poet to partake of the Eucharist. In his chapter on George Herbert in *England's Antiphon* (1868), MacDonald says: "Amongst the keener delights of the life which is at the door, I look for the face of George Herbert, with whom to talk humbly would be in bliss a higher bliss" (193).

29. See "The Conjunction," in *Mysterium Coniunctionis*, par. 676. Jung is aware that the conjunction can happen in stages.

30. "A Study in the Process of Individuation," *Archetypes*, par. 612. The sacrificial nature of the fire is emphasised by the Queen's having earlier laid her hand on Lina's head (*PC* 226), as Aaron treated the sacrificial goat in Leviticus 6:21.

31. "Religious Ideas in Alchemy," *Psychology and Alchemy*, par. 334.

32. Sourced from Wikipedia, History.Com etc.

33. The original participants in the gold rush were known as "forty-niners" (Wikipedia). Could this have anything to

do with the fact that there are forty-nine Uglies? I merely proffer a tentative thought . . . In *Guild Court* MacDonald refers to seven as "the mystical number" (146), so the forty-nine may be a multiple of this ("there were seven present [in the church] when Lucy and Mattie entered and changed the mystical number to the magical" [*GC*]).

34. See William Raeper, *George MacDonald*, 305.

35. An account entitled "The Wreck of the Golden Mary," by Charles Dickens and Wilkie Collins, appeared in the Christmas number of *Household Words* in 1856 (see the Broadview 2011 edition of *At the Back of the North Wind*, ed. McGillis and Pennington, 112n).

36. "[F]ill thine hand with coals of fire from between the cherubims, and scatter them over the city," a heavenly visitant is instructed in an earlier chapter of Ezekiel (10:2); and although it does not happen in *The Princess and Curdie*, there is a connection with Queen Irene's (benign) fire in *The Princess and the Goblin*—"a fire which burned in the shapes of the loveliest and reddest roses, glowing gorgeously between the heads and wings of two cherubs of shining silver" (*PG* 145)—and which carries over (minus the cherubim) to *The Princess and Curdie* (92), later becoming a rose fire which first purifies the king ("a living sacrifice" [*PC* 295]) and eventually, in a chamber transferred from the original castle to the palace in Gwyntystorm, sends Lina to eternity (319). The intermittent allusions to Ezekiel (starting with the allusions to king Tyrus from Ezekiel Ch. 28 in *At the Back of the North Wind*) constitute one important link between the three major fantasies.

37. In a chapter entitled "Fairy Tale Versus Myth: Optimism Versus Pessimism," in *The Uses of Enchantment*, Bruno Bettelheim says that in myths "the ending . . . is nearly always tragic, while always happy in fairy tales," and this is in large part why "[t]he myth is pessimistic, while the fairy story is optimistic, no matter how terrifyingly serious some features of the story may be" (37). *The Princess and Curdie* comes somewhere between the two—and according to Jack Zipes, in "Fairy Tale as Myth/Myth as Fairy Tale," "the classical fairy tale has undergone a process of

mythicization" anyway: "Any fairy tale in our society, if it seeks to become natural and eternal, must become myth. Only innovative fairy tales are anti-mythical," he affirms (in *Cross-Culturalism in Children's Literature: Selected Papers from the 1987 International Conference of the Children's Literature Association*, 107).

38. A reversal of Jesus's question in St. Matthew's Gospel: "[W]hat man is there of you, whom if his son ask bread, will he give him a stone?" (Matthew 7:9, and see also Luke 11:11).

39. *Lilith A*, a transcript of the original manuscript, is incorporated into the Johannesen edition of *Lilith*, 365-539; 539.

40. I cannot forbear relating an anecdote of Jung's in *The Spirit in Man, Art, and Literature:* "I had an uncle whose thinking was always direct and to the point. One day he stopped me on the street and demanded: 'Do you know how the devil tortures the souls in hell?' When I said no, he replied: 'He keeps them waiting.' And with that he turned and walked away" ("Psychology and Literature," par. 165). [N.B. Jung thought of this when he was reading James Joyce's *Ulysses* for the first time].

41. Glenn Edward Sadler, *An Expression of Character: The Letters of George MacDonald*, 344.

42. Cit. in Raeper, *George MacDonald*, 361.

43. *An Expression of Character*, 303.

ENDNOTES TO CONCLUSION

1 David Holbrook, introduction to *Phantastes* (Everyman's Library, 1983 edition), xxiv. And this not only applies to his fantasies; William Raeper says of him that "his greatest achievement is as a novelist of the unconscious, giving expression to the inner workings of the mind and grasping at a dimension of human experience which has been largely ignored or rejected as indescribable" (*George MacDonald*, 213). The distinction between the genres is admittedly blurred in MacDonald's case.

2   As Jung says, "consciousness did not exist from the beginning; in every child it has to be built up anew in the first years of life. Consciousness is very weak in this formative period . . ." ("Psychotherapists or the Clergy," in *Psychology and Religion,* par. 533). In *Ranald Bannerman's Boyhood* the narrator says: "I cannot tell any better than most of my readers how and when I began to come awake, or what it was that wakened me. I mean, I cannot remember when I began to remember" (*RBB* 12). In "A Sketch of Individual Development" MacDonald refers to "the dawn of consciousness" (*Orts* [43]).

3   See *Later Manuscripts,* ed. Janet Todd and Linda Bree (Cambridge, 2008), 146, in *The Cambridge Edition of the Works of Jane Austen* (Cambridge, New York, Melbourne etc.: CUP, 2005-2008).

4   "Conscious, Unconscious, and Individuation," in *The Archetypes and the Collective Unconscious,* par. 490. Jane Austen predates Jung too—but who would think so?

5   Diamond, in *At the Back of the North Wind,* sees a somewhat similar situation from a child's perspective. He is aware that the drunken cabman next door in Bloomsbury has surrendered to the instinctual drives of his darker unconscious: "Baby's daddy takes too much beer and gin, and that makes him somebody else, and not his own self at all," he tells the child he is nursing (181). He himself inspires the cabman to begin to integrate his 'two selves' so that his consciousness has the upper hand (183-184).

6   Mr. Wingfold does this by making Arthur practice observation of the outside world of nature at stipulated times for several weeks, on each occasion writing down what he has noticed, until "[h]e delighted in the grass and the wild flowers, the sky and the clouds and the stars, and knew, after a real, vital fashion, the world in which he lived. He entered into the life that was going on about him . . ." (*TB* 360). This complements the dulling of consciousness exhibited by Curdie, who, at the beginning of *The Princess and Curdie,* "took less and less notice of bees and butterflies, moths and dragon-flies, the flowers and the brooks and the clouds" and "was gradually changing into a "commonplace

man" (*PC* 22).

7   "The Symbolism of the Mandala," *Psychology and Alchemy* par. 247.

8   See, e.g., "The Battle for Deliverance from the Mother," *Symbols of Transformation*, par. 459: "The task [of keeping the libido, or psychic energy, in a state of progression] consists in integrating the unconscious, in bringing together 'conscious' and 'unconscious.' I have called this the individuation process." Jung considers the individuation process "the central problem of modern psychology" ("Flying Saucers: A Modern Myth," in *Civilization in Transition*, par. 809).

9   "A Study in the Process of Individuation," in *Archetypes*, par. 620.

10 "Life," in *Unspoken Sermons, Second Series*, 298.

11 C.S. Lewis, preface to *George MacDonald: An Anthology*, xxxiii.

12 He does, in *What's Mine's Mine* (1886), express disapproval of "a certain [unnamed] lady novelist" whose novels, "to speak with due restraint, do not tend to profitable thought" (*WMM* 93).

13 *Weighed and Wanting*, 313-319, 474-484; *Pride and Prejudice*, ed. Pat Rogers, in *The Cambridge Edition* (Cambridge, 2006), 391-397.

14 It is possible that there is an echo of Jane Austen's *Emma* in *The Princess and the Goblin*. When Emma is devastated by a sudden insight into her own misjudgements and the miseries they may bring upon herself and others, her feelings are reflected in nature: "The weather added what it could of gloom. A cold stormy rain set in." The next chapter begins: "The weather continued much the same all the following morning; and the same loneliness, and the same melancholy, seemed to reign at Hartfield—but in the afternoon it cleared; the winds changed into a softer quarter; the clouds were carried off; the sun appeared; it was summer again. With all the eagerness which such a transition gives, Emma resolved to be out of doors as soon as possible. Never had the exquisite sight, smell, sensation

of nature, tranquil, warm, and brilliant after a storm, been more attractive to her. She longed for the serenity they might gradually introduce"—and sure enough, she meets 'Prince Charming,' Mr. Knightley, outside, and everything culminates in a promise of marriage (*Emma*, ed. Richard Cronin and Dorothy McMillan, in *The Cambridge Edition* [2005], 462). In *The Princess and the Goblin*, Irene's failure to find her grandmother on her second venture up the tower stairs "not only disappointed her, but made her very thoughtful. . . . [S]he thought it very sad not to have been able to find her when she particularly wanted her" (*PG* 42). The weather has been too wet for her to go out for the past two days, but things change almost immediately: "The next day the great cloud still hung over the mountain, and the rain poured like water from a full sponge. . . . But the mist was not of such a dark dingy grey; there was light in it; and as the hours went on, it grew brighter and brighter, until it was almost too brilliant to look at; and late in the afternoon, the sun broke out so gloriously that Irene clapped her hands" and went out with Lootie (43)—to meet Curdie and eventually promise him a kiss. Emma virtually plays 'nursie' to her father, so she doesn't need to bring him with her—but allowing for the difference between child and adult, there is a certain similarity between the two situations.

15 In *At the Back of the North Wind*, set as it is to a considerable extent in the Primary World, Diamond's education is, by contrast, minutely described. Miss Coleman gives him a picture book which teaches him to recognise different animals (*ABNW* 124); Joseph teaches him to read from a book provided by North Wind (192); Mr. Raymond gives him a book of his own writing, "full of pictures and stories and poems" (211), and the Bible is both a subject of family discussion (201) and Diamond's chosen private reading (323). And it doesn't stop there; Diamond teaches Nanny to read and Joseph listens to them both (311). Catherine Persyn, in a discussion of the number seven in *At the Back of the North Wind*, demonstrates from textual evidence that it took Diamond seven weeks to learn to read ("A Person's Name and a Person's Self, or: Just *Who* is North Wind,"

North Wind 22 [2003], 72).

16 The image of the siren is certainly present (see Ch. 9, n34, 296 above). Hugo Rahner, in *Greek Myths and Christian Mystery*, says: "The sirens of Holy Scripture are nocturnal, demonic bird figures that live in the desert" (359) and "it was held—wholly in the spirit of [Homer's] myth—that the purpose of Scripture was in this case to express the fact that these God-forsaken places had been given over to the power of the demons" (360).

17 And he continues: "I tell you, I know you not whence ye are; depart from me, all ye workers of iniquity" (Luke 13:25, 27). MacDonald's allusion gives a deeper resonance to the laird's fear. What might almost be termed his philosophy of bewilderment is summed up in the second chapter, "The Mad Laird": "I dinna ken whaur I cam frae, and I dinna ken whaur I'm gaun till; but I ken 'at I'm gaun *whaur* I cam frae" (*M* 8).

18 The slightly later *Wilfrid Cumbermede* (1872) draws on the same image. In the chapter tellingly entitled "The Ice-Cave," Wilfrid at first finds the cave in the valley of the Grindelwald delightful. His friend Charley Osborne's terror, however, changes Wilfrid's view: "Charley's face was that of a corpse. The brilliant hue of the cave made us look to each other most ghastly and fearful" (142). In the next chapter but one, "Again the Ice-Cave," Wilfrid and Charley return to the ice-cave with Clara, and Wilfrid becomes a witness: "[T]here stood Clara and Charley—staring at each other with faces of ghastly horror." Wilfrid's conjecture is that "Clara took fright at [Charley's] fear, her imagination opening like a crystal to the polarized light of reflected feeling; and thus they stood in the paralysis of a dismay which ever multiplied itself in the opposed mirrors of their countenances" (163). *Wilfrid Cumbermede*, at least in the case of Charley Osborne, shows fear getting out of hand. Clara comes out of the cave in "a dumb show of the resurrection," so MacDonald's preferred trajectory is in some degree followed—but for Charley the impression of death is too strong. "That lovely face!" he says to his friend: "To see it like that—and know that is what it is coming to!" (164) His vision of the future is of death, not resurrection,

and so death grows all-powerful with him.

19 *The Uses of Enchantment*, 91, 96. In view of the fact that Queen Irene pulls the emerald out of the rocky floor of the cavern *(PC 76)* and says that "if a thief were to come in here just now, he would think he saw the demon of the mine" (77), it is interesting that Joan Evans cites De Boot's seventeenth century lapidary, *Gemmarum et Lapidum Historia*, as saying that one property of the emerald is to repel demons (*Magical Jewels of the Middle Ages and the Renaissance*, 153).

20 There's a page who makes a brief appearance in *Lilith* too, but he's a nasty little creature, as befits his darker context (*L* 179).

21 Mr. Smith, the narrator in *Adela Cathcart*, speaks for MacDonald when he says "I love the common with all my heart, but I hate the common-place" (*AC* 31).

22 W.H. Auden, in the afterword to the Bodley Head edition of *The Golden Key* in 1967, says: "To me, George MacDonald's most extraordinary, and precious, gift is his ability to create an atmosphere of goodness about which there is nothing phony or moralistic. Nothing is rarer in literature" (86).

23 Daniel Gabelman, in *George MacDonald: Divine Carelessness and Fairytale Levity*, describes both Diamond and Gibbie (and their forerunner Colin in "The Carasoyn") as "holy fools" (138).

24 A figure of Scottish legend, never seen by day (*SG* 112), endowed with toeless feet (113, 124) and "thumbed but fingerless hands" (124).

25 There is a suggestion of this in *Alec Forbes of Howglen*, when one evening Curly, "flitting along from tree to tree just within the deeper dusk of the wood," makes "awful sounds, like the subdued growling of wild beasts" to amuse himself. "'I thocht ye was a wild beast!' said Annie" (*AFH* 224).

26 Another book which is about the main character's boyhood, but seen largely from an adult perspective, is *A Rough Shaking* (1891). Clare Skymer, whose name has celestial overtones which rather put him in Diamond's league, lives

in a world in which mothers drug their unwanted babies and throw them into water-butts to drown quietly (*RS* 147ff) and in which rats, given the opportunity, nibble a baby's toes (185). But just as he seems to be "[l]ike a child the sport of an evil fairy" (376), he finds his father (380).

27 Moxy falls down the outside cellar steps in the dark and breaks his leg, forcing his homeless family to take refuge in the Raymounts' cellar which is also a hiding-place from a policeman passing by (*WW* 405-408). This could pass as the 'shadow' side of Diamond's descent of Old Sal's cellar steps in search of Nanny, watched over (unknown to him) by a kindly policeman (*ABNW* 203-207; policemen [only instituted in London in 1829; a royal commission in 1839 recommended wider police areas] always make a good showing in MacDonald's works). But even in the desperate situation of the Franks family the immanence of the divine is suggested. Before the family settles down for the rest of the night, Mr. Franks, Moxy's father, says to his wife: "It's some sort of a cellar—p'r'aps at the bottom of a church. It do look as if it wur left open jest for us!—You *used* to talk about *him* above, wife!" (*WW* 407). And, wakeful and desolate, he has a strange and never-to-be-explained experience: "In about an hour [he] . . . heard the door open softly and stealthily, and seemed aware of a presence beside themselves in the place. He concluded some other poor creature had discovered the same shelter; or, if they had got into a church-vault, it might be some wandering ghost; he was too weary for further speculation, or any uneasiness. When the slow light crept through the chinks of the door, he found they were quite alone" (408). The title of the novel, *Weighed and Wanting*, is drawn from the Book of Daniel, in which the disembodied fingers of a man's hand write on the wall at King Belshazzar's feast foretelling the destruction and dispersal of his kingdom: "Thou art weighed in the balances, and art found wanting" (Dan. 5:27).

28 MacDonald cites these words of Jesus in his essay "Light," in *Unspoken Sermons: Series Three*: "[M]y father and your father, my God and your God" (549). The whole situation is one example, among many, of that "re-echoing" of truths

the importance of which is expressed by MacDonald in "The Imagination: Its Functions and its Culture" (*A Dish of Orts*, 22 and elsewhere) and discussed by Gisela Kreglinger in *Storied Revelations*. She focuses on his recognition of the need to "re-echo" biblical symbols with which we have grown too familiar, and adds that "for MacDonald the imagination . . . plays a central role in this recasting of scriptural truth" (147). Another case in point is the chapter in *The Princess and the Goblin* headed "The Little Miner," in which Irene and Lootie become lost on the mountain after dark and are escorted home by Curdie (a re-working of the scriptural 'lost and found' motif already applied to the princess). This incident is 're-echoed' strikingly in the chapter entitled "The Beast-Boy," in *Sir Gibbie*; Ginevra, separated from the servant, Nicie (a name quite close to "nursie") on the mountain, becomes lost and at first runs away in terror from the "beast-boy" of local gossip—actually Sir Gibbie, who is trying to rescue her and eventually sees her safely to Nicie's home.

29   Roderick McGillis, introduction to *George MacDonald: The Princess and the Goblin* and *The Princess and Curdie*, ix.

30   Some themes and symbols figure in the earlier works but do not fundamentally interest or attract MacDonald and are later dropped; mesmerism, famous at the time because of Mesmer's use of hypnotic techniques for medicinal purposes, is one such. It looms large in MacDonald's first novel, *David Elginbrod*, which, as William Raeper points out, contains many elements of the vogue for sensation fashionable at the time (*George MacDonald*, 198); Von Funkelstein/Halkar gains control over Euphra's spirit until shortly before her death. But mesmerism was never likely to have enduring appeal to such a freedom-loving spirit as MacDonald's, even though it plays a significant part in Coleridge's "The Rime of the Ancient Mariner"—"than which what more marvellous?" says MacDonald in his dedication to the ghost story *The Portent* (1864). The short story "The Cruel Painter" features pseudo-vampirism (perhaps a sign that MacDonald was beginning to take Gothic sensationalism less seriously). In MacDonald's last novel, *Salted With Fire* (1897), there is a cataleptic trance,

followed by an improbable resurrection. This is probably a reminiscence of Edgar Allan Poe, who is specifically mentioned in *David Elginbrod*, though not in a favourable context; Von Funkelstein, who bets Hugh Sutherland that he won't spend a night alone in a reputedly haunted chamber, advises him to take "Edgar Poe's Tales" with him as reading material (*DE* 261). While there are definite Gothic elements in *Phantastes* and *Lilith*, they are not, of course, found in the children's fantasies, except for a little somnambulism (in Martha's estimation at least) in *At the Back of the North Wind*.

31 The Collins Line ship SS Arctic, which had been built only four years earlier, had luxurious accommodation and was very large and very fast. Among the dead were members of the families of the founder of the Collins Line and of a partner; apparently 20 male passengers and about 60 crew members were saved. Public outrage over the treatment of women and children resonated for decades and gave rise to the tradition of "women and children first." NB: The other ship was smaller, but survived; unlike the Arctic, it had a steel hull. (Source: "The Sinking of the Steamship Arctic," website).

32 Nor was he the only author to do so. "The Wreck of the Golden Mary," by Charles Dickens and Wilkie Collins (see Ch.10, n35, 304 above) was about a ship lost while transporting hopefuls to California to take part in the gold rush—apparently a conflation of two major events, the gold rush and the shipwreck.

33 In *AFH* 282-293 there is an echo of the Moray Floods of 1829, fixed in the memory of the four-and-a-half-year-old George (see Raeper, *George MacDonald*, 28-29). Tibbie Dyster and Murdoch Malison the schoolmaster, with his pupil Truffey, were drowned in the flood (*AFH* 289-290; 291); a similar flood in *Sir Gibbie* sees Gibbie saving the life of Angus, the gamekeeper who has treated him brutally (*SG* 254-256).

34 "Ye're jist an angel unawares," Robert tells her when she not only offers to give him lessons but invites him to practise on her piano (*RF* 196), and he also thinks of her

as "a protecting angel" (396). To the dying Ericson she appears to be "[a] strong she-angel with mighty wings" (358). Other 'angel' references occur, and are consistent with the associations of her name with the Mother of God and the beloved disciple, John. But there is also a more human dimension to Mary St. John, who, but for other circumstances, "might have found no little attraction in the noble bearing and handsome face of young Falconer" (331).

35 See, e.g., Colin Manlove, "Circularity in Fantasy: George MacDonald," in *The Impulse of Fantasy Literature*, [1]-36.

36 The hero's stepmother, Lady Ann Lestrange of Mortgrange, on the other hand, is a character MacDonald seems actively to dislike. In some respects this book is subjective almost to the point of self-indulgence.

37 When they wintered in Algiers in 1856-57, the MacDonalds lived in a house the upper floor of which was occupied by Archdeacon Wix of New Zealand and his family. The two families became friends, but it is the Leigh-Smith girls, whom they also met at this time, who are likely to have influenced the portrayal of Barbara as unconventional (see Kathy Triggs, *The Stars and the Stillness*, 63-64).

38 At one point Richard feels himself, in comparison with Barbara, to be "an earthy pebble beside a celestial sapphire" (368).

39 See Margery Fisher, "Signs of the Times," in *Children and Literature: Views and Reviews*, ed. Virginia Haviland, 127-128.

40 "Fairy Tale Versus Myth: Optimism Versus Pessimism," in *The Uses of Enchantment*, especially 37. Daniel Gabelman has a different perspective: "MacDonald reverses the joyous fairytale conclusion ["Irene and Curdie were married"] almost instantly," and the reader is reminded that "the hold of goodness in this age is tenuous. We must battle evil and champion goodness until the blissful end. In this way, MacDonald extends the fairytale into the everyday, hinting that fairytale temporality verges upon the lives of his audience" (*Divine Carelessness and Fairytale Levity*, 140).

41 "Miracles of Healing Solicited by the Sufferers," in *The Miracles of Our Lord*, 304.

42 In *Thomas Wingfold, Curate* (1876), the fate of Gwyntystorm is anticipated in microcosm in the perceived destiny of the two dwarves. Mr. Polwarth tells the curate that he and his niece Rachel are as they are because of the misdeeds of their ancestors. "The results of their lawlessness are ours: we are what and where you see us. . . . There are none of the family left now but myself and Rachel. God in his mercy is about to let it cease" (82); but it will only cease in *this* world.

43 "I think [Lady Catherine] will be pleased with the hermitage," says Mrs. Bennet (*PP* 391). The wilderness at Sotherton, in *Mansfield Park*, does not go quite this far, though in one respect much further; it is "a planted wood of about two acres . . . and though laid out with too much regularity, was darkness and shade, and natural beauty, compared with the bowling-green and the terrace" (*MP*, ed. John Wiltshire, in *The Cambridge Edition* [Cambridge, 2005], 106-107).

44 Barbara Wylder, in *There and Back,* is described in similar terms at one point: "Barbara was like a heath of thyme and wild roses and sudden winds" (95). NB: Her name, though it intriguingly suggests "wild" (this is presumably deliberate, as at one point she is described as a "divine little savage" [82]), is actually pronounced "willder"—probably because of Barbara's strength of will. We know this through the offices of Miss Malliver, the unpleasant governess in the Lestrange family, who jokes grimly that "the house was very much B. Wyldered" by the newcomer (81).

45 In *The Flight of the Shadow* (1891) MacDonald deals with the question of the ending by entitling the final chapter of the book "The End of the First Volume." The last chapter of *Wilfrid Cumbermede* (a sad book in which misunderstandings and disappointed hopes are not overcome) is rather bleakly entitled "Conclusion"—but even here hope timidly raises its head, though it has no definite focus.

46 Introduction to *George MacDonald: The Princess and the Goblin and The Princess and Curdie*, xviii. In "Fantasy as Miracle: George MacDonald's *The Miracles of Our Lord*,"

McGillis says that *The Princess and Curdie* "ends with a vision of cleansing so effective that everything is clean, the world begins again" (*George MacDonald: Literary Heritage and Heirs*, 201-202). Catherine Persyn, in "'In My End is My Beginning': The *fin-negans* Motif in George MacDonald's *At the Back of the North Wind*," notes "[t]he characteristic hooking-up of the last words of the book 'the back of the north wind' with its title," already found in the last words of Chapter 9 and the title of Chapter 10 (*Mythlore* 24 [2006], 68n19). This is often found in hero myth, of which *At the Back of the North Wind* has elements; Richard Adams's *Watership Down*, for example, begins with the sentence "The primroses were over" and concludes: "[T]he first primroses were beginning to bloom." Colin Manlove, in "Circularity in Fantasy: George MacDonald," takes this circularity, or returning from the end to the beginning, to be "an image of the preservation of things as they are, and thus one expression of fantasy's delight in 'being'" (*The Impulse of Fantasy Literature*, [1]). Later he says: "Most fantasies seek to conserve those things in which they take delight: indeed it is one of their weaknesses that they are tempted not to admit loss" (*IFL* 31)—a temptation to which neither *At the Back of the North Wind* nor *The Princess and Curdie* succumbs and which is circumvented in *The Princess and the Goblin*. Carl Schrock, in "From Child to Childlike: The Cycle of Education in Novalis and George MacDonald," says: "We move . . . from a childhood of potential, through a process of 'becoming,' into a fully realized childhood" (*North Wind* 25 [2006], 63). In Rosemary Jackson's opinion, however, the "more conservative fantasies" of such authors as MacDonald, Kingsley, Morris, Tolkien, Lewis etc., "simply go along with a desire to cease 'to be,' a longing to transcend or escape the human" (*Fantasy: The Literature of Subversion* [London and New York, 1981], 156).

47 "Light," in *Unspoken Sermons, Series Three* (552).
48 *Good Words for the Young*, June 1871, 420.

When he had eaten his breakfast, she took a pouch made of goatskin, with long hair on it, filled it wqith bread and cheese, and hung it over his shoulder. Then his father gave him a stick he had cut for him in the wood, and he bade them good-bye rather hurriedly, for he was afraid of breaking down. As he went out, he caught up his mattock and took it with him. It had on the one side a pointed curve of strong steel, for loosening the earth and the ore, and on the other a steel hammer for breaking the stones and rocks. Just as he crossed the threshold the sun showed the first segment of his disc above the horizon.

Chapter 9, "Hands"
illustration by Helen Stratton

WORKS CITED

PRIMARY SOURCES

MacDonald, George. *The Complete and Original Works of George MacDonald*. Whitethorn, California: Johannesen, 1991-97, and subsequent reprints. First references to books other than *At the Back of the North Wind*, *The Princess and the Goblin* and *The Princess and Curdie* will normally include original publication dates.

Primary texts by other authors are referenced in endnotes where appropriate.

SECONDARY SOURCES

Apter, T.E. *Fantasy Literature: An Approach to Reality*. London & Basingstoke: Macmillan, 1982.

Atterbury, Paul. *Wonder Book of Trains*. Newton Abbot & Cincinnati: David & Charles, 2012.

Auden, W.H. Afterword to George MacDonald's *The Golden Key*. London: Bodley Head edition, 1967.

Authorized Version of the Bible, 1611

Avery, Gillian. "George MacDonald and the Victorian Fairy Tale," in *The Gold Thread: Essays on George MacDonald*, ed. William Raeper. Edinburgh: Edinburgh University Press, 1990: 126-139.

---------------."George MacDonald," in *The Oxford Companion to Fairy Tales*, ed. Jack Zipes; 2nd ed. Oxford: Oxford University Press, 2015: 371-373.

---------------"The Return of the Fairies," in "British and Irish fairy tales." *The Oxford Companion to Fairy Tales*, ed. Jack Zipes. 2nd ed. Oxford: Oxford University Press, 2015: 80-84.

Bettelheim, Bruno. *The Uses of Enchantment: The Meaning and Importance of Fairy Tales*. New York: Alfred A. Knopf, 1976.

Book of Common Prayer, The (Anglican).

Briggs, K.M. *The Fairies in Tradition and Literature.* London: Routledge & Kegan Paul, 1967.

Bubel, Katharine. "Knowing God 'Other-wise': The Wise Old Woman Archetype in George MacDonald's *The Princess and the Goblin, The Princess and Curdie* and 'The Golden Key'." *North Wind: A Journal of George MacDonald Studies,* 25 (2006): 1-17.

Burt, Michael. "Books in *Phantastes*" in "*Phantastes* and the Development of the Imagination." *North Wind: A Journal of George MacDonald Studies,* 35 (2016): 99-100.

Buttrick, George Arthur, and others, eds. *The Interpreters' Dictionary of the Bible: An Illustrated Encyclopedia.* New York: Abingdon Press, 1962.

Carpenter, Humphrey. *Secret Gardens: A Study of the Golden Age of Children's Literature.* Boston: Houghton Mifflin, 1985.

-------------------, and Mari Prichard. *The Oxford Companion to Children's Literature.* Oxford and New York: Oxford University Press, 1984.

Chesterton, G.K. Introduction to *George MacDonald and His Wife,* by Greville MacDonald. Whitethorn, California: Johannesen, 2005 (2nd ed.; from George Allen & Unwin, London 1924).

-------------------. From "George MacDonald and his Work," *The Daily News,* London 1901; cit. in "Appreciations," in *The Gospel in George MacDonald, Selections from His Novels, Fairy Tales, and Spiritual Writings,* ed Marianne Wright. New York, England and Australia: Plough Publishing House, 2016: 306-311.

Cope, Gilbert. *Symbolism in the Bible and the Church.* London: SCM Press Ltd., 1959.

Creed, Daniel. "Connecting Dimensions: Direction, Location and Form in the Fantasies of George MacDonald." *North Wind: A Journal of George MacDonald Studies,* 33 (2014): 1-20.

Crockford, Ally. "Sitting on the Doorstep: MacDonald's Aesthetic Fantasy Worlds and the Divine Child-

Figure," in *Rethinking George MacDonald: Contexts and Contemporaries,* ed. Christopher MacLachlan, John Patrick Padziora, and Ginger Stelle. Glasgow: Scottish Literature International, 2013.

Cruden, Alexander. *Cruden's Complete Concordance to the Bible,* ed. C.H. Irwin, A.D. Adams, S.A. Waters. Guildford and London: Lutterworth Press, 1977 (for 1737).

Cusick, Edmund. "MacDonald and Jung," in *The Gold Thread: Essays on George MacDonald,* ed. William Raeper. Edinburgh: Edinburgh University Press, 1990:56-86.

David, Deirdre, ed. "Chronology," in *The Cambridge Companion to the Victorian Novel,* 2nd ed. Cambridge: Cambridge University Press, 2012.

Day, A. Colin. *Collins Thesaurus of the Bible.* London: HarperCollins, 2002.

Dearborn, Kerry. *Baptized Imagination: The Theology of George MacDonald.* Aldershot, U.K., and Burlington, U.S.A.: Ashgate Publishing, 2006.

Dickens, Charles. *Dickens Journals Online.* Website.

Douglas-Fairhurst, Robert. *The Story of Alice: Lewis Carroll and the Secret History of Wonderland.* London: Harvill Secker, 2015.

Duffy, Maureen. *The Erotic World of Faery.* London, Sydney, Auckland, Toronto: Hodder and Stoughton, 1972.

Easton, M.G. *The Illustrated Bible Dictionary.* Revised Ed. London: Bracken Books, 1989.

Evans, Joan. *Magical Jewels of the Middle Ages and the Renaissance, particularly in England.* Oxford: Clarendon Press, 1922.

Fiedler, Leslie. Introduction to *Beyond the Looking-Glass: Extraordinary Works of Fairy Tale and Fantasy,* ed. Jonathan Cott. New York: Overlook Press, 1973.

Fisher, Margery. "Signs of the Times," in *Children and Literature: Views and Reviews,* ed. Virginia Haviland. Glenview, Illinois, & Brighton: Scott, Foresman

& Co., 1973: 126-130.

Franz, Marie-Louise, von. *Shadow and Evil in Fairy Tales.* Zurich: Spring Publications, 1974.

Frazer, Sir J.G. *The Golden Bough: A Study in Magic and Religion,* 3rd ed. London: Macmillan, 1915.

Freud, Sigmund. *Totem and Taboo.* Vol. X111 of *The Standard Edition of the Complete Psychological Works of Sigmund Freud.* Ed. James Strachey, Anna Freud, Alix Strachey and Alan Tyson. London and Toronto: Hogarth Press and Institute of Psycho-Analysis 1955 (for 1913-14).

Fromm, Erich. *The Art of Loving,* ed. Ruth Nanda Anshen. New York: Bantam, 1963.

Furness, Hannah. "How dawn of the railway left a lasting impression." *Daily Telegraph,* Jan. 26th 2015.

Gaarden, Bonnie. *The Christian Goddess: Archetype and Theology in the Fantasies of George MacDonald.* Lanham, Maryland: Fairleigh Dickinson University Press, 2011.

Gabelman, Daniel. "'Divine Alchemy': *The Miracles of Our Lord* in its Context." *Rethinking George MacDonald: Contexts and Contemporaries,* ed. Christopher MacLachlan, John Patrick Pazdziora and Ginger Stelle. Glasgow: Scottish Literature International, 2013: 18-35.

----------.*George MacDonald: Divine Carelessness and Fairytale Levity.* Waco, Texas: Baylor University Press, 2013.

Gardner, Martin, ed. *The Annotated Alice: Alice's Adventures in Wonderland and Through the Looking-Glass by Lewis Carroll.* Revised ed. Harmondsworth, Middlesex: Penguin, 1970 (from Clarkson N. Potter, Inc., 1960).

Gaster, Theodore. *Myth, Legend, and Custom in the Old Testament: A comparative study with chapters from Sir James G. Frazer's "Folklore in the Old Testament."* New York: Harper & Row, 1969.

Grant, William, and David Nunn, eds. *The Scottish National Dictionary,* Vols 3, 6. Edinburgh: The Scottish

National Dictionary Association, Ltd., 1952, 1965.

Gray, William. "George MacDonald, Julia Kristeva and the Black Sun," in *Death and Fantasy: Essays on Philip Pullman, C.S. Lewis, George MacDonald and R.L. Stevenson*. Newcastle: Cambridge Scholars Publishing, 2008: [9]-24.

--------------- "George MacDonald's Marvellous Medicine," in *Fantasy, Myth and the Measure of Truth: Tales of Pullman, Lewis, Tolkien, MacDonald and Hoffmann*. Basingstoke, Hampshire, and New York: Palgrave Macmillan, 2010: 25-60.

"Great Exhibition, The." *Wikipedia*. Website.

Green, Melody. "Death and Nonsense in the Poetry of George MacDonald's *At the Back of the North Wind* and Lewis Carroll's *Alice* Books." *North Wind: A Journal of George MacDonald Studies*, 30 (2011): 38-49.

Hardwick, Michael and Mollie. *The Charles Dickens Encyclopedia*. London: Futura Publications Ltd., for Osprey Publishing, Ltd., 1973.

Harvey, Sir Paul, compiler and ed. *The Oxford Companion to English Literature*. 4th ed (revised by Dorothy Eagle). Oxford: Clarendon Press, 1967 (from 1932).

Hayward, Deirdre. "The Mystical Sophia: More on the Great Grandmother in the *Princess* Books." *North Wind: A Journal of George MacDonald Studies* 13 (1994): 29-33.

Hein, Rolland. *The Harmony Within: The Spiritual Vision of George MacDonald*. Grand Rapids, Michigan: Christian University Press (Eerdmans), 1982.

Helson, Ravenna. "The Psychological Origins of Fantasy for Children in Mid-Victorian England." *Children's Literature: The Great Excluded* (later entitled *Children's Literature*), 3 (1974): 66-76.

Holbrook, David. New introduction to *Phantastes*. London, Melbourne and Toronto: Everyman's Library, 1983 edition.

Irwin, W.R. *The Game of the Impossible: A Rhetoric of*

Fantasy. Urbana, Chicago and London: University of Illinois Press, 1976.

Jackson, Rosemary. *Fantasy: The Literature of Subversion.* London and New York: Methuen, 1981.

Johnson, Kirstin Jeffrey. "Curdie's Intertextual Dialogue: Engaging Maurice, Arnold and Isaiah," in *George MacDonald: Literary Heritage and Heirs,* ed. Roderick McGillis. Wayne, Pennsylvania: Zossima Press, 2008: 153-182.

Jung, Carl Gustav. *The Collected Works of C. G. Jung,* trans. R.F.C. Hull. London: Routledge & Kegan Paul, various dates. Ed. Sir Herbert Read, Michael Fordham, Gerhard Adler. Occasional executive Ed. William McGuire.

Vol. 5: *Symbols of Transformation.* 2nd ed.

Vol. 6: *Psychological Types*

Vol. 7. *Two Essays on Analytical Psychology.* 2nd ed.

Vol. 8: *The Structure and Dynamics of the Psyche.* 2nd ed.

Vol. 9 i: *The Archetypes and the Collective Unconscious*

Vol. 9 ii: *Aion: Researches into the Phenomenology of the Self*

Vol. 10: *Civilization in Transition.* 2nd ed.

Vol. 11: *Psychology and Religion: West and East.* 2nnd ed.

Vol. 12: *Psychology and Alchemy.* 2nd ed.

Vol. 13: *Alchemical Studies.* 2nd ed.

Vol. 14: *Mysterium Coniunctionis.* 2nd ed.

Vol. 15: *The Spirit in Man, Art and Literature*

Vol. 18: *The Symbolic Life: Miscellaneous Writings*

Kingsley, Charles. "The Coal in the Fire." *Town Geology,* 1872. *The Literature Network, http://www.online-literature.com/charles-kingsley/town-geology/4*

Knoepflmacher, Ulrich C. *Ventures into Childland: Victorians, Fairy Tales, and Femininity.* Chicago: University of Chicago Press, 1998.

Kreglinger, Gisela H *Storied Revelations: Parables,*

Imagination and George MacDonald's Christian Fiction. Eugene, Oregon: Pickwick Publications, 2013.

Le Guin, Ursula K. *The Language of the Night: Essays on Fantasy and Science Fiction*, ed. Susan Wood. New York: George Putnam's Sons, 1979.

---------------- Preface to *The Princess and the Goblin.* Puffin Classics: Harmondsworth, Middlesex, 2010.

Levine, Amy-Jill, and Marc Zvi Brettler, eds. *The Jewish Annotated New Testament.* New Revised Standard Version Bible Translation. Oxford and New York: Oxford University Press, 2011.

Lewis, C.S. Preface to *George MacDonald: An Anthology.* London: Fount Paperbacks, 1983 (first published by Geoffrey Bles, 1946).

-------------- Introduction to *Phantastes and Lilith.* London: Victor Gollancz, 1962.

Lindblom, J. *Prophecy in Ancient Israel.* Oxford: Basil Blackwell, 1962.

Litten, Jonathan. "*Phantastes:* All Mirrors are Magic Mirrors." *North Wind: A Journal of George MacDonald Studies*, 35 (2016), 104-125.

Lochhead, Marion. *Renaissance of Wonder: The Fantasy Worlds of J.R.R. Tolkien, George MacDonald, E. Nesbit and Others.* San Francisco, Cambridge, London, etc.: Harper & Row, 1977 (first published in the U.K. as *The Renaissance of Wonder in Children's Literature*).

Luthi, Max. *Once Upon a Time: On the Nature of Fairy Tales.* Bloomington and London: Indiana University Press, 1976 (for 1970).

MacDonald, Greville. *George MacDonald and His Wife.* Whitethorn, California: Johannesen, 2005, from 2nd edition of George Allen & Unwin, London 1924.

MacDonald, Ronald. "George MacDonald: A Personal Note," in *View From a Northern Window*, ed. F. Watson. London: Nisbet & Co., 1911: 55-113.

Makman, Lisa Hermine. "Child's Work is Child's Play: The Value of George MacDonald's Diamond," in

Behind the Back of the North Wind: Critical Essays on George MacDonald's Classic Children's Book, ed. John Pennington and Roderick McGillis. Hamden, CT: Winged Lion Press, 2011: 109-127. From *Children's Literature Association Quarterly* 24.3 (1999): 119-129.

Manlove, Colin. Afterword to "On the Nature of Fantasy." *The Aesthetics of Fantasy Literature and Art*, ed. Roger C. Schlobin. Notre Dame and Brighton: University of Notre Dame Press and Harvester Press, 1982: 16-35.

--------------- "A Reading of *At the Back of the North Wind*," in *Behind the Back of the North Wind: Critical Essays on George MacDonald's Classic Children's Book*, ed. John Pennington and Roderick McGillis. Hamden, CT: Winged Lion Press, 2011: 148-174. From *North Wind: A Journal of George MacDonald Studies* 27 (2008): 51-78.

--------------- *Christian Fantasy: From 1200 to the Present*. London and Basingstoke: Macmillan, 1992, and Notre Dame, Indiana: University of Notre Dame Press, 1992.

--------------- *The Impulse of Fantasy Literature*. London & Basingstoke: Macmillan, 1983.

--------------- "MacDonald and Kingsley: A Victorian Contrast," in *The Gold Thread: Essays on George MacDonald*, ed. William Raeper. Edinburgh: Edinburgh University Press, 1990: 140-162.

--------------- "MacDonald's Shorter Fairy Tales: Journeys into the Mind." *SEVEN: An Anglo-American Literary Review* 22 (2005): 11-28.

--------------- *Modern Fantasy: Five Studies*. Cambridge: Cambridge University Press, 1975.

--------------- "*The Princess and the Goblin* and *The Princess and Curdie*." *North Wind: A Journal of George MacDonald Studies* 26 (2007): [1]-36.

Martin, Thomas L. "God and Laughter: Overcoming the Darkness in Modern Fantasy Literature." *North Wind: A Journal of George MacDonald Studies* 34 (2015): 4-12.

McCrie, George. *The Religion of Our Literature: Essays Upon Thomas Carlyle, Robert Browning, Alfred Tennyson, etc.* London: Hodder and Stoughton, 1875.

McGillis, Roderick, and John Pennington, eds. Introduction and "Comparison of Serial Version and First Edition of *At the Back of the North Wind*," in *At the Back of the North Wind*. Several locations: Broadview, 2011: 35-38.

McGillis, Roderick. "Fantasy as Miracle: George MacDonald's *The Miracles of Our Lord*." In *George MacDonald: Literary Heritage and Heirs*, ed. Roderick McGillis. Wayne, Pennsylvania: Zossima Press, 2008: 201-215.

--------------- "The Fantastic Imagination: The Prose Romances of George MacDonald." PhD diss., University of Reading, 1973.

--------------- "George MacDonald's *Princess* Books: High Seriousness." In *Touchstones: Reflections on the Best in Children's Literature*, ed. Perry Nodelman. ChLA Publishers: West Lafayette, Ind., 1985: 146-162.

--------------- Introduction to *The Princess and the Goblin and The Princess and Curdie*. Oxford and New York: World's Classics, Oxford University Press, 1990.

--------------- "Language and Secret Knowledge in *At the Back of the North Wind*." In *For the Childlike: George MacDonald's Fantasies for Children*, ed. Roderick McGillis. Metuchen, N. J., and London: Children's Literature Association and Scarecrow Press, 1992: 145-159.

--------------- "Outworn Liberal Humanism: George MacDonald and 'The Right Relation to the Whole.'" In *Behind the Back of the North Wind: Critical Essays on George MacDonald's Classic Children's Book*, ed. John Pennington and Roderick McGillis. Hamden, CT: Winged Lion Press, 2011. From *North Wind: A Journal of George MacDonald Studies*, 16 (1997): 5-13.

Mendelson, Michael. "The Fairy Tales of George MacDonald and the Evolution of a Genre." In *For the*

Childlike: George MacDonald's Fantasies for Children, ed. Roderick McGillis. Metuchen, N.J., and London: Children's Literature Association and Scarecrow Press, 1992: 31-49.

New Jerusalem Bible, The. London: Darton, Longman & Todd, 1985.

Onions, C.T., ed. *The Oxford Dictionary of English Etymology.* London: Clarendon Press, 1966.

Parsons, Coleman O. "The Progenitors of Black Beauty in Humanitarian Literature." *Notes & Queries* 19 (April 1947): 156-58. In *Behind the Back of the North Wind: Critical Essays on George MacDonald's Classic Children's Book*, ed. John Pennington and Roderick McGillis. Hamden, CT: Winged Lion Press, 2011: 1-5.

Patterson, Nancy-Lou. "Kore Motifs in *The Princess and the Goblin.*" In *For the Childlike: George MacDonald's Fantasies for Children*, ed. Roderick McGillis. Metuchen, N. J., and London: Children's Literature Association and Scarecrow Press, 1992: 169-182.

Pazdziora, John Patrick, and Joshua Richards. "The Dantean Tradition in George MacDonald's *At the Back of the North Wind.*" *SEVEN: An Anglo-American Literary Review* 29 (2012): 63-78.

Pemberton, Marilyn. "The Ultimate Rite of Passage: Death and Beyond in 'The Golden Key' and *At the Back of the North Wind.*" *North Wind: A Journal of George MacDonald Studies*, 27 (2008): 35-50.

Pennington, John. "Alice at the Back of the North Wind, or the Metafictions of Lewis Carroll and George MacDonald." In *Behind the Back of the North Wind: Critical Essays on George MacDonald's Children's Book*, ed. John Pennington and Roderick McGillis. Hamden, CT: Winged Lion Press, 2011: 52-62.

------------ "Muscular Spirituality in George MacDonald's Curdie Books," in *Muscular Christianity: Embodying the Victorian Age*, ed. Donald E. Hall. Cambridge: Cambridge University Press, 2006 (from 1994); 133-149.

Perkins, David, ed. *English Romantic Writers.* New York, Chicago, San Francisco, Atlanta: Harcourt, Brace & World, Inc., 1967.

Persyn, Catherine. "And All About the Courtly Stable / Bright-Harnessed Angels Sit": Eschatological Elements in *At the Back of the North Wind.*" *North Wind: A Journal of George MacDonald Studies,* 20 (2001): 1-29.

------------- "A Person's Name and a Person's Self, or: Just *Who* is North Wind." *North Wind: A Journal of George MacDonald Studies,* 22 (2003): 60-83.

------------- " 'In my end is my beginning': the fin-negans motif in George MacDonald's *At the Back of the North Wind.*" *Mythlore,* 24 (Winter-Spring 2006): 53-69.

Phillips, Michael R. *George MacDonald: Scotland's Beloved Storyteller.* Minneapolis, Minnesota: Bethany House Publishers, 1987.

Philo. *De Fuga et Inventione.* Vol. V of *Philo,* transl. F.H. Colson and G.H. Whitaker. London and Cambridge, Mass: William Heinemann and Harvard University Press, 1958.

Pickering, David, comp. *Dictionary of Superstitions.* London: Cassell, 1995.

Prickett, Stephen. Preface to *At the Back of the North Wind,* ed. Roderick McGillis and John Pennington. Several countries: Broadview Editions, 2011.

------------- *Romanticism and Religion: The Tradition of Coleridge and Wordsworth in the Victorian Church.* Cambridge: Cambridge University Press, 1976.

------------- "The Two Worlds of George MacDonald," *North Wind: A Journal of George MacDonald Studies,* 2 (1983): 14-23.

------------- *Victorian Fantasy.* 2nd ed. Waco, Texas: Baylor University Press, 2005.

Pridmore, John. "George MacDonald and Spiritual Development." *North Wind: A Journal of George MacDonald Studies,* 22 (2003), 1-2. From an essay in the *International Journal of Children's Spirituality*, 7, No. 1 (2002).

Raeper, William. *George MacDonald*. Tring, U.K: Lion, 1987.

------------- "Diamond and Kilmeny: MacDonald, Hogg, and the Scottish Folk Tradition," in *Behind the Back of the North Wind: Critical Essays on George MacDonald's Children's Book*, ed. John Pennington and Roderick McGillis. Hamden, CT: Winged Lion Press, 2011: 41-50. From *For the Childlike: George MacDonald's Fantasies for Children*. Children's Literature Association and Scarecrow Press, Metuchen, N. J., 1992: 133-144.

Rahner, Hugo, S.J. *Greek Myths and Christian Mystery*. London: Burns and Oates, 1957.

Reis, Richard. *George MacDonald*. New York: Twayne Publishers, 1972.

Robb, David. *George MacDonald*. Edinburgh: Scottish Academic Press, 1987; republished as *God's Fiction: Symbolism and Allegory in the Works of George MacDonald*. Eureka, CA: Sunrise Books, 1989. Part of the chapter entitled "Fiction of the Child" has been published in *Behind the Back of the North Wind: Critical Essays on George MacDonald's Classic Children's Book*. Hamden, CT: Winged Lion Press, 2011: 26-32.

Rosenberg, Joel. "The Closing Chapters of 2 Samuel," in "1 and 2 Samuel." *The Literary Guide to the Bible*, ed. Robert Alter and Frank Kermode. London: Collins, 1987: 138-140.

Ross, David, and Gavin D. Smith, compilers. *Scots-English, English-Scots Dictionary*. New Lanark: Geddes & Grosset, 2007.

Roukema, Aren. "The Shadow of Anodos: Alchemical Symbolism in *Phantastes*," *North Wind: A Journal of George MacDonald Studies* 31 (2012): 48-63.

Rowland, Beryl. *Animals with Human Faces: A Guide to Animal Symbolism*. London: George Allen & Unwin, 1974 (for1973).

Ruskin, John. *The Ethics of the Dust.* 1866: CPSIA digital reprint.

Sadler, Glenn E., Ed. *An Expression of Character: The Letters of George MacDonald.* Grand Rapids, Michigan: William B. Eerdmans, 1994.

Schrock, Carl. "From Child to Childlike: The Cycle of Education in Novalis and George MacDonald." *North Wind: A Journal of George MacDonald Studies,* 25 (2006): 58-76.

de Selincourt, Ernest, ed. *The Letters of William and Dorothy Wordsworth: The Early Years, 1787-1805.* 2nd ed; revised by Chester L. Shaver. Oxford: Clarendon Press, 1967.

Sherman, Cordelia. "The Princess and the Wizard: The Fantasy Worlds of Ursula K. Le Guin and George MacDonald." In *For the Childlike: George MacDonald's Fantasies for Children,* ed. Roderick McGillis. Metuchen, N. J., and London: Children's Literature Association and Scarecrow Press, 1992: 195-205.

Shorter, Clement. *The Brontes' Life and Letters.* Website.

Sigman, Joseph. "The Diamond in the Ashes: A Jungian Reading of the 'Princess' Books." In *For the Childlike: George MacDonald's Fantasies for Children,* ed. Roderick McGillis. Metuchen, N.J., and London: ChLA and Scarecrow Press, Inc., 1992: 183-194.

-------------- "Death's Ecstasies: Transformation and Rebirth in George MacDonald's *Phantastes.*" *English Studies in Canada,* 11. 2 (1976): 203-226.

Smith, Lesley (Willis). "Old Wine in New Bottles: Aspects of Prophecy in George MacDonald's *At the Back of the North Wind.*" In *Behind the Back of the North Wind: Critical Essays on George MacDonald's Classic Children's Book,* ed. John Pennington and Roderick McGillis. Hamden, CT: Winged Lion Press, 2011: 33-40. From *For the Childlike: George MacDonald's Fantasies for Children,* ed. Roderick McGillis. Metuchen, NJ, and London: ChLA and Scarecrow Press, 1992: 161-168.

---------------- "MacDonald's Crystal Palace: Diamonds and Rubies, Coal and Salt in *At the Back of the North Wind.*" *North Wind: A Journal of George MacDonald Studies*, 34 (2015): 13-57.

---------------- " 'Born Again': The Metamorphosis of Irene in George MacDonald's *The Princess and the Goblin.*" *Scottish Literary Journal: A Review of Studies in Scottish Language and Literature* 12. 1 (1985): 25-39.

Soto, Fernando. "Cosmos and Diamonds: Naming and Connoting in MacDonald's Work." *North Wind: A Journal of George MacDonald Studies*, 20 (2001): 30-42.

---------------- "Kore Motifs in the Princess Books: Mythic Threads Between Irenes and Eirinys." In *George MacDonald: Literary Heritage and Heirs*, ed. Roderick McGillis. Wayne, Pennsylvania: Zossima Press, 2008: 65-81.

---------------- "The Two-World Consciousness of *North Wind*: Unity and Dichotomy in MacDonald's Fairy Tale." In *Behind the Back of the North Wind: Critical Essays on George MacDonald's Classic Children's Book*, ed. John Pennington and Roderick McGillis. Hamden, CT: Winged Lion Press, 2011: 128-147.

Sutherland, John, ed. Introduction and note on composition of Wilkie Collins's *The Moonstone*. Oxford and New York: Oxford World's Classics, 1999.

Tanner, Tony. "Mountains and Depths—An Approach to Nineteenth-Century Dualism." *Review of English Literature* 3. 4 (Oct. 1962): 51-61.

Tolkien, J.R.R. "On Fairy-Stories," *Tree and Leaf* in *The Tolkien Reader*. New York: Ballantine Books, 1966; originally published by Unwin Books, 1964.

Tomalin, Claire. *Charles Dickens: A Life*. London and elsewhere: Viking, 2011.

Trexler, Robert. "Dombey and Grandson: Parallels Between *At the Back of the North Wind* and *Dombey and Son*." *North Wind: A Journal of George MacDonald Studies*, 29 (2010): 70-76.

Triggs, Kathy. *The Stars and the Stillness: A Portrait* of *George MacDonald*. Cambridge: Lutterworth Press, 1986.

de Vries, Al., compiler. *The Dictionary of Symbols and Imagery*. London and Amsterdam: North-Holland Publishing Company, 1974.

Wansbrough, Henry, Gen. Ed. *The New Jerusalem Bible*. London: Darton, Longman & Todd, and New York: Doubleday & Co., 1985.

Warner, Marina. "Toads, Tongues and Roses." Review. *Times Literary Supplement*, Nov. 16th 2012.

Watkins, Gwen. "A Theologian's Dealings with the Fairies." *North Wind: A Journal of George MacDonald Studies*, 7 (1988): 5-14.

Webb, Jean. "Realism, Fantasy and a Critique of Nineteenth Century Society in George MacDonald's *At the Back of the North Wind.*" In *Behind the Back of the North Wind: Critical Essays on George MacDonald's Classic Children's Book,*" ed. John Pennington and Roderick McGillis. Hamden, CT: Winged Lion Press, 2011: 175-191. From *"A Noble Unrest": Contemporary Essays on the Work of George MacDonald*, ed. Jean Webb. Newcastle: Cambridge Scholars Publishing, 2007: 15-32.

Willard, Nancy. "The Goddess in the Belfry: Grandmothers and Wise Women in George MacDonald's Books for Children." In *For the Childlike: George MacDonald's Fantasies for Children,* ed. Roderick McGillis. Metuchen, NJ, and London: Children's Literature Association and Scarecrow Press, 1992: 67-74.

Willis, Lesley (Smith). See Smith, Lesley.

Wolff, Robert Lee. *The Golden Key: A Study of the Fiction of George MacDonald*. New Haven: Yale University Press, 1961.

Wood, Naomi J. "Suffer the Children: The Problem of the Loving Father in *At the Back of the North Wind.*" In *Behind the Back of the North Wind: Critical Essays on George MacDonald's Classic Children's Book*. Hamden,

C.T. Winged lion Press, 2011 (from *Children's Literature Association Quarterly*): 63-81.

Woodward, Sir Llewellyn. *The Age of Reform, 1815-70*. Vol. 13 of *The Oxford History of England*, ed. Sir George Clark. 2nd. ed. Oxford: Clarendon Press, 1962.

Wordsworth Classics (no Ed.) "Tattercoats," in *English Fairy Tales*. Ware, Herts,1994.

Wright, Marianne, ed. "Appreciations," in *The Gospel in George MacDonald: Selections from his Novels, Fairy Tales, and Spiritual Writings*. New York, England and Australia: Plough Publishing House, 2016, 305-314.

Zipes, Jack. Ed. and introduction to *The Oxford Companion to Fairy Tales*. 2nd ed. Oxford: Oxford University Press, 2015.

------------ "Fairy Tale as Myth / Myth as Fairy Tale," in *Cross-Culturalism in Children's Literature: Selected Papers from the 1987 International Conference of the Children's Literature Association*, 107-110.

INDEX

Page numbers in bold type indicate references deemed to be of particular significance by the author.

Adams, Richard, *Watership Down*, 227n31, 273n21, 316n46

alchemy, esp. 9, 32, 39, 144, critics on alchemy in MacDonald, 230n49, 255-256n33

anima, *definitions*, 151; outside time, 152; 167, 263n6; archetype of the feminine, 288n31; personified unconscious, 290n44; personification of inferior functions which relate man to collective unconscious, 295n29

anointing, 113, 114

Aquinas, St. Thomas (quoted), 12, 43, 153

Arctic, SS, 210, 313n32

Auden, W.H., 221n9, 310n22

Austen, Jane, 37, 108, **199**, 201-202, 307-308n14

baptism, baptismal, 75, 113, 122, 279n28, 280n32, 282n14

beginnings and endings, theories of critics listed, 315-316n46

Bettelheim, Bruno, *The Uses of Enchantment*, 90, 91, 95, 146, 194, 205, 213, 267n28, 268n6, 269n11, 278n21, 301nn18,19, 304n37

Bible, *Authorized Version of King James*, 1611

Amos, crushing of summer house, **39**, **251n14**; summer house, pestilence, sword, **50**; selling the poor for a pair of shoes, **51**; 251n14; the powerful destroyed, 258n1

Colossians, 282n14

Corinthians, 1 Cor. 105, 146; 2 Cor. 62, 254n26

Daniel, resurrection, 10; influence of, 49; North Wind on night of storm resembles Daniel's visitant, **52-53**; understanding, and its importance to MacDonald, **55**; Diamond reading chapter 3, **56**; stars at end of Daniel, 59; Revelation, 60, 260n18; 60; 'for thou art greatly beloved,' **62**; 66; rest and resurrection, 67; 148; psychiatrist, 156; 190, 193; burning fiery furnace, 243n39, 294n23; 259n11; 311n27

Exodus, 19; adornment of high priest's breastplate, 41, **42**; **43**, "I AM," 96

Ezekiel, 10, 39, 40, expulsion of merchant king Tyrus, **41**; king's adornment, **41**; whirlwind out of the north, **49**; merchandise leading to sin, **174**; 192, 193, 215; prophet's heavenly visitant like Daniel's, 258n7; hole in wall, 265n17; 266n25, 280-281n2; mother, also Israel, seen as vine planted in wilderness, **294n21**; 302-303n24; coals of fire from between the cherubim, **304n36**

Galatians, law and pedagogue, **105, 277n11, 106**

Genesis, 281n5

Habbakuk, 65

Hebrews, 133

Hosea, 262n31

Isaiah, importance of in *The Princess and the Goblin*,10, 231n54; 61, 66, 89; primacy of light over darkness, 95, 273n20; 96, 101, 109, 117; fire guarded by seraphim, 119; 122, 136; stone of stumbling, 172; 231n56; thou shalt be brought down . . . to the sides of the pit, 266n25; 277n15; as birds flying, God will defend Jerusalem, 297n36; precious corner stone, 298n4; 303n27

James, First General Epistle, 108; "Mother of Light,"149; Father of lights,233n65

Jeremiah, 26, 39, 43, 49; 50, 258n3; prophecy of death, 60; 62, 65; death prophecy fulfilled without sting, 66-67; 84, 186; drunken sleep, 214

See also Lamentations *below.*

Job, 25, 66; 69, 262n1; 85; riding on wind, brought to death, 69, **262n1**; 146; God brings hidden things to light, 148; where wisdom and understanding to be found, 157; 166, 193, 199; "The Voice of Job," 146, 287n.15

John,

First Epistle: 10, 62; "the Word . . . made flesh," **95**; anointing, 114; God's forgiveness, 118; 130; quoted, 135, 136; we love him because he first loved us, 266n21; 284n26

Gospel: 66; feminine Wisdom of God, 95, 273n21; 96, 97, 103, 113-114, 130, 131; John quoted, 134-135; born, not of will of man, but of God, 136; 145; operations of spirit, 152; spirit of truth, 153;

189, 205, 208, 240n21; 'light of the world,' 241n28; wind blows (spirit breathes) where it chooses, 266n24; special "I AMs," 274n25; doves and Holy Spirit, 115, 280n32; Lazarus's tomb, 282n11; not to be left comfortless, 288n25

See also Revelation *below*.

Judges, 192; Samson's strength, 266n26

Jude, blackness of darkness, 288n25

Lamentations 39, 62, 186

Leviticus 184; sacrificial goat, 303n30

Luke, my master's interests, 25, 243n36; emblems of evangelists, 26-27, 244n41; 38; 63, 261n28; resurrections, 69, 274n27; egg and scorpion, 103, 276n7; doves and Holy Spirit, 115, 280n32; no storehouse or barn, 143, 285n6; 146, 164, 189; resurrection, 157, 290n45; where do we come from, 203, 309n17; Queen's identity revealed at banquet, 214, 240n22; love of neighbour, 177, 300n12; stone for bread, 194, 305n38; 261n28

Mark, emblems of evangelists, 26-27, 244n41; doves and Holy Spirit, 115, 280n32; forsaken, 122, 282n12; love of neighbour, 177, 300n12

Matthew, the light of the world, 22, 241n28; needn't eat for tomorrow, 63, 261n28; those in darkness saw great light, 89, 268n5; 101, 109; doves and Holy Spirit, 115, 280n32; forsaken, 122, 282n12; 146, 163; walking on water, 128, 283n20; no storehouse or barn, 143, 285n6; resurrection, 157, 290n45; love of neighbour, 177, 300n12; cast into outer darkness, 180; 187; stone for bread, 194, 305n38

Micah, 'when I fall, I shall rise again;' 118; Queen's forgiveness, 280n1

Obadiah, 65

Peter, 3, 42, 109, 187; living stone, 30, 246n54

Philippians, 97, 136

Proverbs, the name of the Lord is a strong tower, 118; Wisdom of God female figure, 273n21

Psalms, 11 (Ps 104, 18); 51 (Ps 65); 52 (Ps 72); 81 (Ps 104); 116 (Ps 4); 117 (Ps 112); 133 (Ps 85); 185

(Ps 78)

Revelation, 10, 42, 44; horses, 60, 61; 62, 83, 97, 122, 128, 145; rider of red horse, 169; stone clear as crystal, street pure gold, 172; punitive beasts, 179, 180; cage of unclean and hateful birds, 182; 185; alas for their city, like Babylon, 186-187; 190, 193, 242, 253, 260, 279, 287, 296, 297, 302

Romans, 107, 118; death in baptism leads to resurrection, 282n14

Samuel,1, 1 Sam. 283n21, 2 Sam. 10, 11, 81; 231n56

Carroll, Lewis (Dodgson, C.L.), 1, 32, 103, 114; 146, 286n13; 235n9

Chesterton, G.K., effect on of *The Princess and the Goblin*, 3; 136, 201, 224n15, 226n28, 233n61, 286-287n14; justice and mercy, preferences for, 180, 301n18 (quoted)

childlike, **1**, 22, 36, 93, 126, 145, 193, 203, 206, 213, 219nn3,4

Coleridge, S.T., 291; "Christabel," **115, 116**, 216, 280nn30, 31, 32; "Kubla Khan," 258n4; "The Rime of the Ancient Mariner," 144-145, 216, 312n30

Collins, Wilkie, 18, 192, 237-238n15, 304n35, 313n32

comforting or protective narrator, 4, 98, 101

commerce, negative aspect of, 40-41; connection with violence, 173-174

consciousness and the unconscious, collective; conscious and unconscious need to be integrated in both collective and individual areas, **9**, 17; Raeper's definition of collective unconscious, 230n48

consciousness and the unconscious, personal; see, e.g., 6, **7-8**, 72, 133; disjunction between consciousness and unconscious, 8, 199; primary function of consciousness, **9**; dawning consciousness, 10, 199; instinctive forces of unconscious to be dominated by consciousness, 28; contact with unconscious, 43; total self into consciousness, **44**, 147; ruled by unconscious, 45, 46; psychiatrist, 55; king's relationship with unconscious, 112, 177, 178-179, 181; God and unconscious, 141; possession by unconscious without divine enlightenment,

147-148; total personality, conscious and unconscious, 151; inspiration of Spirit for growing into consciousness, 153; unconscious ultimate source of consciousness, 155; psychic danger of remaining superficial, 165; possibilities of Curdie's unconscious, 167; once made conscious, unconscious contents can't revert to former state, 168; darker side of unconscious becomes source of strength, 170; confrontation with the unconscious, 177; forcing awareness of unconscious, 179-180; destructive drive in unconscious, 181; MacDonald reaching parts of unconscious not reached by other authors, 200

Cope, Gilbert, *Symbolism in the Bible and the Church.*, 43n25, 44, 239, 243, 266, 293, 295, **301n16**, 302n21

Dante, Alighieri, 246-247n57, 253n23, 260n17

darkness, as symbol of death, 92, 97; of unconscious, 92, 270n14, 116, 158; nigredo state, **150, 288nn25, 26**; mystery, 152; darkness of soul, 183

darkness and light, see, e.g., 7, 9, **12**, 89, 95, 117, **118**; Messianic task, 122-123; fear of dark, light shining in darkness, 130; John quoted, 135; hidden things of darkness brought to light, 146; Daniel quoted, **148**; **162**; God's invitation, **217**; references to darkness and light in other works, **233-234, n.65**; Matthew, **268n5**

Darwin, Charles, 300n10

death, e.g. alchemical Great Work to be completed by second death, 55 (Catherine Persyn on, 259n 10); second death, 97, critics on, 263n3, goblin queen and second death, 128-129; symbolic deaths, 89; spiritual death, 92

demons, symbolise psychological and spiritual death, 97; dead jealous of living, **98**; distorted view, 149-150, 186; representing negative qualities of unconscious, 165; king's warning from unconscious, 178; sirens, 296n34, 309n16

Dickens, Charles, 17, 40, 192; dawning consciousness, 199; 231, 234n6, 236, 249; *Dombey and Son*, **252**; Nanny's debt to Little Dorrit, 256n34, 304n35, 313n32

Earth Mother (or Great Mother), variations of same

archetype, 74; old princess as, **149**; occasionally related to moon, 150; connected with instinctual level of unconscious and with source of consciousness, **151**; offence against the Great Mother, **167**; bees and Great Mother archetype, 243n38; widely varying types of mother-goddess, see critics on, 265n15; animals belong to Great Mother, **267n28**

Elementargeister, or Kobolds; German influence, 270n13

fairy tale, note of consolatory hope in, 3; express unconscious processes and connect conscious and unconscious, **7**; MacDonald concerned with miracle rather than magic in, **12**; symbolism can reduce fearfulness, 36; Tolkien's theory, **69, 90-91**; rejection of children, Bettelheim, 90; suitable medium for religious truth, 90-91; 'typical' fairy tale, 94; serious fantasy, 101-102; flexibility, 106; taboo, 107; sacrosanctity of promise, 108; traditional question, 129; Bettelheim quotes Carroll's test question, 146; fairy tale tradition, 187; myth and fairy tale timeless, 191; Bettelheim's distinction between myth and fairy tale, 194; compatible with religious faith and observance, 220n8; W.H. Auden on *At the Back of the North Wind* as part fairy tale, 221n9; critics on MacDonald's fairy tales, 223-224n14; G.K. Chesterton on MacDonald's tales of real life as allegories of fairy tales, 233n61; good or evil? 269n11; physical malformation standing for evil, 278n21; optimism in fairy tales, pessimism in myths (Bettelheim), 304n37; Zipes on fairy tales becoming myths, 304-305n37

father, God "the father *I* of this my *I*," 9; Father of Lights, 12-13, 233n65, 287n19; framework of fatherhood in *PC*, 142; father-attributes, 164, 292n17; "home to the house of our Father," 208

Fisher, Margery, 213

forgiveness, Nanny teaches Diamond, **47**; Irene's faith confirmed by Queen's forgiveness, **118**; repentance and forgiveness, 144-145; instinctual forces know nothing of forgiveness, 167; importance of experiencing, 206; Queen's capacity for, 280n1

Franz, Marie-Louise von, 167

Frazer, Sir J. G., *The Golden Bough*, properties of witches, 81-82

Freud, Sigmund, *Totem and Taboo*, children's perceptions of name, 22, 276n8; relation of living to dead, **97-98**; prohibition and desire, **106**, shifting prohibition, 108; fear of demons, 165

Fromm, Erich, *The Art of Loving*, 284n24

Gaarden, Bonnie, 188, 214, 264n14, 269n10, 272n17

Good Words for the Young, 5, 141, 219n3, 245n51, 247n59, 254n27, 278n23, 279n26

grandmother, see Great Mother, Mother Goddess and mother archetype under *mother*, below; Queen Irene, 94; position of honour, 175

Great Exhibition, The, of 1851, 17-18, 235-237nn8, 9, 11

hawthorn tree, shadow of old princess, **165**; possible crucifixion, 168; shadow birds tried to encircle old princess's shadow, 169; complemented by dogs and butchers, 174; negative superstitions associated with hawthorn, 293n19

Herbert, George, 303n28

hero myth, "note of consolatory hope" muted in, 3; connecting conscious and unconscious, 7; night sea journey in, **43, 160**; place of perspective, **51-52**; strong element of, in the three fantasies, 102; *Princess and Curdie* more like than fairy tale, 146; myth and fairy tale timeless, 191; no resolution, **194**; dark end of spectrum of myth, 212; ending nearly always tragic, **213**; mythic fairy tale, see critics, 223-224n14; hero often has androgynous dimension, 273n21; critics on Yggdrasil as source of tree-magic in George MacDonald, 293n20; Rahner on spirit of Homeric myth, 296n34; Bettelheim and Zipes on fairy tale and myth, 304-305n37

high priest's breastplate, Diamond's name in, 19; 25, 41; meaning of, **42**; judgement, 43

horse, Curdie's inner, 162-163

Hughes, Arthur, illustrator, portrays MacDonald as Irene's father, 4; Old Sal, 44; rock as skull, 122; family connection, 224n19; makes Horse Diamond black, 242n32

imagination, see MacDonald, *A*

The Downstretched Hand: Individual Development in

Dish of Orts
individuation process, e.g. 1; connection between conscious and unconscious, 7; means to final end of oneness with God, 8; consciousness of own shadow forwards individuation process, 151, 288n32; journey to full individuation in eternity, 195

isolation, Diamond's growing, in family, 29; threat of isolation rather than individuation for Curdie, **168**; independence can end in isolation, 212; Jung (quoted), individuation must lead to collective relationships, not isolation, 230n48; Jung (quoted), contrast between isolation and individuation, 296n35; unconscious makes no distinction between good and evil, 186, 303n25

Jung, Carl.
  Aion: Researches into the Phenomenology of the Self, magic exercises compulsion, 12, 233n62; threesome as defective quaternity, 24, 29, 242-243n33; complement of quaternity, 31; ego must be anchored in consciousness, 82; 227n36; myths and fairy tales further connection between conscious and unconscious, 7, 227n36; danger of being dominated by instincts, 27, 245n47; St. Thomas Aquinas (quoted), 253n21; anima and animus, 263n6; left corresponds to feminine, 264n10; Christ represents divine totality, 273n19; Lina as psychopomp, 166, 295n29; king symbol of self, 177, 300n13; 186, 303n25

  Alchemical Studies, 239n19; mountain and tree symbols of personality and self, 293nn18,19; relation of birds to tree, 295 n31

  The Archetypes and the Collective Unconscious, instinctive forces of unconscious brought into unity within mandala, 28, 245n46; relationship with stars symbolises eternity, 32, 246n57, 59, soul comes from stars and returns there, 71, 264n9; rebirth, 75, 265n16; women can represent aspects of mother archetype, 93, 270n16; Earth Mother always chthonic, 149; occasionally related to moon, 150; mother presides over place of transformation and rebirth and over underworld, 151, 288n33; anima timeless when appears clearly, 152, 288n34; anima varied, 152; negative side of mother archetype, 167, 295-296n32; isolation contrasted with individuation, 168, 296n35; symbolism of falling into water, 176, 300n11; Wise Old Man archetype, 178, 300-301n14; sacrificial fire, 190, 303n30; unconscious phenomena manifest themselves in behaviour, 199; becoming whole, 200; anima psychological expression of totality of self, 234n1

Civilization in Transition, civilization depends on individuals who integrate unconscious contents, 171; individuation central problem of modern psychology, 229n40, 307n8

Mysterium Coniunctionis, dog representing threat, 23, 241n29; moon associated with unconscious, 23, 242n30; no coniunctio where both elements male, 28, 245n45; qualities of bitterness and wisdom in salt, 43, 46, 253n22; salt pervades everything, 44; salt representing feminine principle of Eros, bringing everything into relationship, 44; darkness of the unconscious, 92, 270n14; green attributed to Holy Spirit as creative principle, 149; Lina connected with both moon and sun, 165-166, 294nn24, 25, 26; psychological difference between masculine and feminine, 298n5; union of opposites symbolising wholeness, 189, 303n29

Psychology and Alchemy, connection between psychology of unconscious and alchemical symbolism, 9, 230n50; diamond is *lapis*, ultimate symbol of completeness, 17, 234n3; soul rules mind and mind rules body, 19, 239n18; moon and unconscious, 23, 242n30; fiery agony of furnace, 25, 243n39; "chymical wedding," 28, 245n48; mandala most complete union of opposites possible, 30; spirit separated from body and then put back, 31; *lapis aethereus*, 31; *lapis invisibilitatis*, 32,

200, 289n40; Diamond Body, 32; *prima materia*, 39, 251n12; dark world of unconscious, 92, 270n14; mandala symbolism, 125; alchemy undercurrent to Christianity, 144; nigredo state, 150; self or total personality, 151; watery abyss region of danger, 176, 300n11; disintegration of personality into separate functions of consciousness, 177; rubedo follows from albedo when fire hottest, 190, 303n31; magical travelling companion, 294n23

Psychology and Religion, West and East, St. Thomas Aquinas on Holy Spirit, 12; Trinity most distinctive and fundamental Christian doctrine, 12; snake associated with venom and transformation, 181, 302n21; stable in which the Lord is born, 21, 240n23; fourth added to Trinity results in totality, 24, 30, 242-243n33; 'inferior' personality compounded of 'disobedience,' 24; Christ as archetype, 95, 273n19; shadow and individuation process, 151, 288n32; self is psychic totality, 289n40; transformation or initiation associated with hairless head, 299n6; consciousness to be built up in child, 306n2

Psychological Types, anima contains qualities lacked by conscious attitude, 151

The Spirit in Man, Art and Literature, archetype of Wise Old Man can also be negative, 178, 300-301n14

The Structure and Dynamics of the Psyche, ancestor worship protection against malice of dead, 274n28

The Symbolic Life: Miscellaneous Writings, anima personification of inferior functions relating man to collective unconscious, 295n29; city symbolises totality of man, 171, 298n1

Symbols of Transformation integrating conscious and unconscious in individuation process, 8, 229n40; totality of man's being reaches through animal and human to divine, 19, 239n18; night sea journey, **43**, 253-254n24; negative associations of three-legged horse, 61, 260n22; soul comes from the stars, 71; animals can be symbols of unconscious and belong to Great Mother, 82, 267n28; danger of negative attitude to unconscious, 92, 270n15, and see 147, 287n18 and 179, 301n15; parallel to dying and rising being lost and found, 101; sexual symbolism can signify something else, 110, 278n18; fight against grip of unconscious calls forth creative powers, 111; negative mother imago can turn into lamia, 115, 280n30; unconscious symbolised by mother but infinitely greater, 151, 288n30; horse signifies man's energy, 162; hero and horse symbolise man and animal instinct, 163 and see 239n21; father-attributes may fall to son, 164, 292n17; tree shadow of old princess, 165, 293-294n20; offence against Great Mother, 167; birds images of evil spirits, 167, 296n34; if had lost fight, hero could have been killed and possessed by demon, 168; 'strange' probably expresses peculiar emphasis or numinosity, 169, 297n37; forest and tabooed tree, 169, 297n39; tabooed and beneficent trees in forest, 170, 297n40; anthropoid psyche, 170, 297n41; city mother archetype, 171, 298n2; in sleep underwent process like dreams auguring death, 183, 302n23; individuation process central problem of modern psychology, 200, 307n8; Spirit and wind, 240n21

Two Essays on Analytical Psychology, Jung defines individuation process, 200, 306-307n8

Jungian criticism, 228-229n37

Kingsley, Charles, 220-221n8, 238n16, 250-251n9; Wise Woman in Victorian fantasy, 74, 264n14; endings, 216, 316n46

Koh-i-Noor Diamond, the, 17, 18, 24, 32, 238n15

lamp, see moon below

lapis, 17, 44, **aethereus**, 31, 32; **invisibilitatis**, 23, 200, 289n40; Lapis-Christ parallel, 243n39

law (Galatians), 106, 107, 277n11; king's law, 112; tries to keep Irene in realm of consciousness, 112

Le Guin, Ursula K., 7, 8, 152, 227n34; animal instincts

eventually to be sacrificed so true self may be reborn, 245n47; old Sal's kindred, *The Tombs of Atuan*, 255-256n33; tower place of perspective in *A Wizard of Earthsea*, 275

Lewis, C.S., effect on, of reading *Phantastes*, 200-201; 238-239n17; time experience, 254n26,

light, all light comes from Father of Lights, 12-13; Mother of Light, 149, 164, 292n17; God's invitation to come into the light of home, 217n47; "God alone is the light, and our light is the shining of his will in our lives," 241n28; see also **darkness and light**, above, and **moon**, below

Lina, given to Curdie as helper, 160; seeming to come from sun, 165; name and nature; psychopomp; connected with moon, sun and shadow of sun (consciousness), 166; defends Curdie from birds, 167; fights Uglies for him, 170; helps Curdie integrate feminine aspects of psyche, 173; fights butchers' dogs with Curdie, 174; consumed by Queen's fire in redemptive process, 186; a shapeless terror through a guilty mind, 190

Luthi, Max, 12

MacDonald, George. Works other than the major children's fantasies:

Adela Cathcart, 201; 220-221n8; suicide, 222n13; 256n34; dreams and personal unconscious, 259n15; gnomes of terror in unconscious, 278n19; common and commonplace, 287n17; 310n21

Alec Forbes of Howglen, 210; suicide, 222-223n13; 270n15; 283-284n22; 285, 294n27, 310n25

Annals of a Quiet Neighbourhood, 232n59; Father of lights, 287n19

"Butcher's Bills, The," see *Stephen Archer and Other Tales*, below

Castle Warlock, 202, 237n13, 291n8

David Elginbrod, 5, 32, 102, 144, 156, 199, 210, 211, 244n43, **245n50**, 246n56, 251n11, 252n17, 258n6; "Rime of the Ancient Mariner," **286n8**; 312-313n30

Diary of an Old Soul, A Year's, in *Rampolli*; plea not to be left unindividuated, 8, 229n45; God "the father *I* of this my *I*," 9; beast till love as God loves, 82, 267n29; shadow and shining, 159; need to struggle against negative impulses of unconscious, 182-183; 262n30; 278n24

Dish of Orts, A, "The Fantastic Imagination," 12, 286n10; writing for the childlike, 241n26; "The Imagination: Its Functions and Its Culture," 5, 225n23; 72; main function of imagination, 264n13; work of art has larger origin than man who produced it, 278n22; re-echoing of truths, **311-312n28**; "A Sermon," loving and thinking, 224n17; 8, 229n44; "A Sketch of Individual Development," relationship between self and God, 2; second, third and possibly fourth birth, 275n1; "True Christian Ministering," obedience, 282n10; "Wordsworth's Poetry," 72-73; 264nn11, 12; 291n5

Donal Grant, 96, 159, 208

England's Antiphon, George Herbert, 303n28

Flight of the Shadow, The, 79, 215; Belorba Day, 241n28; horse called Thanatos, 260n19; thin horse looks like Old Diamond, 261n25; ending, 315n45

"Golden Key, The," see *The Light Princess and Other Tales* below

Guild Court, 36, 45, 210, 211; mention of suicide, 222n13; Poppie resembles Nanny, 225n24; underground railway, 240n24; Lucy's ring, 252n17; Poppie forerunner of Nanny, 256n34; Poppie fights boys with broom, 257n37; nine magical number, 282n13; seven mystical number, 304n33

Hope of the Gospel, The, becoming, 1, 17; growth in understanding, 7, 55, 227n32; universe home of true children, 215; not conscious of full self, 229n39, 234n2; see 241n28 and "The Salt and the Light of the World," HG 162-175; danger of recidivism, 275n5; out of harmony with nature because not complete, 285n6; 157-158, 290n46; constant strife with nature till we're true children, 291n9

Light Princess and Other Fairy Tales, The, "The Carasoyn," talking through hole in head of bed, 265n17; losing and finding, 275n2; "The Golden Key," 69, 75, 196; key central symbol, 219n1; animals talking, 243-244n40; 265n15, 272n17; baptismal experience, 279n28; attacked by tree, rescued by air-fish, 296n32; "The Light Princess," equates death with love, 79, 266n23

Lilith, 5, 6; development of complex self, 8; 32, 84; Novalis quoted, 117; relative value of dreams, 127; "Revelation of St. George," 145; 163; Gwyntystorm foreshadows Bulika, 194; original Lilith ends with hoping and waiting,195, 305n39; from dark self to light, 199; just beginning to become an individual, 200; ending, 216; 219n4, 225n24, 226-227n30, 230n49; Vane came to know he was himself, *Lilith A*, 231n53; 252-253n19; resurrection morning, 262n2; masculine horse out of feminine moon, 294n22; 295n28; in *Lilith A*, Raven's wife shoots through dark like shining white pigeon, 297n37; 300n10, 305n39, 310n20,

313n30

Malcolm, 203, 233-234n65, 287n19, 302n22

Marquis of Lossie, The, 89, 101, 224n20; second birth, 89, 267n3

Mary Marston, 18, 291n6

Miracles of Our Lord, The, 9; infinite hope in darkness of future, 12, 233nn 64,65; individual and nation, 159; nation only changes through individuals, 171, 213, 315n41; 213, 226n26, 227n32, 229n47; divine alchemy, quoted, 230n49; 233nn64, 65; 247n59, 250n9

Paul Faber, Surgeon, suicide, 223n13; red and black horses, 242n32

Phantastes, 5, 6, 12, 84; C.S. Lewis's conversion of spirit, **200-201**; waiting, 217; fairy tale for adults, 219n4; attempted suicide, 223n13; library experience, quoted, 227n30; 228n37, 229n37, 230n49, 239n18, 255n30, *PG* goblins toned-down version of *Phantastes* goblins, 269-270n13; forest contains tabooed Ash more than balanced by beech, 297n40; shapes hard to see in wood, 298n43 (cf. 170); 313n30

George MacDonald's Major Fantasies for Children

Portent and Other Stories, The, "The Portent," 221n8; three kinds of resurrection, 267-268n4; 312n30

Ranald Bannerman's Boyhood, 5, 7, 229n38; dawning consciousness, 10, 306n2; 209, 226n26, heavenly ceiling, 277n12; Mr. Sun, 295n28

Robert Falconer, developing faith, 9-10; 36; strong son seeks weak father, 142; home to our Father's house, 208; ship sinking, 210; value of peace, 211; Mary St. John prelude to Queen Irene, 211-212; redemption of sinners in hell, 214; suicide, 223n13; belief *in*, not *about* Jesus, 224n17; 225; holy will of Father of Lights, 233n65; black and red horses, 242n32; 244n43; Nanny's debt to Nancy Kennedy, 256n34; 273n22; means of bringing highest nature to birth, 275n1; spider's thread potential guide to mission, 290n43

Rough Shaking, A, 192; boyhood seen from adult perspective, 310n26

Salted With Fire, attempted suicide, 223n13; spiritual resurrection of James Blatherwick, 262n2; improbable resurrection of Isy, 312n30

Seaboard Parish, The, 232n59; "God's baby," 245n49; novel aglow with theme of resurrection, 262n2

Sir Gibbie, 46; common good uncommonly developed, 207; house built on a rock, 284n22; 295n28; beast-boy, 312n28; flood, 313n33

Stephen Archer and Other Tales, "The Butcher's Bills," lack of awareness of unconscious, 8, 229n43; 199, 235n6; Dempster's life not yet reduced to ashes, 252n18; "If I Had a Father," 255n31

There and Back, extending consciousness, 200, 306n6; another Barbara, 213, 314n38; 216; father of lights, 233n65; dying pigeon, 286n8; 315n44

Thomas Wingfold, Curate, 315n42

Unspoken Sermons, Series I, God utters himself in nature, 35; new name, 247n58; 274n24; Series 2, individuation means to oneness with God, **8, 229n41, 200, 307n10**; quaternity represents wholeness of self, 24, 227n33; passage from

Job underlies *ABNW*, **69**, 262n1; God works behind our consciousness, **141**; MacDonald on Job, 287n15; Series 3, great diamond, 17, 234n4; 20, 35; justice, judgement and love, 145, 286n11; 311n28; invitation to come home, 217, 316n47

Vicar's Daughter, The, trilogy, 232n59; Marion Clare, 273-274n22

MacDonald, Greville, 2,4,5,6,49,79,145,202, 220, 248

MacDonald, Ronald, 37,133

magic, see esp. magic v. miracle, **12**; understanding of animals' speech, 69, 243n40; Magical (face) towards Nature, 90; trickery of magic, 116; magical objects that turn out to be mandalas, 91; magical object, **150, 205**; nature of magic (critics quoted), **268n7**; 282n13; magical travelling companion, 294n23

mandala, esp. definition of, and Diamond's role as central mandala, 30, 234n1; moon as mandala, 242n31; 247n58

Manlove, Colin, 84, 208, 220n8, 230n49, 248,n3, 264n13, 268n7, 271n17, 272-273n18, 292n14

McGillis, Roderick, 35, 112, 209, 216, 222n13, 248n3, 278nn20,21, 298n5, 315n46

Mesmer, Franz, 312n30

Milton, *Paradise Lost*, 110, 132

miracle, contrast with magic, **12**; Sir Gibbie's miracle, 207-208

mission, see esp. Irene's mission, 121; Curdie's fitness for mission, 160, 206; obstacles to Curdie's, 167, 170; fundamental purpose of mission, **171**; 179; nature of mission, 213; obedience without information, 282n10

moon, esp. Nanny and moon, 23; moon lady's bees, 25; 28, 46; Nanny's rejection of her dream, 57; Diamond takes over Nanny's interest in, **58**; presides over desolation, but less important than sky, 59; in context of death imagery, 80; moon lamp seldom seen, 97; moon lamp sharpens sight, 114; faith needed to see moon lamp, 119; large globe of silvery light, 130; Mistress of Silver Moon, 150; Lady of Silver Moon, 154; moon lamp, 154; moon inside or outside, 155; moonlight vanishes, 157; moon represents unconscious,

165; 166; moon condition raised to sun condition, 190; 259n15; 260n16

mother, e.g., mother-image of cave and cradle, 21; Curdie's mother 'just like my own grandmother,' 133; Great or Earth Mother, 149; Earth Mother sometimes related to moon, 150; symbol of unconscious and source of consciousness, **151, 288n30, 155**; slaying of wild animal offence against Great Mother, 167; city mother archetype in communal aspect, 171; association of bees with Great Mother archetype, 243n38; Great Mother (quoted), 265n15; Mother Goddess often associated with tree (critics quoted), 293-294n20; negative side of mother archetype, 295n32

name, e.g., significance of Diamond's, **17-19**; Queen and Princess Irene, **96**; Prince of Peace, 109; doesn't matter how many names if person is one, 153; great difference between *Princess* books shown by treatment of Queen's name, 154; Queen resumes right name, 154

nameless, e.g. nameless brother, **29**; nameless horse, 60; North Wind refuses to tell Diamond most dreadful name, 60; Wise Old Man archetype not given name, 178; loss of name indicates loss of identity, 194, 196

nature, e.g. God utters himself in nature, 35; in *The Princess and the Goblin* it straddles Primary and Secondary worlds, 103; Curdie separated from nature by shooting pigeon, **143-144**; dark side of nature, 165, 167

Novalis, 117, 223n14, 287n16

obedience, 77; "love and faith and obedience … sides of the same prism," **96**; unqualified obedience, 121; from obedience to initiative, 141; trust and obedience, 158

Pennington, John, 141, 262n33

Philo, *De Fuga et Inventione*, feminine Wisdom and masculine Word of God, 273n21

Poe, Edgar Allan, 312-313n30

postage, cheap, 37

Prickett, Stephen, 142, 159, 222n3, 248n3, 250n9, 271n17

Primary and Secondary Worlds, see Tolkien, J.R.R.

protective narrator, 4, **98, 101**; father seeks son, 162

psychopomp, definition, and

Lina as, **166**

Queen Irene, nature of, 12, 75, 91, **94-95**; association with Jesus, **96**; resurrection, **97**; 104-105, 108-109, 113, 114; forgiveness, 118; **130**; 133-134; theories of several critics listed, 271-272n17; as old princess, 149; association with Holy Spirit, **152**; 153-154, 189, 194; silence about goblins, 202

Raeper, William, esp. 49, 117, 144, 192, 209, 212, 228n37, 230n48, 281n7, **305n1**, 312n30

railways, 2, 36-37; underground railway, 1863, 240n24; railway development, 1850s and 60s, 249n6; Diamond's first fare to King's Cross station, 37, 250n8

rebirth, by being pulled through hole at head of bed or by baptismal bath, **75, 265n16**; second birth, 89; Queen essential to Irene's rebirth, 94; challenge of death and rebirth, 98; second birth of sonship and liberty, epigraph, 101; second, third and fourth birth, 101, **275n1**; Irene's symbolic death and rebirth through rescuing Curdie, 122; bath with baptismal overtones of death and rebirth, 122, 282n14, 113, 279n28; spiritual rebirth, **127**; 133, **134**; place of rebirth presided over by the mother, 151; Jung connects Spirit and wind in rebirth, 240n21

resurrection, Daniel, 10; *PG* deals with, 11; Diamond and, **32**; Diamond's whole life tends towards, **37**; Diamond's resurrection, **67**; whole book tends towards, 69; North Wind threshold to eternity, **70**; faith that death followed by resurrection, 89; resurrection theme of *PG*, 89; Queen living resurrection, **97**; symbolic resurrection, **113**; Irene made over again, **122**; Queen exists in eternity, **127-128**; spiritual rebirth eventually moves into eternity, **134**; Irene continually reborn, **136**; continuous resurrection, 159; immanence of resurrection in *ABNW*, 209; 247n59, 259n13; resurrection perennial theme for MacDonald, **262n2**; three kinds of resurrection in "The Portent," 267-268n4; series of rebirths merge with concept of resurrection, **275n1**; 279n28; 283n20; old princess's song of resurrection, **156-**

157, 290n45; *Wilfrid Cumbermede*, 309n18; improbable resurrection, 313n30

Ruskin, John, 236n11, 249n6, 250n9, 255n30

Scott, Sir Walter, Cuddie Headrigg, 163; 292n11

self, mystery to be explored, 1-2; much of self is unconscious, 7-**8**; individuality develops in context of collective, **9**; relationship between God and self, 10; wholeness of self, 12; moon as symbol of aspect of self, 23; trinity and quaternity as symbols of self, 24; fourth element of psyche source of energy, 25; 28; total self into consciousness, 44; symbol of self and non-self, 147; total personality, conscious and unconscious, never completely knowable by conscious self, 151, 288n28; king symbolic head of self, 177; the crust of self, 182; inferior functions of personality brought into harmony with total self, 182; *lapis invisibilitatis*, 289n40

shadow, Lootie's inner shadows, 124; shadow of death, 89, 129, 136; Curdie becoming conscious of own shadow, **151, 288n32**; Chapter 9, "The Shadow," 159-170; hawthorn tree shadow of old princess, **165**; shadow thrown off by consciousness, 166; strange birds shadows of pigeons,167; 169; shadow projections, 174; shadow forms in Gwyntystorm, 175; shadows of shadows, 186; Gibbie, 207; 208, 311n27; Uglies part of shadow of collective unconscious, 298n42

sun, 295n28

suicide, possibility of suicide discussed, 3, **222-223n13**; discussion of, and actual, 144

taboo, Koh-i-Noor, 18; 24, 27, 28, taboo against Irene's going out after dark, 90, 92; evil and death linked, 97; taboo violated, **105, 106, 107**; heath taboo, 164-165; **169**; falling into water taboo, 176, 192; law only of use while taboo in force, 105, 277n11; 282n9. Taboo in *Phantastes*, 297n40. *See also* Freud, *above*.

Thackeray, William Makepeace, 202, 221n8

thread, 120-121; critics on significance of, 281-282n7

threat, element of, in fairy tale, **91**, 92; Irene unaware of threat, 131; 167, 170, 194

The Downstretched Hand: Individual Development in

time, relationship of anima to, 152

Tolkien, J.R.R. "On Fairy-Stories," Primary World and Secondary Worlds, 2-3, 221n9, 10; 35, **36**; wish fulfilment in fairy tales, **69, 243n40; 70**; 'God is Lord . . . of elves,' **90**; supports taboos, 107, 235n7; 263n4; *The Hobbit*, 107

tower, importance of towers to MacDonald, 4; biblical treatment of tower as refuge, 10, 11; point of vantage from which perspective may be gained, 30, 31, 58, 64-65; tree struck, 66; North Wind visits through windows of tower room, 84; Queen seldom leaves tower, 94; 95; place of perspective which must be climbed by hero in hero myth, 102, 275n3; perspective on world of nature, 103; 104, 110; king climbs tower, 112, 126; workroom represents everyday reality, 113; washing, bathing and anointing in bedroom, 113-114; sleeping in grandmother's bed, 115; grandmother at home in tower, 115; unconscious shows Irene her way up tower, 117; 'the name of the LORD is a strong tower,' 118; 124, 131; servants didn't search tower, 143; old princess associated with nature in tower, 149; old princess doesn't stay in tower, 152-153; tower rooms different in *The Princess and Curdie*, 154-155; tower haven, 157; old princess wants Curdie to come alone, 164, 292-293n17; neglected tower defenceless, 173; 175, 176

trinity, Holy Trinity, 11-12; symbolic trinity of diamonds, 19; trinity incomplete symbol of self, 24; trinity turned into quaternity, 28; intersecting trinities, 30; trinity of rooms at top of tower, 102; third person of Trinity, 153; MacDonald's Trinitarian faith, 232n60; 240n23; if Trinity understood as process, addition of fourth would bring absolute totality (Jung, quoted), 242-243n33

unconscious, dangerous possibilities of instinctual level of, 107; Lootie's unconscious, 124; Curdie doesn't realise how much darkness still within him, 157-158; 206. *See also* 'consciousness and the unconscious,' above.

understanding, our whole life must be growth

in, 7; Daniel a man of understanding, 55; Gabriel tells Daniel to understand the vision, 62; Irene realises importance of understanding others, 123; Job on where wisdom and understanding to be found, 157; full understanding in visionary future, 217

unknown, the, beyond this world, 84; our unknown being, 141; an unknown but trusted future, 208; unknown territory in Diamond's dream, 215-216

universal context, individuation only possible within context of universal meaning which leads to transcendence, 1; individual must be rooted in universal context, 7; Diamond's psyche now centred in universal context, 22-23; human life in context of universal nature, 147, 149; old princess's song situates world in context of universe, 157; individual develops in universal context, including events, 210

washing, symbolic significance of, 113; baptismal bath, 113; reminder of washing of disciples' feet at Last Supper, 189

wheel, Queen Irene's spinning wheel, 117; like Aeolian harp blown on by wind, 152; spinning wheel hypnotic, 154; mother's wheel compared with old princess's wheel, 155; wheel of fire, 155, 289n42; and unconscious, **156**

Wise Old Man archetype not given name, 178, 300-301n14; can have negative components, 181; colonel of the guard, 184

Wise Woman, North Wind in tradition of, 74; has something in common with Great Mother, 74, **264-n14, 265n15**; Queen distinct from other manifestations of Wise Woman, 94

witches, characteristic attributes of, **81-82**

Wolff, Robert Lee, 69, 248n3, 265n15, 271n17

Woodward, Sir Llewellyn, 36, 249n6; 37

worlds, two, 35, theories of critics, 248n3

Wordsworth, William, "Ode: Intimations of Immortality," 22, 241n27; 72-73, 264n11,12; 160, 291n5; MacDonald made line "The Child is Father of the Man" the motto of Good Words for the Young, 241n27; "Michael," **160-162**

OTHER BOOKS OF INTEREST

Phantastes by George MacDonald: Annotated Edition
John Pennington and Roderick McGillis, Editors

Phantastes was a groundbreaking book in 1858 and continues to be a seminal example of great fantasy literature. Its elusive meaning is both alluring and perplexing, inviting readers to experience a range of deep feelings and a sense of profound truth. This annotated edition, by two renowned MacDonald scholars, provides a wealth of information to better understand and enjoy this masterpiece. In addition to the text, there are 184 pages containing an authoritative introduction, life chronology, textual notes, book reviews, and comparative source materials. With 354 footnotes to explain obscure words and literary references, this enhanced edition will benefit any reader and provide a solid foundation for future scholarship.

> A good critical edition of George MacDonald's *Phantastes* has long been needed, and now we have it. This fine, comprehensive edition provides an accessible and illuminating introduction to this profound work.
>
> —Colin Manlove, author of *Scotland's Forgotten Treasure: The Visionary Novels of George MacDonald*

C. S. LEWIS

C. S. Lewis: Views From Wake Forest - Essays on C. S. Lewis
Michael Travers, editor

Contains sixteen scholarly presentations from the international C. S. Lewis convention in Wake Forest, NC. Walter Hooper shares his important essay "Editing C. S. Lewis," a chronicle of publishing decisions after Lewis' death in 1963.

"*Scholars from a variety of disciplines address a wide range of issues. The happy result is a fresh and expansive view of an author who well deserves this kind of thoughtful attention.*"
  Diana Pavlac Glyer, author of *The Company They Keep*

The Hidden Story of Narnia:
A Book-By-Book Guide to Lewis' Spiritual Themes
Will Vaus

A book of insightful commentary equally suited for teens or adults – Will Vaus points out connections between the *Narnia* books and spiritual/biblical themes, as well as between ideas in the *Narnia* books and C. S. Lewis' other books. Learn what Lewis himself said about the overarching and unifying thematic structure of the Narnia books. That is what this book explores; what C. S. Lewis called "the hidden story" of Narnia. Each chapter includes questions for individual use or small group discussion.

Why I Believe in Narnia:
33 Reviews and Essays on the Life and Work of C. S. Lewis
James Como

Chapters range from reviews of critical books , documentaries and movies to evaluations of Lewis' books to biographical analysis.
"*A valuable , wide-ranging collection of essays by one of the best informed and most accute commentators on Lewis' work and ideas.*"
  Peter Schakel, author of *Imagination & the Arts in C. S. Lewis*

C. S. Lewis: His Literary Achievement
Colin Manlove

"*This is a positively brilliant book, written with splendor, elegance, profundity and evidencing an enormous amount of learning. This is probably not a book to give a first-time reader of Lewis. But for those who are more broadly read in the Lewis corpus this book is an absolute gold mine of information. The author gives us a magnificent overview of Lewis' many writings, tracing for us thoughts and ideas which recur throughout, and at the same time telling us how each book differs from the others. I think it is not extravagant to call C. S. Lewis: His Literary Achievement a tour de force.*"
  Robert Merchant, *St. Austin Review*, Book Review Editor

In the Footsteps of C. S. Lewis: A Photographic Pilgrimage to the British Isles
Will Vaus

Over the course of thirty years, Will Vaus has journeyed to the British Isles many times to walk in the footsteps of C. S. Lewis. His private photographs of the significant places in Lewis' life have captured the imagination of audiences in the US and UK to whom he has lectured on the Oxford don and his work. This, in turn, prompted the idea of this collection of 78 full-color photographs, interwoven with details about Lewis' life and work. The combination of words and pictures make this a wonderful addition to the library of all Lewis scholars and readers.

Speaking of Jack: A C. S. Lewis Discussion Guide
Will Vaus

C. S. Lewis Societies have been forming around the world since the first one started in New York City in 1969. Will Vaus has started and led three groups himself. *Speaking of Jack* is the result of Vaus' experience in leading those Lewis Societies. Included here are introductions to most of Lewis' books as well as questions designed to stimulate discussion about Lewis' life and work. These materials have been "road-tested" with real groups made up of young and old, some very familiar with Lewis and some newcomers. *Speaking of Jack* may be used in an existing book discussion group, to start a C. S. Lewis Society, or as a guide to your own exploration of Lewis' books.

Light: C. S. Lewis's First and Final Short Story
Charlie W. Starr
Foreword by Walter Hooper

Charlie Starr explores the questions surrounding the "Light" manuscript, a later version of story titled "A Man Born Blind." The insights into this story provide a na ew key to understanding some of Lewis's most profound ideas.

"As literary journalism, both investigative and critical, it is top shelf"
    James Como, author of *Remembering C. S. Lewis*

"Starr shines a new and illuminating light on one of Lewis's most intriguing stories"
    Michael Ward, author of *Planet Narnia*

C. S. Lewis & Philosophy as a Way of Life: His Philosophical Thoughts
Adam Barkman

C. S. Lewis is rarely thought of as a "philosopher" per se despite having both studied and taught philosophy for several years at Oxford. Lewis's long journey to Christianity was essentially philosophical – passing through seven different stages. This 624 page book is an invaluable reference for C. S. Lewis scholars and fans alike

C. S. Lewis' Top Ten: Influential Books and Authors, Volume One
Will Vaus

Based on his books, marginal notes, and personal letters, Will Vaus explores Lewis' reading of the ten books he said shaped his vocational attitude and philosophy of life. Volume One covers the first three authors/books: George MacDonald: *Phantastes*, G.K. Chesterton: *The Everlasting Man*, and Virgil: *The Aneid*. Vaus offers a brief biography of each author with a helpful summary of their books.

"Thorough, comprehensive, and illuminating"
  Rolland Hein, Author of *George MacDonald: Victorian Mythmaker*

C. S. Lewis' Top Ten: Influential Books and Authors, Volume Two
Will Vaus

Volume Two covers the following authors/books: George Herbert: *The Temple*, William Wordsworth: *The Prelude*, Rudopf Otto, *The Idea of the Holy*.

C. S. Lewis' Top Ten: Influential Books and Authors, Volume Three
Will Vaus

Volume Three covers the following authors/books: Boethius: *The Consolation of Philosophy*, James Boswell, *The Life of Samuel Johnson*, Charles Williams: *Descent into Hell*, A.J. Balfour: *Thiesm and Humanism*.

C. S. Lewis Goes to Heaven:
A Reader's Guide to The Great Divorce
David G. Clark

This is the first book devoted solely to this often neglected book and the first to reveal several important secrets Lewis concealed within the story. Lewis felt his imaginary trip to Hell and Heaven was far better than his book *The Screwtape Letters*, which has become a classic. Readers will discover the many literary and biblical influences Lewis utilized in writing his brilliant novel.

C. S. Lewis Goes to Hell
A Companion and Study Guide to The Screwtape Letters
William O'Flaherty

The creator and host of "All About Jack" (a podcast feature of EssentialCSLewis.com) has written a guide to *The Screwtape Letters* suitable for groups or individuals.

WWW.WINGEDLIONPRESS.COM

Joy and Poetic Imagination: Understanding C. S. Lewis's "Great War" with Owen Barfield and its Significance for Lewis's Conversion and Writings
Stephen Thorson

Author Stephen Thorson began writing this book over 30 years ago and published parts of it in articles during Barfield's lifetime. Barfield wrote to Thorson in 1983 saying, ""...you have surveyed the divergence between Lewis and myself very fairly, and truly 'in depth...'". This book explains the "Great War" between these two friends.

Exploring the Eternal Goodness: Selected Writings of David L. Neuhouser
Joe Ricke and Lisa Ritchie, Editors

In 1997, due to David's perseverance, the Brown Collection of books by and about C. S. Lewis and related authors came to Taylor University and the Lewis and Friends Colloquium began. This book of selected writings reflects his scholarship in math and literature, as well as his musings on beauty and the imagination. The twenty-one tributes are an indication of the many lives he has influenced. This book is meant to acknowledge David L. Neuhouser for his contributions to scholarship and to honor his life of friendship, encouragement, and genuine goodness.

Inklings Forever, Volume X: Proceedings from the 10th Francis White Ewbank Colloquiunm on C. S. Lewis & Friends
Joe Ricke and Rick Hill, Editors

In June 2016, the 10th biennial Frances Ewbank Colloquium on C. S. Lewis and Friends convened at Taylor University with the special theme of "friendship." Many of the essays and creative pieces collected in this book explore the important relationships of Inklings-related authors, as well as the relationships between those authors and other, sometimes rather surprising, "friends." The year 2016 marked the 90th anniversary of the first meeting of C.S. Lewis and J.R.R. Tolkien – a creative friendship of epic proportions

> What a feast! It is rare that a book of proceedings captures the energy and spirit of the conference itself: this one does. I recommend it.
>
> > Diana Pavlac Glyer, Professor of English at Azusa Pacific University and author of *The Company They Keep* and *Bandersnatch: C. S. Lewis, J. R. R. Tolkien, and the Creative Collaboration of the Inklings*

Mythopoeic Narnia: Memory, Metaphor, and Metamorphoses in C. S. Lewis's The Chronicles of Narnia
Salwa Khoddam

Dr. Khoddam offers a fresh approach to the *Narnia* books based on an inquiry into Lewis' readings and use of classical and Christian symbols. She explores the literary and intellectual contexts of these stories, the traditional myths and motifs, and places them in the company of the greatest Christian mythopoeic works of Western Literature.

Christian Living

Keys to Growth: Meditations on the Acts of the Apostles
Will Vaus

Every living thing or person requires certain ingredients in order to grow, and if a thing or person is not growing, it is dying. *The Acts of the Apostles* is a book that is all about growth. Will Vaus has been meditating and preaching on *Acts* for the past 30 years. In this volume, he offers the reader forty-one keys from the entire book of Acts to unlock spiritual growth in everyday life.

Open Before Christmas: Devotional Thoughts For The Holiday Season
Will Vaus

Author Will Vaus seeks to deepen the reader's knowledge of Advent and Christmas leading up to Epiphany. Readers are provided with devotional thoughts for each day that help them to experience this part of the Church Year perhaps in a more spiritually enriching way than ever before.

"Seasoned with inspiring, touching, and sometimes humorous illustrations .... I found his writing immediately engaging and, the more I read, the more I liked it. God has touched my heart by reading Open Before Christmas, and I believe he will touch your heart too."
  The Rev. David Beckmann, The C.S. Lewis Society of Chattanooga

God's Love Letter: Reflections on I John
Will Vaus

Various words for "love" appear thirty-five times in the five brief chapters of I John. This book invites you on a journey of reading and reflection: reading this book in the New Testament and reflecting on God's love for us, our love for God, and our love for one another.

Jogging with G.K. Chsterton: 65 Earthshaking Expeditions
Robert Moore-Jumonville

Jogging with G.K. Chesterton is a showcase for the merry mind of Chesterton. But Chesterton's lighthearted wit always runs side-by-side with his weighty wisdom. These 65 "earthshaking expeditions" will keep you smiling and thinking from start to finish. You'll be entertained, challenged, and spiritually uplifted as you take time to breath in the fresh morning air and contemplate the wonders of the world.

"This is a delightfully improbable book in which Chesterton puts us through our spiritual and intellectual exercises."
  Joseph Pearce, author of *Wisdom and Innocence: A Life of G.K. Chesterton*

GEORGE MACDONALD

Diary of an Old Soul & The White Page Poems
George MacDonald and Betty Aberlin

The first edition of George MacDonald's book of daily poems included a blank page opposite each page of poems. Readers were invited to write their own reflections on the "white page." MacDonald wrote: "Let your white page be ground, my print be seed, growing to golden ears, that faith and hope may feed." Betty Aberlin responded to MacDonald's invitation with daily poems of her own.

> *Betty Aberlin's close readings of George MacDonald's verses and her thoughtful responses to them speak clearly of her poetic gifts and spiritual intelligence.*
> Luci Shaw, poet

George MacDonald: Literary Heritage and Heirs
Roderick McGillis, editor

This latest collection of 14 essays sets a new standard that will influence MacDonald studies for many more years. George MacDonald experts are increasingly evaluating his entire corpus within the nineteenth century context.

> *This comprehensive collection represents the best of contemporary scholarship on George MacDonald.*
> Rolland Hein, author of *George MacDonald: Victorian Mythmaker*

In the Near Loss of Everything: George MacDonald's Son in America
Dale Wayne Slusser

In the summer of 1887, George MacDonald's son Ronald, newly engaged to artist Louise Blandy, sailed from England to America to teach school. The next summer he returned to England to marry Louise and bring her back to America. On August 27, 1890, Louise died leaving him with an infant daughter. Ronald once described losing a beloved spouse as "the near loss of everything". Dale Wayne Slusser unfolds this poignant story with unpublished letters and photos that give readers a glimpse into the close-knit MacDonald family. Also included is Ronald's essay about his father, *George MacDonald: A Personal Note*, plus a selection from Ronald's 1922 fable, *The Laughing Elf*, about the necessity of both sorrow and joy in life.

Informing the Inklings: George MacDonald' and the Roots of Modern Fantasy
Michael Partridge and Kirstin Jeffrey Johnson, Editors
Preface by Stephen Prickett

In the summer of 2014, the George MacDonald Society held a conference at Magdalen, C.S. Lewis' old college in Oxford. Twelve papers from the conference were selected for publication, some written by established MacDonald scholars and others by a new generation of scholars who continue to mine the depths of the rich correlations between fantasy writers of the 19th and 20th centuries.

Behind the Back of the North Wind: Essays on George MacDonald's Classic Book
Edited and with Introduction by John Pennington and Roderick McGillis

The unique blend of fairy tale atmosphere and social realism in this novel laid the groundwork for modern fantasy literature. Sixteen essays by various authors are accompanied by an instructive introduction, extensive index, and beautiful illustrations.

Through the Year with George MacDonald: 366 Daily Readings
Rolland Hein, editor

These page-length excerpts from sermons, novels and letters are given an appropriate theme/heading and a complementary Scripture passage for daily reading. An inspiring introduction to the artistic soul and Christian vision of George MacDonald.

Shadows and Chivalry:
C. S. Lewis and George MacDonald on Suffering, Evil, and Death
Jeff McInnis

Shadows and Chivalry studies the influence of George MacDonald, a nineteenth-century Scottish novelist and fantasy writer, upon one of the most influential writers of modern times, C. S. Lewis—the creator of Narnia, literary critic, and best-selling apologist. This study attempts to trace the overall affect of MacDonald's work on Lewis's thought and imagination. Without ever ceasing to be a story of one man's influence upon another, the study also serves as an exploration of each writer's thought on, and literary visions of, good and evil.

Crossing a Great Frontier: Essays on George MacDonald's Phantastest
John Pennington, Editor

"This is the first collection of scholarly essays on George MacDonald's seminal romance *Phantastes*. Appropriately to the age of its hero Anodos, here we have twenty-one of the best essays written on *Phantastes* from 1972 onwards, in which straightforward literary analysis works together with contextual, psychological, metaphysical, alchemical and scientific approaches to the elucidation of this moving and elusive work."

    Colin Manlove, author of *Scotland's Forgotten Treasure: The Visionary Novels of George MacDonald*

A Novel Pulpit: Sermons From George MacDonald's Fiction
David L. Neuhouser

Each of the sermons has an introduction giving some explanation of the setting of the sermon or of the plot, if that is necessary for understanding the sermon. "MacDonald's novels are both stimulating and thought-provoking. This collection of sermons from ten novels serve to bring out the 'freshness and brilliance' of MacDonald's message." *from the author's introduction*

Pop Culture

To Love Another Person: A Spiritual Journey Through Les Miserables
John Morrison

The powerful story of Jean Valjean's redemption is beloved by readers and theater goers everywhere. In this companion and guide to Victor Hugo's masterpiece, author John Morrison unfolds the spiritual depth and breadth of this classic novel and broadway musical.

Through Common Things: Philosophical Reflections on Popular Culture
Adam Barkman

"Barkman presents us with an amazingly wide-ranging collection of philosophical reflections grounded in the everyday things of popular culture – past and present, eastern and western, factual and fictional. Throughout his encounters with often surprising subject-matter (the value of darkness?), he writes clearly and concisely, moving seamlessly between Aristotle and anime, Lord Buddha and Lord Voldemort.... This is an informative and entertaining book to read!"
—Doug Bloomberg, Professor of Philosophy, Institute for Christian Studies

The Many Faces of Katniss Everdeen: Exploring the Heroine of The Hunger Games
Valerie Estelle Frankel

Katniss is the heroine who's changed the world. Like Harry Potter, she explodes across genres: She is a dystopian heroine, a warrior woman, a reality TV star, a rebellious adolescent. She's surrounded by the figures of Roman history, from Caesar and Cato to Cinna and Coriolanus Snow. She's also traveling the classic heroine's journey. As a child soldier, she faces trauma; as a growing teen, she battles through love triangles and the struggle to be good in a harsh world. This book explores all this and more, while taking a look at the series' symbolism, from food to storytelling, to show how Katniss becomes the greatest power of Panem, the girl on fire.

Myths and Motifs of The Mortal Instruments
Valerie Estelle Frankel

With vampires, fairies, angels, romance, steampunk, and modern New York all in one series of books, Cassandra Clare is exploding onto the scene. This book explores the deeper world of the Shadowhunters. There's something for everyone, as this book reveals unseen lore within the bestselling series.

Virtuous Worlds: The Video Gamer's Guide to Spiritual Truth
John Stanifer

Popular titles like *Halo 3* and *The Legend of Zelda: Twilight Princess* fly off shelves at a mind-blowing rate. John Stanifer, an avid gamer, shows readers specific parallels between Christian faith and the content of their favorite games. Written with wry humor (including a heckler who frequently pokes fun at the author) this book will appeal to gamers and non-gamers alike. Those unfamiliar with video games may be pleasantly surprised to find that many elements in those "virtual worlds" also qualify them as "virtuous worlds."

BIOGRAPHY

Sheldon Vanauken: The Man Who Received "A Severe Mercy"
Will Vaus

In this biography we discover: Vanauken the struggling student, the bon-vivant lover, the sailor who witnessed the bombing of Pearl Harbor, the seeker who returned to faith through C. S. Lewis, the beloved professor of English literature and history, the feminist and anti-war activist who participated in the March on the Pentagon, the bestselling author, and Vanauken the convert to Catholicism. What emerges is the portrait of a man relentlessly in search of beauty, love, and truth, a man who believed that, in the end, he found all three.

"This is a charming biography about a doubly charming man who wrote a triply charming book. It is a great way to meet the man behind A Severe Mercy."

Peter Kreeft, author of *Jacob's Ladder: 10 Steps to Truth*

Remembering Roy Campbell: The Memoirs of his Daughters, Anna and Tess
Introduction by Judith Lütge Coullie, Editor
Preface by Joseph Pearce

Anna and Teresa Campbell were the daughters of the handsome young South African poet and writer, Roy Campbell (1901-1957), and his beautiful English wife, Mary Garman. In their frank and moving memoirs, Anna and Tess recall the extraordinary, and often very difficult, lives they shared with their exceptional parents. Over 50 photos, 344 footnotes, timeline of Campbell's life, and complete index.

Harry Potter

The Order of Harry Potter: The Literary Skill of the Hogwarts Epic
Colin Manlove

Colin Manlove, a popular conference speaker and author of over a dozen books, has earned an international reputation as an expert on fantasy and children's literature. His book, *From Alice to Harry Potter*, is a survey of 400 English fantasy books. In *The Order of Harry Potter*, he compares and contrasts *Harry Potter* with works by "Inklings" writers J.R.R. Tolkien, C. S. Lewis and Charles Williams; he also examines Rowling's treatment of the topic of imagination; her skill in organization and the use of language; and the book's underlying motifs and themes.

Harry Potter & Imagination: The Way Between Two Worlds
Travis Prinzi

Imaginative literature places a reader between two worlds: the story world and the world of daily life, and challenges the reader to imagine and to act for a better world. Starting with discussion of Harry Potter's more important themes, *Harry Potter & Imagination* takes readers on a journey through the transformative power of those themes for both the individual and for culture by placing Rowling's series in its literary, historical, and cultural contexts.

Hog's Head Conversations: Essays on Harry Potter
Travis Prinzi, Editor

Ten fascinating essays on Harry Potter by popular Potter writers and speakers including John Granger, James W. Thomas, Colin Manlove, and Travis Prinzi.

Repotting Harry Potter: A Professor's Guide for the Serious Re-Reader
Rowling Revisited: Return Trips to Harry, Fantastic Beasts, Quidditch, & Beedle the Bard
Dr. James W. Thomas

In *Repotting Harry Potter* and his sequel book *Rowling Revisited*, Dr. James W. Thomas points out the humor, puns, foreshadowing and literary parallels in the Potter books. In *Rowling Revisted*, readers will especially find useful three extensive appendixes – "Fantastic Beasts and the Pages Where You'll Find Them," "Quidditch Through the Pages," and "The Books in the Potter Books." Dr. Thomas makes re-reading the Potter books even more rewarding and enjoyable.

Sociology and Harry Potter: 22 Enchanting Essays on the Wizarding World
Jenn Simms, Editor

Modeled on an Introduction to Sociology textbook, this book is not simply about the series, but also uses the series to facilitate the reader's understanding of the discipline of sociology and a develops a sociological approach to viewing social reality. It is a case of high quality academic scholarship written in a form and on a topic accessible to non-academics. As such, it is written to appeal to Harry Potter fans and the general reading public. Contributors include professional sociologists from eight countries.

Harry Potter, Still Recruiting: An Inner Look at Harry Potter Fandom
Valerie Frankel

The Harry Potter phenomenon has created a new world: one of Quidditch in the park, lightning earrings, endless parodies, a new genre of music, and fan conferences of epic proportions. This book attempts to document everything - exploring costuming, crafting, gaming, and more, with essays and interviews straight from the multitude of creators. From children to adults, fans are delighting the world with an explosion of captivating activities and experiences, all based on Rowling's delightful series.

POETS AND POETRY

In the Eye of the Beholder: How to See the World Like a Romantic Poet
Louis Markos

Born out of the French Revolution and its radical faith that a nation could be shaped and altered by the dreams and visions of its people, British Romantic Poetry was founded on a belief that the objects and realities of our world, whether natural or human, are not fixed in stone but can be molded and transformed by the visionary eye of the poet. A separate bibliographical essay is provided for readers listing accessible biographies of each poet and critical studies of their work.

The Cat on the Catamaran: A Christmas Tale
John Martin

Here is a modern-day parable of a modern-day cat with modern-day attitudes. Riverboat Dan is a "cool" cat on a perpetual vacation from responsibility. He's *The Cat on the Catamaran* – sailing down the river of life. Dan keeps his guilty conscience from interfering with his fun until he runs into trouble. But will he have the courage to believe that it's never too late to change course? (For ages 10 to adult)

www.ingramcontent.com/pod-product-compliance
Lightning Source LLC
Chambersburg PA
CBHW021428080526
44588CB00009B/456